1400
99BB

Principles of
Human Relations

APPLICATIONS TO MANAGEMENT

Principles of Human Relations

APPLICATIONS TO MANAGEMENT

NORMAN R. F. MAIER

Professor of Psychology, University of Michigan

JOHN WILEY & SONS, INC., NEW YORK

CHAPMAN & HALL, LIMITED, LONDON

Library of Congress Catalog Card Number: 52–7008

Printed in the United States of America

To my three sons
Richard, Carl, and John

Preface

This book is written for persons who are interested in human relations problems, and as such it concerns itself with overcoming communication barriers, preventing misunderstandings, and developing the constructive side of man's nature. The examples and applications are pointed toward industry, but the principles apply to all situations where leaders must deal with groups or individuals. Since a leader interacts with people, principles are derived from social psychology, group dynamics, and clinical psychology. Some of the principles are new, but perhaps the greatest contribution of this book results from the fact that I have been permitted by industry to use existing industrial organizations as my laboratory to evaluate certain experimentally derived techniques. Thus it may be said that industry has contributed its facilities for the advancement of social psychology while at the same time gaining itself because of recent developments in social psychology and group dynamics.

The scope of this book includes discussion of problems of human relations in industry, new techniques and approaches to them, and the problems involved in training persons to practice the effective techniques. Training in human relations is a complex matter. One must not only have effective procedures to offer, but one must also motivate people to use the effective procedures that are available. The latter problem is the more difficult because it requires changes in established habits as well as changes in attitudes.

Many persons in industry will feel that they are unwilling or unable to apply all the methods discussed in this volume. It is granted that the program is advanced and progressive, but I should like it to be viewed as a guide or blueprint for the future. It may also serve to evaluate some of the methods that are now used to influence employee and public opinion. Although less elaborate methods and training programs may seem more economical than a more detailed program such as I have described, the question of economy can hardly be decided until the relative returns are taken into account.

There is a great difference between what a program is designed to teach and what is learned from it. Because a program of training seems logical and reasonable to persons who prepare it or buy it, it does not follow that it will be seen in the same way by persons who are subjected to it. Those who advocate and those who receive training have different attitudes, and this means that the effects often may be quite opposite to those anticipated. Thus lectures and training films often not only fail to accomplish the desired purpose but produce hostility instead.

The whole problem of human relations training is complicated by the fact that conflicts in attitudes are involved. Attitudes are always loaded with feelings, and the logic of feeling is different from the logic of thinking. Until these two kinds of logic are treated for what they are, misunderstandings cannot be corrected by facts. A basic requirement for human relations training therefore is an attitude change on the part of the person who is to practice human relations. It is this aspect of training that is most frequently overlooked. Once the attitude change is accomplished the leadership and interpersonal relationship skills described in this volume make a new kind of sense and take on the appearance of practicability.

In obtaining case material for this book I am indebted to several industries and a large number of individuals. Although it would be impossible to mention all the persons who have aided me directly or indirectly, I feel I owe most to A. Derks, W. N. Haas, G. H. Selke, Howard F. Shout, L. F. Zerfoss, S. J. Rogers, and the late Richard P. Buchman. Persons who have contributed most in creating opportunities for work in developing this material include H. F. Lange, W. L. Cisler, H. H. Schroeder, S. F. Leahy, B. K. Swartz, R. E. Schwab, H. E. Byrne, and the late J. H. Walker.

For aid in the preparation of the manuscript I owe much to A. R. Solem and to my wife, Ayesha A. Maier. They gave freely of their time and were frank in their criticism.

The presentation of case material frequently includes the names of persons. This has been done to make the case studies more readable. It goes without saying that I have substituted fictitious names for real ones in order not to identify persons or companies.

NORMAN R. F. MAIER

Ann Arbor, Michigan
April 14, 1952

Contents

There can be no peace or calm in this world
until there is full honor and respect of one
individual for another.

Edvard Beneš

1*

Introduction

Industry's Need for Supervisory Training

At the present time industry is becoming keenly aware of the importance of employee morale. Management willingly concedes that the state of employee morale affects production, labor turnover, absenteeism, and public relations, all of which can be translated into dollars and cents. However, the impetus for improving morale comes primarily from a desire to increase job satisfaction and day-to-day human relationships. Undoubtedly the strength of the unions has made this need apparent, and the leadership of management feels itself to be in competition with the union leadership for the loyalty of its employees.

That the first level of supervision is an all-important determiner of employee morale and loyalty is recognized, but that a similar problem is present at intermediate and higher levels is not so well appreciated by top executives. As a consequence, most attention is given to training first-line supervisors in human relations problems. In most such training programs emphasis is given to developing a friendly personal touch, and sometimes techniques for preventing misunderstandings are considered. Stress also is placed on the desirability of getting men to want to do things rather than to fear not to do things. These programs undoubtedly have improved supervision, but management often feels that a great part of the benefit wears off rather quickly.

* Parts of this chapter previously appeared under the title "A Human Relations Program for Supervision," and were published in the *Industrial and Labor Relations Review* (36); other portions were taken from an article entitled "Improving Supervision through Training," published in *Psychology of Labor-Management Relations* by the Industrial Relations Research Association (37).

There seem to be three main reasons why many training programs fail to be sufficiently effective to produce lasting results:

1. Officials in top management positions expect supervisors at lower levels to practice a more and more considerate approach to employees without seeing that the supervisors in turn require the same consideration from persons to whom they report. It is difficult to practice consideration toward those below oneself when one is denied the same treatment from above. As a matter of fact, employees in lower management positions are often more subject to fear than are rank-and-file employees. They have no union to go to when they feel themselves abused, and they cannot obtain comparable positions by leaving the company. As a consequence they are less free in the expression of grievances, and management is left quite unaware of the extent of discontent that exists among them. In interviewing both rank-and-file employees and management personnel the author was unable to escape the conclusion that employees in supervisory positions are less free in expressing their true feelings than are nonsupervisory employees.

2. The training frequently fails to change basic attitudes. In a discussion of human relations a foreman may readily concede that friendly and considerate treatment should be given to employees, but when the supervisor is on the job he encounters situations in which he feels he does not have the time for such treatment; he often feels he is dealing with individuals who are unreasonable; or he is too greatly concerned with his own condition to consider the emotions of others. In such cases he perceives his situation as an exception to the rule presented in training classes. Unfortunately, the exceptions increase in number. On-the-job training seems to be the best way to reduce this condition because it requires the supervisor to apply the training principles to his own cases, not just to cases which the instructor presents and in which the supervisor has no emotional involvement.

3. Unless a supervisor's attitudes toward the rights of employees are changed, training in new procedures requires him to act out a role. Human relations techniques then become a cloak to be worn when problems arise. Thus training that does not change fundamental attitudes becomes nothing more than a sugar-coating for the supervisor, and this coating is either recognized as such by employees or soon wears off.

Basically, this third factor also incorporates the second because the attitude toward the rights, privileges, and superiority of supervisory positions determines when and in what cases consideration is warranted. The factor of attitude also influences the first point because top management's attitude may exclude it from the group that needs training in human relations. One who has succeeded in reaching high places in business under keen competition is not ready to concede that his methods have suddenly become inadequate. He may recognize that there have been changes in attitudes regarding the rights and privileges of the rank-and-file worker and that these new attitudes may explain why the type of relations that previously were successful are no longer adequate. However, he is not ready to accept this change as one with which to reckon because he feels that the questions of "right" and "wrong" or "good" and "bad" enter the picture. That "right" and "wrong" judgments are interpretations produced by conflicting attitudes is a psychological problem that a serious supervisory training program must take into account. To avoid it is to miss a fundamental attitude problem.

Any approach to the problem of human conflict must begin at a point where these judgments are not yet felt. When the judgments appear, both sides of the conflict have principles and ideals to defend, so that each feels he is fighting a holy war. Basically, supervisory training is a preventive program in the control of attitudes.

Workable attitudes must become company policy, and in this sense they may be considered a philosophy of management. This aspect of a supervisory training program makes it imperative that top management wholeheartedly accept the type of attitude that is at the base of human relations training.

The Problem of Attitude in Supervisory Training

In approaching the problem of training in human relations, one must clearly distinguish between the techniques that are found to be useful and the attitude of the supervisor who practices the techniques. For a person to be credited with honesty and sincerity, his actions must conform to the impression other people gain of his attitude. Although attitudes may be communicated by actions, it is questionable whether actions will invariably reflect a consistent impression if the proper attitude is not present to integrate the actions. It appears that an attitude is conveyed by a pattern of action rather than by specific actions themselves.

A supervisor who does not like people will have difficulty in practicing techniques designed to reflect an interest in people. He may be trained to greet employees when they report for work, to smile when he speaks to them, to discuss problems with employees, to refrain from showing favoritism, not to lose his temper, and, in general, to behave in ways that ordinarily indicate an interest in people; yet it is unlikely that his true attitude will remain unknown. On the other hand, a supervisor who has an honest interest in people will, without training, do many things that reflect this interest, and he may make many mistakes in technique without having his true attitude toward employees misunderstood. Thus two supervisors may make the same remark to their employees and yet produce different effects because the remark has different meanings, depending upon what each group sees as the attitude of its supervisor. Words and actions communicate content and feelings, and the feelings that are communicated greatly depend upon the attitude of the person who expressed the words and actions. Much misunderstanding arises because employees react unfavorably to a supervisor's attitude rather than to his actual deeds. Since actions depend so greatly upon attitudes and since actions alone will not prevent misunderstandings, it is apparent that a most important aspect of supervisory training is attitude training. With the proper attitude, training in techniques becomes natural, and each person can more readily reflect his own personality in his techniques.

The attitude of the supervisor is highly important in another respect. Not only do his actions tend to reflect his attitude, but his attitude also influences the way he will view or interpret the behavior of employees. For example, loafing, insubordination, failure to cooperate, disregard of company property, and unwillingness to do a full day's work are largely supervisory interpretations of actions that might also be interpreted, respectively, as resting, face saving, lack of skill, an accident, and a reluctance to begin a job that cannot be completed. The differing interpretations are highly important, since the problem that confronts the supervisor depends on his interpretation rather than on the actual behavior. The procedure that the supervisor will follow depends in turn upon the problem he sees, so that inaccurate interpretations invariably result in inadequate procedures.

Herbert Meyer (43),* one of the author's students, developed tests for the selection of supervisors in a public utility. He gave a battery

* Numbers in parentheses refer to items in the bibliography, pp. 457–459.

of tests to a group of the best supervisors and a group of the poorest supervisors on the bases of ratings supplied by higher management. He found that the most discriminating test was one that explored a supervisor's attitude toward employees. Interpretations of behavior are greatly influenced by an attitude of suspicion. When employees do not trust supervisors and supervisors do not trust employees, misunderstandings in great numbers are created. Grievances that seem small and childish to management are seen as fundamental issues by workers. When mutual trust is present, grievances are rare, and, when they do appear, remedies are easily found. Trust is an attitude that must be developed, and, when the supervisor has this trust, his attitude is recognized and develops mutual trust.

Human Relations and Preventing Misunderstandings

If we assume that our problems with people are due to the nature of people we make a value judgment. This judgment may be reasonable or unreasonable. However, regardless of whether we are justified in our judgment or not, a good solution to the problem is not forthcoming. A reasonable supervisor may regard it as his responsibility to go halfway in getting along with people. But with some people this is not enough. When parents are in charge of infants, they consider it their responsibility to furnish all of the understanding and reasonableness and expect no such understanding from the infant. As a child grows older one expects from him some responsibility for understanding the parents' problems. In marriage we usually consider it a 50–50 responsibility. Does a supervisor have to go farther than this? Perhaps somewhat, because he is selected for his ability to understand and get along with people. But how far should he be required to go?

In following this approach supervisors may be willing to go more than halfway in making concessions and overlooking faults. Finally they reach the point where a certain number of employees still are too uncooperative. The solutions that then suggest themselves are to discipline, warn, and finally discharge the worst offenders.

All these approaches raise new problems. Frequently discipline produces hostility instead of improvement; or improvement in the disciplined area may occur, but other undesirable behaviors may increase. Grievances and even walkouts may occur as a consequence of disciplining one employee. The same may result from warnings. Discharge at least rids one of the employee, but management loses an investment in training, other employees feel insecure, and added problems may have been created with the union.

Generally speaking, solutions that create new problems are not satisfying, and hence they are used as a last resort. Thus the solution is applied to extreme cases only, and as a result many problem individuals remain to aggravate the supervisors. As long as we, as supervisors, blame the other fellow for our problems we locate a source of difficulty, but no remedy suggests itself. We may wish we had no such people to deal with, but the fact that such persons cross our paths remains with us.

If, however, we assume that problems with people are due to misunderstandings then we can seek to discover the sources of misunderstandings. In following this approach we soon find that there are numerous sources of misunderstanding. Since employees and supervisors are in different situations, the work, the company objectives, rules, and regulations all have different meanings to employees and supervisors. Individual attitudes likewise cause various employees to see things differently, so that what is regimentation to one person means order to another. We also misjudge people because we are unaware of their specific needs. A man wants a promotion because he needs prestige, another wants it because he needs more money, still another because he doesn't want to be overlooked. For each need there is a different substitute, yet the same substitute may be given to several men because the supervisor assumes he knows the reason for the desire for the promotion. Frustrated employees likewise are misunderstood because the problems off the job may not be considered. With proper evaluation of such factors many of these sources of misunderstanding can be prevented or greatly reduced. As a matter of fact, the mere understanding of the reasons behind the behavior results in a changed attitude in the supervisor, and this helps him as well as the employee.

This approach thus suggests that there is something we ourselves can do to reduce problems in misunderstanding. As soon as we recognize that there is something we can do to prevent or remove misunderstandings, many problems become soluble without resort to methods that create problems themselves. We can do something to change ourselves so that we are not misunderstood and are not inclined to misunderstand others, even if we cannot change the nature of the other fellow.

This approach in no way implies that supervisors are in the wrong and that employees are right. The question of justice is beside the point if we wish to seek to remedy a situation. Justice is a legal and moral issue and must be distinguished from psychological descriptions of why people behave as they do. If two people misunderstand each other, either one of them could do something to reduce the misunderstanding, and it just happens to be more economical to train supervisors at all levels to develop skills in human relations than to train rank-and-file employees.

The program that we have developed to solve some of the human relations problems may be more extensive and more extreme than the reader may feel is desirable or necessary at this time. This difference in opinion, however, does not change some of the basic problems in human relations training. All training implies that people must be changed, and an important aspect of this change is attitude change. A training program that does not alter people may be interesting, but it is exposure and not training. A good training program must not only change people but must change them in the way that is intended. The procedures described as training methods in later pages have a value apart from the content of the training program. One must therefore distinguish between the objectives of training reported in this book and the training methods themselves. Since the training objectives of our program require rather radical changes, it can be assumed that the training problems are made more difficult. Hence if the methods described are effective under difficulties they should be as effective, at least, when fewer difficulties are present.

New Concepts in Supervision

For some time it has been recognized that participation is an effective method to achieve interest and cooperation. We all recognize that we work better when we feel we are part of a group effort and know what objective we wish to achieve. The value of participation has become fully apparent through the experimental work of Lewin, Lippitt, and White with children (25). These experiments revealed that cooperative and constructive behavior in children could be greatly increased if the leader permitted the children to participate in all the decisions made on their play project. In the light of these findings there have been a number of attempts to adapt the discussion method to the solving of practical problems.

Lewin (23) reports that by holding group discussions and attempting to lead the groups to reach a group decision it was possible to get housewives to change their food habits. During the war it was highly desirable that beef hearts, sweetbreads, and kidneys be utilized. However, the use of such foods is counter to deep-seated attitudes. It was found, on the one hand, that skilled lecturers who pointed out the high nutritional value (vitamin and mineral content) of these foods, described new ways of preparing these foods, supplied recipes, and made emotional appeals, were quite ineffective. They aroused interest, but a follow-up a week later showed that only 3 per cent of the women served one of the foods never served previously. On the other hand, discussion meetings held with similar groups and conducted by Alex Bavelas, a psychologist skilled in group discussion methods, resulted in 32 per cent of the participants using one of the new foods. He permitted the women to talk about the problems involved in using the new foods, but preparation methods and recipes were not supplied until the group became involved sufficiently to be interested in overcoming their obstacles. Other experiments along this line showed that group decision was from 2 to 3 times as effective as the lecture method and about twice as effective as individual instruction. Lewin further points out that groups, after making a decision, behave as group members and feel a responsibility toward the group, whereas in individual decisions a person acts primarily on the basis of his own personal preferences.

Another illustration of group decision conducted by Bavelas (as reported by Lewin [23] and Maier [35]) concerns groups of women workers on a sewing operation. The women worked on a group incentive basis. Bavelas chose one of the superior groups and asked them if they would like to set a production goal for themselves. Before this the group's production varied from 70 to 78 units per hour and averaged 74 units. After some discussion the girls unanimously agreed that they would like to set their goal at 84 units per hour. Within 5 days this goal was exceeded. Another meeting was held for the purpose of making any desired changes in the goal. This time the girls set their goal at 95 units. During the next 3 days they fell somewhat short of this goal. At the third meeting the girls were ready to set a relatively permanent production goal at 90 units.

During the next 6 months this group's production varied between 80 and 93 units, with an average of 88. The fact that the production did not taper off during the next recorded 6-month period indicates the staying quality of group decision and also shows that excessive fatigue was not induced. Further, the girls reported no added fatigue problems.

Other methods were used in an attempt to change the production of comparable groups. When the same leader attempted to suggest goals, promising that standards and rates would not be changed, he seemed to get a friendly response, but production improvements were insignificant. Holding discussions with the girls but not asking them to set specific goals likewise had no effect. Thus it seems that a discussion without a group decision leads to little change in action, although it may contribute greatly to attitude change.

In another study Coch and French (12) report the striking success of the use of discussion in overcoming resistance to a job change. The company in which the experiment was performed found that difficulty arose whenever a change in a job was made or whenever employees were transferred from one job to another. In each case the employees had to change their work patterns, and, although piece rates would be based on standards of like difficulty, the employees had difficulty in getting back to their previous rates. As a matter of fact, transferred employees required 8 weeks to learn a new job, whereas new employees required only 5 weeks. Methods of offering monetary rewards, dealing through the union, etc., had failed to prevent hostility, grievances, low production, and quitting.

On one occasion changes were to be made which involved a large number of groups. The changes were necessitated by manufacturing and competitive conditions. One group was handled in the usual way. The employees were told the reasons why the change was necessary, how new rates in the job were established, and how the new job would permit the same earnings. Thus the new condition was described to the employees after the problem was solved by management.

Two other groups were handled quite differently. Each was presented with the need for a change in operation. The groups then participated in planning for the change with the time-study man. Certain of the group representatives were involved in setting the new rates.

Still another group was handled by a method part way between the two above-mentioned methods. This group was told about how management would like to go about setting up the change. There was no real participation in the planning, but the group was told about the changes before the changes were made and found them acceptable.

The results of the three methods are quite different. Where employees were merely told about the change, there was the usual hostility toward supervisors, time-study engineers and management; there was the usual slow job improvement; and 17 per cent of the group quit within 40 days.

In the two groups where participation was greatest there was no evidence of dissatisfaction. Recovery of production was rapid and soon exceeded the production held before the change. There were no quits.

The group given partial participation also seemed satisfied with the change. Their recovery was not so rapid as in the groups participating fully, but there were no quits.

Later the group dissatisfied with the previous change experienced another job change. This time the group participated, and now the behavior after change was like that of the other groups in which the same procedure was used.

These experiments illustrate the possible practical benefits that may be obtained from group decision and participation methods. How generally can these principles be used? If the method is effective for solving some problems, may it not be considered as a general method to be utilized in the day-to-day job operation? If so, it would be necessary to train supervisors. In the above instances psychologists with specialized skills were used. Can supervisors be trained to use the methods and will the training permit the day-to-day operations to proceed without the development of suspicious attitudes and without a loss in the necessary controls?

Implication of New Concepts to Training

Since 1945 the author has been working with four large industries in an attempt to improve supervision. The program centers around what has been called democratic leadership in management (4, 5, 9, 36). The basic feature of democratic leadership is to shift the functions and responsibility for decisions from the supervisor to the group. In making this shift, one changes the leadership from the autocratic type to the democratic type. However, this change in the placement of responsibility for solutions raises some other problems. If, for example, a group solves problems, how is one to decide which of the solutions suggested represents the group? One method is to use a majority vote. When this is done, the group is divided into a majority and a minority, and as a consequence one may develop two or more opposed subgroups. Another method (Lewin, 22, 24, 25) is to attempt to obtain agreement by group decision as discussed above. In order to accomplish a full meeting of minds free discussion is essential, and the supervisor develops a new leadership role. His effectiveness becomes primarily one of being able to conduct a problem-solving conference. It is this type of leadership that seems essential if the group is to remain unified and constructive. To achieve this effect the supervisor must develop skills in sensitivity and permissiveness. At the same time, he must not permit himself to become a passive leader but must be able to exert controls. Permissiveness and controls seem somewhat contradictory activities, and the interpretation of these becomes one of the important problems in training and an important area of investigation. For the present, it seems clear that some of these controls are as follows:

1. Problems presented to a group must fall within the supervisor's area of freedom. The concept of the area of freedom will be described in detail in the next chapter. For the present it is sufficient to point out that at each level of supervision there are problems that a supervisor may decide himself. It is these problems that he can share with the group that reports to him if the group members have interest. Thus, decisions cannot violate company practices or policies (unless the supervisor involved is at the policy-making level), and they cannot violate working agreements, since problems involving these factors do not ordinarily fall within the supervisor's area of freedom (36). Frequently, the "how to do a job" rather than the "what job to do" is the problem that can be solved.

2. Presenting the subject for discussion in such a manner that it is a problem rather than a criticism of the group or an individual in the group. Whether or not a group becomes defensive or interested in solving a problem is largely a matter of the way the problem is presented. Just how important the manner of presentation is we do not know, but it is clear from case studies that the incidence of defensive reactions can be traced to the supervisor's statement of the problem. On one occasion the supervisor stated as his problem the fact that certain members of the group failed to close file drawers. Immediately the group requested new files which operated more smoothly. Considering the condition of the files, this appeared to be a defensive reaction.

3. Serving in the role of an expert. The supervisor frequently has much background and information which is of value in solving a problem. Instead of using this information as a way for discrediting solutions and thereby having an advantage over group members, the supervisor can give the group the benefit of his experience by present-

ing the information at his disposal (36). For example, he can point
out how much space the group will have in the new office location
and ask them to help plan the office arrangement. If he withheld
this information and the group planned an office arrangement that required too much space, he would be in the position of having to reject
certain solutions. Soon his position would be one opposed to that of
the group. If all relevant facts are given at the outset the problem
becomes more interesting because it is more difficult.

4. Reducing hostility by permitting free expression. In permitting
the expression of hostile reactions one reduces frustration and encourages motivated behavior. The author's research in this field indicates
that frustration and motivation are opposed processes (38). By reducing frustration one reinstates problem-solving behavior. Rogers' work
(52) also supports this contention.

5. Encouraging all members to participate in the discussion. This
technique causes members of a group to interact. In interacting the
members learn their areas of disagreement, they learn about group
fairness, and they learn that each cannot have things his way. It is
in free discussion that social pressure can operate. Social pressure
is always present in social behavior. The leader can use social pressure for constructive purposes by seeing to it that all feel free to participate. Certain dominant individuals must become aware of their
role as listeners, and certain reticent individuals must learn that they
owe it to the group to speak their minds. The leader can play an
important part in bringing about these awarenesses.

6. Protecting the minority. The leader can do much to relieve hostility and to bring deviants back into the group by showing special
consideration to minority positions. Frequently, a few persons refuse
to go along with the group because they feel excluded. By giving
this group of individuals special attention, demonstrating a desire to
have them in the group, and giving their opinions the most favorable
interpretation possible, the leader can make them feel that they have
not been excluded from the group.

7. Making the group responsible for agreeing on a solution. A
group may attempt to escape the responsibility of working as a group
and continue to disagree. In practice this is much more rare than is
usually anticipated. When it occurs, however, the supervisor can
bring this responsibility to awareness. He can point out that a new
problem has arisen, which is, "How can we get together on a solution?"
Since the objective is to obtain a meeting of minds, the problem cannot be settled by taking a vote and following the majority. Thus,

when full agreement is the objective, the leader becomes reluctant to split the group and holds out for keeping the group intact. This makes the leader and group members more permissive. It also forces each person to realize his responsibility as a group member. Social pressure operates in a constructive manner and one hears such remarks as, "Oh, Bill, why don't you give the idea a try?" and "Come on, Jim, don't be so damn selfish." In such instances the group, not the supervisor, is applying pressure.

8. Keeping the discussion on the subject. Whether or not progress is experienced in group discussion depends, to some extent, on whether or not extraneous matters are discussed. The responsibility of keeping a discussion problem-centered belongs to the leader. However, this can easily lead to regimentation. Enough leeway should be permitted so as not to introduce into the discussion an atmosphere of pressure or strictness. Further, the supervisor must be careful not to judge whether something is irrelevant. He might ask the person whether his ideas are tied in with the problem. If the person feels they are not, he can ask whether the issue raised should be discussed at a future time. Thus again, a balance must be struck between a rigid and fully controlled discussion and one that is loose and disorganized.

It is apparent that the types of control discussed above are different from those used by an autocratic leader, and yet it can be seen that they are techniques that are psychologically sound in their effectiveness.

The techniques of sensitivity and permissiveness likewise deviate from those ordinarily used by an autocratic supervisor. These may be listed as follows:

1. Sensitivity to feelings rather than to words or logic. The supervisor must be trained to realize that the reasons a man gives for being for or against something frequently are irrelevant rationalizations. A man doesn't like something, and the dislike is a fact that must be accepted with understanding. Often the objections to something are fears, but the words expressed are criticisms. To require proof or evidence in such instances merely increases insecurity. The fact of fear must be accepted and respected. Fears can best be overcome by permitting fears to be expressed and recognized for what they are (52). Thus, the supervisor must react to the feeling tones and not to the words. This sensitivity to feelings must be developed through training.

2. Permissiveness must be developed. A permissive supervisor is not on the defensive; he has no "face-saving" reactions, and he is primarily concerned with the way the group members feel. Basically he believes that the group, through free discussion, can integrate their various interests better than he can. He believes that a group is more able to solve its problem than is an outsider. As a consequence, the permissive supervisor becomes an active listener. The function of permissiveness in a group discussion is fundamentally the same as in nondirective counseling (52).

3. Reflecting the feelings expressed. As in counseling (52), the technique of reflecting feelings demonstrates permissiveness, it encourages discussion, and it brings feelings out in the open where they can be freely examined and explored. It is an aid to insight in that only through the explorations of ideas and feelings can new relationships be discovered. It is desirable for the supervisor to use a blackboard for this purpose. By writing opinions on the board he shows acceptance and permits further exploration since he now can ask, "Are there other ideas on this matter?"

Further exploration is one of the best ways of having poor ideas rejected. The supervisor must learn not to discredit poor ideas. If he puts a poor idea on the board and then requests other ideas or reactions he can get poor ideas rejected without acting as a censor or critic.

4. The use of exploratory questions. Problem solving can be enhanced in a group by the use of analytical questions. Such questions as, "How could that be done?" and "Would that plan be useful under emergency conditions?" help explore issues further and bring out additional details. Care must be exercised so that the questions asked do not discredit, degrade, or indicate an objection to the idea.

5. Summarizing ideas and solutions. The value of summaries from time to time is to see to it that all members properly understand the issues. Summarizing also serves as a means of holding interest in that it permits progress to be experienced.

The techniques of listening and reflecting are in direct contrast to the techniques of selling employees on a solution. Frequently supervisors confuse the idea of giving up autocratic techniques with the development of skill in selling ideas to employees. As a consequence they employ sales techniques and believe they are using the democratic technique. Such supervisors sometimes are more difficult to train than many autocratic supervisors because the autocrats are not confused in their distinctions.

It is important to note that the above-mentioned leadership techniques are entirely a matter of the leader's behavior. He controls the situation by how he does things, not by any authority his position gives him. An autocratic leader must control by the power he possesses, whereas a democratic leader controls by utilizing forces that are in the group. Thus he is influential rather than powerful.

Some conference leaders who wish to increase participation put problems to a group but arm themselves with ground rules that are previously agreed upon. Thus it is agreed that none of the persons must talk too much, points brought up must be on the subject, personalities must not be attacked, etc. Such ground rules may seem reasonable, but it should be noted that they represent a rule that the leader may invoke at his own discretion and that this rule is something in addition to his technique.

In other conferences it is supposed that the group must previously be trained to be good conferees. Here again a kind of restriction is set up (through training) which makes it more easy for the leader to dominate by resorting to influences outside his office as a leader.

These and other methods may have virtues, but they have been carefully excluded from the views presented here because they restrict free expression. In order for a group of people to reach agreement their differences must come to the surface; otherwise one only can obtain "apparent" agreement. True agreement is reached when differences are resolved. Hence any procedures that submerge or bypass disagreement cannot produce true unity.

Some Training Problems

It is apparent that the training problems involved in instituting the type of program described are very large. The supervisor must undergo a great deal of change, and, as we know, a *change* is frequently met with resistance. At the present time, it is clear that the democratic technique is one of the best *change* techniques yet devised. It is desirable, therefore, to use it as a means of obtaining acceptance of the democratic concepts themselves. In this respect it seems necessary to disagree with Lewin (24), who has expressed the opinion that autocratic methods may be necessary to achieve democracy.

The change required, in this instance, is a fundamental one and actually amounts to a personality change. The supervisor must not only view employees differently, but he must also view himself and his position in a new light. The change in attitude toward employees is not so difficult as the change in attitude toward oneself or one's position. This is evidenced by the fact that one can obtain the ready acceptance of higher management for the program when they view it as a program for supervisors beneath themselves, but when the program is given for them to practice they seek ways to demonstrate that the program is not adapted to their positions. Likewise, lower levels of supervision react by wanting to know why their boss doesn't practice democratic leadership. Thus, generally, the program can be accepted as applying to others before one can see it as applying to oneself. This observation leads to two basic requirements in training:

1. Higher management must practice the democratic method in order that those below can experience it firsthand and, incidentally, in order to supply the motivation that higher management's support may give.

In one training unit, which included three levels of supervision, we had succeeded in motivating the first-line supervisors to try out the group-decision technique. These attempts were successful in that the men reacted favorably and the results were good. Some weeks later, however, interest declined, and further illustrations of its use were not forthcoming. Private interviews with first-line supervisors revealed that they, as a group, had rebelled because the men to whom they reported had failed to practice the group method with them. For example, when a foreman went to the general foreman with an idea, he found his ideas rejected before they were examined. He was told that a plan was already worked out and that this plan would be followed. In another instance a supervisor was so pleased with the results of his problem-solving discussions that he invited his superior to visit one of his discussions. His superior visited him on two successive weeks. Some time later the superior made a third visit and after listening to another discussion for 20 minutes he arose and said, "I've been out here on three occasions, and each time I found you fellows chewing the fat. We have a job to do. Now get out and do it." Such an experience creates countermotivation, and even though higher management may support a program it must realize that intermediate supervision can defeat its purpose.

2. Role-playing procedures (Chapter 4) and discussions (Chapter 3), using problems supplied by the group, must be used to create the

experience that the method applies to the group members' problems. Such experiences can then be extended by having a group decision in which all agree to try the method the following week.

In the previous case, in which the first-line supervisors rebelled, this step was missing for the higher levels of supervision. The role-taking and group-decision phases were applied to the first-line supervisors, and higher levels merely gave their consent and support.

The value of role playing and discussion as change agents for attitudes is most difficult for management to accept. Industry has been sold on visual aids and sees role-playing and discussion procedures as time consumers. Unless one experiences their value personally they are not convincing. Since higher management frequently judges the program on intellectual grounds, they are not easily convinced. Even when such individuals consent to observe these procedures, this observation is given limited time, usually just enough to arouse hostility because the observers experience a threat to their own attitudes. Hostility passes when roles are played a number of times, and then one can be satisfied that a major step has been reached. However, this added time often cannot be obtained.

It has been the author's experience that attempts to cut the program invariably take the form of reduction of role-playing and discussion time. In one industry, the abbreviation of the training time is now being corrected by a follow-up program consisting largely of role-playing and discussion procedures.

It has been indicated that attitude change, which is akin to personality change, is a basic training problem. This does not mean that the usual training problems are not also present. Some of these may be evaluated in passing.

1. It is apparent that effective training must be preceded by creating a *need* or a desire for training. At the present time this is not a difficult problem. If supervisors are asked on what phase of the job they feel they most need help, there is almost complete agreement that help in the area of dealing with people is most needed.

2. Knowledge about psychology is important. Such subjects as individual differences, frustration, attitudes, motivation, fatigue, and counseling are of vital interest to supervisors and can, in part, be taught by the lecture method. For this type of training, time is readily made available. These subjects have a value in encouraging an

analysis of human relations problems, and they permit the use of the discussion method.

3. Skills must supplement this knowledge. In order to develop skills, practice on the job, interviews with trainees, and role playing are needed. When the basic attitude change is accomplished, the opportunity for developing skills is no longer difficult to obtain.

4. Certain aptitudes must be present in the trainees. However, these requirements seem not to be very great. Although persons with above-average intelligence absorb the knowledge content more readily than others, their attitudes are not more easily changed. In many instances very autocratic personalities change attitudes more readily than the friendly paternalists. It is desirable to investigate this problem in detail, since it is quite possible that the traits that make for good supervision, when a company does not train its supervisors in democratic methods, may be quite different from the traits that are essential to good democratic supervision. It seems that some men are autocratic merely because they have not given attention to human relations, but when they see these relationships as problems they develop a real interest. Thus men with engineering training can become interested in psychological problems when scientific concepts are incorporated in the training.

2*

A Human Relations
Training Program

Introduction

In order to understand the problems and results of democratic supervision it is necessary to outline briefly the intellectual content of the program as well as to give some indication of the procedures. In our opinion it is difficult to appreciate the full significance of democratic supervision unless one has background in certain psychological concepts. For this reason our training program has included training in psychological subjects as well as training in techniques. In the industries in which we have used the program the presentation of actual subject matter required 12 to 13 half days (3-hour periods), spaced a week or more apart. Approximately an equal amount of time was used for discussions, reports of experiences, and role playing. During the interval supervisors in the training group were encouraged to analyze job problems in terms of the principles under discussion and to practice the techniques on the job.

The subjects treated and the proportion of training time devoted to the subject in the two industries where the training has been most complete are given in Table 1.

The differences in percentages are due to the fact that in Industry A the program was slightly longer than in Industry C and the subjects of causation, individual differences, and fatigue were treated in greater detail. The time saved by these changes reduced the program to 12 periods, and proportionally more time was given to democratic supervision concepts and counseling procedures in Industry C.

---

* This chapter is an expansion of some of the material previously published by the author under the title "A Human Relations Program for Supervision," published in *Labor Relations Review* (36). For additional details on the treatment given the subjects of causation in behavior, attitudes, frustration, motivation, and fatigue, see Maier (35).

TABLE 1

DISTRIBUTION OF TIME DEVOTED TO VARIOUS TOPICS

Topic	Approximate Percentage of Time for Topic	
	Industry A	Industry C
Democratic leadership	25	34
Causation in behavior	$7\frac{1}{2}$	4
Individual differences among people	15	8
Nature of attitudes	$7\frac{1}{2}$	8
Frustration and its effect on behavior and attitudes	$7\frac{1}{2}$	8
Morale and group structure	$7\frac{1}{2}$	4
Motivation	15	15
Fatigue and boredom	$7\frac{1}{2}$	4
Employee contacts, interviewing, and counseling	$7\frac{1}{2}$	15

A brief summary of the points of emphasis in each of the topics will give the reader a general idea of the concepts covered and their relation to democratic supervision.   In presenting these summaries, proportionately more space is devoted to democratic leadership and counseling than appears in the training program.   This seems necessary because the subject matter of this volume centers around democratic leadership, and the other subjects serve primarily to clarify this approach.   The type of treatment given to other topics in the program is presented in detail elsewhere (35, 52).

Democratic Leadership

Basic Principles.   The section on democratic leadership is a presentation of an over-all viewpoint of a supervisor's activities in dealing with people.   The concepts utilized are based upon the work of Lewin and his students (4, 9, 22, 24, 25, 26), which subsequently led to the establishment of the Research Center for Group Dynamics at the University of Michigan.   Their experimental work with children (25, 26) demonstrates that many important personality traits are not only functions of the individual but of the type of leadership as well. In experimentally arranged clubs, children, aged 10–12, had either an authoritarian leader who gave orders and made all decisions, a democratic leader who encouraged participation and discussion of all matters, or a laissez-faire leader who supplied information only when requested but otherwise was a nonparticipant and permitted complete freedom. The experiments demonstrated that the democratic leadership situation was conducive to constructive, cooperative, and friendly behavior. Thus the notion of *leadership climate* as a factor in behavior is established.

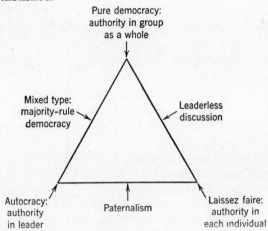

FIG. 1. The basic difference between various types of leadership. The location of authority or the place where decisions are made differs in pure democracy, autocracy, and laissez-faire situations. These extreme locations are shown as the angles of a triangle. Intermediate locations are also possible, and these can be described as falling on the sides of the triangle. Majority-rule democracy would seem to fall between pure group decision and autocracy because it implies both participation and imposition of a majority upon a minority. A paternalistic kind of leader is both autocratic, in that he makes decisions, and laissez faire, in that he considers the wishes of individuals, and so may be described as being a point on the base of the triangle. Since a leaderless discussion involves discussion but does not make for organized action, it may be described as a condition between pure democracy and laissez faire. Any leader may be described by his placement on this triangle.

A leader might also fall within the triangle. This would indicate that he showed all characteristics. He might do this by imposing some decisions on the group, practicing group decisions on other issues, and letting individuals do as they pleased on others. Thus the leader's act describes his style of leadership for a given situation.

Lewin (22) distinguished between the types of leadership on the basis of differences in the location of authority. In the autocratic type of social situation authority resides in the leader; in laissez-faire situations, in each individual; in purely democratically led situations it resides in the group as a whole. These distinctions are graphically described in Fig. 1. Between these pure types of leadership there are a number of possible mixed types. The majority-rule type of democracy, the paternalistic type of autocracy, and leaderless types of discussion would be mixtures according to this viewpoint.

It is important to consider the group as something different from a collection of individuals. Through democratic leadership, problems are solved by group decision. Thus democratic leadership training becomes positive training in techniques of obtaining the group's participation in making decisions and solving problems. Merely to influence group leaders to refrain from autocratic methods would be negative training and could easily result in the laissez-faire type of situation and its resulting disorganization. The objective of discussions under democratic leadership is to obtain *unanimous* agreement, and the skilled leader can obtain this degree of agreement in a high percentage of instances.

There are important reasons for emphasizing 100 per cent agreement rather than settling for a majority opinion. A majority opinion tends to divide a group into two or more subgroups. In essence, the majority functions autocratically in that it imposes its solution on others and thus produces divided interests and loyalties as well as some hostilities so common in autocratically led groups. However, even more important in the stress placed on full agreement is the effect that it has on the leader and on the participants. Everyone in the group is important when his agreement is required. Thus the leader will tend to respect minority opinions and will attempt to get at the bottom of conflicts. Group members are motivated to keep the minority members with them and therefore become less inclined to exclude anyone from the group. It is only when a person feels he no longer belongs to a group that he becomes actively hostile and uncooperative. Seeking full agreement also discourages trickery by which groups get together beforehand and plan on how they can obtain a quick majority decision.

Once the importance of full acceptance is understood one can deviate from it and settle on the best fit. The important thing is that the discussion be a sincere attempt at resolving differences.

Since democratic leadership implies the resolving of differences and the obtaining of common goals, one may suppose that workers will determine policies and run the factory and that all of the worker's time will be devoted to discussions. Neither of these conclusions necessarily follows from the concepts of democratic supervision.

Since the type of leadership is often thought of in terms of the amount of freedom offered, the above definitions of leadership must be re-examined in the light of the amount of freedom afforded and the manner in which freedom is curtailed. Only the laissez-faire situation would be purely free in that each individual would act as he pleased, and such a condition would exclude cooperative effort. Both autocracy and pure democracy restrict freedom, autocracy by imposing the leader's will on the group, and democracy by social pressure. The one is a force imposed from outside the group and implies that the leader has power. The other is a set of forces which act from within the group and implies that group members must consider the wishes of each other. The desire to be well thought of by one's

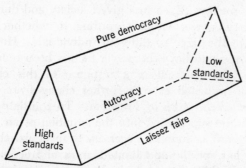

FIG. 2. Differences in the efficiencies of groups form a third dimension. A prism is here used to picture this aspect of group functioning and at the same time to describe the various locations of a decision-making function. It follows that efficiency or standards can be high or low in any type of leadership. An important problem is to determine which type of leadership can achieve high standards most easily. The prism may be used to describe not only a group's leadership but also the performance of groups under different leadership styles.

fellows makes each of us considerate of others and represents a positive force. We don't always do what we want to, but give up some of our freedoms to remain a group member. Thus it follows that the autocracy and democracy differ, not in that one permits more freedom than the other, but in that one restricts freedom through fear and the other through a positive choice.

Another viewpoint associated with definitions of leadership is that of outcome. It may be said that one must be autocratic to get results. According to the above definitions, outcomes of high and low efficiency represent a different dimension. Autocratic situations may be either efficient or inefficient in that the leader may have high or low standards. The same is true of laissez-faire situations. Individuals in a group might have either high or low standards depending on their individual motivations. In pure democracy a group might likewise set high or low standards, depending on the motivations existing in the problem situation. The manner in which efficiency relates to the type of leadership is diagrammed in Fig. 2. The important question is, "In what type of leadership are high standards most easily achieved?" The answer to this will partly depend upon the amount of power an autocratic leader possesses. Considering the limited power invested in supervisors in a modern industry, autocratic leadership might be inadequate for obtaining high efficiency. Thus it is conceivable that in one society autocracy may be more effective than other approaches because the power possessed by management varies from society to society. Even in a given society and during the same period in history, power varies according to whether owners and management are the same or different individuals. Has our society changed its values, and have the power factors been reduced through unionization? Was paternalism a response to this change? Can prerogatives be protected even if further changes are necessitated?

The Concept of the Area of Freedom. To translate the point of view of democratic supervision into the situation of an operating industry (36), the author found it necessary to recognize that each level of supervision has specific and limited areas of freedom. Thus the nature of the job, the existence of higher levels of supervision, problems requiring experts, union contracts, and labor legislation exclude a number of activities from a first-line supervisor's authority. These limitations of the area in which the supervisor may operate are diagrammed in Fig. 3. The large circle represents the limitations that the job situation imposes. Thus the supervisor cannot permit employees the freedom to decide on the type of work they do or to determine what products the company should manufacture. Even within the work situation there are certain limitations. Company policies ($C. Po.$) and company practices ($C. Pr.$) do not fall within the first-line supervisor's authority, and therefore he cannot share such problems with his group. These limitations are diagrammed as rectangles in Fig. 3. Problems of policy and practice do, however, fall within the area of freedom of higher levels of supervision, and such problems can be decided by the group that reports to the level of management having such authority. Union contracts ($U.C.$) and legislation ($L.$) likewise restrict the authority of each level of supervision, and these restrictions are shown as triangles in Fig. 3. Finally, some problems fall within the scope of an expert's responsibility, and to the extent that problems are solved by experts ($E.$), the supervisor's freedom of activity is limited. This limitation is shown as a square.

Other limitations of freedom also are possible. For example, a second-line supervisor may restrict a first-line supervisor by absorbing some of his functions and making some of his decisions. The encroachment of higher levels of supervision on the area of freedom of lower levels is shown in the figure by the pocket indicated by *H.L.* The

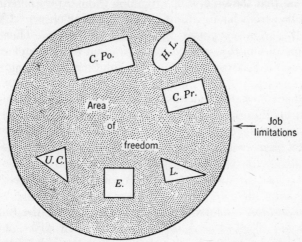

Fig. 3. The area of freedom for the practice of democratic leadership. The circle represents the limitations that the job situation imposes upon activity; *C. Po.* and *C. Pr.* represent the limitations imposed by company policies and company practices, respectively; *U. C.* and *L.* represent activity areas removed by union contracts and legislation, respectively, and *E.* represents problem areas solved by experts. *H. L.* represents the possible interference that a higher-level supervisor may impose by encroaching on the freedom of a supervisor who reports to him. The remaining area falls within the authority of a given level of supervision, and problems in this area may be solved by group techniques. This is a given supervisor's area of freedom. In most instances less than an hour per week in group discussion would solve the problems that concern the group.

size of this pocket will depend upon the degree to which a higher-level supervisor restricts the freedom of those reporting to him. Although this may be deemed an undesirable practice in management, it represents a reality that should be recognized and is a practice that higher levels may impose merely. because of their position in the management hierarchy.

The remaining region represents the authority given to the supervisor. Only problems in a given supervisor's area of freedom can be solved by group participation. The limitations on the area of freedom do not seem to interfere with the success of democratic leadership. The reasons for this will become more apparent in subsequent chapters.

The Role of the Expert. The training also recognizes that the supervisor himself is often in the position of an expert. In his capacity of an expert he may share his knowledge with the group. Thus his superior information is made available to the group so that group decisions can be made on a realistic level.

It is clear that the supervisor's function as an expert must be clearly distinguished from his functions as a leader. As an expert he neither leads a discussion nor passes opinions or judgments. Thus in democratic supervision the supervisor's extra knowledge and experience are incorporated into solutions, yet the solutions still remain the product of the group.

With these limitations clearly understood, the supervisor is able to approach his duties and create a work climate that induces the type of behavior found in the experimentally induced democratic climates. When the democratic concepts are presented with the limitations clearly stated, the fear that employees will make unreasonable decisions is greatly reduced, and supervisors can be induced to make experimental trials with the procedure.

The Importance of First-Hand Experience. After the fundamental concepts are clarified and distinctions between different types of leadership are understood, a number of industrial illustrations of the democratic type of supervision used in the company are presented. A variety of cases are given to show that all types of problems lend themselves to the method. The fear that the leader gives up something when he uses the method of group decision is partly lost when supervisors learn the way employees respond and how problems with which they themselves are concerned lend themselves to solution; but more important in overcoming this fear is a personal experience with the procedure. Throughout the program the conviction gradually grows that democratic leadership increases the importance and influence of a supervisor. He becomes powerful because of his effective influence, not because of his ability to instill fear. It is important, therefore, that each member of a training class obtain first-hand experience with the technique.

The Operation of Democratic Supervision at Various Management Levels. Although the problems falling within the area of freedom vary with different levels of supervision in accordance with the company's organizational structure, the principles of democratic supervision remain the same. Each level of supervision has its responsibilities and its problems, but the supervisor in each instance can lead the group of individuals that report to him in such a manner that the solutions to problems become the group's product. Thus if all levels of supervision practice democratic leadership the first-line supervisor

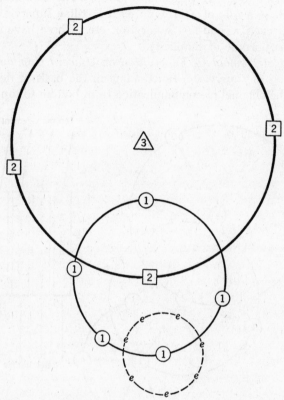

FIG. 4. Representation of levels of organization under democratic management. Only the first, second, and third levels of management are here pictured, and these are indicated by numerals. The center of the circle represents the leader, and the level of supervision reporting to the leader is shown on the circumference of the circle. Each level of supervision may solve its problems by group methods. By this arrangement a given individual in management may be the leader of one group and a participating member of the next group. The symbol *e* represents rank-and-file employees who report to the first level of supervision. To complete the diagram the *e*'s reporting to each of the first-line supervisors should be drawn. Similarly, the constellations for each of the second-line supervisors should be included.

becomes the leader of the group that reports to him, and he in turn becomes a member of the group that is led by the second level of supervision. This relationship between different levels of supervision is diagrammed in Fig. 4. This figure is incomplete, however, in that it begins with the employees (e) and carries the structure to the third level (3) of supervision only. The completed picture would continue the arrangement to the top executive group. The complete picture also would show a ring of e's around each first-line supervisor, a ring of 1's around each second-line supervisor, etc. These have not been drawn for the purpose of simplicity.

The Effect of Democratic Supervision on Upward Communication. With all levels of supervision functioning on the basis of democratic leadership, the channel of communication from bottom to top is facili-

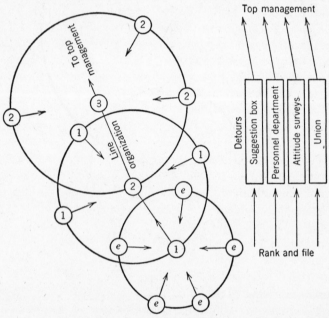

Fig. 5. Lines of communication upward. The arrows indicate the directions of communication. Thus the e's communicate to 1's, the 1's to 2's, and the 2's to 3's, etc. All these lines result in an upward trend in communication. Without proper upward communication detours develop. Such detours as the suggestion box, personnel functions, surveys, and unions are ways for communicating upward when the line organization is inadequate for communication purposes.

tated, since each level of supervision is influenced by the forces from below. The communication line upward is shown in Fig. 5. The arrows indicate the direction of communication. The first level of supervision learns about the feelings and attitudes of the rank and file, and he reflects them when he meets with the second-line supervisor. Likewise, the third level learns of the problems existing below him from the second-line supervisors who report to him. This set-up represents a channel of communication within the line organization, which too frequently is lacking. In the absence of such communication various detours have arisen to supply this need. The suggestion box, personnel functions, attitude surveys, and the union office represent examples of upward communication channels outside the line organization.

Too often top management has had to learn about employee attitudes and needs by these means, and frequently they are inadequate. With facilitated communication within the line organization these alternate channels could be used for more constructive functions.

The Effect of Democratic Supervision on the Area of Freedom. When all levels of management practice democratic supervision there is a tendency to increase the areas of freedom at lower levels because of two changes. In the first place, there is less encroachment on the areas of freedom from those above to those below, thus reducing the size of the *H.L.* pockets shown in Fig. 3. In the second place, areas of freedom are increased because the problems of persons reporting to a given supervisor receive consideration. In autocratic supervision, with lines of communication functioning primarily downward, most of the problems raised for consideration are those of management. When problems originating at lower levels are given consideration by higher levels the problem-solving area is increased, and the area of freedom is expanded.

Some Common Misconceptions. Because the group-decision method is new and because people tend to fit new experiences into old categories we have prepared a list of things that group decision is not, in contrast with what it really is. The list shown in Fig. 6 contains the kinds of items the author has found from experience to be stumbling blocks. It is hoped that this list will aid the reader to appreciate the unique character of the group-decision method, which is at the core of democratic supervision.

A brief discussion of democratic supervision is likely to give the impression that a great deal of time is consumed in frequent group discussions. It should be remembered that decisions apply to changes and that these are relatively infrequent in an organized job situation. A supervisor who is alert to dissatisfaction in a group and who is willing to have employees participate in solving problems that concern them would find one short meeting a week to be very adequate. Higher levels of supervision already hold conferences, and it is pos-

sible that actual conference time in many instances would be reduced
if group decisions were followed.

It should also be pointed out that the distinctions between different
types of leadership emphasized at this point are for purposes of clarity.
Once these distinctions are understood, modifications and adaptations
to special conditions and to specific problems can be made more easily.
It is not necessary to assume that because one method of leadership

Group Decision Is Not	Group Decision Is
1. Abandoning control of the situation.	A way of controlling through leadership rather than force.
2. A disregard of discipline.	A way of group discipline through social pressure.
3. A way of giving each individual what he wants.	A way of being fair to the job and all members of a group.
4. A way of manipulating people.	A way of reconciling conflicting attitudes.
5. A way of selling the supervisor's ideas to a group.	Permitting the group to jell on the idea it thinks will best solve a problem.
6. Sugar-coated autocracy.	A way of letting facts and feelings operate.
7. A matter of collecting votes.	Pooled thinking.
8. Consultative supervision in which mere advice is sought.	Cooperative problem solving.
9. A way of turning the company over to employees.	A way of giving each person a chance to participate in things that concern him in his work situation.
10. Something anyone can do if he wishes.	A method that requires skill and a respect for other people.

FIG. 6. The group-decision method compared with other methods.

is superior under certain conditions it will be superior under other
conditions.

In subsequent chapters various problems in the use of the group-
decision method will be given special consideration, and a clearer
over-all picture of the procedure and its values will be gained.

Causation in Behavior

As the section on democratic leadership serves to furnish a general
outlook on supervision, the section on causation furnishes a point of
view on behavior problems (35). The central point of the discussion
is to demonstrate that behavior (B) is the product of an interaction
between the stimulus or situation (S) and the person or organism (O).

These relations are represented by the formulation $(S \leftrightarrow O \rightarrow B)$. Further, it is the behavior which in turn accomplishes something. Confusion often arises because another person reacts to the individual's accomplishment rather than to his behavior. Thus a mother reacts to milk being spilled rather than to the child moving his arms, and a foreman reacts to the amount of damage when an employee has an accident rather than to the behavior that accomplished the damage. This point is made by extending the formulation to read $S \leftrightarrow O \rightarrow B \rightarrow A$, in which A represents accomplishment or the result of behavior.

If all behavior is caused, then emphasis must be placed on analysis rather than on fault finding. The prevention of a repetition of undesirable behavior rather than punishment for past behavior is an important attitude change. The techniques for analyzing behavior problems are discussed and cases analyzed. This treatment covers what might essentially be called the psychological approach to behavior.

For discussions one utilizes cases and illustrations to show that behavior can be altered by changes in either the S or the O. Discussion is also used to show that the same behavior may have a variety of causes and the same cause may produce a wide variety of behaviors. Thus correction requires analysis. There is no one cure for a given behavior defect.

It was evident from discussions that the point of view presented in this section had a direct bearing on attitude change. Situations that previously were sources of irritation can become interesting problems. In addition, the topic serves a useful purpose in suggesting constructive attacks on problems. When an individual is blamed for behavior, one is inclined to overlook the opportunities for altering behavior by changes in the situation in which the behavior occurs. The supervisor also is always an important part of the situation, and changes in him may lead to improvement. An acceptance of this fact makes the supervisor aware of his own contribution to an employee's behavior. When the analysis of a problem suggests that changes should be made in the organism, the causation view throws the emphasis on the use of techniques that will modify the organism in such a way that future behavior will be altered. This approach is in contrast to that shown when the attitude of blame is present. In such instances the techniques used are designed to punish for what has been done. Punishment for past behavior may not be the best way to prevent a recurrence of the undesirable behavior, so that it is important to approach a problem with a desire to prevent rather than to punish. The prevention approach throws the emphasis on influencing behavior by changes in the S (situation) and away from endeavors to change the O (person), which are associated with the blame approach. When the value of changing the S is fully appreciated, the effect of different kinds of supervision on behavior is more readily apparent and acceptable.

Human Abilities

This section consists of two parts and is largely informational in the sense that a knowledge of the origin and nature of human abilities is analyzed (35). It becomes a study of O in the $S \leftrightarrow O \rightarrow B$ sequence. The first part of the presentation deals with individual differences and is the usual type of elementary treatment of distribution curves of ability and the importance of the distinction between aptitude and achievement.

Emphasis is placed upon the degree of difference in ability and the importance of proper placement. Employees who fail on a job are frequently treated as if they had poor attitudes. Often these attitudes arise because the employee is protecting his inability to perform. Failure on a job should be analyzed. Since ability to produce is a function of aptitude, training, and motivation, and since each of these factors requires different treatment, the cause of the deficiency must be known before a remedy will suggest itself.

Supervisors readily recognize cases in which they have used the wrong remedy, and lateral transfers are seen as possible solutions for misfits on a job. A common error in supervision is to promote individuals who succeed and leave on the job those who do not improve. When carried to its logical conclusion, this approach moves employees along until they get on a job they cannot do well. Finally, each job is performed by persons having the least aptitude for the job.

The recognition that motivation as well as ability to do a job influences production is extremely important to supervision. In comparing production distribution curves and ability distribution curves, one finds the former to be less widespread than the latter. From such facts one can develop, in a group of supervisors, the facts that (a) employees showing low production are more highly motivated than those showing high production and (b) employees showing high production have more ability than those showing low production. These facts lead to the conclusion that the productivity of a group can be improved by using the proper motivation techniques on the superior workers and by using training or placement procedures on inferior workers. Ordinarily the supervisor uses motivation methods on the below-average persons, who respond to the pressure by becoming hostile toward the high producers. In order to protect the low producers the most capable men are required to hold back on production. Thus in motivating the less capable men the supervisor actually motivates the more capable men in the direction of lower production. This common-sense method is best altered if the foregoing conclusions are developed through group discussion.

The second part of the human abilities section is concerned with (a) developing an appreciation of the natures of specific human abilities, (b) creating an interest in job analysis, and (c) developing skills in merit rating. Merit is defined in terms of an employee's value to the company, and includes both productivity and such attitudes as make him a cooperative and dependable employee.

The Nature of Attitudes

The importance of attitudes in industry is brought out by a discussion of the investigations by Roethlisberger and Dickson (51) at the Hawthorne plant. The nature of attitudes and the factors that influence them is then clarified by studies in social psychology. Attitude is treated as a frame of reference, and emphasis is placed upon the fact that management personnel and employees naturally have different frames of reference because of their different backgrounds and interests (35). The role of social pressure in influencing attitudes is illustrated by experimental studies and is related to the social groups within the company. Since employees and management are in different social groups, employees are less responsive to management pressure than to employee pressures. Thus employees may refuse to cross a picket line even though they may have no dissatisfaction with their employer.

The practical aspects of this section are directed toward developing an appreciation of the fact that human relations problems largely stem from misunderstandings that have their basis in different frames of reference. The behavior of another person becomes clear only if it is analyzed in terms of his own frame of reference. This means that an understanding supervisor must discover the way employees think and the values they live by, and this can be achieved by listening sympathetically to employees' views. The values of the nondirective counseling technique and interviewing methods are mentioned in this connection but are developed later in the program.

That logic and argument do not change attitudes, but that these are the ways by which people justify their attitudes, is a fact developed in discussion. The conclusion that employees' attitudes change through job satisfaction, considerate treatment, and opportunities to express their dissatisfactions is readily developed through discussion. Ordinarily, supervision attempts to influence attitudes by giving employees more facts and by telling them where they are wrong. The presentation of the material on attitudes greatly reduces this tendency, as is apparent from reports on assignments made. Practice in interviewing also gives the supervisor first-hand experience with the factors that influence attitude and the misunderstandings that arise when people with different frames of reference discuss a problem on the job.

The relationship between democratic leadership and the group attitudes is analyzed to show that the democratic leader conducts himself in the light of prevailing attitudes and to point up the fact that leadership climate is an important determiner of attitudes. Some individuals who are reluctant to accept democratic leadership as a philosophy of supervision are ready to do so after the analysis of attitudes. Thus this section enriches the concept of democratic leadership and extends the training of the leader.

Frustration and Its Effect on Behavior and Attitudes

Motivated problem solving and frustration reactions to a problem situation are clearly distinguished (12, 38). In a motivated condition, behavior is variable and goal-oriented. When a problem becomes too stressful, frustration occurs, and then behavior shows the characteristics of aggression, regression, fixation, and resignation. Variability is replaced by fixated or stereotyped behavior, and constructive goal-oriented behavior is replaced by nonconstructive regression and destructive aggression. These behaviors also reflect themselves in attitudes by making them antisocial, childish, and stubborn.

With the recognition that frustrated behavior shows certain characteristics, supervision becomes more tolerant of such behavior. Instead of regarding the frustrated person as a disagreeable individual, he is recognized as one who has a problem. A trained supervisor now sees few if any cases of insubordination. Instead of aggravating a condition he seeks to discover the problem behind the behavior.

The values of nondirective counseling also become more apparent, since the expression of frustration is one of the ways for relieving the state of frustration. The supervisor often can help the employee find nondestructive ways of expressing his frustration. He can also appreciate factors in the work situation that give rise to frustration and can often correct the situation. Subsequent training in counseling supplies him with skills that aid others in making life adjustments.

The understanding of frustration also transfers to the home situation. In a number of cases marital problems in the lives of supervisors have been corrected by insights into frustration. Behaviors of their children have been remedied by giving the children more affection and understanding and by listening to their problems. The important appreciation generally obtained is that punishment for an act induced by frustration increases frustration and fails to correct behavior; rather, kindness and understanding become the techniques a person uses when he appreciates the nature of frustration-induced behavior.

The importance of the distinction between motivated and frustrated behavior also has important implications for the training of supervisors in human relations. In Chapter 3 it will be shown how conference skills must be geared to the condition of the group. On the one hand, when frustrations and fears are present in a group one cannot use the same procedures, with hope of acceptance, that one follows when a group is motivated to solve a problem. On the other hand, the techniques that are effective for dealing with emotional resistance are unnecessary and time-consuming when a group is motivated to solve a problem.

Morale and Group Structure

The treatment of morale consists of defining morale, demonstrating the importance of good morale to industry and, through discussion, developing the point that the leader (or supervisor) is a key figure in determining the state of good morale. The factors of mutual sacrifice, participation, experience of progress, tolerance, and freedom are discussed and related to both autocratic and democratic types of supervision (35).

This section again strengthens the belief in the fundamental soundness of the democratic type of supervision, and usually most of the remaining skeptics become convinced that psychological principles all point to the technique of democratic supervision.

Group structure is approached from the view of sociometry, and some experiments are described. The importance of recognizing the mutual choices, cliques, stars, and isolates in the work situation are stressed. It is recommended that the supervisor attempt to discover these relations in the group by observing the social interrelationships on and off the job.

Splits in the group when employees fall into two opposing subgroups are also discussed. The color line seems to be less important than is usually supposed in industry. However, the split that exists between younger and older employees is often not recognized for what it is. During the depression few employees were hired, and as a consequence two groups were formed: the predepression employees and the postdepression employees. Since World War II, which followed the depression, resulted in the hiring of many new employees, these new employees became a threat to the older employees, and this, in some offices, resulted in considerable hard feeling. Having older employees sponsor new employees was found to be an effective method for bridging the gap.

Sometimes there is fear that the actual making of sociograms of the job situation might create undesirable results. Supervisors, therefore, were not encouraged to make them without approval from above, but rather were advised to become sensitive to the existence of the social structure and to appreciate its importance in determining social values. The work of Roethlisberger and Dickson contains many illustrations found useful (51).

Motivation and Work

The treatment of motivation is similar to an elementary treatment in an introductory textbook of psychology. Emphasis, however, is placed upon acquired needs, since failure to appreciate them as real leads to a critical attitude toward our fellow man (35). No one can properly judge another since needs are within the person and he responds to these personal needs, which may differ from those of the one who passes judgment. The importance of the ego need and its recognition in aiding people to save face is discussed in detail.

Choice behavior and the implications of the concept of "level of aspiration" are introduced and applied to the job situation. Individual differences are likewise brought out, particularly in connection with different responses to jobs, social prestige, working conditions, and supervisors.

The use of positive and negative incentives is given particular emphasis. Punishment is regarded as a poor training aid and an inadequate tool for disciplinary procedures because it is not constructive and may produce resentment and frustration. The discussion method is used to discover constructive techniques to motivate. Praise, financial rewards, goals, and methods for introducing experiences of progress on the job are discussed in relation to different types of work.

The discussion of this subject tends to free the supervisor of the opinion that loafing on the job is a goal. Rather, loafing is unpleasant, and, if employees are found to engage in loafing it is because there is an incentive for doing so or because loafing is an expression of aggression toward the company. Then the remedy is to remove the cause of loafing. When one regards loafing as a pleasant activity, one has difficulty in finding an effective remedy, because the behavior is inherent in human nature, and in such cases the desire to use punishment prevails.

The section on motivation is an important one for influencing supervisory attitudes in the direction of constructive approaches to the job situation. The desire to make a job attractive and work relations pleasant becomes an important objective. The use of penalties and other forms of disciplinary action disappears from discussions, and democratic leadership receives further appreciation, since it encourages constructive controls of the situation through the desire of individuals to conform to group decisions. As a matter of fact, the group decisions become an important positive incentive.

Fatigue and Boredom

In this presentation, attitudes are again emphasized to bring out the fact that misunderstandings arise when rest pauses are regarded as gifts or concessions rather than as methods for increasing efficiency; or when work stoppages are interpreted as loafing rather than as resting. The presentation of experimental material is used to influence attitudes as well as to suggest methods for reducing fatigue.

Boredom is included as a form of psychological fatigue and is considered just as real and just as disruptive to efficiency as muscular fatigue (35). Techniques for reducing boredom emphasize the uses of subgoals (assuming that wages and reaching the end of the day are the major goals). Rest pauses, music, the setting up of hourly quotas by the employees themselves, the breaking up of long tasks into smaller units, the bunching of repetitive tasks into larger units, and the completion of tasks are suggested techniques for introducing subgoals. Methods for introducing variability into jobs are also suggested, and these often seem to go contrary to efficiency methods. It is found, for example, that job satisfaction and production can be

improved in a repetitive job if girls are periodically required to cross
a room to a filing cabinet rather than use one at their elbows. Changes
in the situation which make for variety are sound from the point of
view of reducing monotony, although they may go contrary to some
concepts in motion and time study.

Emphasis is given to the notions that repetitive activities are boring
because they do not give the experience of progress toward a goal and
that the completion of a task is an important goal. Interruption of
tasks produce emotional tensions, and supervisors are cautioned to
appreciate this fact, since it explains why employees resist starting
assignments toward the end of a day and why poor human relations
often arise when a supervisor interrupts work or gives one employee's
unfinished assignments to another.

Employee Contacts, Interviewing, and Nondirective Counseling

Interpersonal Relations. The relationships between a supervisor
and those reporting to him are divided into three general classifications: (1) *Employee contacts* are considered to include casual contacts, training on the job, service measurements, job assignments, etc.
The purpose of such contacts is to use them as opportunities to (*a*)
treat employees as individuals, (*b*) create rapport and free expression
in employees, (*c*) constructively motivate employees, and (*d*) become
familiar with individual employee attitudes and values. The democratic attitude and the principles of motivation make up most of the
pertinent subject matter in this connection, and these concepts are
applied to the handling of the different types of contacts. (2) *Interviews* are scheduled meetings and are used in connection with employment, resignations, merit ratings, and job changes. Since the
greatest value of an interview resides in discovering attitudes, the
techniques of developing mutual interests and letting the employee
do the talking are emphasized. The subject of attitude is regarded
as the most pertinent subject matter in this connection, and the role
of attitudes in different types of interviews is discussed and practice
opportunities are offered in the form of assigned roles acted out by
members of the group. (3) *Counseling* is regarded as the area that
deals with disturbed and excited individuals. The subject of frustration furnishes the most pertinent principles in such cases. The methods of nondirective counseling (releasing expression and reflecting
feelings) are discussed and practice assignments are given (52).

Employee contacts and interviewing will be discussed at greater length in Chapter 12. The basic skill requirements in these areas depend greatly on recent developments in nondirective counseling, and, as a consequence, the principles of this type of counseling need further clarification. On the following pages, the underlying concepts of nondirective counseling are presented. In Chapter 13 the techniques for training supervisors in counseling skills will be given detailed consideration.

Some Training Problems. The important thing is to train supervisors to distinguish between fact and feeling. A person who feels he has been overlooked should be permitted to express this feeling regardless of whether the facts he reports are accurate or even fair to management. To argue the facts in the case prevents free expression. It is through expression that the frustration is relieved, and it is through expression that feelings become clarified and understood in their proper perspective. A study of cases helps to demonstrate how listening and reacting to feelings stimulate expression.

Likewise it is important to permit a disturbed person to solve his own problems. A person only acts to solve his problem when he accepts the solution. When solutions are supplied by another person they may: (1) produce resistance and stifle expression because the troubled person is made to feel inadequate; (2) make the person dependent and less able to cope with future problems; (3) not fit the values, needs, and attitude of the person who must act on the solution; (4) be given before the person advised is ready for the action suggested; and (5) prevent the person from developing the insights necessary for the proper execution of a solution.

Thus the necessary attitude of a supervisor in a counseling situation is that every person can best solve his own problems, provided he is supplied with a situation that encourages him to express his feelings freely. To advise or to express opinions stifles the process.

The needed skills in counseling are difficult because they go contrary to previous experience and because they require a new attitude. It is difficult to pay attention to feelings when we are used to paying attention to ideas. Likewise it is difficult to refrain from giving advice when another requests it or when we feel we know the answer. To develop skills in counseling one must develop substitute responses for the old ones. These substitutes are such responses as, "You feel you would like someone to tell you what to do," "You feel that the company hasn't always treated you fairly," "You feel that I as your supervisor have been too critical of your work."

Such responses indicate acceptance of and respect for feelings. They encourage further expression and eventually the expression of feelings carries the analysis to earlier experiences. One can be quite sure that if a person's disturbance is in excess of what the situation warrants there are earlier experiences that have contributed to the condition. These earlier experiences must become linked with the present feelings to permit the necessary insights and understanding.

The Use of Counselors vs. Supervisors for Dealing with Disturbed Employees. Clinical counselors often feel that counseling cannot proceed effectively when the counselor is in a position of authority. It has been our experience that the democratic supervisor can do a great deal in this area. Supervisors who use this method for the first time find that they obtain expression far in excess of that previously obtained. The employee benefits when the supervisor is trained to listen, and the supervisor becomes more sensitive and understanding with employee behavior when he practices nondirective counseling procedures.

Naturally the counseling interview is handicapped when the supervisor himself is involved, but even in such cases better understanding is obtained. Although an industrial counselor might, in some cases, be in a better position than a supervisor to counsel, it is also possible that in other instances the supervisor has an advantage. He is on the job when a disturbance occurs, and in many instances he can use the counseling technique when the situation is ripe. An incident that sets off an act of aggression may serve to relieve buried or suppressed aggressions as well as bring them to light and permit insight.

The supervisor has a second advantage in that his role in the work situation need not be interpreted to employees. Industries that introduce counselors into the work situation must spend a good deal of time in having them inducted and accepted by employees.

It is not intended that supervision should replace industrial counselors; rather, supervisors may serve to supplement a counseling program or function as an alternate program until a more complete program is adopted. Certainly supervisors that are familiar with the values and techniques of counseling will be more receptive to a counseling program that may be introduced later to make a human relations program more complete. Having knowledge of the nature and values of counseling, supervisors will not feel that their authority is being undermined or questioned by a counseling program.

It has been our experience that supervisors can be effectively trained to become good listeners and to refrain from advising employees on how to feel or think. Many of our supervisors have become skilled in the use of the listening and reflecting procedures.

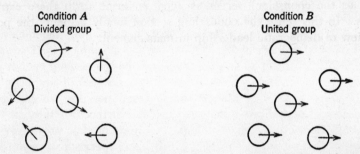

Condition *A*
Divided group

Condition *B*
United group

FIG. 7. Conflicting and integrated group interests. Individuals in a group often have conflicting interests or action tendencies, as in condition *A*. This condition is shown in the diagram on the left. The democratic leader stimulates group discussion, and this expression eventually results in a meeting of minds. This altered condition is shown in the figure on the right and describes the team spirit existing under condition *B*.

Difficult problems have been solved by such persons, and, in the process of seeing problems from another person's side, supervisors grow more understanding, more tolerant, more interested in people, and better integrated.

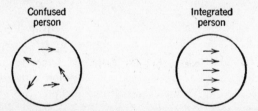

Confused
person

Integrated
person

FIG. 8. Conflicting and integrated-action tendencies within the individual. On the left the individual is shown with impulses leading to different actions. On the right the action tendencies have been integrated. The second condition is achieved when the counselor causes feelings to be expressed and examined freely.

Comparison of Counseling and Group Leadership Skills. The nondirective counseling viewpoint is consistent with the democratic type of supervision. In reaching group decisions a group of individuals become integrated. This condition is illustrated in Fig. 7. In counseling the integration must be achieved within the individual, and in disturbed cases one must deal with a person whose impulses and values are unclear and in conflict. This condition is illustrated in Fig. 8. In both cases the integration is achieved by permitting the opposed forces to come to expression, and the democratic leader (as well as the counselor) serves as agent to bring forth these expressions. In this sense the counseling section finally cements the point of view of democratic leadership in management.

3

Discussion Methods

Introduction

Training implies that an individual is being subjected to change or behavior modification. Recent evidence (38) indicates that there are two possible types of conditions under which a change in an individual occurs, changes under motivation conditions and changes under frustrating conditions. This suggests that training methods may also have to be of two different types. If this is a likelihood, it becomes necessary to examine the two basic conditions of behavior modification. Let us examine, therefore, each of these conditions and their implications for training. In the first, a person has a set of habits and attitudes which he has previously acquired, and these tend to persist because they are stronger than alternatives. If one wishes to induce a change under such a condition, one must build up alternative habits and attitudes and make them stronger and more attractive than the former responses. Thus habits A will be given up for habits B when the B responses are made stronger. This implies that both drill and sales (motivational) procedures could be used. It is this type of condition that is usually assumed in learning theories and around which most training procedures are built. Standard training films repeat steps and procedures and do everything to show the virtue of the new procedure. This condition is also implied when one uses lecture methods, visual aids, and emotional appeals. It is assumed that people will change when more attractive alternatives are presented. Thus any method that brings alternative procedures or behaviors to attention or makes them attractive assumes that one kind of behavior will be substituted for another when the substitute is known, understood, and desired. The limiting condition for change under this state of affairs becomes one of finding ways to motivate a person and the degree of learning ability of the individual who is to be changed.

43

However, this view does not explain the many instances of failure to produce a desired change when both motivation and learning ability are adequate. One finds cases in which there is active resistance to change. Thus some behaviors and attitudes seem to have a quality of persistence or stubbornness that cannot be explained by supposing that alternatives are unknown or are unattractive. For example, the person who has a phobia for snakes may fear a picture of a snake, knowing full well that the fear is inconvenient and that a picture of a snake can do no injury. Attempts to train the person out of this fear by methods designed to convince him that pictures of snakes do no harm have been entirely ineffective. In such an instance the fear behavior has a compelling property, and the person cannot give up the behavior by choosing to do so or by being trained in a different behavior. This compelling characteristic is found in behaviors associated with anxiety and worry, and in extreme instances it forms the basis for abnormal behavior. Behavior of this kind persists because a person is trapped by his old responses, not because he does not know or desire alternatives. This degree of rigidity or stubbornness has long been recognized in emotionally disturbed people, and techniques other than those used for training when the individual is receptive have been found useful. Methods for changing such behaviors have been the techniques of mental therapy.

Experimental evidence (1, 38, 52) has supported the view that this type of persistence is not an exception to a general rule in that it is confined to the abnormal, but rather it represents a different kind of mental condition to which all of us are subject. When dealing with the problem of changing habits in a group of people one must recognize two types of mental conditions: (a) the generally recognized condition in which a habit persists until a stronger substitute is learned; and (b) a less commonly understood condition in which old behavior persists even when it is inadequate and despite a knowledge of attractive alternatives. The first of these conditions is found when the conditions for acquiring the first response were rational rather than emotional and the person was interested in using the behavior to attain some goal. The second is found when the conditions for acquiring the first response were frustrating or when the conditions for introducing a change contain threats or fears and thus develop frustrations at a later time.

Methods for changing behavior under the two conditions necessarily differ. In the first case the usual training methods are adequate because they can be used to train the individual to develop new or substitute behaviors. In the second case training procedures must be designed to reduce the compelling strength of the old response before efforts to develop substitutes can become effective. These training procedures become primarily fear-reducing and threat-reducing procedures. Some of them take the form of creating opportunities for expressing the fears so that they can be seen and recognized for what they are. This is a common procedure in therapy (1, 2, 52). Other techniques take the form of changing the person's perspective so that he can view his own situation differently and thereby see it without the threats to his security. Still other techniques are designed to let the person discover the possible alternatives, and when he himself discovers them they contain no fear element (23, 52).

It is because so many of our resistances to changing in basic ways involve a fear of losing something that management training requires the use of methods that reduce fear and frustration and techniques that allow the person to discover the solution himself. In order to illustrate some of these procedures we will use them in the context of some of the training content. The important problem for the trainer is to be sensitive to the subject matter likely to meet with resistance so that he can adapt his procedures to the conditions he will face.

Often a participant asks a question and the trainer or conference leader answers it. Questions that show a true desire for information may safely be answered, but frequently a question shields doubt, fear, or a challenge that covers some hostility. In such instances the answer to a question may do more harm than good. For example, a group member may ask, "What would you do with a fellow that . . . ?" One may be quite sure that the questioner is emotionally involved and that he has attempted many approaches without success. To supply a remedy or solution would indicate that he has been inadequate. Now one has a *face-saving* problem to deal with in addition to the problem presented. Frequently the participant will withhold enough facts or so alter circumstances that he can refute a suggested solution. Then the trainer is placed in a face-saving situation. Questions of this sort readily lend themselves to various forms of group participation, and it is not uncommon for the questioner to discover for himself the solution to his problem. The procedures discussed in the following pages are methods for reducing resistance to change and developing acceptable solutions to problems.

The Developmental Discussion

Directing Discussion in Positive Action Channels. In a developmental discussion the leader attempts to guide a discussion along a particular line, but not to carry it beyond the point of acceptance. Thus this type of discussion is geared to the pace of the group's development. A certain background of information for which there is little or no resistance is first supplied by lecturing or by having the group supply information. Then by stimulating questions the group is made to react to the relevance of this information to other things. Thus the leader might ask, "How does this information relate to the problem of job transfers?" Such a question clearly points the way along a particular line of thinking. The leader thus controls the direction of the discussion and so carries the thought further, but along a particular line.

Suppose for example that the leader has presented evidence to show that morale is better in groups in which participation is relatively high, where supervision makes a serious attempt to learn what the group considers fair, where ways for experiencing progress are present, and where freedom is not unnecessarily restricted, but that morale tends to be relatively low in groups where these factors are operating to a lesser degree. These facts are not met with resistance, and usually such a list is memorized or supervisors feel that they already have the desired conditions present in their groups. However, the leader can make these principles more alive if he says, "Now let's take the first of these and see if we can find ways for increasing opportunities for participation on our job. Can any of you think of a way of increasing the participation of workers on your job?" Such a question clearly directs the discussion into new territory and also into a particular kind of territory. The group is not told how to run their jobs, nor are they made to feel that they have been inadequate. Rather they are confronted with an interesting problem, and each can speculate on possible improvements. Ideas can be suggested by group members, recorded by the leader on a blackboard to show that a contribution has been made, and then have the group evaluate each idea by a rather free exchange of experiences. Thus potential practices may be discovered, but they are developed in the group as the group's ideas and carry none of the threats and pressures present when an authority makes suggestions.

In a similar manner one could develop practices for the other specific principles. This procedure would clearly show progress, and the progress would arise primarily from group development.

The reader might ask whether the original list of principles should not have been developed by this procedure. This raises the question, "If developmental discussion has value should it not always be used?" It seems that conference methods have their optimum value when used in situations in which they have the best chance of being effective and are worth the time that they consume. Using different procedures also offers variety, which has attention value. If the developmental method were used to develop a list of morale principles the situation would not have been sufficiently shaped to prevent the discussion from spreading in many directions. Such a discussion does not permit the experience of progress. It is also clear that principles, particularly when developed through research or systematic thinking of experts, are more likely to be well defined and mutually independent of each other than if developed in general discussion. Finally, the principles themselves can be clearly stated and will be accepted with little or no resistance, so that their presentation by an expert is more efficient because less time is required than if attempts are made to develop them. Thus the lecture and demonstration methods are effective when no resistance is encountered and when a sufficient variety of procedures is present to hold attention and interest. Group participation methods develop attention and maintain interest, but only when such discussions permit progress in thinking. Thus in some instances the lecture method may have more interest value than a group discussion.

It follows, therefore, that a developmental discussion has greatest value when (a) the group has experiences and opinions that are present to such an extent that the members feel they can contribute; (b) these experiences and opinions are pertinent to the further development and exploration of the topic; (c) the question can be specifically put so that forward progress can be made; and (d) resistance to the forward progress is present, because it leads away from previous practices. The method can also be used to test whether or not the leader, in his presentation of a subject matter, has gone beyond the group's acceptance. In case this has happened the method can be used to systematically explore alternatives. Such an analysis might reveal that the group is united in opposing a new idea, but it might also reveal that the group is strongly divided on the alternatives. Often group members feel that they agree because they are opposed to the same thing, but true agreement is present only when there is agreement on the acceptance of something.

Directing Discussion toward Resistance Points. In order to show how the discussion method may be linked to a problem of resistance toward ideas presented by the lecture method it is necessary to supply some background material. Let us suppose that the leader of a training group has presented experimental findings that show that the *democratic* leadership situation is superior to that of the *autocratic* and *laissez-faire* leadership situations. These experiments (25), as already indicated (Chapter 2), were performed with children in a play situation. Groups of children were carefully matched. In the democratically led group all decisions were made through group discussion, including the decision of what to do, what the club should be called, how the work should be planned, and how assignments of activities should be made. In the autocratically led group the leader made all the decisions and imposed them on the group. However, he attempted, as much as possible, to impose solutions that matched those that the democratically led group had developed. Thus the nature of his decisions was not contrary to the interests of the children; rather the decisions were characterized merely by the fact that the leader made them. In the laissez-faire situation the leader was passive and answered questions but volunteered no services. However, the play environment was so planned that the materials and equipment present would encourage children to ask questions about the materials and to play with them. Thus if a mask-making project was decided on in the democratic or autocratic situation the appropriate materials were in the room during the laissez-faire situation.

The laissez-faire situation may be dismissed quickly because no one in the group would hesitate to accept the finding that cops-and-robbers play was present as much as mask making and that the children soon tired of the club activities and fought with each other. However, the democratic and autocratic situations should be compared in detail.

Some of the findings are summarized in Table 2. It will be noted that the findings demonstrate that under democratic leadership the behaviors of the children are distinctly more desirable than under autocratic leadership. Supervisors like to see initiative, a sense of responsibility, and cooperativeness in their employees, but in the past they have attributed these traits to certain people. Thus, despite the fact that they are interested in the experiment and in the behavior of children, the accumulation of the evidence begins to cause them to reflect on their own leadership. Thus by the end of the factual presentation many members begin to feel a threat to their security.

TABLE 2

COMPARISON OF BEHAVIOR TRAITS REVEALED UNDER TWO DIFFERENT
TYPES OF LEADERSHIP

Behaviors More Frequent under Democratic Leadership	*Behaviors More Frequent under Autocratic Leadership*
1. Initiative (going ahead on their own, finding things to do, etc.)	Dependency (asking trivial questions, depending on leader's approval, etc.)
2. Participation (entering into spirit of activity, cooperation, etc.)	Isolation (times when person is not part of group)
3. Responsibility (work continues when leader leaves, etc.)	Irresponsibility (work deteriorates when leader leaves, etc.)
4. Group unified (sticks together if outsider interferes)	Cliques (subgroups fail to cooperate with each other)
5. Friendly group spirit (spirited talking, smiles, etc.)	Hostility (tendency to fight and blame each other)
6. "We" feeling (use term "we," want to help others, etc.)	"I" feeling (use term "I," show signs of selfishness, etc.)
7. Liked leader and project	Passive or disliked leader and project

At this stage one may assume that resistance is being built up. The group feels that the leader is suggesting that supervisors become democratic supervisors. For this reason the leader himself carefully draws only a minimum conclusion. He concludes that the differences described are personality differences in behavior. Children acted very differently in the two situations. Further he interprets by saying that the leader thus plays a part in determining the personality of a child. The leader creates a *social climate,* and children behave differently in different social climates.

Now he backtracks to get to a discussion question. "Obviously these experimental findings were obtained with children and in a play situation. You, however, work with adults in a work situation, and these are important differences." (At this point there is an active nodding of heads.) "Let us then explore some of the differences between children and adults, and between play and work situations. In doing this we might better understand any practical values that these experiments may furnish."

The points of difference developed from a question of this sort clearly reveal defensive reactions to change. The differences are greatly exaggerated and obviously exceed those that would be obtained if this question were asked before such a presentation. The author has tried presenting some case results of practical tests of the democratic leadership techniques (see Chapter 8) before raising the above discussion question and has found that such evidence is ignored. Every possible difference between a given supervisor's work situation and the setting in which the case evidence was obtained is brought out to show that the case is not relevant. Thus it may be pointed out that in the illustration women were used, pay was employed as an incentive, the group tested had no union problem, etc. Because the group tends to look for differences as a means of defense against the new ideas it seems important to make the criticizing of the illustration as easy as possible. It is for this reason that it seems preferable, at this stage of the presentation, to use the experiment with children when dealing with industrial personnel and to use the adult evidence when dealing with counselors in a children's camp. The camp counselors point out that the method probably works with adults, and supervisors point out that the method probably works with children. That the procedure will work for a group that is presented with the idea is generally questioned, and yet interest remains high.

The discussion of the question of differences between the experimental conditions and the job conditions creates a list of differences, many of which are unimportant. However, the experimental findings can now be accepted, and there is also general agreement that a group's personality is influenced by the leader. This degree of acceptance is all that is needed for the next step, which utilizes the free-discussion procedure. This method will be discussed later in this chapter.

Solving Case Problems by Directing Discussion into Logical Steps. As a final illustration of the use of developmental discussion let us see how it is adapted to the analysis of case histories. For this analysis we have chosen the case of Viola Burns.* The case should be acted out in order to make it realistic. The script for the case is given below.

Characters:
  Mr. Birdsall, paymaster.
  Miss Burns, typist.
  Mr. Randall, employment manager.

In June, 1935, Viola Burns was hired directly upon her graduation from high school and placed in the payroll office as a typist. She was intelligent, quick, cheerful, energetic, and had a pleasing manner but looked delicate and somewhat unprepossessing at first sight and somewhat lacking in self-confidence. The paymaster had asked for a girl

* By permission from *Social Problems in Labor Relations* by Pigors, McKenney, & Armstrong, 1939, McGraw-Hill Book Company, Inc. (48).

who was good at figures, could type with reasonable speed and accuracy, and do shorthand. Viola more than met these qualifications. There were twenty girls in the paymaster's office, and Viola readily made friends with all of them. She not only adapted herself quickly to the job but evidently enjoyed the work. She was usually the first to arrive in the morning and was frequently spoken to for her failure to quit work at noon or at night. She became an asset to the department head and within a year had demonstrated to the employment manager that she was in line for promotion. Consequently, when Mr. Randall received a requisition for a secretary to one of the sales executives, Viola Burns immediately came to his mind. He went to the paymaster, Mr. Raymond Birdsall, and suggested Viola's release for transfer.

RANDALL: Ray, I have a requisition from Jim Wagner's office for a bright girl to replace Agnes Brown, who is leaving to be married. I think Viola Burns is just the girl for the job.

BIRDSALL: Hell, Randall, that girl is practically indispensable to me. She's one of the best girls I ever had. You don't think I'm going to let her go, do you?

RANDALL: How much are you paying her, Ray?

BIRDSALL: Forty dollars.

RANDALL: But you're not going to stand in her way if she has a chance for a better job and more money, are you?

BIRDSALL: Well, maybe I could pay her more money myself.

RANDALL: Maybe you could, Ray. But you're limited to the top rate for her present job classification. You can't pay her what she may eventually receive as a private stenographer.

BIRDSALL: No, of course not. Damn it all, the good girls always go. I sometimes wonder if I'd be better off to take girls that aren't quite so good, so I could keep 'em around here after I've spent time and money training them.

RANDALL: Well, here's your chance to decide. If I take Viola, you'll need a girl to replace her. Tell me what you want and I'll find just the right candidate for you.

BIRDSALL: Well, I suppose there's only one answer. You'll have to take Viola. After all, I've got to give her the break. But you find another girl as good as she is, if you can. I guess I'm better off to hire bright girls even if there is a chance that I may lose them.

Later in the day Viola Burns was called to see Mr. Randall in his office.

RANDALL: Good morning, Miss Burns. Have a chair. I have a suggestion to make which, I believe, will please you. Do you know Miss Brown in Mr. Wagner's office?

BURNS: Not very well, but I know who she is.

RANDALL: Well, she's leaving us very soon—getting married—perhaps you have heard? I have suggested that you be considered to take her place. But whether or not you get the job depends on three conditions. The first is Mr. Birdsall's consent to release you; the second, your own willingness to give it a try; and the third, Mr. Wagner's acceptance. Now I want to tell you something about this job before you make up your mind. If you do well you would become Mr. Wagner's private stenographer, and be the only girl in his office. This is quite a change from your present job and you might feel rather lonesome. Mr. Wagner's work requires a considerable amount of detail. You would have to get acquainted with many customers, their accounts and requirements, with styles, prices, and discounts. You would handle his correspondence, keep his files, and run the office when he is out of town. This would involve contact with customers in person as well as over the telephone. If you should be transferred to this job you would receive a slight increase in salary at once, and more later if you do well. Do you think you would like to try this job?

BURNS: Really, I don't know, Mr. Randall. It sounds like a lot to learn, and so different from what I've been doing. I'd hate to fail. You know more about it than I. Do you think I could do it?

RANDALL: I'm very sure you can do it if you want to.

BURNS: Is there much dictation?

RANDALL: Yes, there's a good deal. But I'm sure you can handle that part of it. And, of course, Miss Brown would be with you for a couple of weeks to show you the ropes. How about it, would you like to give this a try?

BURNS: Well—it's awfully hard to say, Mr. Randall. Could I think it over and let you know later?

RANDALL: Certainly, Viola, just let me know in a day or so when you've made up your mind.

At the end of two days, Mr. Randall had heard nothing further from Miss Burns. He spoke to Mr. Birdsall during the lunch hour.

RANDALL: Oh, by the way, Ray, has Viola said anything to you about taking the job in Wagner's office?

BIRDSALL: No, she hasn't, but I certainly hope she'll make up her mind about it pretty soon. She's not much good to anybody since you spoke to her. She goes around looking like she's lost her last friend. She even cries about it. I believe she feels she ought to take a chance but hates to leave the department and her friends.

For our purpose let us ignore the issue of whether we think the interview with Viola was properly conducted. The practical question is whether it is wise to promote Viola Burns on the basis of the facts available.

If the discussion leader put to a group the broad question of whether Viola Burns should or should not be induced to take the job he would find a group definitely divided. For example, 34 groups of 6 undergraduate students, when asked to discuss the issue and make a decision on the case, decided as follows: 20 groups were unanimous for promotion, 4 groups were unanimous against promotion, and 10 groups remained divided in their opinions. Even a group of graduate students in psychology is divided near middle on this issue, with most persons favoring promotion.

If persons are permitted to present their reasons for the decision we find that the various individuals have reacted to different aspects of the case. Their final judgment is based upon a general impression and is mostly determined by whether they like or do not like Viola, as described in the case; not upon a utilization of the principles of psychology. The reason why persons who argue for promotion win out most frequently in discussions is that, in case of lack of proof, they give Viola the benefit of the doubt. Those who oppose promotion likewise do so to protect Viola in that they fear she will be unhappy if promoted to the new job. Thus Viola, not Viola's ability in relation to job requirements, is the central issue. This fact prevents the reaching of a solution based upon psychological principles.

With this type of discussion a good group decision is difficult to reach. Suppose, however, the discussion leader made his questions more specific and directed the discussion into a sequence of steps. His first question might be, "What are Viola's present duties?" This question would supply a list of duties that will be agreed upon.

The next question might be, "Which of the duties are performed well?" Here agreement is again reached in that practically all the duties are well performed by Viola.

The third step is to develop a list of duties in the new job. The script should be referred to so that the new duties have a factual basis. Some disagreement may arise, but usually the factual references clarify the duties, and agreement is reached.

The fourth step is to indicate the duties on the new job which Viola will be able to perform well, those in which she is likely to be ineffective, and those about which there are reasonable doubts. The question of which duties Viola will like and which she will dislike should also be raised.

The fifth step is to lead the discussion in the direction of locating the important duties. "On which of the duties is Viola's new boss most likely to judge her?" Here the importance of making decisions, working alone, and meeting strangers emerge as important.

After this analysis the judgment of a group is usually unanimous and against putting Viola on the new job. Methods for helping Viola to reach this decision are likewise agreed upon.

It therefore appears that by directing the discussion the leader causes all members of a group to go through a more complete analysis and thus not to make an impressionistic judgment. The discussion leader does not impose his judgments on the group, but rather he causes the group to think systematically. Additional illustrations of ways in which the discussion leader can upgrade a group's problem solving will be given in Chapters 10 and 11.

Description of the Process. The developmental discussion is a form of discussion in which the leader influences the direction of thinking by the use of specific questions or problems. Thus he causes all group members to consider similar issues and phases. He remains a central figure in that he puts the question, and responses tend to be directed toward him. Although there is some talk between group members this interaction between members is the exception rather than the rule. The process may be diagrammed as in Fig. 9. The leader serves as the center for the clearing up of differences, and he accepts all ideas.

It is his responsibility to get full participation in the discussion. By looking toward certain quiet persons, asking for a show of hands, and inquiring of certain persons whether they have views on the matter, he encourages participation. Likewise, it is the leader's responsibility to see that certain individuals do not dominate the discussion. This control must be performed gently so that a face-saving problem does not develop. Usually encouraging others to participate or making such a comment as, "I think we understand your position. Now let's see how some of the others view the issue," will be sufficient. With encouragement from the leader each member's responsibility for contributing and participating will gradually create a balance and cause the dominant individuals to learn to listen. The findings in group dynamics research (29) reveal that through training and experience group discussions become much more efficient. The leader can do much to hasten this process of causing members to listen to each other if he is tolerant and makes participation easy. It should be remembered that the excessive talker in a group may have a feeling of inferiority. By recognition of his contributions and by generosity this inferiority is decreased, but in criticizing him we may increase his inferiority. If the excessive talker is an individual with ideas and a sense of responsibility he is no real problem and will actually help others to enter the discussion if the leader shows an acceptant attitude.

The leader also must be sensitive to group interests to see that discussions on minor issues do not take too much time. He has nothing to lose if he points out that there seems to be disagreement on a point and suggests that the group go on to something else. Summarizing, reviewing, and pointing out highlights and areas of agreement and disagreement are likewise his responsibility. In carrying out these

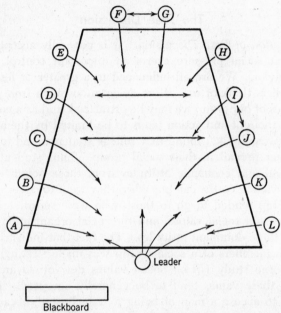

Fig. 9. Interaction in developmental discussion. The circles represent conferees sitting around a conference table. The leader is the center of discussion in that he initiates issues, and most responses are directed toward him. The arrows indicate the responses and their directions. The leader stimulates responses by the use of questions. When responses are given he is acceptant and records them as well as clarifies ideas when necessary. He endeavors to get all members to participate in these discussions. He may prevent certain individuals from dominating the discussion by requesting the views of others, by asking the dominant individual if it would be wise to explore other viewpoints, etc. The purpose of the developmental discussion is to lead the thinking forward into areas that are new and therefore are reluctantly entered.

functions he permits the discussion to move along and helps the members experience progress.

The developmental method thus lends itself to a group's participating in the development and exploration of ideas, the analysis of conditions that are barriers or interferences to action, and the solving of problems for which there is adequate experience but for which there is lack of agreement or a tendency on the part of individuals to arrive at judgments on an impressionistic basis. However, before one considers the developmental method as complete in itself one must consider the values of some other techniques. In actual practice one may wish to combine the procedures as the needs for them arise.

The Free Discussion

The Function of Free Discussion. It is generally accepted in psychology that social pressure exerts an important control over individual behavior. We are all influenced to a greater or lesser degree by what others think of us. If we deviate too much from the values and attitudes of our group we may be ostracized, and as a consequence freedom of thought and action tends to be limited by the approval of others. Newcomb (46) found that college students tend to adopt the attitudes that prevail in their social group. Thus students changed their political and economic attitudes from those acquired at home to those prevailing on the campus when they went to college. Prestige and leadership tended to go to those who were sensitive to prevailing attitudes and social values, and the social organization tended to perpetuate these dominant attitudes. The fact that industrial workers likewise are members of a social group was made strikingly clear by the Hawthorne study (51). Social values develop in an industrial group, and these values tend to be generally accepted. Thus for a companion to accuse a man of being a "rate buster" because he has high production more than offsets a supervisor's praise, provided the man identifies himself with the work group rather than with management.

The influence of the opinions of others on our own behavior and attitudes is known as social pressure. Whether we think that social pressure operates for making conditions better or worse is beside the point. It is a force that influences behavior, and as such it must be recognized. It should also be understood that social pressure does not merely operate as a restraint or as an encouragement of behavior. Newcomb's study demonstrated that its influence was deeper than a show of approval or disapproval in that the behaviors produced by social pressure were consistent with the beliefs of the person. Thus after a woman left the campus her campus-acquired attitudes continued to be expressed for some time.

One of the important functions of free discussion is to permit attitudes and values to come to expression in a conference so that all members can become fully aware of them. Frequently certain individuals feel that they know what others think, they assume that others feel as they do, or they fear to change because others have not changed. If views are freely expressed the existing forces are clarified, and each person is made more aware of the relation between his values and the values of others. In the day-to-day relations between people attitudes and opinions are communicated and behaviors are observed, but in the proper kind of discussion these processes are facilitated and a larger number of individuals is included. Thus each individual is influenced by relatively realistic social forces rather than by assumed or imagined forces. In other words, free discussion is a method that recognizes the already existing social influences, brings them into the open, and then uses them to serve a constructive and useful purpose.

An important finding reported by Lewin (23) is that it is easier to change the attitudes of a group of people than to change the attitude of one person. One person may resist change because he will have to move alone from his present attitudes. In a group he has company. Each person may make gradual changes without losing his security in the group. However, in order for each person to perceive his position in the group there must be interaction and free expression. Thus a person might feel that certain attitudes would be unacceptable to others, but when he can see other persons change with him he is not retarded by vague fears. For example, a supervisor may fear that withholding punishment is not the right thing to do even if he is unable to understand why, but if he finds that others in the group tend to move away from punishment techniques he can also make the move. It appears that each individual helps another change his attitude, and security is felt because each is a group member.

A second function of the free-discussion method is to permit the expression of hostile attitudes, fears, and suspicions. It is generally recognized in therapy that tensions, fears, and frustrations are reduced through their mere expression (2, 38, 49, 51, 52). One phase of therapy, known as *catharsis,* is the creation of opportunities and of stimulations for the release of expression. The free-discussion technique likewise is designed to encourage the release of expression, but it is a group rather than an individual method. However, the benefits derived are similar to those obtained in the permissive type of counseling.

The free-discussion method is most efficiently used when the problem of acceptance is involved, when there are fear barriers to action, or when the group is in violent disagreement. Instead of attempting to guide the discussion, the leader lets the discussion spread and permits each individual to introduce any kind of material or express any attitude he feels is relevant. This permissive procedure permits a large number of attitudes and values to be expressed. Individuals may agree or disagree with each other. They may be united against the leader, or they may be united against something else. The purpose of the free discussion is to get everything out in the open. Any attempt to guide, control, or lead the discussion would tend to block the expression of feelings aroused in the group. Thus the objective of free discussion is to reconcile differences, not to move forward to a further development in thinking. This means that free discussion must probe the areas of disagreement and that the leader should conduct himself so as to bring disagreement to expression. Unexpressed differences cannot become reconciled.

Some Illustrations. To better understand the discussion leader's role let us examine some situations in which free discussion is of particular value. Suppose the leader has developed the notion of autocratic and democratic leadership and someone asks, "Do you think the democratic method is always better?" This is a loaded question and indicates doubt on the part of the questioner, but there is no way of knowing what specific situation he has in mind. If asked whether he has a situation in mind he may be evasive or deny that he has anything in particular in mind. The leader, however, may respond to the question by saying, "Let's explore this question a bit. It is possible that autocratic and democratic methods each have their time and place. Under what conditions do you think that the autocratic method might have an advantage?" Such a question may reveal that the group feels that autocratic decisions are required during emergency conditions; at times when quick decisions are needed; on jobs having long-range planning needs; on hazardous work which requires enforcing safety rules; for production-line problems; in situations that require the coordination of groups reporting to different supervisors; on shift problems; or in work situations having irresponsible employees. Any one of these situations may then be discussed in detail, and one usually finds group members disagreeing with each other when the issue becomes specific. If they all agree, however, the leader may carry the analysis further by asking how the autocratic method works out in such instances. Now some members are likely to be satisfied and others to be dissatisfied with the results. As soon as disagreement is found the leader can withdraw from the discussion and let the members interact.

It is the interaction of group members which permits social pressure to operate. A person may be sure, for example, of his position that safety must be enforced, but when others with similar experiences in the company disagree with him he realizes that he is not reflecting a company viewpoint or one that seems obvious and self-evident. An outsider or a person lacking in certain day-to-day experiences may disagree with him without shaking his convictions, but when his own associates fail to agree with him he is exposed to social pressure.

Such discussions should not be carried to the point of seeking agreement. This would involve face-saving problems. Rather the disagreement should be expressed and left as an unsolved problem. The effect of social pressure requires time, and the confused state of affairs in the group serves its purpose of loosening up viewpoints. It is the leader's responsibility to terminate the discussion when no further progress is being made. He can do this by summarizing the various viewpoints expressed and by pointing out areas of agreement and disagreement.

If the viewpoints of most of the group are against an individual member and in harmony with the general position of the leader it is best for the leader to protect the minority individual. To gang up on one person will exclude him from the group and make him hostile. To prevent this the minority individual should be given extra time to express himself, and the leader can help to keep the individual a group member by nodding his head in an understanding way and by adding comments to make the position taken by the individual more plausible.

All questions having to do with values, justice, fairness, etc., are material for free discussion, since these involve emotional attitudes. In such cases both expression and group interaction are more important than immediate solutions. As long as resistance is present, solutions, regardless of their attractiveness, have little value. The important thing is to achieve a constructive attitude, and when this is accomplished the solution phase is relatively simple.

The value of mere expression as a means of reducing resistance and hostility may be illustrated by an example.

A supervisor was having difficulty with a couple of girls, whose job it was to open flattened cartons for packing small objects. The problem arose after the job procedure had been changed and the girls refused to cooperate in following the improved method. Finally the problem reached the stage where a grievance was threatened, and so the problem was taken to Mr. Clay, the works manager.

The foreman and the personnel director were invited to attend a meeting of the girls, a union representative, and Mr. Clay. Mr. Clay planned his procedure and decided that the best approach would be to do a good job of listening. He decided to hear the whole story from the girls and was determined not to disagree or disapprove of anything that was said. He requested the foreman and the personnel director to help him by letting the girls do all the talking and to cooperate in his plan of listening.

When the girls arrived at Mr. Clay's office they were given a friendly reception, invited to be seated, and offered cigarettes (which were accepted). Mr. Clay first chatted about the company picnic held sometime previously, then turned to the problem by saying, "Well, tell me about this little difficulty you had this morning." One of the girls began to talk about the problem in a calm manner. Soon, however, various hostilities came to expression. The new method wasn't any good, it caused any number of inconveniences, the methods man was not fair, the supervisor didn't consider them, and they just weren't going to do it the new way. After she had finished he smiled and looked at the second girl, indicating he would like to hear from her. She told a similar story with much excitement. When she had finished Mr. Clay asked if they would show him the old and the new ways of doing the job. This was done. He nodded understanding and indicated that he could see what they meant. After the unfavorable features had been pointed out several times Mr. Clay asked if there were some other things that were bad, whether there were some other difficulties involved. After some hesitation one girl said, "Yes, we don't like to be told that we've got to do something." After a little further expression and whispering between themselves the first girl smiled and said, "I guess that takes care of things. We really don't mind doing it the new way. I don't think you'll have any more trouble. We just had to talk to someone and get things off our chests." The girls smiled when they left, and no further trouble was reported.

This is a clear case in which expression alone relieved hostility. No actual solution was needed because, with the girls' changed attitude toward the company, the problem no longer existed.

Description of the Process. The technique of the leader in free discussion is primarily one of listening permissively, respecting the right of each person to feel or express himself as he does, and being able to accept each person as an important and useful member of the group. In developing skills in listening the leader must learn to pay attention to feelings more than to ideas or facts. He should ask himself, "What is the feeling behind that remark?" From time to time he may reflect feelings expressed by making such comments as, "You feel that you would lose something if you did that?" "It seems to you that things would not work out the right way?" and "Your experience makes you doubt what some of the others have said?" Such comments should reflect an attitude or a feeling that an individual

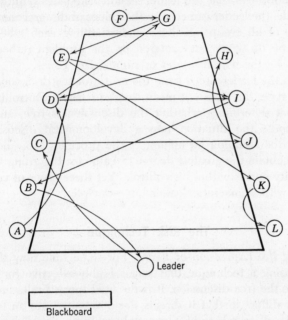

Fig. 10. Interaction in a free discussion. The circles represent conferees sitting about the conference table. The arrows indicate the course the conversation might follow. Note that the leader initiates the discussion but that thereafter the conversation flows between members of the group. Free discussion permits social pressure to operate, and it relieves fear and tension by permitting the free expression of attitudes.

has expressed and when they do, they demonstrate that the leader understands and accepts the feelings. There is no implication in such "reflecting" remarks which make a person feel he must prove or justify his views, and, as a consequence, the group is made to feel more free to express themselves.

When a free and permissive situation is present, expression of views becomes more and more uninhibited, and soon the leader can withdraw from the center of discussion and permit group interaction. The leader's role thus becomes one of stimulating interaction between all group members. This condition is diagrammatically illustrated in

Fig. 10 and may be contrasted with the developmental type of discussion shown in Fig. 9.

If social pressure becomes abusive and the group turns on a particular individual it becomes the leader's responsibility to protect the abused person, regardless of whether or not he seems to deserve it. This does not mean that the leader should take sides. Rather, by his own attitude, the leader can convey the values of disagreement and the importance of all group members' understanding each other, and he can keep the disagreement centered on the problem rather than on individuals by the way he states or summarizes issues.

Although the leader drops from the center of the discussion when it is the free type, this does not mean that he is not a controlling factor. It is he that determines whether the discussion is free, and he can readily change the situation into a developmental discussion. By controlling the situation he influences the process. How he budgets the time to obtain the greatest degree of value for the group thus is his responsibility and is within his control. Yet these types of control are consistent with democratic leadership principles.

The Risk Technique

Releasing the Expression of Fear. For some time now the author has been using a technique that seems highly effective for reducing fears. Like the free discussion, it is directed toward releasing expression, but it differs in that it directs the discussion into an expression of fears. If all members of a group have fears, some clear-cut and some vague, then each can help the other by expressing the fears he can locate and communicate. The group's expression thus serves to clarify fears and at the same time creates a situation where such expression is acceptable. When all members express some fears, further expression of fears is facilitated so that even the lesser fears can become expressed. The risk technique amounts, in part, to the nondirective counseling method (see Chapters 2 and 13) applied to groups and is based on the assumption that our fears are not the opposite of our goals (38). For example, the fear of a union shop does not necessarily reflect a desire for an open shop. Rather, the avoidance of the one alternative leaves the person in the open-shop camp. Sometimes it is only because the union wants the union shop that suspicion is aroused. Likewise, the union may fear to lose its gains, and management's opposition to the union shop arouses fear. Analysis of the fears of each reveals a different problem than an analysis of the goals each side of a controversy attributes to the other side. When labor and management argue such an issue, management accuses labor of having as its goal the acquisition of management's prerogatives, whereas labor accuses management of having as its goal the destruction of the union. Each might honestly deny having such hostile motives, since it is quite possible for management to be satisfied to retain the union and for labor to be satisfied with present methods of bargaining. Thus it seems that the fears are based upon the imagined goals of the opposition and that neither side has the goals attributed to it.

Fears in general tend to reflect the *imagined* goals of our enemy so that anything that benefits the enemy represents a defeat for us. However, when each reacts to his own goals it is quite possible for both parties to gain something at the same time. An increase in union membership could increase union revenue and permit the management to bargain with union leaders who represented a larger number of employees. Thus the union and management conferences would represent the interests of a larger number of employees, and this would make for more realistic problem solving from the points of view of both parties. The barrier to such constructive conferences is distrust and fear, and when fear enters the picture frustration dominates behavior. Under frustration behavior is hostile, childish, and stubborn rather than of a constructive problem-solving nature (6).

Likewise, the fear of the group-decision technique is not the same as a desire for autocratic methods. Thus, the problem in training is not a matter of demonstrating that the democratic method is superior to the autocratic, but rather the problem is one of removing the fear of a change. To reduce fears one must release expression, and this is the crux of the *risk technique*. The situation is so structured that group members talk about dangers or risks involved in a change and disregard, for the time, any discussion of possible gains. Once these fears have been expressed they serve a further value in that they can be re-examined from time to time and re-evaluated.

Illustration of the Risk Technique. After a conference training group has been presented with a description of the differences between autocratic, laissez-faire, and democratic techniques and of the experimental results from the studies on children by Lewin, Lippitt, and White (25), they are asked, "If supervisors practiced democratic leadership on the job, what are some of the risks that management would take which would not be taken if other methods were used?"

The question is discussed to make it clear that even if democratic supervision might have potential values one must also examine the price one would have to pay to obtain such values. It is pointed out that in all decisions there are favorable and unfavorable aspects, and it is important to examine the unfavorable possibilities very carefully so as not to be misled. For practical purposes one may have to make modifications or additions to the concept of democratic leadership as outlined in the children's experiment in order to avoid running serious risks. Comments of this kind make it clear that the discussion leader is also aware of dangers and that he is receptive to having the risks spelled out.

Each risk presented is recorded on the blackboard. Frequently, the risk is reworded by the discussion leader to point up the issue. This procedure is similar to the type of responses used in nondirective counseling in which the counselor reacts to or reflects the feelings expressed. As in counseling these responses should mirror the feelings behind the remark rather than be a reaction to the content of the remark. Suppose someone remarks, "The supervisor won't be able to get a job done if he can't ask someone to do it. There has to be some kind of integration. You just can't let people do what they want to. Everything will be a mix-up." The leader's response to this might be, "You feel that democratic supervision would result in loss of discipline or control?" If the answer is "yes" he records "loss of discipline and control" on the board. If the answer is "no" the leader should request further elaboration until the basic idea can be specifically recorded.

The leader might also ask questions to point up a risk. Someone says, "The method is too inefficient." Since there are many types of inefficiency the leader might ask, "In what ways would it be more inefficient than other methods?" This question might lead to such specific factors as "time wasted in discussions" and "failure to meet deadlines." If two sources of inefficiency are indicated they should be recorded as separate items.

A little discussion follows each risk to determine the amount of support for and the degree of feeling toward the statement written on the board. The leader uses his office to support the reasonableness of the risk in case the majority of the group opposes it. By this method the group soon feels free to express risks, and the leader ceases to be an individual who is trying to sell them something. Group members also can recognize unreasonableness in each other. In this respect social pressure may function somewhat as in free discussion.

A group of 18 to 28 usually finds 13 to 22 risks with a mean of 18 in 45 such groups. The risks include statements indicating that production goals will be poor, quality will decline, the union will oppose the method, morale will drop, supervisors will lose prestige, the union will get control, the decisions will be selfish, planning will be inefficient, time will be wasted in discussions, etc.

The effect of producing a list of risks tends to clarify attitudes. It is not uncommon for members of a discussion group to come to the leader after a meeting and say that the list of risks is really misleading and that the democratic method is not really that bad. Others remark that their comments were exaggerated. Persons who seemed hostile toward the idea are more friendly toward the leader and refer to the meeting as a good one. In general this method tends to make the group less reserved and more friendly.

In testing the method with student groups one finds a distinct reduction in the number of persons who are doubtful about how they feel toward democratic leadership in management. Thus before the risks are recorded 7 groups totalling 134 students were asked to vote "yes," "no," or "doubtful" on the issue of whether they would recommend democratic methods in supervision as outlined in laboratory studies. After making a list of the risks they were again asked to express their opinion. The results obtained are given in Table 3.

TABLE 3

EFFECT OF DISCUSSING RISKS ON ATTITUDE TOWARD DEMOCRATIC
SUPERVISION

Would Recommend	Before Discussion of Risks	After Discussion of Risks
Yes	53	68
No	29	43
Doubtful	52	23

Since both the "yes" and "no" votes increased by similar amounts and at the expense of the "doubtful" votes, it seems that an immediate effect of the risk discussion is to crystallize an opinion. Of interest is the fact that a discussion of dangers or risks does not decrease the number of "yes" votes. Apparently the clarification of risks does not make the feeling of danger any greater.

It is probable that the greatest values of the risk method occur later. If a person, on the one hand, voted "yes" at the outset and did not change as a result of the discussion of risks, it is unlikely that he will be susceptible to influence by opinions of others who voice the fears already covered in the risks. If a person, on the other hand, voted consistently "no" it is possible for him to change if certain specific protective measures are incorporated. By being aware of the risks he can be alert and can determine whether the proper protective measures have been taken. He has no face-saving problems if he changes his mind because he can always point to the fact that the method has been changed.

It is also of interest to note that, if one precedes the discussion of the risks with the presentation of certain controls (area of freedom and functions of an expert) that logically overcome certain risks, this added material has little effect on the content or number of risks that a group presents. Even the report of cases showing that the method works on the job fails to influence the number and kind of mentioned risks to an appreciable degree. However, there is a reduction in the number of persons who support a risk that is in contradiction with the material presented, but this difference is offset by the fact that other risks receive more support. It is the writer's experience that the presentation of the controls should follow the expression of risks, since it is at this stage that the group is receptive and will give the controls a proper evaluation.

Although developing a list of risks clarifies thinking and serves to reduce hostility and fear through expression the risk technique has further values. These arise when the group is asked to pass judgment upon the risks on later occasions. At two or three regular intervals in a 12-week program (1 day per week), the list of risks is re-examined and, whenever there is unanimous agreement that a risk no longer applies, it is removed from the list. This procedure allows social pressure to operate. The group members interact with each other, and the leader finds himself in the position of having to protect minority individuals who still have fears. Of importance is the fact that the risks gradually are removed. Even the discussion on individual differences, during which the democratic method is not mentioned, is followed by a reduction in the list of risks. The discussion on counseling, which occurs last, usually serves to remove the last items. When all are not removed, it is because one or two persons still wish to retain one or two risks.

The technique of removing risks in subsequent discussions causes the group values to come to the fore so that the trainer no longer is in a position of defending the program. Rather, the support for the program comes from the group membership, who soon assume the responsibility of reducing the list of risks. Frequently, it is claimed that they initially did not understand what was meant by a risk. With changed attitudes many of the risks begin to appear ridiculous.

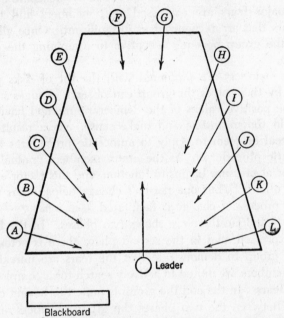

Fig. 11. Interaction in the risk technique. The circles represent conferees seated around a conference table. The leader proposes a question having to do with the dangers or risks inherent in a change. All conferees can react to this question in their own particular way. Thus a flow of reactions is initiated by the leader. As in the free discussion the leader contributes little in the form of directing thinking in the group, and as in developmental discussion he remains a central figure. The objective is to release the expression of fear and to clarify those fears. These fears are re-examined from time to time to permit the experience of change.

Description of the Process. Although the risk technique has many of the benefits of the free discussion it is more specific in that it is used to cause fears to be expressed and clarified. Thus instead of emphasizing interaction between members it encourages a flow of reactions from all members to the leader. Figure 11 illustrates the direction of the interaction. Sometimes hostility toward the leader's ideas may be expressed, but because of this expression the hostility is reduced. As a consequence the ideas can be examined for what they are rather than in terms of the imagined threats that the ideas carry.

The process of releasing fears in a group perhaps has greater value than the expression of such fears by an individual alone because the group situation offers security in expression and makes each member feel less atypical. Furthermore, each person's expression serves as a relief for each of the others so that the catharsis effects are cumulative. Soon all major fears are expressed, and members find themselves voicing fears that are recognized as insignificant. Once all fears are expressed the group becomes receptive to examining the other side of the issue.

If group members are presented with the list of risks previously developed by themselves the group can observe changes in attitude. Some of the positive values of the democratic method have been experienced in the meantime and make sense. As a result the risks seem less real or seem to apply to autocratic procedures as well as to democratic procedures. As the group members gradually change attitudes social pressure begins to function, and this factor encourages changes in others. Thus one person's change helps others to change so that the process of change is facilitated.

The risk technique therefore shows two phases. In the first phase fears are expressed, and in the second phase there is actual motivation in the group to demonstrate that the fears are unreal. At the outset all members are united to actively search for a complete expression of the fears. In the end the group is united in having eliminated the fears. Between the two phases the group members are in conflict and they disagree on the risks that should be removed. It is during this intermediate condition that free discussion may be used to some degree. However, care must be taken not to permit too much interaction, since the social pressure may become intense and produce stubbornness in the remaining hesitant persons. Merely asking for a vote on each of the risks seems to be appropriate to indicate where the group as a whole stands. The leader always refrains from discrediting a risk and supports those who wish to keep an item in the list.

The complete removal of the risks generally becomes a group's goal. Members search for information in material presented in other parts of the program and use it to refute a risk. Others examine their experiences with the democratic method to test the risks. Thus the leader is freed from the responsibility of supporting the democratic method, and his contributions remain those of an expert on the facts.

*Analysis of Risks Submitted.** Although the risk technique has a value as a process in influencing attitudes, the data obtained may also be used to study the nature of fears. Since a primary concern of this book is the practical aspects of democratic supervision, a large number of risks submitted on this issue have been analyzed in order to determine whether the fears reflect the fact that democratic supervision is impractical and unadapted to the real work situation or whether the fears reflect attitudes and emotional resistance.

It seems that if fears reflect purely technical difficulties inherent in industry one would postulate that the risks submitted by supervisors in industry (at all levels in the organization) would show some characteristics not found in the risks submitted by college students. Thus college students and industrial personnel would be very much alike in their intelligence and logical thinking, but they would be quite different in their industrial experiences. If risks submitted by the two groups are different in certain ways one would be inclined to conclude that industrial experiences in supervision and management problems influenced the fears. However, if the risks submitted by the two groups are basically alike one would tend to conclude that the risks reflect a fear of the idea. In other words, the risks would reflect an attitude not grounded in industrial experience. The risks would become logical criticisms leveled at an idea and would then be a form of justification for not accepting a new idea. Ability to rationalize or justify resistance would be primarily a matter of intelligence, and in this respect the groups would be similar.

For the purpose of comparison it was necessary to divide the risks into general categories, since groups tend to word their objections differently. These categories give one the general area of resistance. Within each category the more specific statements of risks could be classified. For example, a category might be lower production resulting from democratic supervision. The specific risks classified as forms of lower production might be as follows:

1. Time lost in discussion would not be made up.
2. Group would set lower production goals.
3. Group would tend to make it easy for themselves.
4. Men would do less work.
5. Men would have no reason for wanting to do a good job.

* Readers not concerned with experimental data on this subject should proceed to p. 73.

In order to measure the similarity between management and student groups one may compare them on the basis of the number of risks submitted, as well as on the basis of the types of risks submitted. The qualitative comparisons can be made by analyzing the categories in which the specific risks fall. Thus the number of items in each category and the percentage of groups that list items in each of the categories would permit comparisons of the types of fears as well as their relative importance.

The risks submitted by 35 groups of college students and 7 management groups have been used in order to make these comparisons. The students used were from the laboratory sections of a course devoted to training in management, and the management groups were selected from higher management personnel in three utilities where similar training was being introduced. Only the risks named by management groups trained before the company accepted the program were used, since it was felt that a company's acceptance of the program would influence the risks submitted. Seven other large groups of management personnel also were used, but the method of developing the risks was different. The results of these groups will be considered in the next section.

Student and management groups show striking similarities in the number of risks developed. The student groups (consisting of 18 to 30 students) submitted an average of 19.9 risks, whereas the management groups (consisting of 18 to 22 members) submitted an average of 18.1 risks.

For the purposes of comparing the types of risks we divided the risks into 9 categories. The management and student groups have been compared for each of these categories in terms of:

a. The average number of items in each category, or

$$\frac{\text{Total number of risks in a category}}{\text{Number of groups}}$$

b. The percentage of risks falling into a given category, or

$$\frac{\text{Total number of risks in a category}}{\text{Total number of risks}}$$

c. Percentage of groups expressing at least one risk in a category, or

$$\frac{\text{Number of groups expressing a risk in the category}}{\text{Total number of groups}}$$

The results of these data are summarized in Table 4. It is apparent that both management and student personnel consider the problem

TABLE 4

COMPARISON OF RISK DATA OBTAINED FROM 35 GROUPS OF COLLEGE STUDENTS (697 RISKS) WITH CORRESPONDING DATA FROM 7 MANAGEMENT GROUPS (127 RISKS)

| | Students | | | Management | | |
| | A | B | C | A | B | C |
Category	Average Number of Items	Percentage of Risks	Percentage of Groups	Average Number of Items	Percentage of Risks	Percentage of Groups
1. Supervisor will lose something (authority, prestige, morale, respect of men, etc.)	2.1	8.9	86	2.4	9.5	71
2. Worker's morale will suffer (bickering, formation of cliques, suspicions, etc.)	3.2	15.8	100	2.2	10.1	86
3. Company will lose integrative functions (coordination, planning, discipline, nonuniform practices, safety controls, etc.)	3.6	15.4	86	3.2	15.0	86
4. Poor-quality decisions (workers lack necessary ability, knowledge, and information; may act selfishly, etc.)	2.9	14.3	97	2.7	12.5	86
5. Low production goals (workers will set goals too low, time lost in discussions, irresponsibility, poor work, etc.)	2.0	10.0	100	1.7	9.5	100
6. Union interference (unions may take control, may object to program, more friction with union, etc.)	1.4	6.0	86	1.4	5.5	71
7. Technical problems and difficulties (too hard to get unanimous agreement, all supervisors cannot be trained, training too costly; emergency conditions could not be handled; not adapted to all problems; foreman will abuse technique, etc.)	2.5	12.5	91	2.6	14.4	100
8. New problems created (workers increase their demands, bad effect if decisions reversed, democratic technique may fail and one cannot return to old methods, company practices in flux, etc.)	2.7	13.4	100	3.6	19.6	100
9. Outside objectors (competitors, stockholders, public will disapprove)	1.6	3.7	46	1.3	3.9	57

of introducing democratic supervision from the point of view of its effects on: (1) the supervisor (category 1); (2) the worker (category 2); (3) management's interests (categories 3, 4, 5, 7, and 8); (4) the union (category 6); and (5) public relations (category 9). Details of administration, coordination, training, and the possibility that new problems will be created likewise are not overlooked by either management or student groups. The surprising thing is the degree of similarity obtained. Only in three categories are the differences worthy of mention, and these are not significantly different. The student groups seem more inclined to feel that workers will not respond favorably to the method (see category 2) than do management groups. This is evidenced by the fact that student groups put (a) more items in this category (3.2 vs. 2.2); (b) make it a larger proportion of their risks (15.8% vs. 10.1%); and (c) include it more often (100% vs. 86%) than do management groups. Thus management seems to be less fearful of the employees' unfavorable reactions than are students, perhaps because management personnel is likely to feel that employees will not object rather than because they are less concerned with employee morale than are students.

Students also feel somewhat more critical of solution quality, as evidenced by an examination of the data under category 4. In all three measures the student figures slightly exceed those of management personnel. If these differences were somewhat greater we might argue that students had more confidence in management's ability to make good decisions than did management personnel. When combined with category 2 one might argue that students tend to have less understanding and respect for workers than does management. However, the differences are too small to indicate that this difference in attitude is a trend. Of importance is the fact that the trend is not reversed. One cannot say that the experience of dealings with employees has made management less respectful of the ability and judgment of the common man.

Category 8 shows management personnel to be somewhat more concerned with the possibility that new problems will be created. This category received a higher average number of items (3.6) and a larger proportion of items (19.6%) than any other category. Although all student groups and all management groups list an item in this category the management groups give it the greater emphasis. It is likely that, in this respect, business experience has been helpful. With experience more specific items can be pointed out. To some extent the same is true of category 7, and in this category the management groups also supply a larger proportion of risks than the student groups.

If we reflect on the general trend of the results the conclusion seems to be that management and student groups submit strikingly similar lists of risks. This is true even when the subheadings of the categories are compared. If this conclusion is accepted it means that the risks are not the product of business experience. Rather they are logical deductions of what might happen if a change were introduced. In this sense the risks become fears of what might or could happen. When one explores what could happen if we made a change, one explores all existing conditions and discovers that each of these could be worse. Students and management both have this mental agility and hence must make the same listings. A different conclusion could be reached with the same kind or quality of thinking. One could explore existing conditions and conclude that a change might make all things better. Which way our ingenuity takes us thus becomes a matter of attitudes, and apparently these attitudes are not a result of business experience. It is the existence of the attitude that the risk technique tends to reflect, bring to expression, and clarify. As training in human relations continues, one develops a better understanding of people and a greater faith in human nature, and as a consequence the risks become less real. It is impossible to prove that the area of freedom protects certain phases of management's interests as long as an attitude stands in the way. However, a change in the attitude makes it unnecessary to prove this because proof is no longer demanded.

Phillips 66

A Method for Widespread Participation in Large Groups. In large groups it is difficult to capture the values of participation and ego involvement so effective in small groups. From time to time one may put questions to an audience and by a show of hands have the group participate by registering a choice. For example, one may ask how many consider the stated risk as serious, how many consider it as not applying, and how many have neither of these opinions. The number of hands raised permits some communication and allows social pressure to operate. One may go so far as to permit samples of opinion to be voiced; nevertheless an actual exchange of ideas and full involvement are never very great. This method of participation is limited also in that only issues that can be put in the form of a vote are subject to this procedure.

To meet the need of more personal participation, J. D. Phillips (47) has developed a method, which has become known as Phillips 66, that is quite effective. The plan is to divide an audience into groups or committees of 6 and let the groups discuss a question for 6 minutes.

It is from this procedure (6 persons, 6 minutes) that the method develops its name. However, the 6-minute time limit need not be taken too seriously, and one may use smaller or somewhat larger groups if conditions warrant.

The idea is to break up a formal lecture situation into discussion committees and permit committee members to interact with each other on an issue or problem. Each committee is asked to take a minute or two to get acquainted, to choose a chairman who encourages contributions from everyone, and to elect a secretary-spokesman who will record and report the group's ideas. A carefully worded problem or issue should then be discussed. The choice and wording of an issue must be clear-cut and specific if all committees are to perform similar activities. The issue should involve attitudes so that differences in opinion are generated, interest is stimulated, and the members are made to feel competent to have an opinion. The committee process is most successful if each person is first expected to express his views. After this expression the various views are then evaluated so that the most valuable ideas can be selected for the spokesman's report. Thus true interaction appears after some general participation has been stimulated. The method of Phillips 66 is easy to set up, and groups readily respond to the situation. It may be used to obtain opinions, to contribute values, to give reasons for action, or merely to formulate questions to be directed to a speaker.

In addition to its value as a means of obtaining participation, the procedure serves to get a group acquainted, utilize social pressure, and learn about an audience's thinking. It is superior to having questions or reactions from the floor, not only because it causes all persons to be involved, but also because it screens out reactions that are not representative or to the point of issue. Its effectiveness is apparent from the fact that groups take pride in the reports of their spokesman and watch for the lecturer's or the audience's reactions. Thus subsequent comments from the floor receive better attention.

The Use of Phillips 66 in Supervisory Training. The author's training program always utilizes small groups for the discussion of experiences and applications to the job, but for presentation meetings both large and small groups have been tried. It is in the large presentation meetings that Phillips 66 has been found to be helpful. Since it is most economical when taking management personnel off a job to devote a whole morning to presentation rather than have two or three hourly meetings, the method offers an opportunity to break up the monotony of a formal presentation, and serves a value in its being a participation procedure. The author has found the method useful for having each group contribute its opinion on the most important reason why the company should be interested in employee morale. Each group is requested to make a list and place the most agreed-upon items in their order of importance.

After the groups have reassembled the group reports are presented from the floor and recorded, much the same procedure as in the developmental discussion. When any group finds that its first item has already been reported it may contribute the next item on the list. Evidence of involvement and interest is seen by (a) the businesslike manner in which various groups discuss and argue; (b) the repeated use of "we" in the reports; (c) later comments of individuals who have participated; and (d) the disappointment registered when another group has already covered a group's major items. It is almost a necessity to obtain reports from groups in a reverse order when the method is used a second time, in order to eliminate the accusation of favoring one side of the audience. The quality of the group's reports is also very high. The report of the various groups on the subject of morale is as complete as any that can be found in a textbook, and the contributions are devoid of irrelevant ideas. Apparently the weak items are screened out in the discussions.

A second useful application of the method is to introduce it in connection with the risks (see pp. 62–72). The list of risks contributed by this method is at least as complete and specific as in a good developmental discussion with a small group.

Although the groups may be constituted differently on successive occasions because of changes in seating, this fact does not seem to interfere greatly with the continued improvement of the participation within the groups. As the method is repeated the groups get down to business more quickly, and full participation becomes more the rule rather than the exception.

On later occasions the method is used to pass judgment on the risks developed previously. Each group is asked to delete first the items from the list of risks which are unanimously agreed upon to be superfluous and then to discuss those on which there is disagreement. Such discussion will result in agreement to delete others. When reporting back to the group as a whole, the spokesman gives the numbers of the items his group has unanimously agreed to remove from the list.

Description of the Process. The processes in Phillips 66 are a combination of those operating in the free-discussion method and the risk technique. Its unique value is that it introduces some of the benefits of these processes in a large group situation. Although these benefits are reduced because each process cannot be exploited to its full value, the gains apply to a large number of persons. The method thus fulfills a need that arises because of the fact that one must sometimes deal with large groups.

In breaking up a large group into committees one permits free discussion on a single issue, and if this single issue is important and central to a program it serves a value in proportion to the value of the issue. Unlike free discussion the method does not permit the exploration of many issues, and unlike the free-discussion method one must be satisfied with lesser discussion-leader skills. However, it does permit the use of social pressure to some extent, and it does supply in part the values of the participation processes that occur in all types of discussion.

In illustrating the flow of interaction in a committee discussion the diagram is similar to that made for the free discussion in Fig. 10. The course of the conversation goes from one person to another in an irregular pattern without the leader's intervention. In Fig. 12 the interaction of five different committees is illustrated.

The clusters of circles represent groups of individuals, and the connecting lines indicate the order in which persons may have participated. In each group the connecting lines are patterned differently to illustrate the obvious fact that no two groups will interact in the same way.

After the committee discussions reports are made to the floor. Although the committee arrangement is disbanded at this time, the individuals remain psychological groups. For this reason the lines have been drawn from the committees to the lecturer to indicate that the report actually comes from the committee. Since these reports are directed to the leader of the large group, we have one-way communication from groups to leader. This process is indicated in Fig. 12 by the long arrows. To the extent that these reports reflect doubts, fears, or hostilities they serve the values similar to those obtained by the risk technique. Since the spokesman merely reports the group reaction, hostile reactions can be expressed quite freely. As the reactions are the product of a committee, no one feels a personal danger in the expression of a true feeling. Although only the spokesman reports, the fact that his report is that of the group gives him security. Ego involvement for all members is present, so that they have an interest in the report their leader makes. In this manner some total participation is extended throughout the whole process.

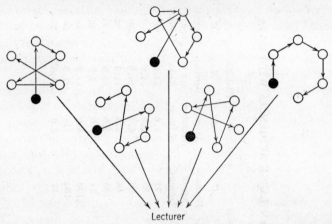

Lecturer

FIG. 12.   Interaction in Phillips 66.   This method for obtaining widespread participation was developed by J. D. Phillips (47).   A large group of about 150
persons may be divided into committees of 6.   These committees then hold a discussion for 6 minutes on a common issue or question, which is stated from the
floor.   Six persons discussing for 6 minutes gives the method its name.   By this
method a large group of persons may actively participate in a discussion and
interact with other persons.   Since each group reports its conclusions or opinion
to the chairman of the meeting as a whole, every member of the audience experiences ego involvement.   The groups of circles indicate groups of 6 discussing with
each other.   The fact that all participate makes these committee discussions the
free type of discussion.   After a time interval of approximately 6 minutes the groups
break up, and their spokesmen report the committees' ideas to the meeting as
a whole.

*Risks Developed by Method of Phillips 66.** When an audience is
broken into 16 or 20 groups of 7 or 8 persons and each group is permitted to supply one risk, one can suppose that relatively minor risks
will not appear.   This procedure thus offers selectivity not only because each group or committee performs a screening function in reporting the risk it considers most important, but also because the
accumulated items are not an exhaustive list, there being only as many
risks as there are committees.   Table 5 includes not only the risks
already reported in Table 4, but also the risks obtained by the method
of Phillips 66 in seven audiences of management personnel.

From Table 5 we can see that items supplied in category 1 by
Phillips 66 differ slightly from those obtained by the usual method in
that a possible loss to the supervisor is mentioned in every one of the
seven audiences (column *C*) and in that this category contains a

* Readers not concerned with experimental data should proceed to p. 83.

TABLE 5

COMPARISON OF RISK DATA OBTAINED BY PHILLIPS 66 METHOD IN SEVEN LARGE AUDIENCES WITH DATA OBTAINED BY USUAL RISK METHOD

	Students			Management			Phillips 66		
	A	B	C	A	B	C	A	B	C
Risk Area	Average Number of Items	Percentage of Risks	Percentage of Groups	Average Number of Items	Percentage of Risks	Percentage of Groups	Average Number of Items	Percentage of Risks	Percentage of Groups
1. Supervisor will lose something	2.1	8.9	86	2.4	9.5	71	2.6	14.0	100
2. Worker's morale will suffer	3.2	15.8	100	2.2	10.1	86	2.6	14.0	100
3. Company will lose integrative functions	3.6	15.4	86	3.2	15.0	86	4.4	24.0	100
4. Poor-quality decisions	2.9	14.3	97	2.7	12.5	86	2.5	11.5	86
5. Low production goals	2.0	10.0	100	1.7	9.5	100	2.0	10.9	100
6. Union interference	1.4	6.0	86	1.4	5.5	71	1.0	2.3	43
7. Technical problems and difficulties	2.5	12.5	91	2.6	14.4	100	3.0	14.0	86
8. New problems created	2.7	13.4	100	3.6	19.6	100	1.4	7.8	86
9. Outside objectors	1.6	3.7	46	1.3	3.9	57	2.0	1.5	14

higher proportion of the risks. Category 2, which relates to worker morale, shows a trend much like the ones obtained by the usual methods and is one of the frequently represented categories. Category 3, which deals with some loss in company integrative functions, stands out as the most important risk when the Phillips 66 method is used, but it is also one of the high-ranking risks with the other methods. However, category 4, which deals with poor-quality decisions, becomes relatively less important by the Phillips 66 method than it was by the other procedures, but the absolute figures are similar. Category 5, which deals with low production goals, shows results practically identical with those obtained by the standard methods. The same is true of category 7, which deals with technical difficulties. In categories 6 (union interference), 8 (new problems created), and 9 (outside objectors) the greatest differences are obtained, and those differences are due to the fact that the Phillips 66 method makes them less important than the usual method.

It is perhaps safe to assume that the risks in these areas would be most effectively eliminated by participation methods since the Phillips 66 process causes them to decline in importance. The risks falling in categories 6, 8, and 9 accounted for 23.1 per cent of the risks supplied by students and 29.0 per cent of those supplied by management personnel, but when management groups discussed the problem in small groups these categories accounted for only 11.6 per cent of the risks. Since these categories contain risks that would be very difficult to eliminate by personal experience and by factual information, it is fortunate that they seem subject to change by discussion procedures. Many of the items in other categories cease being risks when a supervisor gives the method a trial. The elimination of such items therefore greatly depends upon the supervisor's experience with the group decision method.

The very fact that Phillips 66 causes some risks to remain unexpressed represents a limitation of the procedure. In order to obtain acceptance a situation must permit the expression of senseless fears as well as real fears. Insofar as Phillips 66 performs a screening function one elevates the level of the things discussed, but one does not permit the expression of feelings that cannot be defended but that nevertheless represent real and personalized fears.

An Illustration of the Removal of Risks. It will be recalled that in developing the list of risks by the Phillips 66 method each committee of 5 to 8 was permitted to report the one they considered most important, and that a second or third choice could be recorded only if their more important risk already had been reported. One audience of 126 contributed the list shown in Table 6. This audience was divided into 18 committees, and 16 risks were reported. In two groups all the risks they had listed were previously reported.

TABLE 6

RISKS ENTAILED IN DEMOCRATIC LEADERSHIP
18 GROUPS

| | *Number of Groups That Ask Removal of Risks at* | |
Risks	End of 7 Weeks	End of Program
1. Supervisors lose prestige and position of authority	16	18
2. Unacceptable group decisions	9	16
3. Difficulty in obtaining decisions would lead to laissez faire	17	16
4. Lower production because of time lost in discussions	14	14
5. Poor-quality decisions	11	17
6. Group often lacks essential knowledge and ability	14	17
7. Discussions would divide workers into cliques	13	16
8. Many decisions do not permit discussion time	6	13
9. Difficulty in obtaining agreement would produce poor morale	12	15
10. Misapplication of technique would result in loss of control	5	13
11. Unofficial leaders might get control	11	16
12. Group would lose faith in supervisor's ability	14	17
13. Older employees would have difficulty in adjusting to democratic technique	14	16
14. Management might lose control	15	17
15. Too much freedom; no controls	15	17
16. Laissez faire more likely with democratic supervisor	13	17
Average number of groups per item	12.4	15.9
Percentage of groups per item	68.8	88.3

At the midpoint of the training program the list of risks developed by this group was presented, each person receiving a copy. The audience was again divided into 18 committees, with the instruction to check the risks that they could unanimously agree no longer applied and should be removed from the list. The procedure suggested was to first remove all items on which agreement for removal was obtained without discussion. The next step was to discuss briefly the items on which there was near agreement for removal, and finally, if time permitted, to discuss any others they wished to consider for removal. Only 15 minutes were permitted for these discussions.

From Table 6 it can be seen that an average of 12.4 of 18 committees agreed to remove each risk, the range being 5 to 17. Items

8 and 10 showed the fewest recommendations for removal. Item 8 refers to certain instances in which the method seems not to be applicable or practical, and Item 10 refers to a lack of skill in the use of the method. Items that reflect a distrust or lack of confidence in employees (items 2, 5, 6, 7, 11, 13, 15, and 16) are removed by an average of 12.5 groups, which is close to the group average. Items 1, 12, and 14, which refer to the loss a supervisor may experience, however, are removed by an average of 15.0 groups.

When the risks were reconsidered in a similar manner at the end of the program, the items were removed by an average of 15.9 of the 18 groups, an average increase of 3.5 groups. Items 8 and 10, which were the most persistent, each rose to 13, but were still the lowest. The 8 items that reflected a distrust or lack of confidence in employees rose from an average of 12.5 to 16.5 and faired slightly better than the average item. Items 1, 12, and 14, which reflected a loss for supervision, rose from an average of 15.0 to 17.3 and, although the gain is not great, this figure represents almost a complete recommendation for their removal.

In examining the final reports of the groups we find considerable variation. At one extreme 9 groups recommended the removal of all risks, whereas 1 group recommended the removal of 1 (item 1). The remaining 8 groups retained from 2 to 4 risks.

It must be remembered that one individual in any group was able to prevent the removal of any risk. In the group that removed only one risk this was primarily accomplished by one person. Thus the percentage of groups retaining a risk is definitely greater than the percentage of persons retaining the risk.

A General Analysis of the Removal of Risks in Seven Large Groups. The procedure of examining the risks in the middle and at the end of the program was followed in two other groups. In four more groups the risks were examined at the end of the program only. The results of these groups are summarized in Table 7. In group *A* (already reported in Table 6) we found that the percentage of risks removed rose from 68.8 on the first evaluation to 88.3 on the final evaluation. For group *B* the corresponding percentages were 66.0 and 82.5, and for group *C* they were 52.1 and 63.6. The lower figures in group *C* seem to be due to the fact that many persons belonging to groups *A* and *B* changed over to group *C* and hence did not evaluate the risks they had helped to formulate. (Attendance figures revealed that groups *A* and *B* had approximately 10 per cent absences, whereas group *C* had a slight excess number in attendance. Thus about half

TABLE 7

RISKS REMOVED BY 7 GROUPS USING PHILLIPS 66

			Average Percentage of Groups Requesting Removal of Each Risk at	
Group	*Number of Risks*	*Number of Groups*	*End of 7 Weeks*	*End of Program*
A	16	18	68.8	88.3
B	19	20	66.0	82.5
C	19	15	52.1	63.6
D	19	20	Not tested	64.5
E	20	19	Not tested	61.6
F	18	11	Not tested	82.2
G	17	17	Not tested	77.7
Average	18.3	17.1	62.3	74.3

the persons absent in groups A and B made up the lecture by attending group C, which was a smaller group and permitted make-up opportunities.)

Four other groups were similarly tested the following year, but they evaluated the risks only at the end of the program. The percentages of risks removed by these groups were 64.5, 61.6, 82.2, and 77.7. In this case the groups were urged to attend their regular groups, and it will be noted that the last group showed no decline. The average for these four groups is 71.5 per cent, as compared to the final average of 78.1 per cent for the other three groups. Although the difference in percentage is not great, it favors the group that examined the risks both during the middle and at the end of the program. The trend suggests that examination of risks in the middle of the program facilitates their final removal, particularly when we take account of the fact that group C was not typical in attendance. Disregarding the difference in treatment of these groups we find that, on the average, 74.3 per cent of the groups removed each risk. This represents a high degree of acceptance, particularly since the reservations or doubts are primarily confined to the details in procedure. The type of reservations obtained from the analysis of group A are typical of what was found in other groups.

The removal of mental reservations, however, does not insure action, but it does eliminate an important barrier to action. The important remaining barrier is one of skill; and the method of role playing, to be discussed in Chapter 4, is one of the best methods for developing skills.

Posting Problems

Introduction. A frequent problem that a discussion leader must face is how to deal with questions which demand simple methods for dealing with problem employees. The trainer previously may have demonstrated how differences in attitudes cause misunderstandings and how attempts to understand attitudes can reduce such misunderstandings. A questioner then asks, "What should one do with an employee who sneaks off the job and goes to sleep in a corner?" This is obviously a hostile question, the hostility being indicated in the description of the employee and in the challenge directed to the trainer. Avoiding answering the question by tabling it might be successful only temporarily.

Questions of this sort pose a disturbing problem. To avoid such questions leaves an unfavorable impression with the group, and answering them successfully may point up the incompetence of the questioner and increase his hostility. Usually attempts to answer such questions require the obtaining of more information, and this process leads to further difficulties and diversions.

In the process of supplying information the hostile questioner is not cooperative. He intentionally or unintentionally withholds information which he can use later to refute suggestions, and he carefully avoids supplying evidence of his own contribution to the misunderstanding. He meets offered suggestions by saying, "I tried that," or "That won't work because . . ." It becomes apparent too late that the questioner is not seeking aid of the type the trainer is likely to supply. Rather, he frequently is seeking support for disciplinary action he would like to take and for which he is not supported by the union or higher management. In other words, he is presenting an insoluble problem and is using it to demonstrate the inadequacy of the training program.

In a discussion with L. F. Zerfoss and T. A. Kotila at the Detroit Edison Company, the problem of dealing with questions that sidetrack the topic under consideration became a real issue because there was a need to train unskilled leaders for dealing with such questions. It is from this conference that the procedure of posting problems emerged as a special discussion technique.

Procedure. Early in any human relations program (or even at the time that a question demanding a simple remedy for dealing with a problem employee arises) it is desirable to put the following project to a training group:

All of you undoubtedly have problems with employees that trouble you a lot, and you would most like a program like this one to help you on problems that give you the most trouble. A knowledge of these problems will be an aid to us for measuring our progress and for evaluating this program. Let's take some time out, therefore, to list the types of problems on which you as supervisors would welcome help.

The leader then develops from the group a list of their problems, which he posts on the easel. Each problem suggested is discussed to clarify its meaning, and members are encouraged to give illustrations if this seems desirable in order to make its implications clear to others. If group members disagree on whether an entry is worth considering it is either entered with a question mark following it or is deleted if the member suggesting the problem consents.

When the list is complete the leader points out that he will have duplicate copies made so that each member will have a personal list of the posted problems.

The list is then duplicated on a form which allows a space for each participant to fill in his name. Following each item there should be a series of columns. These columns are used for rating later discussions on how much they helped in solving the types of problems shown on the list.

The prepared form should be passed out to the participants at the end of the next meeting. The members are reminded of the list and asked to cross out all the problems they do not consider real. They are then asked to fill in the first column indicating the degree to which the current discussion helped them on the remaining problems. If the discussion topic helped little or not at all on a problem listed they should rate the current discussion "0" for that problem; if it helped a reasonable amount it should be rated "1"; and if it helped a great deal it should be rated "2."

When all members have finished rating each of the problems the leader obtains the results for each item by asking, "How many gave the first problem in the list a '1' or '2'?" This should be followed by some discussion so that members can exchange ideas on ways in which the discussion helped or did not help. The same procedure is used for each of the items listed.

At the end of the discussion the leader collects the forms, pointing out that the group members will evaluate subsequent discussions in the same way so that they, as well as the leader, can gauge the value of the program and perhaps improve it for future groups.

This evaluation procedure is repeated at the conclusion of each major topic in the program. The tendency for members to give favorable ratings may be expected to increase both because of improvement in attitude and because the various units tend to supplement each other and produce a cumulative effect.

The concluding meeting should allow time for summarizing the tally sheets and discussing any problems that seemed to receive little or no help from the program.

If at the end of the program a number of problems remain unresolved and if group members still are not receptive to suggestions, it would seem safe to conclude that the program is in need of improvement.

Value of the Procedure. The method of posting problems has a number of potential benefits in addition to preventing and dealing with hostile questions. These may be outlined as follows:

1. Group members are given a chance to voice problems in which they are involved emotionally and to have them recognized and accepted. This leaves them free to take their minds off these problems and to pay attention to the topic under consideration. Like the "risk" technique, it permits hostile behavior to be expressed and thereby gives the relief that permits motivated problem solving to come to the fore.

2. Highly resistant members may feel they are receiving no help as the program progresses. However, if the other members of the group begin to give topics such as attitudes, motivation, listening skills, participation, etc., credit for aiding many of the problems listed, the resistant individual is exposed to group pressure without being placed on the defensive.

3. Responsibility for receiving help on personal problems is placed in the lap of each individual. The discussion leader does not find himself in the situation of telling supervisors how to run their jobs, but instead finds himself in a situation where group members grope to use his material to solve their own problems.

4. In examining their own problems from time to time group members can experience that progress is being made. They may also discover that their own problems take on different meanings as the program progresses and that the hostility present at the outset has declined.

5. The leader obtains a record of the value of and the reception given of various topics in the program. He thus can determine what the group is getting out of the program.

6. The tally sheet also may be used to measure the attitude changes of group members. A person who indicates very little help from the program will undoubtedly have an unfavorable supervisory attitude, and a person who indicates that he has been helped a great deal will be likely to have a constructive attitude toward his employees.

7. Finally, a tally sheet which shows that a particular problem has been aided by several of the discussion periods demonstrates something to group members which they may not have expected. This is that no problem can be solved without considering a number of aspects of human relations. Thus excessive tardiness may involve an employee's lack of job interest, his aptitude, his outside interests, his attitude toward the supervisor, his home problems, his health, his motivation to get ahead, his feeling of inferiority, etc. It is because almost any facet of a person's make-up may play an important part in his behavior that there are no general remedies for specific actions. To explain this point to a group when a question is asked makes the group as well as the leader feel he is backing away from giving an answer to a question. It is only when a program has progressed far enough to make the unity and interrelation of human relations principles apparent that the need for tailoring solutions to meet specific situations is discovered. And only then is it believed.

This procedure, like others described in this chapter, is designed to meet specific needs. However, it is consistent in spirit with the others, and the basic elements of the procedure are appropriate for meeting conditions of a similar sort. The discussion leader must be alert at all times to the needs and frustrations of his group so that he can supply the discussion procedure that best solves or resolves the problem at hand.

4

Role Playing

Introduction

The technique of *role playing* is one of creating a life situation, usually one involving conflicts between people, and then having persons in a group play the parts of specific personalities. Since only the situation is given, the dialogue must spontaneously grow out of the situation created, and the end product is fluid in that it will depend upon the way different persons played their roles. The method was first used by Moreno (44, 45) as a therapeutic procedure and was called *psychodrama*. A patient who had conflicts with different people might play the role of himself and subsequently of each of the other people, while other members in the group assumed the remaining roles. By playing different roles a patient gains insights and an understanding of the behavior of others. The role-playing method permits a person to react as his father, his wife, his employer, etc., and thus to get outside himself and thereby view himself more objectively. In playing these different roles attitudes are not only revealed but are also changed. This method gives the therapist a broader view of the client because the approach not only is through verbal communication between client and counselor, but also it utilizes actions and conversations in a lifelike social situation (16).

The potential value of the role-playing method for other situations was quickly recognized. Wherever training in attitudes and interpersonal relations are involved the method offers new possibilities. It has been used for schoolroom purposes (20, 57, 60), home training (28), interview training (3), speech adjustment (17), leadership training (27, 30), and supervisory training (6, 8, 10, 14).

Various workers have used the role-playing method in somewhat different ways, each attempting to adapt it to fit his needs. Generally speaking, there is no rigid procedure, since the objective is to obtain a spontaneous interaction between people in a structured situation. The situation thus offers the starting point for the expression, and from this point on the words that are spoken by each influence subsequent reactions. The major objective is to place a person in a situation with one or more other persons and let them interact as if they were in a real-life situation. In real-life situations a person supplies his own words, gestures, and method of expression. In role playing a similar demand is made upon him. Thus role playing becomes a lifelike approach to problems, and some authors (20, 60) have described the method as *reality practice*.

The reason for structuring the situation is to supply a subject matter for interaction. Thus certain facts should be agreed upon, such as a specific job situation, certain past events, a present event that raises a problem, e.g., an employee making an error, the type of relationship between individuals participating, etc. These objective situational conditions are also present in real-life situations, and enough background should be supplied to give the play situation a realistic basis.

It may be generally assumed that in most instances all members of a group do not play roles at a given time, so that part of a group acts as observers while others act as participants. As the method is continued all members of the group receive the opportunity to play roles. Not only does the presence of observers act as a stimulant for those playing a role so that they are more conscious of their actions, but also persons receive training in the capacity of observers. Both players and observers are useful for analyzing the situation and the way it was played.

The types of variation in approach that have been made tend to fall within the broad specifications of the method. Some of these may be illustrated to clarify the procedure and add detail.

The extent to which a person is himself may be varied. In some instances each person is allowed to play himself completely, and thus reflects his own personality; in others, he is given a specific position in life, e.g., union steward, and must adapt his personality to his position; and in still others he is supplied with an attitude and must react as he would if he had that attitude. The attitude supplied might be insecurity, an intense interest in order and neatness, or extreme sensitivity to race prejudice, such as the part of a Negro working with a white group.

Problems may be set up so that conflicts can be resolved and thus end in some kind of agreement or understanding, or they may be set up without there being any intention of reaching a solution. In the latter type the discussion leader terminates the role playing whenever he feels certain conflicts have come to expression. Thus roles may be set up to illustrate a complete interview, or they may be set up merely for the purpose of showing different ways that an interviewer may begin an interview.

How much reversal of roles takes place also depends upon the training objective. If one wished to produce insights between mother and daughter in a specific problem situation, the switching of roles would have more value than if one wished merely to demonstrate how differently problems are viewed by parents and children.

Also, the question of whether the leader should supply role-playing situations or whether the group should supply specific real-life problems they themselves must solve depends on the needs and objectives of the training. Generally speaking, this question is similar to asking whether problems that highlight principles or specific on-the-job problems should be used. If the objective of training is to develop insights into day-to-day problems, rather than to arrive at a more general understanding and feeling for human relations principles, then one would tend to use problems supplied by the group. If, however, there is a desire to place emphasis on principles the role-playing situation should be planned so that general principles are brought out.

After roles are played there is also the problem of deciding how much of an analysis of the role-playing session should be made. One extreme method is to make no analysis, but let each member of the group draw his own conclusions; the other extreme is to make a detailed analysis, going over what was accomplished, analyzing why a person said one thing or another, classifying hostile *vs.* constructive reactions, showing attitude differences, evaluating the permissiveness of each participant, analyzing the feelings behind the remarks made, etc. In all this analysis the behaviors may be related to principles derived from the study of attitude, frustration, and motivation, as well as to situational factors. The discussion may then be followed by the group's planning how the end result might have been improved by developing skills in sensitivity and permissiveness.

The Training Values of Role Playing

The effectiveness of any training instrument partly depends on the degree to which the method is suited to the training objective. Since role playing is time-consuming and since variety in methods is desirable, it is important to use role playing where and when it will make its most unique and valuable contribution. It, therefore, is desirable to examine some of the unique accomplishments of role playing so that it can be suited to needs as they develop. Since the concern of this volume is with human relations training we will consider role playing from this point of view.

Developing Interest and Needs for Training. Many supervisors are unaware of the fact that good human relations are more than common sense. They may believe that they should treat others as they themselves would like to be treated, but they assume that the treatment they give out is what they would like themselves. Thus they insist that they want to be told when they do something wrong. However, they overlook two points. There may be disagreement as to whether the something a person did was wrong, and on this issue the judge and the accused may differ greatly. In such instances a person wants to be told only if he is not in a defensive position and instead is interested only in improving his behavior and fully trusts his critic's motives. This condition is not frequently met.

The other point overlooked is the importance of *how* a mistake is pointed out to another. A person who insists that he wants to know his weakness overlooks the importance of the procedure that is used. One may want to be corrected, but one may object to being insulted or degraded. Thus, when a supervisor gets a violent reaction (tears, hostility, etc.) after evaluating an employee's work, he may describe his contribution as, "I merely tried to get the girl to switch to a better method. She certainly has a poor attitude if she doesn't want to improve."

There is no more effective way to demonstrate how little details in procedure may determine the receptiveness of an employee to training or changes in work procedures. One may point out the fact that these things are important, but such statements are agreed to without their being related to oneself. Lecturing may convince supervisors that the training is needed by others, but role playing makes them realize it is needed by themselves.

Role playing clearly demonstrates that what a person says and believes are not always reflected in what he does. On the one hand, when on the job, a supervisor may have good intentions when he asks an employee to change his work pattern. Since he had no intention of insulting or degrading the employee, he feels he has been misjudged when this occurs. If his procedure is criticized he feels that the employee, not he, showed poor human relations. This leads to a circular discussion on who is to blame, and improved procedures seldom emerge from such a discussion. On the other hand, when roles are played, the same situation may be played several times, and we may observe different outcomes resulting from different supervisory approaches. Thus a situation may be set up in which a supervisor must correct an employee's behavior. Different supervisors may try out their "tested" approaches which have stood them in good stead, and all may find themselves lacking. The mere fact that all persons are involved throws attention on the procedure and makes for increased awareness of difficulties that previously may have been entirely overlooked.

Pointing up Personal Weakness. Unlike a formal presentation, which is designed to train all persons in one specific area at a time, there is something in role playing that permits each person to learn what he needs most. The bull-of-the-woods type of supervisor learns that his aggressive approach produces hostility, the salesman type of supervisor learns that he isn't trusted, the paternalistic type of supervisor learns that others have more maturity than he credited them with, and the hands-off type of supervisor learns that he does not inspire confidence and respect. Each may learn how much he overlooks opportunities to praise, how much he is on the defense, how much he trusts others. Since role playing reveals attitudes, the person has an opportunity to see his own attitude more as others see it. A supervisor may claim that he doesn't show his anger or dislike of a person, yet when roles are discussed he may find that all were aware of his emotional state. Thus in a role-playing situation a supervisor may have planned a sugar-coated procedure for getting a person to transfer and may have become frustrated when the employee asked him an embarrassing question but may think that both his motive and emotions were undetected. In some situations participants display real emotions without being aware of their expression.

Filling the Gap between Knowing and Doing. We usually judge ourselves in terms of the values we live by and the goals we strive for. That we do not practice what we preach is often overlooked. Thus a parent may believe he should spend time playing with his children, but actually continues reading the paper when his child wants attention.

A supervisor may believe and teach that it is poor human relations to lose one's temper on the job and yet actually do so when sufficient provocation arises. Such instances are overlooked because we can justify our action in each case. There are two basic reasons for our failure to practice what we preach. One is our failure to see or view a situation as relevant to a principle we preach. Thus the parent sees the hour before dinner as newspaper-reading time and not play time, and the supervisor sees the employee's attempt to get out of overtime work as an interference to getting a job done rather than as a reasonable desire. Failure to view a given situation as one in which our beliefs and values apply is a matter of attitude and will be discussed shortly.

The other reason for not being able to practice what we preach is a lack of skill. The golfer may have learned from his coach that the club must be held a certain way, that he must maintain a certain posture, and that he must attend to the ball. However, he cannot do these things until he has practiced them. Developing skill is a matter of practice, which means doing rather than memorizing instructions. Through practice one automatically executes the proper behaviors and need not translate principles into deeds any longer.

A group of supervisors is made more ready to accept training when the gap between ideas and actions is appreciated, and role playing causes performers frequently to remark, "Now why did I do that? I really know better."

Developing Skills in Sensing Another Person's Feelings. There are a number of skills essential to the practice of good human relations. These skills are in the nature of observing or perceiving and in the nature of doing or executing.

The skills in perceiving or observing take the form of increasing a person's sensitivity in recognizing the way another feels. Ordinarily one reacts to what a person says, but behind all our remarks there are feelings not expressed in words. A person whose feelings have been hurt may not say that his pride has been injured; he may doubt what you say but fail to verbalize his doubts; he may say he will co-operate in the future and still not feel like cooperating; and he may feel hostile without putting it in so many words. How is a person to recognize feelings in others that fail to be expressed? Since people express their doubts, their disinterest, their hostilities, and their hurt feelings in different ways, there is no simple formula to follow. After role playing a supervisor may think that he has convinced a person, who played the role of an employee, that he should change jobs. The observers may disagree. The events of the role playing may then be analyzed in terms of what happened, and the behaviors which indicated that the employee was or was not convinced could be pointed up. Such analysis reveals the significance of facial expression, the tone of voice, guarded remarks, pauses, gestures, and postures as factors in determining the nature of the feelings behind the remarks. The person who played the role of the employee may then be asked to report on his feelings to check on the accuracy of the analysis.

Experiences of this kind train a person to pay attention to feelings and to discover significance in the behavior as a whole. Such experiences develop sensitivity for feelings which so often fail to be communicated.

Developing Skill in Permissiveness. The problem of recognizing the feelings of another person is greatly simplified if a person's words can be made to reflect his feelings more accurately. One only permits his feelings to be freely expressed when one feels it is safe and permissible to do so. One way to increase the expressiveness of another is to create a permissive relationship. Thus the supervisor who listens, reacts to feelings, and accepts another's feelings as being understandable and genuine will find that persons talk quite freely. However, the supervisor who criticizes, argues, rejects, and insists on sticking to facts will find that a great psychological distance separates him from the other person.

Permissiveness is a kind of behavior, and it can be improved with practice. To test a person's permissive skill one cannot rely on his intentions. Rather he must learn by having others react to him. Role playing creates this kind of practice situation, and the subsequent analysis not only gives him an idea of his progress but points up his strengths and weaknesses.

Developing Additional Skills in Leadership and Interviewing. In addition to permissiveness the supervisor, as the leader of a group, must develop further conference skills. He must be able to formulate problems in such a way that constructive behavior is stimulated; he must develop techniques for dealing with hostile behavior; he must learn what to do when he is criticized so that a bad situation is improved rather than aggravated; he must be resourceful in accurately reflecting ideas; he must be skilled in dealing with persons who talk too much or too little; he must learn how to repress his own preference for a particular solution; he must learn how to bring differences in attitude to expression so that the discussion is open and aboveboard, and he must be able to make the group feel responsible for reaching agreement. Although many of these skills require the proper conference attitude, good judgment, and resourcefulness, they nevertheless are improved with practice. Actually performing these functions in role-playing situations gives a supervisor the "feel" of these problems, and he discovers, by trial and error, which responses from the group are produced by the various leadership behaviors.

When dealing with individuals the supervisor must learn how to put a person at ease and make him feel free to talk, how to treat a person as an adult by refraining from talking down, how to develop common or mutual interests, how to supply objectives and goals that relate to a person's needs, how to avoid arguments, how to translate his criticisms of employees into constructive training terms by avoiding negative terminology, and how to use positive methods to motivate in place of fear motivation. This all sounds like a large order, and the list is incomplete. However, the above activities are related to each other, and many of them are already known. In experiencing the role-playing process one learns to pay attention to what is done, and it is through increased attention to detail that one improves with practice. It is a general principle in the acquisition of skill that improvement takes place only through conscious attention and effort during performance. The eventual objective, of course, is to make an act of skill automatic, so that attention to detail is no longer necessary.

Discovering Attitudes of Trainees. Role playing reveals attitudes more effectively than most other conference procedures perhaps because the situations are free and stimulate spontaneous behavior. If a supervisor is inclined to be suspicious, hostile, defensive, autocratic, etc., he is likely to reflect this attitude when playing a role. An attitude inconsistent with good human relations becomes apparent not only to the trainer and to the observers, but it soon becomes apparent to the individual himself. The trainer can profit by a knowledge of a participant's attitude by assigning him to roles in which he is on the receiving end of his type of attitude; he can give such an individual more opportunity for expressing his views, and thereby permit him to release his hostilities; he can provide him with face-saving opportunities; and he can supply nondirective counseling when it seems desirable. Other members of the group can be of service in that they exert social pressure by believing in and practicing different attitudes, and the individual can help himself by becoming conscious of his attitude. When an individual becomes conscious of his prejudices, he is at least on the threshold of change.

When an intolerant person is assigned the role of a supervisor and is asked to correct one of his associates, who plays the role of an employee, his own contribution to a misunderstanding is highlighted. His associate in the role of the employee can hardly be set aside as a disgruntled employee, particularly when observers agree that the employee role was played in a normal fashion. Further, when he himself is placed in the role of an employee he finds himself reacting unfavorably to ideas imposed on him. Now he sees supervisory behaviors, some of which he himself has displayed, from a different viewpoint, and as a consequence he recognizes certain supervisory behaviors as capable of arousing feelings he previously had ignored or considered inappropriate. It is these feelings that may be called "gut" feelings, which carry the emotional loadings that are so readily overlooked when one is on the giving rather than on the receiving end of a supervisory-employee contact.

Since different members of a group might have a variety of attitudes that conflict with good human relations, each member is given an opportunity to learn something of unique value to himself. When attitudes of distrust are absent, the training time need not be devoted to changing such attitudes, but instead can be directed toward the changes that are needed.

Changing Attitudes toward Other People. Such attitudes as (a) a respect for other people, (b) a belief that whatever people do or feel has been caused, (c) a true feeling that people have needs which may not correspond to our own, (d) a realization that perhaps all problems with people are matters of misunderstandings, (e) an ability to see the frustrated individual not as bad, but as in need of understanding and help, (f) a tolerance for people who may have less ability than others, but whose feelings may easily be hurt, and (g) a true feeling for the fact that everyone in a healthy state of mind wants to be a member of society and do a constructive job—these attitudes are essential to permissive, acceptant, and understanding behaviors. Such attitudes are in conflict with (a) the inclination to locate and blame someone as a method of correction, (b) the tendency to overlook the contribution of the situation to behavior and to see the individual as the only factor in behavior, (c) the belief that fear motivation is basically sound, (d) the belief that people want to do as little for as much as they can, and (e) the belief that kindness is a sign of weakness.

Role playing readily demonstrates that hostility, threats, and suspicion stimulate hostile and defensive reactions in others, whereas generosity, tolerance, and a desire to see another's point of view stimulate constructive and social behavior in him. It is in experiencing these relationships in reality practice that they can become practical living principles.

One also experiences these relationships in another way when one is at the receiving end of hostile treatment. One sees one's own hos-

tility stimulated by intolerant remarks, and one sees his generosity
stimulated by tolerant treatment. The fact that the point of view
changes as one switches roles also makes one able to see that the
behavior situation determines perception. Thus one begins to seek
possible differing points of view when dealing with people. When a
person can see that different points of view are not only possible but
usually are present, one cannot remain intolerant and rigid in one's
point of view.

Perhaps the most important contribution to attitude change is the
opportunity to express one's pent-up attitudes in role playing. Role
playing furnishes opportunities for harmless aggression, and hence
the aggression need not be expressed later in the real situation. Therefore, role-playing situations that an individual must actually face on
the job prepare him not only in skills but in a state of mind. If he
can dissipate his frustrations in role playing he can face the real-life
situation constructively. Thus it follows that some role playing of
actual job problems with which an individual is faced has a special
value in changing his attitudes toward other people.

A change in one's attitude toward other people represents a profound one, since it is bound to be reflected in all social behavior.
Personality characteristics are primarily social reactions, so that an
attitude change toward people really becomes personality change.
This means that deep emotional effects are involved. The fact that
role playing introduces some of the emotional experiences of real-life
situations facilitates the training of these emotions. Intellectual discussions and lectures tend to by-pass the emotional content, and hence
are unlikely to permit training at an emotional level. One can hardly
expect behaviors that are not expressed in a training situation to be
trained by that situation.

Changing Attitudes toward Oneself. It is easier to change a person's attitude toward other people than to change his attitude toward
himself. Thus, compelling discussions may convince a person of
the value of human relations training, and yet not create a feeling
that he himself needs training. It is for this reason that higher-management personnel may recommend a course of training for others
and not see the value of the subject for themselves. In training
groups in democratic leadership one first obtains acceptance of the
idea that the technique is sound and valuable but that it could not
be used in their jobs. We have also found that supervisors first see
the value of human relations in handling children, but question its
value for handling adults. At the same time, when we attempted

to train counselors in a children's camp there was ready acceptance of the idea for use in industry, but it was regarded as not adaptable to a children's camp.

A high official in one company who had observed the training of three successive groups reminisced that the first time he had been in the program he agreed with the material and was glad that he practiced so much of it; the second time he began to realize how few people practiced it and how badly others were in need of the training; the third time he observed the program he was shocked by the realization that he himself needed the training.

For similar reasons people can see prejudices and needs for counseling in others before recognizing them in themselves. To face the fact that one may be somewhat inadequate is degrading, so that natural protective reactions present themselves.

These observations merely reflect the fact that a considerate attitude toward other people may be developed without essentially changing one's attitude toward oneself. We can feel that we are being fair to other people and yet impose our own estimation of fairness on them. It is when a person discovers that he can influence the success of his social contacts by his own actions, regardless of who the other person may be, that new insights into his role develop. Since all persons feel some degree of inadequacy the problem of face saving is reduced, yet the leader must be observant so that prestige is not lost. If prestige is lost a hostile reaction to role playing develops.

In role playing the emphasis is on what each person does to influence the outcome. Thus each has the power to alter the direction in which a human relations situation may develop. After the roles have been played the subsequent analysis may be used to determine what each party may have said or done to alter the end result. This gives each person the direct experience of seeing his behavior as a contributing factor. It is desirable to permit each participant to evaluate himself and suggest improvements. In this way he can gain prestige by being a good critic of himself.

Changing Attitudes toward the Job. A supervisor quite naturally is inclined to view his position as one of responsibility for getting a job done. As an employee he may have envied those in management positions, and from the point of view of an employee he was inclined to see prestige and power in such a position. It is natural, therefore, that some of this attitude will be carried in his promotions upward. Subsequent experiences also tend to encourage an individual to use the "power" he perceives his position gives him. Actually this process tends to become perpetuated because, within the management hierarchy, each position above seems to contain the power and prestige that is vaguely felt below.

Good human relations demands that persons in management positions exert influence, but the most effective kind of influence may not require the use of power or fear motivation. Thus a supervisor might be made to feel that his position carries responsibility and that part of this responsibility is to build up the morale of his group so that he will have a happy and cooperative team. If he can discover that by developing skills in human relations he can influence the obtaining of these objectives then this view becomes reasonable. A further step then becomes possible. He can learn that by using his office to develop good morale he exerts an important influence on behavior and finds that the group accepts his influence. It is when the group accepts his influence that he develops leadership power. Thus, accepted influence is a kind of power that does not require fear motivation. According to this view, power and prestige are earned by an individual and should not come from the position. The obtaining of a management position then becomes the beginning of an opportunity to develop influence; it is not the achievement of an end or goal.

The development of this point of view depends on experiencing the reality of an influence with people by a method that does not resort to fear; the role-playing method supplies an initial opportunity for experiencing this reality. Being told that such reality exists is not enough. One must actually have it work for oneself before there is enough faith to motivate continued effort.

A person might have the intellectual belief that he can use artificial bait for catching fish. Many people have succeeded, and so there are many cases to support this belief. However, the person may find that he does not continue to practice his belief. After throwing a plug in the water a few times he finds himself using live bait. It is only after he has succeeded that he can persist, and then it is to persist in using the lure that has succeeded for him. Intellectual belief and the faith that leads to action are very different in their effects on behavior.

Developing Action Tendencies. We have already considered the gap between thought and action. Thus a change in ideas does not necessarily lead to action. We may go so far as to consider action, but the time for carrying out the action never arrives. To be effective, training must do more than change attitudes. It must also result in a change in behavior. Role playing carries the training into action, even if the action is only at the level of play. Once an action has been expressed the resistance to a repetition of the action is reduced. This is actually one of the major benefits of laboratory training in connection with a subject. You might be fully trained in a physiology course in how to use a certain instrument to destroy the brain of a frog. You may have observed demonstrations and have a knowledge of the position of the brain and of where to insert the instrument, etc., and yet if you had not actually performed this act it is quite unlikely that you would do so of your own choosing. However, if you had performed this act in the laboratory a basic factor in resistance for future action would have been overcome. Role playing becomes the laboratory part of human relations training.

Illustrating Principles. Sound psychological principles can best be formulated from scientific research. Through research we can discover something about the nature of attitudes, their origins, and their resistance to change. Likewise, one can investigate motivation and find the relationship between needs and need satisfiers, differences in acquired needs among people, principles dealing with substituting one need satisfier or another, and the relative merits of rewards and punishments for influencing behavior. What we know about frustration also comes largely from research so that hostility, stubbornness, and immature behavior are seen as products of frustration. Thus the science of psychology has much of an informational nature to offer, and this knowledge can most readily be presented by lecture and discussion procedures. However, role-playing analysis can be used to make these principles live and help a person to recognize illustrations of principles. To know that a person with low ability rationalizes and protects himself from degradation is one thing, but to recognize an instance of rationalization and to respond to it helpfully is quite another thing. Role playing gives practice in recognizing and diagnosing such conditions. Thus role playing may serve the same function for human relations training as clinical experience serves the young doctor of medicine.

Supplying Answers to Questions. Frequently trainees ask questions that should not be answered because the answer may be unacceptable or may even produce hostility. (This point was discussed in Chapter 3, and the method of posting problems was recommended.) For example, a supervisor who has had considerable training asks, "What should I do with a fellow who absolutely refuses to go along with any new development or method in our office?" He then describes his problems in some detail. The leader may suggest that he present an illustration of a situation in which this individual would fail to cooperate. After such a situation is described the questioner may be asked to play the part of the employee. The leader adds, "In this way the rest of us can get to know the kind of person the employee is." Another supervisor is then asked to play the part of the office manager.

In an instance that this procedure was tried out the person who played the part of the office manager asked the employee to help him on an office problem, and showed an interest in his opinion. The questioner, who played the part of the employee, saw no opportunities to resist, but found himself making constructive suggestions. After a few minutes had passed he announced that his question had been answered and he now knew the nature of his trouble. He was thankful for the help and had not lost face.

Magnifying Behavior. Up to this point the values of role playing have been attributed to the fact that it approaches real-life situations and permits practice without actually disturbing reality. This would imply that the training value of real-life situations would actually be better, except for the undesirable consequences of poor performances. However, there is one major value contributed by role playing which is actually superior to the learning that could be gained from real-life situations. The advantage of role playing is that persons are less inhibited and fearful than in real-life situations. As a consequence they are more likely to express what they feel, so that ineffective or crude procedures are more likely to produce observable unfavorable responses. This amounts to magnifying behavior effects and making them more apparent and less likely to go unnoticed. After a person has seen the magnified reactions in the roles played he is more likely to recognize them in real-life situations where people tend to hide their hostilities, their dislikes, or their fears.

The exaggeration of behavior is likely to make the reaching of agreements more difficult. This is also an advantage since it means that a higher degree of skill is needed for role playing than for real-life situations. If the reverse were true, persons might experience too much failure after training and so abandon the training instead of increasing their skills. Because role playing makes the reaching of solutions difficult it tends to set a goal for a high level of skill.

Summary. We have enumerated fourteen functions that role playing may contribute to training. This does not mean that it is the most valuable training technique. The purpose in making the detailed breakdown in function has been to assist the trainer in using role playing to fit the needs as they arise. Generally speaking, the function of the role-playing method is to train for action. There are what may be called *barriers to action*, and role playing as well as the group-decision method is effective for reducing these barriers.

The major areas in which action barriers are found are in: perception, or the way we view situations and people; attitudes, or the predispositions for certain perceptions which we bring to a situation; the presence of frustration, which prevents a person from solving problems and instead makes a person react in hostile and nonconstructive ways; the fear of change, which arises because of insecurity; the lack of confidence in one's ability to use new methods; and the interference of old habits of action. The values of role playing described above therefore reside in the ways in which perceptions and attitudes can be changed, the ways in which frustrations may be expressed in harmless manners and thereby reduced, and the ways in which a variety of skills may be developed to replace previous behaviors.

Role-Playing Situations and Procedures for Analysis

As an aid to the practice of role playing in industry a number of cases are presented which have been tested and found to produce well-balanced conflict situations. The cases selected are nontechnical and general enough so that they lend themselves for use with almost any group. It is desirable that some of the role-playing situations be on jobs other than those in which participants find themselves. This is to avoid the rigid procedures that the company may have followed over a period of time and hence that do not produce the desired spontaneity and differences of opinion.

The following cases contain two sets of instructions, one for each side of the conflict. These instructions create the situation. In presenting a case, one of the participants may be excused from the room while the other is instructed in the presence of the observers. After one of the parties has been instructed he should feel free to ask questions so that his situation is clear. He is then excused and given the instruction sheet for further study. The other party is then called in and given his instructions in a similar manner. Thus the observers hear both sides of the issue and in this manner are made sensitive to the nature of the conflict.

Variations in the procedure for instructing observers may also be used, particularly on later cases. A third of the group may hear one side, another third, the other side, and the last third may hear both sides. This permits a comparison of the evaluations, based upon different sets of information and identifications.

After the instructions are completed room arrangements and props can be utilized as needed. When the stage is set, the leader gives the signal to begin.

The problem of obtaining participants to play the roles is not a difficult one. We suggest that certain persons be asked if they would be willing to try. Persons who are hesitant to participate, however, should not be pressed into playing a role. Ordinarily one does not obtain volunteers at the beginning of a program, but this does not mean necessarily that all are reluctant. Most persons are anxious to participate if invited. To depend entirely on volunteers is not recommended because some persons may be too hesitant to volunteer and yet would be glad to participate. Of those who volunteer one must be particularly careful not to involve face-saving problems. The person who volunteers may expect to succeed, and frequently roles are too difficult to assure reasonable success.

THE PROBLEM OF "OLD" GIRLS

This case is excellent for the purpose of demonstrating that attitudes rather than facts create certain conflicts between individuals. Thus two persons might be exposed to the same objective information, but one will react only to those facts which fit into his general attitude and the other will react only to such facts as support his attitude. If the attitudes of the two differ they will behave, therefore, as if they had quite differing experiences. In setting up the roles for this case we have given two individuals different attitudes, but the same set of objective facts.

Although the usual procedure with case material is to permit observers to hear the roles supplied to each of the role players, this case is an exception, as the observers will be asked later to see if they can locate the difficulty.

For the purposes of demonstrating the way facts are used to justify a point of view it is not necessary to carry the interview to completion. The discussion leader may break off the interview at the point where the conflict in views has caused all the points listed as facts to be expressed by either one participant or the other, or at the point at which the presentation of facts becomes repetitious. However, there is no objection to continuing the interview until Jones completes it, if one is interested in the type of solution reached.

Role for Mr. Smith, manager of office force (*to be studied by role player in private*): You have had considerable trouble with Mr. Jones in the personnel office. He isn't cooperative with you regarding the kind of employees you want and doesn't help you in obtaining new jobs for those you want to get rid of. Mostly, the issue centers on problems concerning older girls. You refuse to accept girls over 30 years of age, and you try to transfer your old girls whenever you can. You like a young force. You have had dealings with all types of employees, and you and the four supervisors who report to you all agree that old girls are no good. You don't like to deal with them and see no reason why the company should put up with them. However, if the company wants to keep old girls let those who like them take them in their units. As far as you are concerned they aren't worth the pay they get. They are inefficient, undependable, and slow.

You have an appointment with Mr. Jones, who is in charge of the personnel office. He has asked you to come to his office to discuss your views concerning older employees.

Here are the known facts about old girls:

Absenteeism lower.
More time in rest rooms.
Less tardiness.
Less willing to do unpleasant jobs.
Same production.
Less sociable.
Object more to changes.
Can do a greater variety of jobs in company.
Know company set-up.
Adapt slowly to new jobs.

Role for Mr. Jones, director of the personnel office (*to be studied in private*): You have had a persistent problem with Mr. Smith, the manager of a large office group in the company. He objects to older employees and refuses to accept transfers. He also gives poor ratings to older girls and tries to get you to find other places for them. As far as you can tell he is prejudiced. You believe that the older girls make good, stable employees. You find them more conscientious, more dependable, more businesslike, and generally more capable. You can't understand Smith's position and therefore have decided to talk to him to see if you can't convert him. It is about time for him to arrive.

Here are the known facts about old girls:

Absenteeism lower.
More time in rest rooms.
Less tardiness.
Less willing to do unpleasant jobs.
Same production.

Less sociable.
Object more to changes.
Can do a greater variety of jobs in company.
Know company set-up.
Adapt slowly to new jobs.

DIFFERENT APPROACHES THAT MAY BE EXPECTED. Since Mr. Jones of
the personnel department is conducting the interview, his style will
largely determine the outcome. After the usual pleasantries have
been exchanged, Jones may begin by presenting his side of the question and supply certain facts supporting his point of view. Smith then
is likely to attempt to interrupt Jones in order to offer contrary evidence. If the person playing the part of Jones is a skilled interviewer he is likely to introduce the subject of "old" girls by presenting
the company's problem and asking Smith to give his views on the
matter. When Smith begins to present an unfavorable picture of old
girls, even the skilled interviewer is likely to interrupt and supply
evidence suggesting an opposite conclusion. Thus, regardless of the
initial approach, the scene usually turns into one in which Smith supplies the facts that support his point of view and Jones supplies the
facts that support his views. When this condition occurs, the men
usually become argumentative and the relationship deteriorates.

ANALYZING THE INTERVIEW. The first point to discuss after termi-
nating the interview is the over-all evaluation of the progress made.
Did the men get closer together or farther apart as the interview
progressed? What were the reasons for the trend? Did Jones do
anything to determine the trend?

If the men did not get along too well the observers may find a variety
of reasons to explain it. These will include criticism of either individual's conduct, the nature of the instructions given, or differences
in the facts supplied. The discussion leader will want to get around
to the point of asking the observers whether the facts supplied caused
the conflict. Usually, several observers will take the position that the
role players were supplied with different facts. When this occurs the
discussion leader can ask the person who played the role of Jones
to read the facts he was given. He then asks the other participant to
read the facts he was given. It becomes obvious that the facts supplied were the same. The analysis might then be carried out as
follows:

(a) List the facts favorable to old girls.
(b) List the facts unfavorable to old girls.

(*c*) Check the facts that Jones brought up by asking the group to supply them.

(*d*) Check the facts that Smith brought up.

This analysis clearly reveals that each participant contributed the facts that favored his position, thus demonstrating that attitudes select the facts people use.

By this time it is apparent that the conflict produced in the interview was due to the different attitudes planted in the participants. To emphasize this point, it is suggested that the discussion leader read the attitude part of the roles, supplied to Jones and Smith, respectively.

The group may then become interested in the proper way to handle an interview of this sort. The group should be encouraged to discuss this problem. For the benefit of the discussion leader the following is suggested as a good approach for Jones to take:

(*a*) Receive Smith in a friendly manner.

(*b*) Express interest in Smith's views. Ask Smith to enumerate some of the difficulties his office has had with older girls. This question should cause Smith to list unfavorable facts. Accept all points without criticism.

(*c*) When Smith has listed all the unfavorable points, ask him whether he feels that old girls have any satisfactory characteristics. This question should cause Smith to bring out some favorable facts about old girls.

(*d*) When Smith has had an opportunity to express his views fully, ask him to offer suggestions concerning the best use the company can make of old girls.

This procedure will prevent an argument, and it will cause Smith to supply both the good and the bad aspects of old girls. He then is not placed in a position where he must defend his initial position and can more easily become cooperative when the problem of what to do with "old" girls comes up. Even though this procedure may not always cause Smith to cooperate, it will at least prevent the men from becoming less tolerant of each other.

SAFETY-BELT CASE

This role-playing case readily lends itself to a new group and can be used to create an awareness of need for training. It involves the

violation of a safety practice, and supervisors usually have quite definite attitudes in such instances. At the same time there are many
reasons why men violate safety practices. These include hostility
toward a company or supervisor, dislike of a safety practice, desire to
increase production, and the feeling that danger is not always present
and that judgment should be used. Unlikely reasons are: failure
to know of hazards or consequences of injury; failure to know how to
use safe procedures; and failure to know company attitude toward
violations. But, whatever the reason for the violation, it is likely
to be a personal one and to require a personalized procedure. The
case is set up so that the foreman must decide not only whether to
take action on the violation, but also whether to use the contact for
developing future cooperation. Will he decide to discipline before
the complexity of the situation becomes apparent, or will he capitalize
on conditions as they develop? There are sufficient difficulties in the
case so that the need for skills becomes apparent to all. Opinion on
how the problem should be handled will differ widely. The situation
involves a contact between two men, a foreman and one of his men.
The objective of the foreman is to stimulate safe work habits and
to improve cooperation and morale. The objectives of the workman
are to protect himself from criticism and to have a good record in the
company. These objectives are not necessarily in conflict, but if they
are temporarily lost conflict may arise. The roles are as follows:

Role for Jim Welch, foreman: You are the foreman of a repair crew
of a utility company. You have 12 men who go on jobs, and the men
usually work alone or in pairs. As foreman you spend your time visiting the work locations of your men, checking on progress, giving such
help, training, and instruction as is needed. You are also responsible
for the safety of your men, and the company judges you partly on
the safety record of your crew. At the present time the annual company safety drive is just beginning. The slogan is, "No job is so important that it cannot be done safely." The company has passed a
ruling that anyone found violating a safety practice will be laid off
for 3 days.

You have just driven up to the place where Bill Smith is working.
You can stop your car some distance away (you cannot drive directly
to the work location) and see Bill working on top of the pole. As you
stop the car you have a distinct impression that Smith snapped his
safety belt. Apparently he was working without using his belt, and
this is a safety practice violation.

Smith is an employee with 20 years of service. He has four children ranging in age from 5 to 12. He is a good workman, but is quite
independent in his thinking. You feel it is your responsibility to cor-

rect this man and give him a better attitude toward safety, and you also have to operate in accordance with company regulations. You have been the supervisor of this crew for 2 years and don't know too much about Bill's past record. You have 10 years' service with the company.

Role for Bill Smith, repairman: You are a member of Jim Welch's repair crew in a utility company. You have been in the company for 20 years, and for the past 2 years Jim has been your supervisor. You feel you know the job and consider your technical knowledge perhaps somewhat greater than that of Welch, who has worked in the company a total of 10 years. You believe Jim has done a fair job as foreman, but feel that he supervises too closely.

You usually work alone on repair jobs except for several visits a week from your supervisor. You are now working on top of a pole and haven't bothered to snap your safety belt. You are a careful worker and use it when it is necessary, but you find it uncomfortable and in the way, and so you frequently don't bother to snap it.

Welch has just driven up, and so you hasten to snap your belt. There is an annual safety drive on, and the company has threatened to lay men off for safety violations. You can't afford having time off. You have four children, and living expenses use up all your earnings. You are quite sure Jim didn't see you snap your safety belt. He is walking toward your pole now.

DIFFERENT APPROACHES THAT MAY BE EXPECTED. The foreman may or may not assume a violation of company practice. If he accuses the man of a violation the man may deny it or say he was switching positions on the pole. This may lead to argument and poor future relations. If the man admits a violation the foreman must decide whether to invoke the penalty. If he invokes the penalty he is likely to create bad relations and lose the man's entire productivity for the 3 days he is suspended and have less production because of the "bad" feeling that is created. If he does not invoke the penalty he himself is violating company regulations and may run a risk himself. These approaches tend to lead the discussion away from safety and toward the subject of violations.

If the supervisor approaches the workman in a friendly manner and later raises the question of the safety drive, he may ask the man for help in improving safety habits. With this approach the foreman may obtain the workman's point of view and attitude, and together they might work out methods for improving safety. If, however, the foreman lectures on safety, discussing the hazards and consequences of falling, he is merely talking down to the employee, since he is saying things that are already well known to the man.

It can readily be seen that different approaches will greatly influence the nature and value of the employee-foreman contact.

ANALYZING THE CONTACT. After the roles have been played either to the point of a solution, in which case the foreman terminates the interview, or to the point of a deadlock, in which case the leader terminates it, the role process may be made the subject for discussion. The discussion topics suggested below may be found useful. The order in which to discuss them is irrelevant and should be determined by the interests and context of the discussion.

1. *Comparison of first and last half of interview with regard to degree of "good" feeling.* It is apparent that, if the latter half of the interview was less friendly than the first, the interview, instead of solving a problem, created a new one. If the second half was an improvement over the first it indicates that there was some meeting of minds and that the interview served a valuable purpose.

2. *Comparison of the amount that each talked.* If the foreman talked more than the repairman it indicates that he was telling the company viewpoint rather than discovering the workman's attitude and analyzing the causes behind behavior. In the best interviews the foreman spends a good deal of time listening.

3. *Obtaining opinions on whether the workman will improve his safety habits and his job performance.* If neither is improved or if safety is improved at the expense of production, the interview was lacking in effectiveness. The group's opinion should be accepted.

4. *Obtaining opinions on whether the foreman should have approached the safety problem as he did.* This discussion should develop alternatives, with an analysis of what would have happened in response to each. If opinion is sharply divided and very definite opinions are expressed it is sometimes wise to have two other persons play the roles, the foreman being a member who disagrees with the initial approach used. Comparisons between two approaches may then be made.

5. *Determining whether the foreman lectured on the obvious.* Frequently views will be expressed which recommend that the man must be made to realize that an injury to himself will cause his family to suffer, he must be told that falling will cause injury, he must be told the company's position, etc. The best way to handle these questions is to determine whether the man knows these things, what evidence there was in his behavior to indicate that he does. Usually the roles contribute the answers and reveal that many of the things

the foreman said were well known beforehand. Thus much of the foreman's contributions are elaborations of the obvious.

6. *Exploring the interview to determine the type of motivation used.* "Was fear motivation used?" "If so, in what ways?" "What was the response?" "Was positive motivation used in the sense that there was an attempt to get the man to want to practice safety?" "If so, how was this done?" "On what needs in the individual did the foreman capitalize?"

7. *Exploring the interview for evidences of hostile or defensive responses.* "What made the repairman lie or distort?" "Why did he not give his real reasons?" "Did the foreman get angry?" "If so, why?" "Were face-saving conditions present?" "In what way?" "Did the foreman get at the real cause?" "Why not or how?" Questions of this nature point up details and principles.

8. *Is the problem soluble?* Exploring the group opinion to determine the best approach to the problem presented in the case is a good approach. Usually this case stimulates a number of diverse opinions. How direct should the foreman's approach to the problem be? Should he discuss safety at the outset, later in the interview, or not at all? What are the consequences of each? In all these questions the leader should explore and summarize opinions, not impose his views.

Although it is desirable to obtain solutions from the group, it is well for the leader to have constructive ideas in leading a discussion. He may direct the thinking into positive channels by having the group determine just exactly what the foreman might have learned from his observations. Since the foreman is not sure whether a violation occurred, he cannot take a sure stand on the issue. All he knows is that perhaps all his men do not always use safe methods. He also knows that, for every unsafe practice that is observed, there are others that are not observed, and the unobserved violations are as likely to cause accidents as the observed ones. This suggests that safety should not be discussed with the man on this occasion. Rather the foreman should call a democratic safety meeting and ask the men to participate in helping him solve the safety problem. Since a safety campaign is in progress, he can easily do this without seeming to single out any one man. If training in democratic leadership has already been given, this solution can be obtained quite easily.

Another approach would be to ask the group to suggest positive appeals that the foreman might make. This suggests that the foreman might ask the man to help him on the safety drive. He can easily do this without appearing to be selecting this particular individual with an ulterior motive in mind because the man has considerable seniority. For example, he might say, "You know your way around here, and I'd like to have the benefit of your ideas to help me get safety across to the young fellows during our safety drive. Perhaps you can give me some ideas why men don't always go along with safety." This approach recognizes the man's experience and appeals to his pride because his leadership is desired. By this approach the foreman not only motivates but learns about the particular attitudes toward safety that the individual may have.

The first of these two approaches would appear to be the better because the motivations and attitudes of a group are explored rather than those of an individual. As a result, even unobserved safety violations may be corrected and new safety ideas explored.

However, it is not important to obtain acceptance of a particular solution. Solutions of the kind mentioned above may be obtained from an analysis of the case, but many groups of supervisors may not be ready for this type of solution. Then it is best to let the group experience conflicts in opinion and to go to new cases. Perhaps later on the same case can be presented again and the better solutions may be developed from the discussion.

THE STORM-WINDOW PROBLEM

The refusal of a man to do a job is usually considered to be insubordination, and as such seldom receives considerate treatment from supervisors. At the same time, a man must have very strong feelings before he will refuse to do a job. To what extent will the understanding of a case prevent such acts or alter one's interpretation of such refusals? To classify a man's resistance to a job as insubordination is an unfavorable interpretation of behavior, and the supervisor's reactions depend upon the interpretation rather than the act itself. The following case might terminate in insubordination or in improved relations, depending primarily on the type of human relations used by the supervisor. It will reveal how misunderstandings arise when supervisors are insensitive to attitudes, and how a knowledge of a workman's side of the picture changes one's interpretation of behavior. It is a good case to illustrate attitudes or discussions dealing with saving face. The case has to do with giving a work assignment, and it involves a supervisor and a workman. Reference is made to other crew members in the roles supplied, so that when using this case a couple of other persons should be familiar with Jack's role and should be brought into the action to the extent that the case demands. The roles are as follows:

Role for Mr. Brown, supervisor: You are in charge of a crew of 10 men. The company is a state organization which does electrical repair work. Your location is a small town, and you cover the neighboring towns as well as the communities between. You are located in a two-story building. Each year certain extra jobs arise. One of these is washing and putting up storm windows.

Ordinarily the plan you follow is to give these odd jobs to the man with least seniority. You feel that it is only fair to give this work to the man with least seniority.

Jack Jones has least seniority in your crew. He has been with the company for 6 years. During this period he has been given the odd jobs and he has performed them willingly. Jack is a good man and has been on the lowest level type of work this long merely because turnover has been very low. He is married and has two fine children.

At the present time you find that the work has piled up and that someone should work Sunday. The senior men have declined the privilege of working Sunday, and so you have asked Jack to do it. He has agreed to this. You now find that he will have plenty of time on Sunday, and it has occurred to you that he might as well wash the storm windows so that he can put them up the following week as time permits. You are just approaching Jack, who is talking to a couple of the other men. You are going to ask him to wash the windows on his spare time on Sunday so that he can put them up during the week.

Role for Jack Jones, repairman: You work for Mr. Brown, who is in charge of the branch office of a large organization that does electrical repair work. The office is located in a small town and serves the neighboring community. Your job is repair work, but because you have least seniority you are frequently asked to do work around the building. The unpleasant jobs are given to the man with least seniority. Although you have been with the company for 6 years, you find you still have the least seniority. You don't mind doing Sunday work because you can use the extra money, being married and having two children. You have already consented to work this next Sunday. But you do feel that you have enough seniority to get out of some of the more degrading work. One of these jobs is putting up storm windows. Only the other day some of the other men said, "Jack, I guess it's about time for you to put up the storm windows." You replied, "This year some of you guys will do it for a change—I'm through with doing it all alone." The group just laughed it off.

You are talking to a couple of the men right now. Mr. Brown has just come up, and you've stopped talking to see what he has on his mind.

DIFFERENT APPROACHES THAT MIGHT BE EXPECTED. Persons playing the role of supervisor usually use good manners when they begin this problem but soon become frustrated when the man can give no acceptable reason for resisting. The supervisor may either attempt to convince the man that he should follow accepted practice, or he may explore to determine why the man is so reluctant. When the first approach is used things usually move from bad to worse. Some persons recognize this condition and change their approach; others move to the threat of discharge. In the actual case the workman resigned.

When the supervisor is permissive and explores the man's attitude, some form of agreement is usually found. However, this degree of permissiveness is seldom found even among sophisticated supervisors.

ANALYZING THE INTERVIEW. The same type of analysis applied to the case of the safety belt may be used here. However, emphasis should be placed on the part that face saving plays in situations of this sort. The person who played the role of the supervisor might be asked to give his view of why the man didn't want to work. The extent to which he is correct serves as an index of his skill. After the reasons for resistance have been revealed the general issue of whether a supervisor is supposed to have known why the man resisted may be raised. Here the person who played the role of Brown may make some contributions. He can point to remarks which indicated that there was something on the man's mind that wasn't obvious, explain what misled him in his viewpoint, and describe how meanings have changed when he learned the reasons for the man's reluctance.

In developing the best approach to the problem the following should be considered:

1. The importance of asking a man in private to do a job.

2. Reacting to feelings, such as the feeling that the work is degrading.

3. Recognizing that a company practice of seniority privileges may not be popular.

4. Delving deeper into the situation when the expressed feelings seem inadequate for accounting for behavior.

5. Exploring the possibility that if the man had the opportunity to tell his side of the story he might be more ready to do the job.

6. Exploring whether or not the problem was a group, rather than an individual, problem. The fact that the man had to save face with

his group indicates that the group was partly involved. Should the rest of the crew help work out the problem?

Regardless of the agreement reached, insights will be gained from such analyses, and the meaning of insubordination will thereby be changed. It might be found desirable to discuss the group's attitude toward persons having pride of the sort exhibited by the workman. Do group members feel that such a trait is desirable? How much of the problem was created by the fact that the foreman as well as the workman was influenced by pride? What can be done in such cases to help persons save face? Can face-saving situations be prevented?

AN ALTERNATE METHOD OF ROLE PLAYING THE STORM-WINDOW CASE

Facts in a case may also be presented in the form of a play. Thus a case may be dramatized and a new ending may be played. The following skit * is a dramatization of the storm-window case. The parts of the play may be assigned to members of the training group, each receiving a copy of the script. It is desirable to furnish a few props and seat the participants around a table to make the situation realistic. The discussion leader may then read the description of the situation, after which he gives the cue for Jack to open the skit.

The skit should be played to the end so that the undesirable consequences of the interview are clarified. After the dramatization the discussion leader asks for comments and puts the question of whether the supervisor could have handled the problem in a better way. Usually the response is "yes." After a little further discussion he may have the person who played the role of Brown try an approach different from the one in the script. Thus the events that transpired before Brown's entrance would be accepted as the background, and Brown would enter without the script and supply his own lines. Whether he excused Dave, Bill and Steve, asked them to remain, or called them back later should be left to his discretion, and his action in this matter supplies a good topic for later discussion.

In replaying the role of Brown the conferee has a distinct advantage in that he knows the nature of Jack's difficulty and can be on guard. This procedure thus makes the case a relatively easy one and is desirable if the group's degree of skill in human relations is limited.

When conferees are skilled a person who has not witnessed the first part of the play should take the part of Brown, or the case may be

* By Howard F. Shout.

handled as in the previous section. If the skit is used the type of analysis described in the previous section may be used.

Situation (read by discussion leader): Although Jack has been on his job nearly six years, he has the least seniority of anyone in his group. Many of the unpleasant jobs around the place fall to him because he is the newest man. One of these is washing and putting up the storm windows each year. Jack has made no complaint about it.

However, after lunch one day, when he is sitting around with other members of the group, the conversation turns to the storm-window job.

JACK: Boy, that hot coffee really tastes good.

STEVE: Yeah, it's getting chilly outside. Almost had a real frost last night.

DAVE: Yeah! Time to finish my fall plowing in the south forty.

BILL (*reading from paper*): Here's a special on storm windows that looks good. It's time to start thinking of them. By the way, Jack, seems to me we ought to be getting them put up here, too, shouldn't we?

STEVE: Sure, Jack, get out the glass wax and shine 'em up.

JACK: Aw, quiet—you guys are always riding somebody.

DAVE: What's the matter? Don't you like the job?

BILL: Takes all your brains to do it, don't it, Jack?

STEVE: That's a real stiff job! You have to figure which one to wash first and which end is up.

JACK: Why don't you dry up?

DAVE: What's the matter, Jack? Don't you like the job?

BILL: Aw, it can't be that! He's been doing it for years. He must like it.

JACK: You know well enough I don't like it.

STEVE: Well, you keep doing it, don't you?

JACK: I'm going to get out of it, though.

DAVE: This I must see!

BILL: What are you gonna do—jump the seniority list?

JACK: I don't know, but I think it's time somebody else did it.

STEVE: Not me!

DAVE: You don't hook me on it, either. I had my turn.

JACK: For how long? One time—that's all you ever did it.

BILL: And that was enough, too, wasn't it, Dave?

STEVE: What's the matter, Jack? Can't you take it?

JACK: Sure I can take it. I have for five years.

DAVE: Looks like you're gonna make it six years, too.

JACK: Not me—I'm through doing all the dirty work around here.

BILL: What do you mean—dirty? You get your hands clean, don't you?

STEVE: Who do you think's gonna put 'em up—Brownie himself?

JACK: I don't care who does it, but not me any more.

DAVE: Aw, you talk big, but you can't make it stick.

BILL: Yeah, Jackie, you're just asking for trouble.

❖   ❖   ❖   ❖   ❖   ❖   ❖

Mr. Brown, supervisor, enters.

BROWN: Hello, fellows. (*Greetings from the group.*) Say, Jack, could I see you for a minute? I don't want to break up the lunch session. (*Looks at some papers in his hand.*)

DAVE: Oh, no—it's time we were getting back on the job anyway.

JACK: Yes, sure, Mr. Brown. (*Picks up paper bag and waxed paper and throws it in basket.*) Anything wrong?

BROWN: No, Jack, not at all. I just wanted to remind you about the storm windows. (*Laugh from group at the table.*)

JACK: What about 'em?

BROWN: It's starting to turn cold, Jack. I think we ought to get 'em up. Don't you think so?

DAVE: This is where we came in, fellows. Let's go. (*All but Jack leave.*)

JACK: Yeah, I guess *somebody* ought to put 'em up.

BROWN: Will you take care of that, Jack—anytime this week you can manage it.

JACK: I wanted to talk to you about that, Mr. Brown. I'd rather not do it this year.

BROWN: Do what—put up the storm windows?

JACK: Yes, Mr. Brown, I'd rather not do it.

BROWN: Well, Jack, it won't take you any time at all. I'll get you some help to get 'em out when you're ready.

JACK: It isn't that—I just don't want to do it again. I've had it for five years. It's not fair!

BROWN: Well, now, I know how you feel, Jack. I know it's a chore, but somebody has had to do it.

JACK: If you don't mind—count me out this time.

BROWN: But I do mind, Jack. We've got to do what's part of our job. And you're the newest man here. Be a good fellow.

JACK: I've been the goat around here for five years. Let somebody else do it for a change.

BROWN: Now, Jack, the others had their turn.

JACK: For how long? Dave did it once, and so did Bill. I don't think Steve ever had to put 'em up. Why pick on me?

BROWN: Nobody's picking on you. We just have to do our jobs, that's all.

JACK: Well, it's not part of my job—it's not in my job description.

BROWN: It *is* part of your job, and I think we have a right to expect you to do it.

JACK: Count me out.

BROWN: Now be yourself, Jack. I don't want to be unreasonable about this thing, but after all——

JACK: Well, I think I've done my share.

BROWN: We can try to work something out on this next year, but suppose you take care of it this time.

JACK: No, Mr. Brown, I just don't feel I ought to do it.
BROWN: Jack, I think I'll have to say you've got to do it.
JACK: I'm sorry, but I'm not going to do it this time.
BROWN: It's an order!
JACK: Not to me, it's not.
BROWN: You'll take an order, Jack, or get out.
JACK: You're not firing me. I quit, and you can give your dirty job to some of those other guys. I'm through.

THE STUBBORN EMPLOYEE (FEAR)

On the surface this case is similar to the storm-window problem, but the reason for the apparent job resistance is very different. Either case may be used alone, but it is also interesting to use them in succession, since a person might attempt to apply what he learned in the previous case to the present one. It is important that such generalizations are not made. Each case has its unique features, and an interviewer must be trained not to reach conclusions based on initial similarities. The present case requires even more permissiveness on the part of the supervisor than the former one because the man gives poor excuses for not being willing to accept an assignment. Thus the man appears unreasonably stubborn. The two roles for this problem are as follows:

Role for Henry Spring, supervisor of house service crew: You are in charge of a crew of men who do house service work which includes some highly developed skills such as cabinet work and indoor painting. In your crew of 12 men you have a new man, Bill Edwards, who has been with the company for 9 months. Bill is a family man with 2 small children. He is a responsible parent and seems happily married. You have been quite pleased with him because he is very handy and has considerable proficiency in cabinet work and refinishing furniture. He also seems to get along fairly well with the other men, but you feel he sometimes tries to get others to do his work. The other members of the crew have been with you for 4 years or more, and you think you have good morale in your crew. You have always tried to be fair.

It has always been your practice and that of the company to give certain recognitions for seniority. The men with the greater seniority are given the first chance for overtime work if they want it. Furthermore, undesirable jobs, which usually are simple and routine, are given to the men with least seniority.

One of the routine jobs is that of washing and putting up storm windows in a small building. There are 24 windows, 12 on the first floor and 12 on the second. This work has always been done by the man with least seniority. Joe Drake did it for 4 years. You are about to ask Bill Edwards to do the job.

Role for Bill Edwards of the house service crew: You are a member of a crew of 12 men in a house service unit. You do repair jobs in the building, including carpentry, cabinet work, furniture refinishing, and painting. You have been with the company for 9 months. You are a good repairman and like carpentry and painting, but could not go into either of these trades because you are afraid of high places. You figure that in house service work you can avoid high places and still do the type of work you like best. So far you have not had to do work that involved your fear. On one occasion you had a job that required the use of a stepladder. This made you nervous but not panicky, so you were able to cover up.

You are ashamed of this fear and have never mentioned it to your associates. It has been very inconvenient and has greatly interfered with your selection of a vocation. At last, you feel, you have found a job that permits you to use your skills without exposing your fears.

You are happily married and have two children, a boy of two and a girl of four.

You are anxious to get ahead in the company, and so far you feel that the boss approves of your work. You have managed to hide your fear of high places from him, and you hope he never finds out because you fear it might endanger your chances of getting ahead. Abnormal fears aren't things that people understand, and you might be considered a neurotic.

DIFFERENT APPROACHES THAT MIGHT BE TAKEN. The supervisor who approaches this case in an authoritative manner is likely to meet with a straightforward refusal to do the job. If he is less insistent and seeks to know why the man is so dead set against doing the job he is likely to obtain excuses that do not hold up. If he tries selling the man on the idea of cooperating, with everyone doing his share, he is likely to find the man highly cooperative and yet surprisingly stubborn when he approaches suggesting action. On one occasion the foreman assumed he had solved the problem because the man was so agreeable. When the leader requested that he ask the man whether he would do the storm-window job, the foreman was amazed to hear the man say "no."

The case is particularly interesting because no amount of consideration or coaxing causes the man to deviate from his position, and yet the foreman can find no indication of uncooperativeness in other respects.

ANALYSIS OF THE CASE. When the true facts are revealed in the case, the man's behavior makes good sense, and practically no one in a group feels that the man should be expected to do the job. It is also generally agreed that a miscarriage of justice would result if the true facts were not revealed. This leads to a discussion of how the supervisor should have detected that there was something specific about the job that caused the resistance. Evidences from the roles can then be listed. Obviously the degrading features of the job are eliminated because the man showed willingness to do other routine jobs.

If a specific and personal objection is detected one must explore the conditions under which the man would have given his true reason. This usually stimulates suggestions of a permissive nature. The man must be made to feel that a phobia (abnormal fear) is something the foreman will understand, and that the man will lose nothing by revealing it.

Some questions might be raised which have to do with clarifying the condition to the other men. This is a group problem, and this problem might be set up and role played.

PROMOTION INTERVIEW

Before announcing a promotion it is a common practice in industry to interview all the men who were considered or who might have expected themselves to be considered for a job. It is hoped that these interviews will create a better understanding of company practices and policies. Usually management personnel assume that those interviewed have a personal interest in the job, so that such interviews are approached with a specific mental set. At the same time it is known that some promotions are accepted by others without difficulty, whereas other promotions create morale problems. Furthermore, the degree of acceptance or nonacceptance cannot be entirely explained in terms of differences in the way management and employees view the importance of seniority. Sometimes there is trouble when seniority privileges are violated, and sometimes there is trouble when seniority is followed. Satisfaction with promotions seems to have something to do with the personalities involved, and this makes it difficult to formulate an effective policy on the subject. One approach is to attempt to learn beforehand the type of reactions that different promotions might produce, and thereby prevent major dissatisfactions. Another approach is to reduce the degree of dissatisfaction by effective interviewing. The latter approach is tested in the following case.

The interesting angle on this interview is that the supervisor thinks he knows what the workman's viewpoint will be. As a consequence he is likely to forget to explore it. Thus he goes into the interview prepared to meet an objection that does not exist, instead of being prepared to discover the real objection, which, if recognized, could be overcome.

This case makes particular use of the value of permissiveness and the encouragement of expressions of hostility. It is therefore a good case to illustrate frustration or counseling principles. However, the case also has a general value in demonstrating how human relations determine the nature of conflicts.

Each of the following two roles might be given to two persons. If this is done the case can be role played a second time if the first fails to get to the root of the problem. It is perhaps best to have the observers know both roles so that they can better detect the leads that the supervisor overlooks.

The situation and viewpoint of Mr. Smith, the supervisor: You have been asked to recommend one of your men for a foreman's position which has just opened up in another part of the plant. It has been requested that you recommend a man who not only will qualify but who has the ability to go higher in the organization. It is the company's policy to hire and promote a certain percentage of men who have abilities beyond the requirements of the job on which they are placed. Since it is the company's policy to promote from within the ranks, some men have to be promoted more rapidly than others in order to have high-quality men at the top.

You are a college graduate, have been with the company five years, and have been a foreman for two years. You take your responsibilities seriously and have carefully deliberated the promotion recommendation. You have had to choose one of three men that you considered eligible. The names and qualifications of these men are as follows:

Mr. Dick Attwood, a college graduate with three years' service in the company. Attwood is bright, has a pleasing personality, seems conscientious, and has been highly cooperative. You know Dick very well and have spent a good deal of time with him. He makes a good appearance and is at ease in a group. However, he doesn't seem to have much in common with his associates on the job.

Mr. Jim Bowls, a high school graduate with 6 years' service. Bowls is also a very satisfactory employee, with a good personality. He is very popular with the men and seems to have their respect. He has a lot of natural intelligence and inventive ability.

Mr. George Cole, a high school graduate with 12 years of service. Cole is an excellent workman. He is used for training new men, and actually trained both Attwood and Bowls when they started with the company. He also successfully takes over your duties when you are absent. The men seem to like Cole and have confidence in him. Although Cole is highly competent, he isn't too easy to handle. He is sure of himself and sometimes argues about the way a job should be done. He lacks a certain polish and makes mistakes in grammar. He is by no means a problem employee, but, on occasion, he speaks his mind.

After careful consideration you have decided that Attwood is the man for the job. You were influenced by the fact that you were asked to choose a man with added potentialities. All three men would be good foremen, but Attwood could go farther, you believe. Certainly Attwood is a college graduate, and that means something. The fact that Attwood is a graduate of Cornell, your alma mater, did not influence you in your choice.

You recognized that Bowls had leadership ability, but not to the degree that Attwood possessed it. The strong point in favor of Cole was his seniority, and there were no real weaknesses to point to. His personality was not bad enough to be used against him, but he did have a way of putting things bluntly.

You, therefore, have recommended Attwood. Your recommendation has been accepted, but the promotion has not been officially announced. Further, you have told Attwood about it confidentially. Before the promotion is announced you feel you must interview Cole. Next you will interview Bowls.

You have arranged an interview with Cole. Your goal is to get Cole to accept your recommendation. You do not want to create bad feeling in Cole because you must still work with him, and Cole is your best man. Cole is about to enter your office, and you are ready for him.

Point of view of Mr. George Cole, the senior workman: You have heard through the grapevine that a new job is opening up in another part of the plant. You feel that you have a chance at it, but aren't too confident, since you have been passed up a few times. Nevertheless you have, on occasion, taken Smith's place and run the job in his absence, and so you have some reason to believe that you may be considered. However, you do not feel too qualified. You are happy in what you are doing and actually like doing better than directing. You take pride in your skill. If a position for supervisory work is opening up, you feel that the best qualified man is Jim Bowls. In your book Bowls has everything to get ahead in the company. You fear that Bowls may not get the job because you strongly feel that college men are favored, and in addition Bowls lacks seniority.

As for Dick Attwood, you feel that he is an apple polisher and worse. He hangs around the boss, and you believe that he talks about ideas he got from you when he was being trained. Since Attwood is in good with the boss he has spent less time with the men, and you feel that Attwood no longer is as friendly as formerly. You feel that Attwood has changed since he got in good with the boss. Maybe it's natural, since they both went to Cornell. Maybe that's the way to get ahead. You feel that promotions have not been fair and believe that knowing the right people is a factor. But, above all, you don't like apple polishers. Also, you believe that Attwood is unpopular in the group, whereas Bowls is popular.

This is the way it adds up: Your 12 years of service give you the edge on seniority. Bowls, with 6 years' service, has the edge over Attwood, who has 3. However, Attwood has a college degree. Will they promote him just for that? He's bright enough, but Bowls has brains, too, and lots of personality. He would do a good job as a foreman and is more comfortable with big shots than you are. The other men in the crew are out of the running. You trained most of them, including Bowls and Attwood, so you have a good idea of the ability in the crew.

You are about to go to Smith's office for the scheduled interview. You suspect it's about the job. You fear that you may not like the results, but are determined not to get into trouble over it. You consider Smith one of the best foremen you have had, but feel he isn't too experienced in the company. You don't want to get in wrong with Smith, but nevertheless you do have principles.

APPROACHES THAT MIGHT BE TAKEN. The approach most likely to lead to hard feelings is one in which the supervisor presents his decision and tells Cole about his weakness. This approach puts Cole on the defensive and makes him hostile. Perhaps the most common approach is for the supervisor to give a long talk presenting his problem and justifying his decision. Thus the supervisor attempts to sell his viewpoint and forgets to learn how Cole feels. This type of talk is beside the point and hence falls on unreceptive ears. In other instances the supervisor fails to state clearly the purpose of the interview and keeps Cole in the dark. This approach increases Cole's anxiety or causes Cole to interview the supervisor. In a few instances the supervisor presents his problem as if he had not yet made his decision. Then when he asks Cole's advice he finds that Cole holds out for Bowls. Usually Smith has prepared himself for a comparison between Attwood and Cole and feels he can make a good case, but he has not prepared himself for the comparison between Bowls and Attwood. Cole's reluctance to argue for himself leaves Smith at a disadvantage.

Whether Cole will get to the point of talking for Bowls and whether he will be frank about Attwood largely depends on Smith's willingness to listen. Usually he is more willing to let Cole make a case for Bowls than to let him make a case against Attwood. Thus, to get the real point—that Cole is against Attwood—requires the most listening skill.

In most instances the results of the interview are not too satisfactory. Some interviews become heated and others remain superficially friendly, but one or both lose in the estimation of the other.

ANALYSIS. An initial question to ask of the observers is whether Cole went up or down in Smith's estimation. Cole's feeling on the matter might then be requested. Finally Smith expresses his opinion of Cole. By comparing Smith's answer with the observers' opinions one obtains a measure of the sensitivity of the group members to Smith's feelings. The same can be done with Cole's estimation of Smith. If it is found that each has lost in the estimation of the other it becomes apparent that the interview was of questionable value. Usually the group opinion of the feelings of the participants is very accurate.

Individuals in the group may express the opinion that Smith should have sought Cole's opinion before making his decision. Although this procedure may have been desirable and is worthy of discussion, it should not detract from the discussion of the case. Regardless of what Smith should have done, the question of whether the problem, as presented, can be solved is of interest.

The group should also evaluate Smith's skill in listening by determining who talked the most, what remained unsaid, and the extent to which Smith can describe why Cole objected to the decision to promote Attwood. (It should be remembered that Cole's loyalty to Bowls is not so strong a factor as his opposition to Attwood's apple polishing.)

The group might also be interested in determining the good and bad parts of Smith's approach. It is preferable that the person who played the part of Smith be allowed to make criticisms first and to suggest improvements.

In deciding upon the best approach the group should be asked to explore ways in which Smith could have complimented Cole. The fact that Cole was considered for the promotion shows that he is highly rated and worthy of consideration for future promotions. The fact that Cole trained both men and is able to run the job in Smith's absence gives Smith reasons for requesting Cole's opinion and demonstrating his confidence. These acts and a request for Cole's opinion are positive recognitions of Cole's value. They differ from the negative approach of telling a man what is wrong with him. (The use of positive vs. negative approaches ties in with the principles of motivation, and reference to them can be made in this connection.)

How can Smith reconcile his sincerity in these matters with his reaching a decision before talking to Cole? At this point Smith must be somewhat apologetic, and it follows that if he has a good interview with Cole he probably will consult him beforehand in the future. As reasons for not seeking Cole's opinion beforehand, he can indicate the fact that Cole was involved or that his decision was made at a conference, and that he now wants to check up on his decision. He may also admit that he now feels that he should have sought Cole's opinion before reaching a decision, particularly since he finds Cole so helpful. If Cole questions Smith's motives (favoring friends) his best position is to accept the criticisms and express regret that Cole feels that way. If Smith defends himself he is likely to find himself in an argument.

These points usually can be brought out of a group by exploring alternatives. "What would happen if Smith accepted criticism?" "What would happen if Smith defended his action?" A group usually agrees that a man does not lose prestige by admitting that his opinion or judgment may have been wrong. Such an act is hard to perform, and yet it is generally admired. Practice in role playing helps one do it. It is also possible for Smith to want Cole's opinion for future use, for follow-up purposes, and to reassure Cole that he hasn't been forgotten. Any or all of these points can become his main reason for talking to Cole. Each of these items is good interview procedure because they touch on points of common interest. Both men are concerned with the fairness of future promotions.

If Cole speaks well of Bowls, should Smith accept this information as valuable, or should he become defensive and protect his decision? Observers usually agree that the former course is the better. What should Smith do when Attwood is criticized? He can encourage criticism or he can argue. The values to be gained by listening to criticism are: (a) a better knowledge of Attwood; (b) a realization that men on the job see things that management may miss; and (c) emotional relief for Cole.

Once Cole has had the opportunity to express his hostility he will feel better about Attwood. As a matter of fact he is likely to follow his criticism with statements about some of Attwood's good points. Thus after expressing hostility his view of Attwood comes closer to that of Smith. With this opportunity blocked, his view gets farther away from that of Smith's.

The relief gained through hostile expression is a principle in frustration study, and the importance of listening understandingly is part of the training given under counseling. Groups that have been exposed to frustration and counseling principles should recognize their value in this case and should be able to bring them out in the analysis.

NEW-TRUCK PROBLEM

This case serves as an excellent demonstration of the effectiveness of the group-decision method. Whenever a foreman has a new truck (or any new piece of equipment) to pass out to one of his men the problem of fairness is created and, whichever way he decides, some members of the crew are likely to feel dissatisfied. In other words, perhaps no decision that the foreman himself can make will be regarded by the men as a good one. Foremen, therefore, will welcome the opportunity to put the problem of distributing a new truck to the crew for solution. Since the foreman is likely to have no strong feeling concerning who should get the new truck, he can be permissive and, therefore, is likely to do a good job. Thus this case serves as a good introduction to practice in group-decision methods such as is required in the remaining cases in this chapter.

Instructions for Walt Marshall, foreman of repair crew (to be studied by the foreman in private): You are the foreman of a crew of repairmen, each of whom drives a small service truck to and from his various jobs. Every so often you get a new truck to exchange for an old one, and you have the problem of deciding to which of your men you should give the new truck. Often there are hard feelings because each man seems to feel he is entitled to the new truck, so that you have a tough time being fair. As a matter of fact, it usually turns out that, whatever you decide, most of the men consider it to be wrong. You now have to face the issue again because a new truck has just been allocated to you for distribution. The new truck is a Chevrolet.

Here are some brief facts about the situation:

George, 17 years with the company, has a 2-year-old Ford truck.
Bill, 11 years with the company, has a 5-year-old Dodge truck.
John, 10 years with the company, has a 4-year-old Ford truck.
Charlie, 5 years with the company, has a 3-year-old Ford truck.
Hank, 3 years with the company, has a 5-year-old Chevrolet truck.

All the men do city driving, making fairly short trips, except John and Charlie, who cover the suburbs.

In order to handle this problem you have decided to put the decision up to the men themselves. You will tell them about the new truck and will put the problem in terms of what would be the fairest way to distribute the truck. Don't take a position yourself because you want to do what the men think is most fair.

General instructions for crew (to be read to the crew and observers after foreman has left the room): You are repairmen for a large company and drive to various locations in the city to do repair work. Each of you drives a small truck, and you take pride in keeping it looking good. You have a possessive feeling about your trucks and like to keep them in good running order. Naturally, you like to have new trucks, too, because a new truck gives you a feeling of pride.

Here are some facts about the trucks and the men in the crew that report to Walt Marshall, the supervisor of repairs:

George, 17 years with the company, has a 2-year-old Ford   truck.
Bill,   11 years with the company, has a 5-year-old Dodge   truck.
John,   10 years with the company, has a 4-year-old Ford   truck.
Charlie, 5 years with the company, has a 3-year-old Ford   truck.
Hank,   3 years with the company, has a 5-year-old Chevrolet truck.

(It is desirable to write these facts on an easel or blackboard within view of all role players.)

Most of you do all your driving in the city, but John and Charlie cover the jobs in the suburbs.

In acting your part in role playing, accept the facts as given and assume the attitude supplied in your specific role. From this point on let your feelings develop in accordance with the events that transpire in the role-playing process. When facts or events arise which are not covered by the roles, make up things which are consistent with the way it might be in a real-life situation.

Special instructions for each member of the crew (to be read silently by the particular role player):

GEORGE: When a new Chevrolet truck becomes available, you think you should get it because you have most seniority and don't like your present truck. Your own car is a Chevrolet, and you prefer a Chevrolet truck such as you drove before you got the Ford.

BILL: You feel you deserve a new truck. Your present truck is old, and, since the more senior man has a fairly new truck, you should get the next one. You have taken excellent care of your present Dodge and have kept it looking like new. A man deserves to be rewarded if he treats a company truck like his own.

JOHN: You have to do more driving than most of the other men because you work in the suburbs. You have a fairly old truck and feel you should have a new one because you do so much driving.

CHARLIE: The heater in your present truck is inadequate. Since Hank backed into the door of your truck it has never been repaired to fit right. The door lets in too much cold air, and you attribute your frequent colds to this. You want a warm truck since you have a good deal of driving to do. As long as it has good tires, brakes, and is comfortable you don't care about its make.

HANK: You have the poorest truck in the crew. It is 5 years old, and, before you got it, it had been in a bad wreck. It has never been good, and you've put up with it for 3 years. It's about time you got a good truck to drive, and you feel the next one should be yours. You have a good accident record. The only accident you had was when you sprung the door of Charlie's truck when he opened it as you backed out of the garage. You hope the new truck is a Ford, since you prefer to drive one.

APPROACHES TO THE PROBLEM. The manner in which the foreman puts the problem is not too important in this case. The men will soon disagree, and before long they will realize that each cannot have his way. The men will then begin to make constructive suggestions, as this difference in opinion soon leads to plans involving a general exchange of trucks. Usually the solution most acceptable to the crew is an arrangement by which all or most of the men get a better truck, and hence the obtaining of a single new truck becomes an event that permits all or nearly all the men to profit. At the same time the poorest truck is discarded.

The style of different leaders may vary in the degree to which they enter into the discussion, take sides, or offer suggestions. The best procedure is one in which the foreman indicates that he wants to do what is fair and refrains from taking sides and offering plans. His activity is best if he confines himself to summarizing, protecting individuals if the group becomes abusive toward them, and using questions to move the discussion away from a deadlock and into new aspects of the situation. For example, if the group fails to consider the problem of which truck should be discarded, he may cause this point to be considered by raising the question, "Which truck should we discard?" If the group fails to make progress he may summarize the solution under dispute, write it down, and then ask the group to try out a different approach to see if a more acceptable solution can be found.

ANALYSIS OF THE CASE. Since it is highly probable that a satisfactory solution will be reached, the analysis of the case is relatively simple. The following points may be considered to stimulate discussion.

1. The observers may be asked how they think the crew feels about the solution. Their opinions can be checked against the acceptance of the solution by asking each member of the crew how he feels about the solution. Thus the observer's sensitivity to feelings is explored.

2. The observers may be asked what they think would have happened if the foreman had assigned the truck. This permits an evaluation of the democratic method as compared to the autocratic method.

3. The observers may be asked to evaluate the group solution obtained in comparison with what they would have considered "fair" before the roles were played. This discussion will raise the question of fairness as the group sees it and justice as an outsider sees it.

4. General discussion of details of the case should be permitted so that the group can criticize and evaluate. It is desirable to pursue, in detail, behavior data brought up by members. If someone raises a question of why someone was stubborn or too easily satisfied, see if the group can find specific things that were said which caused the behavior. Exploring for cause and effect in the roles emphasizes the importance of minor details.

5. Before the end of the discussion the group may be asked whether they think the solution was determined by the roles. If this is true it would follow that different groups would come up with the same solution. However, the fact is that solutions vary considerably from group to group.

6. It might also be valuable to spend some time to consider other types of problems which create the same type of issues. There are many decisions in which acceptance of a solution becomes a more important issue than the specific nature of the solution.

GROUP COFFEE PROBLEM

This case raises a common problem and is designed to give practice in democratic leadership and to test a leader's skill in developing a group decision. It permits the development of a conflict between a group's set of values and the supervisor's opinion of fairness. The purpose of planting specific roles in group members is to create diversity and to determine the skill of the leader in drawing out the various attitudes. Whether the leader develops in the group a defensive reaction or a sincere desire to solve a problem depends greatly upon his initial approach and upon whether or not he attempts to impose his solution on the group.

The instructions for the case are as follows:

Instructions for Mr. Henderson, the supervisor: You are a supervisor in a large utility and are in charge of a crew of 12 repairmen who leave the garage and go to work in different sections of the city. Your superior has reported to you that there has been too much time wasted by the men, who stop their trucks at restaurants to get coffee in the morning. It seems that groups of them meet at certain places directly after leaving the garage and have a good morning visit over coffee. This condition seems to apply to all groups who work out of garages, so that your group has not been selected as a bad example. However, your boss points out that it has gone too far and that the abuse must be stopped. The company is very sensitive about public opinion and wonders what people will think if several company trucks are parked in front of a restaurant.

Employees who work in offices are given 15 minutes' relief both morning and afternoon. No such arrangement has been made for drivers and outside workers, but it is common for them to take pauses as their work permits. You know men stop for coffee, and you did it yourself when you were a workman. Some supervisors are strict and say that outside workers do not need rest pauses. Thus the issue of rest pauses has not been clearly defined for men who work outside the office building. This, you believe, is the main difficulty. Your boss told you that he didn't object to a cup of coffee now and then, but he did object to the organized stops and the long visits, with cars parked outside.

You have called in your group and want to go over the problem with them. You feel that if an authorized rest pause was allowed in the middle of the morning, you would be able to improve the situation. It is within your area of freedom to define rest pauses for your group. The production of your crew is slightly but consistently above average.

Instructions for the crew as a whole: You are members of a crew who work for a large utility. You do repair work and leave the garage in the morning and return at night. It is your practice to drive off in groups of 3 to 6 and stop your trucks at favored spots for a cup of coffee on the way to your first morning stop. By having your coffee first thing in the morning you have the company of each other before going to your various job locations. When the load isn't too heavy you may spend as much as a half hour having a nice chat. Although the company has never stated a policy on the matter, you assume it is all right. Office workers get 15-minute relief periods both morning and afternoon, and they can visit in the company restaurants. Your boss has never raised a question of coffee stops, and you are not sure that he knows about them. Some supervisors don't permit the men to stop for coffee, but the men do it anyway. The boss has asked you to wait in the garage this morning to discuss a problem. He has these meetings about twice a month.

Each of the 12 members of the crew is then given an individual slip of paper, which states the way he feels about something. The gist of the instructions given to the group and in the presence of the observers is as follows:

Play the part of the kind of person you think you would be under the circumstances. However, these slips give you an additional feeling or attitude which you can make a part of yourself. Do not express this feeling or attitude unless you feel that the situation, as it develops, would cause you to do so. In real-life situations you do not always say the things you feel. Conduct yourself as you would in a real-life situation. Guard your statements, if this seems desirable, or speak up frankly if you feel like it. Do not confine your remarks to the content of the slips, however. These slips merely supply you with additional background. You should also feel free to change your mind if circumstances seem to warrant it.

Opportunity for questions and a chance to read the individual instructions are then given. Next, the leader divides the participants into 2 or 3 groups, with the instructions "you usually have coffee together in the groups I have indicated."

The planted instructions for the crew are as follows:

1. You find that if you go directly to your job, you frequently cannot go to work because customers are not ready and you have to wait. By arriving a bit later you find people more likely to be up and ready for you.

2. You find coffee makes you feel better and you can be more friendly.

3. You like the coffee at the particular restaurant and do not want to get coffee elsewhere.

4. You find that a visit with the crew keeps up your interest in the job.

5. You stop for coffee because everybody else does.

6. At the restaurant you often meet your friends who work for another utility, and you like to kid with them.

7. You need a cup of coffee in the morning. Your wife is an invalid, and you get the kids off to school in the morning. Then you like to relax with the boys over a cup of coffee.

8. You have stomach ulcers and drink a glass of milk rather than coffee. You carry some milk with you, but if you stop for milk in the morning your thermos bottle supply holds out.

9. Your girl friend works in the restaurant where you stop, and you insist on going to this place a half mile from the garage.

10. You like the group you stop with and join them at these stops.

11. You can work much better, you believe, if you stop for coffee. It starts the day out right.

12. It is your understanding that coffee privileges are company practice. Office workers have them. Why shouldn't you get your coffee when you want it? You prefer having it early, particularly on cold mornings.

DIFFERENT APPROACHES. Some persons in the role of a supervisor point to the abuses of coffee privileges, the loss of production, the effect on public relations, or all of these. When this is done the group becomes defensive and places the supervisor in a position of having to prove the charges. Regardless of whether this is done with or without first complimenting the group, it tends to produce defensive reactions. In self-defense the supervisor may become hostile or resort to passing the blame to his superior. A different approach is to make the statement of the problem so vague that the group places the supervisor in an embarrassing situation by asking, "What is the trouble?" "Has someone done something wrong?" "Who is complaining?" In this manner the supervisor tends to lose control of the situation and finds himself, rather than the group, in a problem situation. In still other instances the supervisor works out beforehand what he considers a liberal solution and then attempts to sell it to the group. The roles assigned definitely prevent such a selling job because the supervisor's solution is likely to be one which permits coffee, but places the time in the middle of the day when getting together in groups is either prevented or results in excess travel time. Thus the group can prove to the supervisor that his suggestion is inferior to the procedure now followed. Since solutions worked out ahead of time usually fail to account fully for the needs that exist in the group, it is important that role-playing experiences discourage this approach.

ANALYSIS OF THE CASE. In the analysis of the case the following points are suggested.

(a) Evaluation of the way the problem was put to the group. The crew's reactions to the supervisor's initial remarks may be evaluated in terms of suspicion, hostility, defensiveness, constructive remarks, etc.

(b) Evaluation of the degree of participation. This should bring out the extent to which each person talked, how many attitudes were revealed, how many of the planted attitudes were expressed, etc. The supervisor might list the attitudes he found to be present, and the participants might then be asked to evaluate his items and to complete the list.

(c) Evaluation of the supervisor's permissiveness. To evaluate the permissiveness of the supervisor the group may itemize the number of ideas or opinions the supervisor rejected or by-passed and list the statements he made which discouraged free expression.

(d) Deciding on whether or not the leader had a solution in mind. In this case the observers may give their reasons for believing that the supervisor did or did not have a preferred solution in mind. This opinion may be checked against the opinion of the participants. If there is disagreement between the observers' and the participants' opinions it indicates that the opinion was influenced by the situational differences of these two groups. Finally, the supervisor may be asked whether or not he had a solution in mind. If he did have one in mind he may discover that he was unable to conceal this fact.

(e) The performance as a whole may be evaluated. This means that the group can decide whether the procedure used was autocratic, democratic, or laissez faire; determine the strong or good features of the procedure; point out the procedures that led to difficulty; and analyze the whole performance in relationship to the steps given on pp. 198–203. This may reveal how a problem individual was handled, whether minority individuals were protected, how participation was encouraged, etc.

(f) The proper approach to use in this problem. Although the democratic type of leadership is suggested by this problem, one may still inquire into certain details. How can the leader put such a problem, loaded with attitudes, so that defensive reactions do not occur? Perhaps the problem is insoluble? If the group feels that the problem has been made too difficult the supervisor can feel satisfied that he did as well as any of the others.

A useful approach, which is usually welcome, is to ask the group, "What would have happened if the leader had asked the group to list the advantages and the disadvantages of time out for coffee. This statement permits the group to list the advantages without making such items defensive or argumentative reactions. In listing the disadvantages one may explore the points that the group might contribute. These points probably would include effect on public opinion and abuses of privileges. Under these conditions the employees are likely to list the very items that represent the company's viewpoint. Finally, the problem becomes one of exploring the problem, "How can we best keep the advantages without creating major disadvantages?" This problem becomes a challenge and stimulates constructive thinking.

VACATION PROBLEM

Since a company is not primarily concerned with the details of a vacation plan so long as coverage is proper, it is customary to allow employees a choice. It also allows the company to show consideration for seniority by giving older employees first choice. Frequently the individuals who have first choice have no strong preferences, whereas others might have. On such occasions employees may make certain exchanges among themselves, and these may be acceptable to the foreman. On other occasions the persons with greater seniority use their choices as ways of gaining prestige, and such prestige is obtained at the expense of others. Thus the vacation arrangements achieved by the method of free choice frequently leads to the formation of cliques.

The present case is set up so that the method of group decision may be used. It is not a difficult problem, and hence is primarily concerned with furnishing an opportunity to practice group decision in solving a problem of vital concern to all members of a group.

Two procedures are given in connection with the supervisor's instructions. It is desirable to role play the problem twice, once with procedure 1 and once with procedure 2. Different participants may be used for each procedure, but if the group is too small some or all of the persons may be used for both procedures.

Instructions for George Smith, supervisor of a group of repairmen: In the past you have made vacation arrangements by giving men with seniority their first choice. For the year under consideration the calendar reads as follows:

			June								July			
S	M	T	W	T	F	S		S	M	T	W	T	F	S
				1	2	3								1
4	5	6	7	8	9	10		2	3	4	5	6	7	8
11	12	13	14	15	16	17		9	10	11	12	13	14	15
18	19	20	21	22	23	24		16	17	18	19	20	21	22
25	26	27	28	29	30			23	24	25	26	27	28	29
								30	31					

			August							September				
S	M	T	W	T	F	S		S	M	T	W	T	F	S
		1	2	3	4	5							1	2
6	7	8	9	10	11	12		3	4	5	6	7	8	9
13	14	15	16	17	18	19		10	11	12	13	14	15	16
20	21	22	23	24	25	26		17	18	19	20	21	22	23
27	28	29	30	31				24	25	26	27	28	29	30

The weeks from June 18 through September 9 represent the vacation period for the company. This allows 12 weeks. Each of your men is allowed two weeks' vacation, and only one of them may be gone at a given time. Thus, the 12-week vacation interval should be adequate for your crew. Both July 4 and September 4 are holidays for the company, but vacations falling during these dates are not given an extra day.

The men in your crew and the length of service of each in the company are as follows:

Henry Duff	12 years
Bill Kelly	9 years
Walt Schultz	7 years
Jim Brady	6 years
Ken Roberts	5 years
Jack Williams	3 years

Procedure 1

Vacation schedules are about due, and so you are going to make the rounds of your men and determine their preferences. You believe that the plan of giving preferences in the order of seniority is the most fair, and it has usually worked out fairly well. Study the calendar and make any other preparations you feel are necessary to get the problem settled. Visit each man separately on the job just as you would if they worked in different places.

Procedure 2

This year you have decided to put the scheduling of vacations up to the crew. You have called them together and plan to ask them to participate. You feel that the objective is to get a schedule that is most satisfactory to all. Bring a calendar with you so that you have dates to work from.

Instructions for crew as a whole: You are members of George Smith's crew and are repairmen. The company gives you two weeks' vacation with pay, and in the past you have been allowed to choose your preferred time from among the open dates. The order in which choices for vacation time have been made in the past followed the seniority pattern, and you have already given the matter of how you will choose some consideration.

The lengths of service for different members of the crew are as follows:

Henry Duff	12 years
Bill Kelly	9 years
Walt Schultz	7 years
Jim Brady	6 years
Ken Roberts	5 years
Jack Williams	3 years

Each of you has been given a separate paper telling you who you are and the kind of vacation plans you have made. Act your part as a member of the crew, keeping in mind that you will cooperate or protect your rights as the situation warrants.

Procedure 1

Each of you is working at a different place. Your foreman will visit you on the job, as he frequently does for a variety of reasons.

Procedure 2

Smith has asked all of you to meet with him this morning. You are in his office waiting for him.

Individual instructions:

HENRY DUFF: You have 12 years in the company. You have always had first choice on vacation plans. This year you plan to take the June 25 through July 8 period because you have plans for a trip of several days over July 4th. You also have plans for the weekend of September 1, but have decided in terms of the July vacation period because you particularly want the July 4th dates. Of course, you wish you could do both but that seems out of the question, and you have to give the rest of the gang a break, too.

BILL KELLY: You have 9 years' service in the company and are second to Henry Duff in seniority. In the past you have had second choice of vacation plans, and you want two consecutive weeks in July. On the old plan you are sure to get your wish. You prefer the last two weeks of July over the first two weeks because if you take the first two weeks you lose July 4th as a day off with pay.

WALT SCHULTZ: You have 7 years with the company and are next to Duff and Kelly in seniority. According to the previous method of handling vacations, you have third choice in vacation plans. You have been invited to spend the week of August 20 at a friend's cottage and hope to have this week fall during your vacation. You are planning to make the last two weeks of August your first choice because Duff and Kelly have indicated that they will not choose this time.

JIM BRADY: You have 6 years with the company and are fourth in seniority. Only Roberts and Williams have less seniority than you. In the past the men with greater seniority have had first chance, and as a consequence you have not been able to get the most desirable vacation times. You would like either to split your vacation and take a week off, at both the beginning and the end of the vacation season, or to have two consecutive weeks falling mostly in July. Since you offer two alternatives, you feel you should get one of your preferences. If the July dates are open you will choose them because there will be less likelihood of a mix-up. If you find that Duff and Kelly have split up July so that a single week is left open you will oppose such an abuse of seniority privileges.

KEN ROBERTS: You have 5 years with the company and are fifth in seniority. Only Jack Williams has less seniority than you. You seldom get your vacation when you want it. It comes either early or late in the season. Once in a while you think it is only fair that you should have time off at the height of the vacation period. You are willing to take any two weeks falling mostly in July. You are going to make a strong case for this with the foreman when the matter of vacations comes up. Your wife often has asked, "How long must a man be in the company before he gets some consideration?"

JACK WILLIAMS: You have been with the company for 3 years and have always had the least seniority. You have accepted this state of affairs because that is the way things are. However, you are very much disturbed this year. Your parents are coming from California on a visit. They will be at a cottage from June 25 to July 9. It is important that you see your parents. You are most anxious to spend at least a week with them at this time. However, the chances that your vacation will come at this time are not very good. As a result you are deeply concerned. This is the first time you really feel you should get your vacation when you want it. You think you should get at least one of your weeks when you want it.

DIFFERING APPROACHES. Under Procedure 1 the foreman may follow the seniority pattern and not concern himself with attempting to make adjustments to take care of special needs, or he may follow the seniority pattern but attempt to obtain concessions from senior men if they conflict with the desires of others. If he follows the first course he tends to please the senior men, but if he follows the second course he may create defensive reactions among the senior men.

Under Procedure 2 some supervisors may show a lack of interest in settling the problem, indicating that it is up to the men to work out an arrangement. In such case the leadership of the group will have to be taken over by one of the men. In other cases the supervisor may actually leave the group and thereby create a laissez-faire situation. The best leaders will, of course, be vitally interested in having the group work out a solution. Leaders will also vary in the way they encourage participation, in their method of recording for the group the ideas presented, and in the extent to which they try to solve the problem for the group. How the leader presents the problem and the company regulations (one man off at a time) also may vary and may determine whether the men spend their energies criticizing regulations or solving a problem.

A common mistake is for the foreman to indicate that he wishes to change things so that seniority no longer will be a factor. This approach divides the group so that argument centers around seniority rights rather than solving the vacation schedule. The best approach is to ask the group to help set up the schedule so that it can be settled with everybody satisfied and save them the problem of altering plans to meet special needs. If seniority is felt to be important the group will give it the recognition that it feels is important. Thus a supervisor can prevent the seniority issue from becoming a problem.

ANALYSIS OF RESULTS. It is best to make the analysis after both procedures have been tried out. Participants in each procedure can indicate their degree of satisfaction with the vacation schedule that is finally set up. The degree of satisfaction will then become an evaluation of the procedures.

The group may then discuss ways in which each supervisor might have improved his approach. The question of whether one procedure has an inherent advantage over the other can then be raised and related to the autocratic and democratic types of leadership. The leader should check the degree of satisfaction felt by the men with each procedure.

If the men in the roles of participants do not enter into the situation in a problem-solving manner the roles should be examined to determine the reason. If disputes arose, questions as to what Smith did to reduce or aggravate the condition should be asked. If the situation became confusing, suggestions should be requested as to how better order could have been kept. If the supervisor did not use a calendar and other ways of keeping records the uses of these aids should be brought out.

The present case can be solved so that all men obtain what they want. One such solution is that Duff would split his vacation and take the week of July 2 and the week of August 27; Kelly would take the weeks of July 9 and 16; Schultz would take the weeks of August 13 and 20; Brady, the weeks of June 18 and September 3; Roberts, the weeks of July 23 and July 30; and Williams, the weeks of June 25 and August 6.

THE PARASOL ASSEMBLY PROBLEM

The instructions and roles for this problem are given in Chapter 10. This problem can be used to give the group experience in solving a technical problem. One should not hope for perfect results, since the problem is a difficult one. However, if the group can work out a solution in which others volunteer to help out the slow workers the importance of using group participation to remove fears and develop cooperation will be illustrated.

RESTAURANT PROBLEM

Many problems involve more than one level of supervision. In these circumstances group discussions can be held at two or more levels. Such problems are usually too involved to present for role-playing purposes because too many details would have to be supplied. However, in real-life situations these details are familiar, so that difficulties of this sort are not involved. In order to give an illustration of group problem solving involving more than one level in industry it has been necessary to develop a rather simple situation that can easily be adapted to role-playing purposes. The following case has been used with considerable success. Since the major purpose of the case is to illustrate the manner in which democratic leadership may overlap different levels, the situation is so structured that it encourages the use of the democratic method. Thus the case serves to develop skill but is not designed to influence basic attitudes.

Instructions for Jim Holiday, second-line supervisor (given in the presence of all participants so that they can become familiar with the facts): The company restaurant in a large bank has been losing $25,000 per year even though the space, electricity, janitor service, and the salary of the manager are not included. The main source of the loss is the cost of meat for the special luncheon, which sells for 50¢ and costs the company 75¢. Since only about 500 of the 1000 employees use the restaurant on any given day, this means that the present restaurant policy benefits only those who use it. On the other hand, if everyone used the restaurant the loss would be greater than the company would like to take. The company would like to know what the employees would consider a reasonable and fair plan to follow, and Holiday has been asked to find out how employees feel about the matter.

The restaurant is open all day. It serves meals from 11:30 to 1:30, and coffee (5¢) and snacks (ice cream at 10¢) at other hours.

Jim Holiday, a second-line supervisor, is about to call his group of first-line supervisors together to work out a plan of how to put the problem of restaurant service to the employees. There are many angles, such as smaller portions, change in price of coffee, increased price of lunch, etc., to consider. How would the employees react to such changes in restaurant policy? What can the first-line supervisors do to get the answer? He, therefore, has called a group of first-line supervisors together to consider an approach that they might make to their employees. The first-line supervisors present are:

Gerald Smith, the supervisor of a group of filing clerks (girls), whose wages range from $130 to $150 per month.

Otto Schulz, the supervisor of a group of machine operators (girls), whose salary range is $150 to $200 per month.

Henry Townsend is the supervisor of male clerks, whose wages range from $240 to $300 per month.

Joe Williams is in charge of a group of men office workers, whose salary range is $375 to $500.

Alfred Banks is in charge of a group of house service men, whose wages range from $175 to $215 per month.

The five supervisors who will meet with Holiday are each given the nature of their work groups, including salary range and the number of employees. The number of employees assigned to each supervisor will depend on the size of the group present in the training class. There should be at least four employees in a group. If the available group is less than twenty it is desirable to reduce the number of work groups to four or three.

The meeting of Holiday and his group is then held, and in a short time they usually agree to put the problem to their employees. These meetings are held next, each supervisor presenting the facts and obtaining employee reactions.

Before each meeting of the separate groups each of the employees should receive instructions which describe the nature of their work group, the wages (falling within the range given above), and the extent to which the individual uses the restaurant.

About one-third of the employees should be told that they buy the special luncheon regularly and go to the restaurant for coffee or a snack daily; another third should be told that they frequently leave the building for meals and occasionally use the company restaurant, but that they regularly go to the restaurant during rest pauses; the last third should be told that they seldom use the restaurant for a regular meal, since they usually carry their lunch, but they always use it for coffee and frequently purchase a dessert.

All should be told to supply their own reasons for using the restaurant to the extent that they do.

In each case the instructions are verbally supplied by the trainer. After he finishes his instructions the supervisors hold their meetings in different parts of the room. When these discussions are completed the second-line supervisor calls his group together again to learn what the various supervisors have found out. Persons who played the role of employees are to observe this discussion and should be encouraged to interrupt and correct any of the supervisors' statements that misrepresent them. Thus each supervisor is placed in a situation in which he must accurately reflect his group's feelings.

From the findings obtained the group of supervisors attempts to work out a solution that may be recommended to the company. The objective is to satisfy the interests of the various groups to the greatest possible degree.

Creating Role-Playing Situations

The preceding cases and examples of analysis are adequate for indicating the use of role playing and for designing other cases. It is desirable that the training class be encouraged to create cases of their own, rather than depend on cases supplied from outside sources. It is frequently felt that the problems supplied by outside sources are not typical, and hence greater acceptance is gained if the group participates. A given group may also have the advantage of creating problems in which the many details of the situation are familiar and yet would be complex to those not in the industry.

If the group wishes to create a problem the individuals who will play the roles may be excused. The rest of the group then agree on the details of the situation. Care should be taken to (1) create a problem for which there are differing viewpoints, (2) create a situation in which these viewpoints are relevant, (3) supply instructions which give each an objective or motive, (4) furnish each with enough factual information so that the facts of the case do not become an issue, (5) make all roles as nearly alike in reasonableness as possible, and (6) make the true reasons for the behavior expressed by one participant be due to reasons that are not obvious to the others.

Problems that members of the group are presently experiencing are a good source of material with which to start. The group can then structure the situation so that specific attitudes and motivations are supplied. Even though the roles constructed may not fully conform to the real individuals in the case, the purpose will have been served.

Experience with creating role-playing situations is good training. It demands that both sides of an issue be explored. It permits participation, and it demonstrates that the problems of the training group are soluble by the application of principles presented in the training. Even if the trainer discovers that the roles created by the group are no different from the cases he may supply, he can rest assured that the time spent in creating roles has not been wasted.

Some initial advantage is gained by using prepared problem situations. In addition to their being more satisfactorily prepared, they permit the participants to save face by finding fault with the case. After the need for skill in human relations is accepted by the group they are more prepared to turn to their own problems.

Roles prepared from company cases familiar to all members of the group are a disadvantage. There is likely to be too much of a problem in limiting the facts that various members feel are relevant, and they will lose sight of the basic issue, which is to resolve a specific conflict.

It should also be made clear to a group that in role playing a company case the group has not come up with a solution which can be put into practice in the company. The solution to any problem assumes that it has been preceded by a specific discussion. A different discussion might resolve the conflict in a new manner. However, such role playing may serve to sensitize a supervisor to the kind of conflicts he might expect and thereby make him more open-minded and better able to meet a comparable real-life situation.

5

Role Playing
in Large Groups

Introduction

The role-playing procedures described in the preceding chapter involve only a limited number of persons, so that the method is primarily adapted to small training groups. Sometimes it is desirable to have large-scale participation, and we have therefore explored the possibility of adapting the role-playing principles to meet this need. We have tested three procedures that can be used with large audiences and have found that they effectively meet this need. In addition these methods introduce two new advantages.

When many groups of persons engage in role playing at the same time, the process is facilitated, since all of them enter into it without the embarrassment that comes from feeling that they are being observed. Thus groups that have never experienced role playing quickly get the spirit of the procedure and go into the process in a natural and interested manner. The feeling that the situation is unreal and artificial, which nonparticipants frequently report, is eliminated because all become involved. Since this method reduces self-consciousness, it is particularly helpful for initiating role-playing techniques in supervisory training.

A second value that emerges is the fact that live data are obtained from the subsequent analysis. A single role-playing case may raise the possibility that a certain individual determined the outcome, and so the result may be atypical. By drawing upon various groups, one is able to make comparisons and generalizations which could not be made without this rich background of varied experiences. The idea that solutions are tailored to fit a particular group of personalities is clearly brought home by the fact that solutions vary even when the problem and the roles are identical.

141

Thus we find that, in the process of attempting to induce into a large group some of the benefits of small group discussion and role playing, we not only succeeded in achieving some of these advantages, but captured some entirely new ones. The benefits that are lost are the values obtained from the analysis of the interaction between specific individuals. A group cannot discuss the details of the role-playing process when they have not observed the same process. It seems that role playing in both large and small groups might be more valuable than the exclusive use of either method.

The Skit-Completion Method

In role playing the completion to a skit, one reduces the amount of role playing required and confines it to the crucial conflict area. The preliminary skit follows a script and is used to supply a background of information and to create a situation, thus making it unnecessary for participants to study roles. In dramatizing the preliminary material one can insure better understanding and also help to establish the mood in which participants are to conduct themselves later. This approach leads to somewhat greater uniformity in the way the roles are approached than does a mere description of a situation. Participants also are aware of the uniformity of the background information to which each is exposed, so that they can enter into the subsequent role playing with a better feeling for what they will encounter.

The author has found the method particularly useful in presenting cases involving face-to-face dealings between persons, although there seems to be no reason why it could not be used to set up group discussion problems. It has the disadvantage of requiring a script and players to act out the preliminary action.

. *General Procedure.* Members of an audience are asked to identify themselves with certain characters in the skit presented on the stage. If there are two characters in the skit half the audience is asked to identify themselves with one of the characters, and the other half with the other character. This division in the audience can be obtained by having each row of persons count from left to right and then giving the *even*-numbered persons a blue set of instructions and the *odd*-numbered persons a yellow set of instructions to read. These instructions consist of a sheet of paper, folded in the middle with the open ends stapled together. Persons are asked to read instructions printed on the outside, but not to remove the staples and read the content on the inside until instructed to do so. The first instructions tell the person from which point of view he should view the skit which is about to be presented. The skit is then dramatized on the stage, and a certain background of information is supplied. The dramatization must be one in which a conflict between individuals is created because of differences in motives and attitudes. Just as the situation reaches a deadlock the skit is terminated.

The audience is then asked to unfold their instruction sheets and read a second instruction, which they will find on the inside. These new instructions request each person to change his identification and to put himself in the position of the character other than the one with which he previously identified himself. When he has read his instructions he should wait for instructions from the floor telling him to turn to his neighbor, who will be the other character of the skit, and to carry on the discussion from where the play left off. All persons are told to try to feel their parts and to see whether they can solve the problem created in the skit.

In order to give the reader an idea of the type of material for which this procedure may be adapted, a sample case and the type of analysis suggested are given below.

THE CASE OF BILL AND TED *

Ted, supervisor in drafting department.
Bill, one of Ted's men.
Miss Wood, a messenger.

The scenes take place in a section of an office of a large company. Two tables piled with folders and papers are located at opposite sides of the stage.

First Scene. Midmorning.

Ted and Bill are seated at desks. Ted looks over toward Bill, who is busy working.

TED (*approaching Bill's desk with a folder of work*): Here's something for you, Bill—I believe you're familiar with it.
BILL: Yep!
TED: How's the work going?
BILL: Swell, Ted. Catching up a little.
TED: Good! By the way, how is your mother feeling these days?
BILL: She's about the same—have someone with her most of the time —I wish I could take her out in that new car of mine.
TED: Would be nice if you could. I believe it would make her feel better. By the way, how do you like your car?
BILL: Just fine—it's got a smooth pick-up.

* Prepared by Howard F. Shout.

TED: I don't suppose you've opened it up yet?

BILL: No, I'd like to break it in carefully. Gee, I wish I had more time to use the darn thing.

TED: We sure could use a little more of your time down here, too, Bill.

BILL: Yes, I know, Ted, but I've got so many other things to do—and I've got share riders, too. But I suppose these things should take their turn.

TED: This emergency work we're doing has built up into quite a job —no let-up to it. The other fellows have been staying down regularly, each taking his turn. They've been swell. But this emergency work is something we've all got to share, don't you agree?

BILL: I suppose. I'll try to do better.

TED: I would like to depend on you at least one evening a week.

BILL: Could you let me know in advance?

TED: We have little or no advance notice on emergency jobs, Bill— and the way it looks now it's not going to slack down either. How about managing to work one evening a week? The other fellows would appreciate it, and so would I.

BILL: O.K., Ted. Count on me from now on.

TED: O.K., Bill. I'll be counting on you next week for sure.

Curtain

Second Scene. One week later.

It is nearly time to close up for the day when Miss Wood enters with emergency work. She goes to Ted's desk.

TED: What have you got there?

MISS WOOD: Some more rush work that Mr. Avery wants done tonight.

TED: Holy smoke! (*Looks toward Bill's desk.*) Bill—some emergency jobs just came in this minute. They'll have to be done tonight. I'd like to have you stay with me and get it done.

BILL: Tonight? Why, I can't do it—why can't I stay some other time?

TED: We had some kind of an agreement about your staying down one night a week. Maybe we'd better have a talk about this. Come on over to my desk.

BILL (*approaching Ted's desk*): My share riders are waiting for me. (*Sits down.*) Some of them are at the car now.

TED: There are many things to share. Sharing extra duty is a responsibility to consider, too.

BILL: But you haven't given me any notice—it's late.

TED: I didn't get any notice either, but we both knew it was coming. Besides, you gave me your promise last week. A promise is a promise, Bill.

BILL: Here is another reason I can't stay. My girl friend has arranged a birthday party for me. She's invited a whole gang to her place. You know how she will feel if I don't come.

TED: I appreciate your problem here, Bill, but isn't it a question of which problem comes first?

BILL: But I can't back down on my promise to be there. They're depending on me to be there.

TED: We recognize your responsibilities to your friends, but you have responsibilities to your job and your work group, too. Maybe some of the other fellows would like some time to themselves.

BILL: And we made special arrangements about the sitter for Mother. You mustn't forget she is ill. I've arranged for Mrs. Dow to. . . . What's the matter, have some of the other fellows been complaining about my not working?

TED: The grapevine has it that the men don't like it because you've been shirking extra duty. I've no complaint about your work, understand, but we've got to take the other fellows into account here.

BILL: I know, Ted, but look at all the things I've planned.

TED: They're depending on us—what do you suggest?

Curtain.   Finish through role playing.

Analysis of the Case.   After less than 10 minutes most pairs of individuals will have reached some kind of a solution. At this point it is desirable to interrupt the role playing and make a general analysis of results.

The first question is to determine how many pairs of individuals arrived at a solution to the conflict. A show of hands will supply this answer and give participants the general idea of the total number who solved the problem.

The next step should explore the number of persons who are satisfied with the solution reached and the number of persons who are dissatisfied. A show of hands in each case will show that most groups reached a satisfactory decision.

At this point the question to be explored is whether any members underwent a change in feelings when they were asked to switch their identification from the supervisor to the employee, or from the employee to the supervisor. A number of individuals will indicate that they experienced a change in feeling tone. One can then point out that merely imagining oneself in one situation and then in the other situation causes the outlook on the problem to change; that what is important and what is unimportant is not just a matter of principle, but also a matter of the side of the problem on which one finds himself. The discussion leader can then ask, "How many of you feel that having experienced both sides of the problem has made you more tolerant and therefore better able to get together?" Many persons raise their hands in response to this question.

The next step in the discussion procedure is to obtain some samples of solutions. The discussion leader can write a brief descriptive comment of each on an easel pad. After each contribution the leader can take a vote on the number of duplicate solutions and then explore for different solutions. Usually five or six solutions are volunteered. It will be found that the usual characteristics of the solutions indicate concessions made by both parties. A show of hands can then be requested to demonstrate how many persons regard their solution as having this characteristic.

Since most solutions obtained will represent concessions made by both parties, time should be taken to explore the exceptions. Have those pairs in which one or the other member refused to make concessions supply details. A few cases of this kind will clearly reveal that, when one person refused to do his part, the other also became stubborn. Thus the general feeling that generous behavior in one person stimulates it in the other is demonstrated.

Many persons wish to raise questions about the case, saying that such a situation should never have arisen. They will argue that the supervisor should have different men on call for different nights. This of course is a good point, and already indicates a value that the case has served. The discussion leader should readily agree that problems should be prevented whenever possible. He can then ask, "Isn't it through our experiences with problems of this sort that we learn how to prevent recurrences?" When the group agrees to this conclusion he can ask, "If the supervisor had disregarded the employee's point of view and had ordered him to work or quit, would he have learned how to prevent a recurrence?" To this question the audience readily agrees that the supervisor would have learned less, and the use of the case will have been justified.

Supervisors at all levels generally agree that even if they try to do all they can to prevent problems they still will make mistakes. This means that, in addition to learning how to prevent problems, they need skills in handling problems they are unable to prevent. The purpose of the case material is to study both preventions and cures.

Multiple Role Playing (MRP) *

Multiple role playing was developed to fulfill the need for giving an audience some realistic experiences with the group-decision method in democratic supervision (see Chapter 2). It is difficult to get a few members to put on a demonstration in front of the audience without

---

* This section, with minor adaptations, appeared as an article by Maier & Zerfoss in *Human Relations* (42).

subjecting them to embarrassment, and the use of training personnel in these demonstrations leads to the feeling that the participants were coached ahead of time. However, if the audience is divided into groups and each group role plays the same group-decision problem, these difficulties are avoided. Thus a particular group is not embarrassed, and at the same time everyone is given a first-hand experience, both with role playing and with group decision.

In order to make the group-decision experience a success in a large mixed group it is necessary to satisfy a number of conditions. These are as follows:

1. The supervisor's role should be so structured that he is likely to follow the spirit of the group-decision method by being permissive and unbiased.

2. Difference in attitudes and interests of employees should be such that a true conflict is created.

3. The problem should be one of general interest and understanding.

To satisfy these conditions it is necessary to both select a problem carefully and to create realistic differences in instructions for the role players.

To develop good leadership in conducting the discussion the problem used for the demonstration should be one for which the supervisor is unlikely to have a ready-made solution. Having no preferred solution himself, he is inclined to act permissively and thus encourage free and frank discussion instead of imposing or selling his own views. To produce a lively discussion the problem used must be one that creates a conflict in attitudes.

Multiple role playing deviates from the usual role-playing procedure in that the same roles are simultaneously played by many groups, each without the guidance of a trainer. This absence of specific guidance during the role-playing process makes standardization more essential and requires the use of clear-cut problems. However, it will be seen that these limitations are not serious.

The new-truck problem described in Chapter 4 seems to satisfy these specifications. In setting up the same case for two procedures it is possible to illustrate the different types of contributions that single and multiple role playing can make to training. The new-truck problem is based on an actual case in industry and raises the type of problem that a crew can solve more satisfactorily than can a supervisor. As such, it readily lends itself to a group decision rather than to an autocratic decision imposed on the crew by the supervisor. The way the problem was resolved in an actual case gave each man a different truck, and all felt they had benefited.

THE NEW-TRUCK PROBLEM

1. The first step in the procedure is for the trainer or the person in charge of the meeting to request the audience to divide itself into groups of 6, with 3 persons in one row turning around to meet with

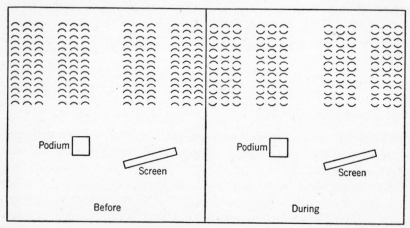

Fig. 13.   Diagram showing audience seating before and during multiple role playing.   When seats are movable, the above seating patterns are readily arranged, each person adjusting his seating in his group to form a huddle.   When seats cannot be moved, it is necessary for the persons in alternate rows to turn about in their seats to form a close-knit group.

3 persons directly behind them.   Assistants can be an aid by helping persons in odd seats to join others in making up these groups.   If the seating rows are arranged in multiples of three the task of organizing the groups is simplified.   In some situations the seats are movable and then it is very easy for the groups of 6 to form a unit.   Figure 13 shows how the seating may appear before and during multiple role playing.

Since the number of persons required in a group is 6, there may be a remainder of from 1 to 5 persons.   Each of these extra persons is asked to join one of the discussion groups and serve as an observer.

2. When the audience has been divided into groups, the trainer announces that each group will receive a set of instructions.   The persons who pass out the material will hand these instructions to one

member of each group. This member will play the part of Walt Marshall, the foreman of a crew of repairmen. The other 5 members of the group will be repairmen who report to Walt Marshall. The foreman is to keep this material until instructed further. In the meantime he may look over the top page, labelled "Walt Marshall, Foreman of Repair Crew." The instructions given to Walt Marshall will be found on p. 124.

3. The trainer then asks the crew members of all groups to give their attention while he reads their instructions. The text of the instructions is given on p. 125 under the title "General Instructions for Crew." After reading the instructions the names of the crew members, their years of service, and the age and make of truck should be written on an easel so as to be visible to all.

4. The foreman is then asked to pass out the material he has been given, which consists of six sets of instructions, his own and one for each member of his crew. He should keep the top set for himself and pass out one set of instructions, beginning on his left, to each of his five crewmen. The sequence of the instructions he distributes should be George, Bill, John, Charlie, and Hank, so that the seating order corresponds to the order of seniority as listed on the easel. (The instructions for the five members of the crew are given on p. 125.)

Members are asked to study their roles until they have a feeling for them. It is perhaps necessary to caution them not to show their roles to each other, but to put them aside when they have finished with them. They can be told that the discussion will be more natural if they refrain from looking at their roles after role playing has begun. The instructions are necessary merely to get started; after that the members of the group should argue things out according to the way they feel.

5. When everyone is ready, the trainer gives the signal for the foremen to stand up. Each foreman should assume that he has called his men together to discuss a problem and that they are waiting in his office. His sitting down infers that he has entered his office, and from this point on he should play his role.

6. About half an hour is adequate for most groups to solve the problem. (If the leader and his assistants observe the groups, they can quite accurately judge when most of them have reached a solution.) Before interrupting the discussion it is desirable to announce from the floor that 3 more minutes will be allowed the groups to settle on some arrangement.

7. At the end of the 3-minute period the members are asked to break off their discussions and join in the analysis of the results.

ANALYZING THE RESULTS. The extent of the analysis need not be confined to the points discussed below, but the analysis should cover the following points:

1. Determination of the number of groups arriving at a solution. (In obtaining this figure only the foremen should vote.)

2. Determination of the number of men who are dissatisfied with the solution. (Only the repairmen of crews that reached a solution should raise their hands.) This figure is important because it indicates the degree of satisfaction obtained from the procedure. The chairman may ask how this degree of acceptance compares with what would have been obtained if the foreman had supplied the solution.

3. Determination of number of crews that discarded Hank's truck. (Only the foremen should raise their hands.) The proportion of the number of times that Hank's truck was discarded becomes a measure of the quality of the solution. The fear that men might fail to discard the poorest truck would constitute one of the reasons why a foreman might hesitate to put such a problem to them. If the proportion of crews discarding the poorest truck is very large it indicates that the danger of not having the poorest truck discarded is more imagined than real.

4. Determination of the number of crews in which the new truck went to various members of the crew. (Only the foremen should vote on the five alternatives.) This analysis brings out the variety of solutions obtained and shows that the same problem with the same roles produces different solutions. Under such circumstances it becomes clear that a company could not work out a policy that would be satisfying to all crews.

This analysis might also be followed by questions such as, "In how many cases did George use his seniority and make a strong demand for the new truck?" "How often did he get it when he was that kind of a George?" "How often did George get the new truck when he did not throw his seniority around?" Such questions frequently reveal that George is more likely to get the new truck when he is a reasonable person and considerate of men with less service than when he is demanding.

5. Determination of the number of crews in which:

(a) All men obtained a different truck.
(b) Four men obtained a different truck.
(c) Three men obtained a different truck.
(d) Two men obtained a different truck.

(e) No exchanges in old trucks were made, and only the man receiving the new truck benefited.

(Only the foreman should vote on these alternatives.) This analysis gives an idea of the extent to which all men were given consideration. If time is taken to analyze these data, it might be found that the foreman's conduct of the meeting determined the number of men who benefited by the addition of a new truck to the crew.

After the analysis of the crews the persons serving as observers should be asked to give their evaluations of the discussion meetings they observed. Their reports may include: (a) the way foremen put the problem, (b) the extent to which he hampered the discussion, (c) the extent to which he imposed his own ideas, and (d) evaluation of things he did to help things along. These reports not only involve the observers in the procedure, but add supplementary material on the different approaches various foremen may have used.

SOME SAMPLE RESULTS. The case has been tested in three audiences. In one of these 17 groups were formed, and in 14 of these all persons were satisfied with the solution they had reached. A total of 5 individuals out of 102 were dissatisfied with the solutions of their groups. In the second group tested, 6 groups were used and 2 persons (in two different groups) out of 42 were dissatisfied. In the third audience 19 out of 21 groups had time to reach a decision, and only one person in each of two groups was dissatisfied. If we combine our groups we find that 42 out of 44 groups reached a decision, and that only 9 out of 220 repairmen (4.1 per cent) were dissatisfied.

In each of three tests of the methods all persons participating readily agreed that nothing approaching the degree of satisfaction shown could have been obtained if supervisors had supplied the solution.

In 41 out of the 42 groups Hank's truck (the poorest one) was eliminated. This result clearly shows that the group decisions were in accordance with the interests of good management. Thus the fear that group decisions might lead to poor-quality decisions was not supported.

The new truck went to George, the senior man, in 20 of the 42 groups. In 16 cases out of 28 times he got it when he did not insist on it because of his seniority, and in 4 cases out of 10 he got it by defending his rank. Thus George gained most when he acted least in his own selfish interests.

A great variety of solutions developed in these groups. The new truck went to each of the individuals in one group or another; the frequency being in the order of George, John, Hank, Bill, and Charlie. In most instances there was a general exchange of trucks. All men got a different truck in 4 groups; 4 men got a different truck in 10 groups; 3 men in 16 groups; 2 in 8 groups; and only 1 got a different truck (the new one) in 4 groups.

From descriptions of the discussion process, there seemed to be a trend in which the general exchange of trucks was greatest when the leader was permissive. The first part of the discussion develops a conflict of interests and, if the leader is permissive at this stage, the idea of exchanging trucks develops. Many men who played the part of the supervisor were surprised at this development because most of them went into the discussion with the idea of getting the new truck assigned to some particular individual and getting the rest of the group to agree on who was most needy. It is this emphasis on the leader's part which prevents the general exchange usually developing out of the free discussion. Thus the idea that all can profit when the crew gets a new truck emerges as a new idea and a group product.

FURTHER USES OF MULTIPLE ROLE PLAYING. The MRP method can be used for all types of role playing, so effective for attitude change and the development of skills. However, one must structure the roles so as to conform to the purpose of the training and the experience of the participants. Thus if one wishes to emphasize (*a*) leadership skills in putting a problem to a group, (*b*) discussion-leading skills, (*c*) sensitivity to the feelings of others, (*d*) ways for dealing with hostile persons, (*e*) skills to upgrade the quality of decisions, and (*f*) methods to cause a group to feel responsible for reaching decisions acceptable to all, one must design role-playing situations that will highlight these performance areas.

MRP also can be used as a tool to evaluate various kinds of leadership approaches, as well as the effect of different kinds of participants on the outcome of a discussion. For example, the leaders of half the groups may receive instructions that differ from those supplied to the other half. These differences may be as follows:

(*a*) Encouraging disagreement in your group *vs.* discouraging disagreement in your group.

(*b*) Suggesting possible solutions to your group *vs.* being careful not to suggest any solutions yourself.

(*c*) Trying to sell a particular solution that seems fair to you *vs.* being careful not to show any preference for any solution suggested.

(d) Having your group explore a variety of solutions before jelling on any one idea vs. hurrying the group along so that leisurely exploration of many ideas is discouraged.

The effect of different kinds of participants can be tested by making the roles slightly different for two sets of groups. For example, (a) George can be asked to insist on getting the truck in one set, and asked to help out Hank's case in the other; (b) one set of groups might be so instructed that they form two cliques, whereas the other set of groups are not so instructed; and (c) one set of groups may have one member who is asked to play the part of a conciliatory individual, whereas in the other set of groups the same individual may be requested to play the part of a belligerent person.

By comparing the outcomes of two sets of groups with similarly instructed leaders and the differences obtained with differently instructed leaders working with similarly instructed groups, one can demonstrate the importance of the injected differences.

The use of the observer can also be expanded by having one or two such persons in each group. (The purpose of two observers is to see to what extent different persons vary in what they see in the same situation. With experience these differences rapidly decline.)

The observers' reports are of particular value in pointing up the effect of each person's remarks on the behavior of others. Their comments would tend to sensitize participants to important details in the discussion process, and the reports of skilled observers would become a valuable training aid to participants. The use of observers would be of special value in the training of individuals who meet repeatedly in conferences.

CHANGING WORK PROCEDURE: A MORE COMPLEX CASE FOR MRP

It is desirable to give a group that is already familiar with group-decision methods an opportunity to see it work on a more difficult problem. The following case is based on a real incident and involves both attitudes and the quality of a decision. This case raises the question of whether the decision of highest quality actually produces the best results. Playing the case tends to lead to the realization that an acceptable decision of lesser quality may be more productive than a decision that is resisted but is of higher quality. The case thus illustrates the value of group discussions in introducing more efficient work methods.

The extent to which workers in the following case will accept a change in work methods depends upon whether the supervisor discovers the source of resistance to change and explores it by letting the men talk. In this case he finds two sources of resistance, the hostility toward the efficiency expert and the need for relief from boredom. The first is overcome by accepting the hostility toward the time-study man and apologizing to the men for not having explained his presence. The supervisor's willingness to listen and not to make any changes that the group does not wish tends to stimulate the men to become problem-minded rather than defensive. Thus the free-discussion method (pp. 56–62) is suited to this phase of the conference.

The problem of boredom can be met if the leader asks the group to consider whether there are ways to overcome boredom other than the method now used. This approach by the supervisor immediately suggests rest pauses and other rotation plans to the men. For overcoming this source of resistance it is apparent that the developmental discussion method (pp. 46–56) is desirable.

Since poor handling will lead to a refusal to change, this case should be used only if many supervisors are already fairly skilled in discussion leadership. When multiple role playing of this case leads to both successes and failures, the results lend themselves to a comparison of the methods used in the successful and unsuccessful cases.

Only four persons per group are needed for this case. The roles supplied to the participants are as follows:

Role for Gus Thompson, foreman: You are the foreman in a shop and supervise the work of about 20 men. Most of the jobs are piece-rate jobs, and some of the men work in teams and are paid on a team piece-rate basis. In one of the teams Jack, Walt, and Steve work together. Each one of them does one of the operations for an hour and then they exchange, so that all men perform each of the operations at different times. The men themselves decided to operate this way, and you have never given the plan any thought.

Lately Jim Clark, the methods man, has been around and studied conditions in your shop. He timed Jack, Walt, and Steve on each of the operations and came up with the following facts:

Time per Operation

	Position 1	Position 2	Position 3	*Total*
Jack	3 min.	4 min.	$4\frac{1}{2}$ min.	$11\frac{1}{2}$ min.
Walt	$3\frac{1}{2}$ min.	$3\frac{1}{2}$ min.	3 min.	10 min.
Steve	5 min.	$3\frac{1}{2}$ min.	$4\frac{1}{2}$ min.	13 min.

$34\frac{1}{2}$ min.

He observed that with the men rotating the average time for all three operations would be ⅓ of the total time, or 11½ minutes per complete unit. If, however, Jack worked in the No. 1 spot, Steve on the No. 2 spot, and Walt in the No. 3 spot, the time would be 9½ minutes, a reduction of over 17 per cent. Such a reduction in time would amount to saving more than 80 minutes. In other words, the lost production would be about the same as that which would occur if the men loafed for 80 minutes in an 8-hour day. If the time were used for productive effort production would be increased more than 20%.

This made pretty good sense to you, and so you have decided to take up the problem with the men. You feel that they should go along with any change in operation that is made.

Role for Jack: You are one of three men on an assembly operation. Walt and Steve are your team mates, and you enjoy working with them. You get paid on a team basis, and you are making wages that are entirely satisfactory. Steve isn't quite as fast as Walt and you, but when you feel he is holding things up too much each of you can help out.

The work is very monotonous. The saving thing about it is that every hour you all change positions. In this way you get to do all three operations. You are best on the No. 1 position, so that when you get in that spot you turn out some extra work and so make the job easier for Steve, who follows you in that position.

You have been on this job for two years and have never run out of work. Apparently your group can make pretty good pay without running yourselves out of a job. Lately, however, the company has had some of its experts hanging around. It looks like the company is trying to work out some speed-up methods. If they make these jobs any simpler you won't be able to stand the monotony. Gus Thompson, your foreman, is a decent guy and has never criticized your team's work.

Role for Walt: You work with Jack and Steve on a job that requires three separate operations. Each of you works on each of the three operations by rotating positions once every hour. This makes the work more interesting, and you can always help out the other fellow by running the job ahead in case one of you doesn't feel so good. It's all right to help out because you get paid on a team piece-rate basis. You could actually earn more if Steve were a faster worker, but he is a swell guy and you would rather have him in the group than someone else who might do a little bit more.

You find all three positions about equally desirable. They are all simple and purely routine. The monotony doesn't bother you much because you can talk, daydream, and change your pace. By working slow for a while and then fast you can set your pace to music you hum to yourself. Jack and Steve like the idea of changing jobs, and even though Steve is slow on some positions, the changing around has its good points. You feel you get to a stopping place every time you change positions, and this almost takes the place of a rest pause.

Lately some kind of efficiency expert has been hanging around. He stands some distance away with a stop watch in his hand. The company could get more for its money if it put some of those guys to work. You say to yourself, "I'd like to see one of these guys try and tell me how to do this job. I'd sure give him an earful."

If Gus Thompson, your foreman, doesn't get him out of the shop pretty soon you're going to tell him what you think of his dragging in company spies.

Role for Steve: You work with Jack and Walt on an assembly job and get paid on a team piece-rate basis. The three of you work very well together and make a pretty good wage. Jack and Walt like to make a little more than you think is necessary, but you go along with them and work as hard as you can so as to keep the production up where they want it. They are good fellows; they often help you out if you fall behind, and so you feel it is only fair to try to go along with the pace they set.

The three of you exchange positions every hour. In this way you get to work all positions. You like the No. 2 position the best because it is easier. When you get in the No. 3 position you can't keep up, and then you feel Gus Thompson, the foreman, watching you. Sometimes Walt and Jack slow down when you are on the No. 3 spot, and then the foreman seems satisfied.

Lately the methods man has been hanging around watching the job. You wonder what he is up to. Can't they leave guys alone who are doing all right?

ANALYZING THE RESULTS. It is desirable to have each group report the solution agreed upon and to indicate the difficulties encountered. The different solutions should be summarized on an easel. The extent of analysis should be adapted to the knowledge of the group, but an analysis should include some reference to methods for overcoming resistance. Emotional resistance requires listening, but the resistance due to a desire to avoid boredom can be helped if the leader asks questions, such as, "Are there other ways to avoid boredom besides our present method?" The fact that the men could not be induced to change when the leader talked about increased earnings should also be clarified. It was not a lack of interest in money that caused difficulty, but rather it was the fear that they would lose something.

TYPES OF SOLUTION REACHED. In 44 groups, in which training in group decision had been given previously to supervisors, 59.1 per cent of the groups agreed to try out working on their best positions, only 4.5 per cent refused to change, and 36.3 per cent agreed on a modified method (spend more time on their best position or have Jack and Walt rotate positions 1 and 3, with Steve holding position 2). Other minor modifications also were included in the solutions of some of the groups (rest pauses, helping each other, etc.). In 36 groups with no training in group decision, the foreman tried to sell the men on working on their best position. He succeeded with 50.0 per cent of the groups; the other groups refused to change, and no modified methods were developed. Thus the knowledge of group decision aided in preventing failures. It is quite possible that the most productive solutions will be the modified ones because boredom is given due consideration.

Also, happier results were obtained in groups with leaders having some training in group-decision methods than in groups having leaders who used the customary supervisory approaches.

Audience Role Playing (ARP) *

One of the problems repeatedly faced by management is that of finding effective ways for improving or changing the attitudes of employees. To achieve this end they develop reading racks, show movies, and give lectures or courses. At the present time there is active interest in giving employees economics training so that they will develop more favorable attitudes toward free enterprise. It is felt that if employees were exposed to the same facts as management their attitudes would be more in harmony with those of management.

Since management personnel select the programs that will be given, the question is raised as to whether persons with one attitude can select material that is appropriate for persons with a different attitude. In training programs one can discuss attitudes at length, pointing out how attitudes select the facts that are convincing and how persons with opposed attitudes select different facts or interpret the same ones differently.

Even though experimental evidence is supplied to support the statement that facts have a very limited effect on changing attitudes, we find persons with knowledge of this principle violating it on many occasions. To point out that attitudes are loaded with feelings and that feelings do not follow principles of logic likewise has little effect on behavior. The fact that people often do not practice what they know when they deal with attitudes creates the need for giving members of an audience a *feeling* for the way attitudes are affected by certain kinds of experience.

* This section was previously published by Maier and Solem (41) in *Human Relations*.

Audience role playing was developed to fill this need on a large-scale basis. The first step in the method is to develop an unfavorable attitude in all members of an audience. After this is accomplished the next step is to introduce some other experience, let the group react to the new events, and record the changes in attitudes produced by the added experience. By giving various kinds of new experiences one can discover which of them tend to alter attitudes most effectively.

When persons are asked to imagine themselves in a certain situation and are told of the experiences they have in the circumstances, they can begin to feel some of the emotions that persons who are in such a real-life situation might feel.

The feelings aroused in the role playing thus correspond to those that an actor might feel when he plays a role on the stage. Notice that in asking an individual to be a particular person in a specific situation and to conduct himself accordingly, one is doing more than asking him how he thinks people will behave under certain circumstances. In the former he is being asked to react on an emotional basis, and in the latter, on an intellectual basis. The purpose of all role playing is to reduce the intellectual judgments and introduce some of the feeling judgments.

In instructing members of an audience in their roles one does not rule out the differences in personality already existing. Persons with the same roles behave differently because each personality interacts with the situation supplied. Thus the products resulting from different persons placed in the same situation are unlike. If we now measure behavior or attitudes of members of an audience placed in a given situation we can attribute the differences obtained to the variations in personalities, and the similarities obtained to the common role or situation supplied to all.

In audience role playing, behavior is measured by asking members to fill out a questionnaire. This questionnaire requires persons to record a number of opinions, and thus information is obtained on how different persons feel about the situation in which they are placed.

After opinions have been measured, added experiences are introduced into the role-playing situation. Thus new facts can be supplied, pleasant or unpleasant experiences can be described, or specific changes in the situation can be made. After each new experience or attitude-change technique is introduced the questionnaire is again filled in by the audience, so that any resulting changes in opinion can be measured.

Each member of an audience can obtain a personal experience of how various types of events influence his feelings and attitudes. In addition the group's results can be roughly recorded at the end of the experiment by asking for a show of hands on how many changed their opinion on a particular item after a given experience. Through observing the different effects of various experiences on opinion changes, each person obtains a firsthand impression of how other members of the audience have reacted.

It is quite possible that artificially produced attitudes do not follow the same pattern or have the same rigidity as true attitudes. It is also possible that any difference obtained is merely one of degree. For this reason it is necessary to test the procedure and determine whether or not a true attitude experience is obtained.

ARP has been tested on two audiences to determine the extent to which artificially induced attitudes follow the principles of true attitudes. A presentation of the case used will not only permit a discussion of the results obtained but will also clarify the details of the ARP technique so that the reader may understand the procedure.

CASE OF THE COMPANY WITH POOR EMPLOYEE MORALE

The audience is informed that they will role play being employees of a company. In order to obtain a realistic experience it is suggested that they imagine themselves to be in the situations described and to let their feelings develop as the situations are described. The initial role is as follows:

You are all employees of the Jones Metal Products Corporation. It is common knowledge among all of you that the company is a success and that its yearly earnings are impressive. It gained its good position in the community through the pioneering efforts of Hiram Jones, whose name was respected in the community. Although the company's wages are as good as the community average, the firm should be able to pay more, with the amount of business it does, especially since the community average is low. Management talks a lot about high labor costs to justify its price increases, but you have a hard time buying the groceries you need.

On its payroll the company has a lot of people for whom you have no respect whatsoever. Many of the supervisors, for instance, are behind the times, arrogant, and inefficient. You know of good employees whose talents are not recognized and who are thoroughly dissatisfied. There are all sorts of untapped skills around the place which management says it needs, but which they are either too ignorant or stubborn to see.

Happy Jones (he's the president of the company and took over when his father died 30 years ago) is also president of the Sociable Golf Club and commodore of the Blue Water Yacht Club, and when he isn't golfing or sailing he's making speeches all over town about all the wonderful things the company has done for the community and for its employees. Somehow we employees, who are doing the work, would give a lot to see a few deeds rather than a lot of words.

The rest of the big brass of course try to ape old Jonesy in every way they know. They copy his manner of dress and sit on their over-stuffed laurels up in their top-floor "penthouse" offices and dictate a lot of useless orders that your boss reads like gems of wisdom and spouts at you every time he has to pretend he's made up his mind about something. The only time those birds ever get out on the floor is when they show some big-shot customer around, and then they take him to lunch in the special executive dining room. There is a company-operated cafeteria, by the way, where you can eat without too much expense, provided you aren't concerned about variety or don't care to walk down the street a ways to a better place.

How a lot of the little brass (90-day wonders, they're called) ever got their jobs is one for the books. They shuffle their papers, hang on the telephone, and jump when they're talked to, and you haven't met one yet who knows the difference between a monkey wrench and a screw driver. Judging from what you've seen of them, it must take an awfully long time to learn how to meet a payroll.

Your boss is typical of most. He is doing his best for the company and regards his job as that of policing the situation and seeing to it that nobody gets away with anything.

After the audience has been instructed concerning their feelings toward the company they are told that management is concerned about employee morale and has decided to conduct a survey. At this point the questionnaire is distributed. Each person is asked to fill out the form, but to place their responses under Column 1. For each question there are three alternatives, one of which should be selected for each of the twelve questions. The questionnaire supplied is duplicated on p. 163.

After the questionnaire is completed the first attitude-change technique is introduced. This technique is in the form of a lecture on the company's development and is used to permit a measurement of this type of lecture on unfavorable employee attitudes.

First Attitude-Change Method: You are attending a lecture in the company cafeteria. The general manager is making the following statement:

"The company feels that every employee is entitled to know some of the inner operations of the company for which he works. You as well as management have a stake in this business. The company has gone to considerable expense to prepare a program for you, presenting to you in an interesting manner the history and development of this company. We want you to be proud of the job we have done together to make this company a success in our community."

At this point the general manager introduced the lecturer, who is an officer in the company. The following is a summary of what he said:

The company has grown, since it was first organized 54 years ago, from a small shop employing less than 100 to its present payroll of 15,350 persons. From the start the business showed promise of success; additional shares of stock were sold, and, with this new capital, expansion of productive facilities was made possible. Efficient management, the introduction of labor-saving machinery and equipment, and the development of a strong sales organization have made us the sound, healthy concern we are today.

Over the years company profits have averaged between 5 and 7 per cent. Last year, for example, profit on investment was exactly 6 per cent. Corresponding dividends have been paid regularly to the stockholders.

A series of charts is presented to show that wages paid by the company are equal to the community average for comparable job classifications. You are shown also that, according to the cost-of-living index for this year and past years, your wages have more than kept up with living costs so that, actually, your present standard of living is 17 per cent above the average for the period 1935 to 1939.

As the lecture goes on you gain, from the speaker and from various tables and charts, an over-all view of company finances; what the total revenues were for the past fiscal year; net earnings before and after taxes; the amount of working capital, fixed capital, depreciation, total salaries to management (which were relatively small as compared to the total figure for wage earners), and so on. Figures are also broken down in terms of the number of cents in each dollar of revenue which is made available from the sales of each product, issuance of new shares, investments, and the like, as well as the number of cents out of each dollar expended in each of the various expenditure items, such as wages, taxes, overhead, and so on.

To conclude the lecture you are shown a film strip, which presents a clear picture of how employees are hired and trained, describes the various employee services, and explains the retirement plan. You are told that it is the company policy to do its level best to be fair to employees and stockholders alike.

Certainly this lecture has informed you concerning the facts of the company's growth and its present financial condition. You have no reason whatever to doubt any of the facts as they were presented to you. How you interpret these facts in the light of your own experiences is your affair.

After the presentation of the first attitude-change technique the audience is asked to fill out the questionnaire again, but to use Column 2 this time. In order to make fresh judgments they are asked to fold their papers so that Column 1 is turned under.

When everyone has completed the questionnaire the second attitude-change technique is introduced. It is in the form of a description of a change in the behavior of their supervisors. Note that it gives a rough description of how a democratic supervisor deals with his men, and is presented to the group in the following manner.

Second Attitude-Change Method: Your supervisor is acting differently lately. One day you mentioned this to a couple of your friends, and they said the same things about their bosses. For one thing, the supervisors seem to be more considerate. Your own boss wasn't a bad guy before, but he sure could raise hell about some things. Even when he wasn't sore it was always, "Joe, do this; Joe, do that." Then if things didn't work out right you got chewed. You weren't treated like a man with ideas and feelings of your own; you were just a badge number.

Now it's different. The bosses actually talk things over when they give you an assignment. When everything is going well they try to keep things that way; but, at the same time, when you are doing a good job they leave you alone. When things go wrong they try to find out what caused it so it won't be so likely to happen again. No more of this business of bawling you out for something that has already happened and wasn't your fault anyway.

Another thing: the supervisors don't try to make believe they are the only ones who know anything around here. The other day when this new job was giving you a lot of trouble, and rejects were clogging things up and nobody seemed to know what to do about it, your boss called you all together and asked for your ideas. Well, Joe Miller came up with a suggestion, and the rest of you talked it over and added to it. The new plan is working out fine, and now the boss is bragging about what a smart, cooperative crew he's got.

You all know how the boss used to hit the ceiling when you'd stay out and not call him beforehand. Well, you know Ed, and the trouble he had at home and how he was out a lot. Ed expected at least a 3-day layoff for that. Instead the boss saw that something was wrong and asked him if he'd like to talk about it; maybe it would help. That floored Ed, but he went in anyway and they had a talk. After that Ed seemed to feel a lot better about his job and got things straightened out O.K. at home.

Something else has happened too. When you complained about something before, the boss would ignore you, make promises he didn't keep, or tell you that's the way it was and he couldn't do anything about it. If he was feeling crabby, he'd jump down your throat. He doesn't do that any more. Even employees who are sometimes a little

OPINION QUESTIONNAIRE

Instructions: Place a check (✓) in the little square opposite the answer that best fits the way you feel about the question. Be completely frank in your answers.

1	2	3		
☐	☐	☐	Yes	1. Do you eat at the company cafeteria?
☐	☐	☐	No	
☐	☐	☐	Sometimes	
☐	☐	☐	Yes	2. Are food prices in the cafeteria fair?
☐	☐	☐	No	
☐	☐	☐	On some items	
☐	☐	☐	Yes	3. Is the food as good as you wish?
☐	☐	☐	No	
☐	☐	☐	Sometimes	
☐	☐	☐	Excellent	4. Do you consider the company a good place to work?
☐	☐	☐	Fair	
☐	☐	☐	Poor	
☐	☐	☐	More than 6%	5. What do you consider a fair profit for the company on its investment?
☐	☐	☐	About 6%	
☐	☐	☐	Less than 6%	
☐	☐	☐	6%	6. About how much do you think the company earns on its investment?
☐	☐	☐	10%	
☐	☐	☐	15%	
☐	☐	☐	Yes	7. Do you get fair treatment from your supervisor?
☐	☐	☐	No	
☐	☐	☐	Sometimes	
☐	☐	☐	Yes	8. Do you feel that the company divides its earnings fairly between dividends to stockholders and wages?
☐	☐	☐	No	
☐	☐	☐	Don't know	
☐	☐	☐	Too high	9. Do management personnel receive proper wages?
☐	☐	☐	Too low	
☐	☐	☐	About right	
☐	☐	☐	Yes	10. Would you advise your son to work for this company?
☐	☐	☐	No	
☐	☐	☐	Don't know	
☐	☐	☐	Management	11. When management and union differ, which do you believe?
☐	☐	☐	Union	
☐	☐	☐	Sometimes one, sometimes other	
☐	☐	☐	Yes	12. Do you think this company is well managed?
☐	☐	☐	No	
☐	☐	☐	Don't know	

unreasonable get a hearing, and it's surprising how often the boss actually looks into the gripes and tries to get something done about them. Take your cafeteria, for instance; you'd complained about that for a long time and nothing was done. Stew every Monday, hash every Tuesday, year in and year out. Who wouldn't get sick of it? Now there's more variety, and they don't repeat the same menus from week to week any more.

Well, that's just a part of the story, but maybe it's enough to give you a rough idea of what's happened around here lately.

On completion of the presentation of a description of more pleasant relationships with their immediate supervisors the audience is again asked to fill out the questionnaire, this time putting their responses under column 3. In filling out this column they are asked to fold under both the other columns so that only column 3 appears next to the question.

ANALYZING THE RESULTS. After the questionnaire has been completed the audience is asked to examine their questionnaires and note the changes in the three columns. When a little time has been allowed for superficial examination, a general analysis of results is made. The procedure for this analysis includes questions such as those given below:

Question 1: How many of you indicated that you eat more frequently in the company cafeteria after the lecture? (Few hands are raised.)

Question 2: How many indicated that you eat more frequently in the company cafeteria after the supervisors' change in attitude? (Many hands are raised after this question.)

Concluding Statement: Although we get a big difference here, one cannot attribute this directly to an improved attitude because there actually was a change in the cafeteria menus in that variety in food was introduced.

Question 3: How many of you who did not give a "yes" answer to item 2 on the questionnaire in column 1 did so in column 2? (There will be few hands raised.)

Question 4: How many gave your first "yes" answer to this item in column 3? (Here many hands will be raised.)

Concluding Statement: This item, concerning the fairness of prices, does suggest an attitude change toward the company, since greater variety may be appreciated without prices becoming fairer.

Questions 5 and 6: The analysis of item 3 follows the same pattern as for item 2 above, and the results reinforce the idea of a spread in the favorable effect when employees' suggestions concerning the cafeteria are recognized.

Question 7: How many of you gave your first "excellent" answer to item 4 in column 2? (A few hands perhaps will be raised in response to this.)

Question 8: How many of you gave your first "excellent" answer to item 4 in column 3? (Many hands will be raised in response to this question.)

Concluding Statement: It seems that many of you felt the company was an excellent place to work when you had pleasant experiences with your supervisor, and that a company lecture on how well the company was operated had very little effect on this opinion.

Question 9: Item 5 involves both attitudes and some understanding of economics. The company lecture on its financial policies would add to knowledge of economics, whereas the experiences with the supervisor would influence only attitudes. How many of you thought at the outset that a fair profit was more than 6 per cent? How many thought so after the lecture on company earnings? (There probably will be fewer hands raised in response to the second than in response to the first of these questions, showing that the lecture caused the notion of a fair profit to decline and correspond with the actual earnings.)

Question 10: How many of you answered "more than 6 per cent" in column 3, but did not answer this generously in column 2? (A fair number of hands will be raised in response to this question, showing that pleasant experiences with supervisors made the employees more tolerant of high company earnings.)

Concluding Statement: It seems that economic facts do not produce a favorable reaction toward high company earnings, but pleasant experiences with supervisors do tend to have this effect.

Question 11: Item 6 has a factual reference in that it refers to company earnings. How many answered "6 per cent" (column 1) before you had specific information on it? How many more answered "6 per cent" (column 2) after you were given the lecture? (A large increase in the hands raised can be expected.)

Question 12: How many more of you answered "6 per cent" (column 3) after you were told about the change in supervision? (Some additional hands will be raised.)

Concluding Statement: It appears that the presentation of facts does increase the accuracy of expressed opinions even though this fact, when accepted, fails to greatly improve attitudes. The fact that some additional persons answered "6 per cent" when more favorable experiences with supervision were given indicates that a financial statement is more likely to be believed when employees have good experiences with supervisors than when they do not.

Question 13: Item 7 deals with fair treatment from supervisors and hence should be helped by improved supervisory treatment. Let us see how that worked out. How many of you answered "yes" to this in column 2, but did not give a "yes" answer in column 1? (A few isolated individuals may raise their hands.)

Question 14: How many of you gave a "yes" answer to this for the first time in column 3? (Nearly all hands will be raised in response to this.)

Concluding Statement: It appears then that the new treatment given by supervisors was generally accepted as fair. A financial report from top management did not make persons feel better about supervision, but we noticed in previous questions that favorable experiences from supervisors made you feel better about the management of the company. Let us see how the next questions bear this out further.

Question 15: Item 8 deals with the fair division of earnings. How many of you answered "yes" in column 2 and did not do so in column 1? (This question should cause about half the audience to raise their hands.)

Question 16: How many more of you answered "yes" for the first time in column 3? (About a fifth of the audience will respond to this question.)

Concluding Statement: It seems that a financial report carries conviction on this fact, but it is rather interesting to note that conviction is improved considerably when supervision is improved. Since improved supervision has no financial implications, the further improvement must be due to the generalized effect of a more favorable attitude toward the company due to pleasant supervisory experiences.

Question 17: Item 9 deals directly with attitudes toward management. The third category that management's wages are "about right" may be considered for this analysis. How many of you checked this category in column 2 for the first time? (More than one-third of the audience will raise their hands.)

Question 18: How many of you checked this category in column 3 for the first time? (Approximately another third will raise their hands in response to this question.)

Concluding Statement: It seems that a discussion of the company's efficiency convinced quite a number of persons that management was paid about the right wages, but pleasant experiences with supervisors convinced nearly as many more that management was not overpaid.

Question 19: Item 10 samples a general attitude toward the company. Considering the "yes" answers, how many of you answered "yes" for the first time in column 2? (A few scattered hands will be raised.)

Question 20: How many of you answered "yes" for the first time in column 3? (More than half the audience will raise their hands in response to this question.)

Concluding Statement: It appears that most of you would rather have your sons work for a company where supervisors are considerate than for a company that can make a good financial statement.

Question 21: Item 11 deals with faith in management *vs.* faith in the union. How many who checked the category "union" in column 1 did not check it in column 2? (About one-third of the audience will raise their hands in response to this question.)

Question 22: How many who still checked this category in column 2 did not check it in column 3? (About one-quarter of the audience will raise hands here.)

Concluding Statement: It seems that a discussion of company finances and policy does do some good, but notice that pleasant supervisory experiences convinced many remaining "die hards," despite the fact that these experiences have little to do with issues between management and the union.

Question 23: Item 12 is a general question and refers to the management of the company. The lecture bears directly on this point and presents evidence to show how well the company is managed. How many of you who did not answer "yes" in column 1 did so in column 2? (Less than one-fifth of the audience will raise their hands.)

Question 24: How many answered "yes" for the first time in column 3? (About two-thirds of the audience will probably raise their hands.)

Concluding Statement: It seems that factual evidence regarding the management of the company is less convincing than personal experiences with one's supervisor when it comes to forming an opinion on "good management."

General Conclusions: It appears that favorable experiences with one's supervisor tend to cause a great variety of opinions to improve, even those quite irrelevant to the nature of the experiences. Such a change in opinion indicates that the general attitude toward the company has improved. A presentation of facts, however, confines its influence to items particularly covered by the facts, and there is less evidence of a general attitude improvement. This finding is consistent with the way true attitudes are influenced. As a matter of fact, true attitudes follow this pattern even more strictly than our results with artificially produced attitudes. This is because, in playing your roles, you were perhaps more reasonable individuals than persons who really possess the attitudes you played.

It is hoped that this demonstration points up the difference between the way attitudes operate and the way one thinks intellectually. We did not ask you how you thought people would react and then requested you to make intellectual judgments. Instead we asked you to be these people and to respond on a feeling basis. When you did this you came up with more correct results of what actually happens than if you had tried to estimate them.

SOME SAMPLE RESULTS. The standard procedure described above has been tested on both student and industrial audiences, with similar over-all effects. However, in order to test the effects of the order in which the two attitude-change techniques were presented it was also necessary to repeat the procedure with the order reversed. The reversal of the two attitude-change techniques would determine whether the influences on the final attitudes were due to the combined effects of the two attitude-change techniques, or whether improved supervision was the major factor by itself.

The test with the description of the change in supervision preceding the lecture on company finances (reversed procedure) was made on a student audience, and the results will be compared with those from another student audience (drawn from the same population) in which the standard procedure was used. The data for an industrial audience (standard procedure) also have been analyzed and will be included for comparison with the data of student audience in which the same procedure was used.

Table 8 presents the results of the two student audiences in which the order of presenting the two attitude-change techniques was different. In Audience 1 the standard procedure was used, and in Audience 2 the reversed procedure was used. Audience 1 consisted of 149 persons, and Audience 2, of 111 persons. In each group 81 per cent of the audience was men and 19 per cent women.

It will be noted that the *initial responses* of the two audiences were very much the same and that in both instances the greater change took place after the description of the improved supervision (the third column for Audience 1 and the second column for Audience 2).

TABLE 8

ATTITUDE CHANGES AS AFFECTED BY LECTURE AND SUPERVISORY
EXPERIENCES

Items	Response	Audience 1 (149 persons) (Per Cent Checking Each Category)			Audience 2 (111 persons) (Per Cent Checking Each Category)		
		Initial	After Lecture	After Change in Supervision	Initial	After Change in Supervision	After Lecture
1. Do you eat at the company cafeteria?	Yes	24.8	22.8	78.5	24.4	66.7	63.0
	No	19.5	14.8	5.4	17.1	2.7	3.6
	Sometimes	55.7	62.4	16.1	58.5	30.6	33.4
2. Are food prices in the cafeteria fair?	Yes	43.6	41.0	79.2	48.6	67.6	67.6
	No	15.4	6.0	4.0	18.9	3.6	6.3
	On some items	41.0	53.0	16.8	32.5	28.8	26.1
3. Is the food as good as you wish?	Yes	3.4	2.1	65.8	2.7	37.8	35.1
	No	81.2	67.0	7.4	79.3	9.9	8.1
	Sometimes	15.4	30.9	26.8	18.0	52.3	56.8
4. Do you consider the company a good place to work?	Excellent	1.3	4.0	69.8	2.7	29.7	44.1
	Fair	64.4	84.6	27.5	65.8	70.3	55.0
	Poor	34.3	11.4	2.7	31.5	0	0.9
5. What do you consider a fair profit for the company on its investment?	More than 6%	18.8	11.4	23.5	18.9	20.7	15.3
	About 6%	66.3	73.2	73.1	64.0	69.4	73.0
	Less than 6%	14.9	15.4	3.4	17.1	9.9	11.7
6. About how much do you think the company earns on its investment?	6%	8.7	76.5	85.2	10.8	19.9	73.9
	10%	39.6	18.1	11.4	36.9	49.5	20.7
	15%	51.7	5.4	3.4	52.3	30.6	5.4
7. Do you get fair treatment from your supervisor?	Yes	6.7	8.7	94.7	13.5	88.3	83.8
	No	54.3	37.5	1.3	46.0	0	0.9
	Sometimes	39.0	53.8	4.0	40.5	11.7	15.3
8. Do you feel that the company divides its earnings fairly between dividends to stockholders and wages?	Yes	5.4	52.2	71.8	8.1	19.9	60.4
	No	70.4	21.5	4.7	68.5	33.4	23.4
	Don't know	24.2	26.3	23.5	23.4	46.7	16.2
9. Do management personnel receive proper wages?	Too high	77.9	43.6	7.4	69.4	22.5	18.0
	Too low	6.7	2.6	6.1	9.0	9.0	10.8
	About right	15.4	53.8	86.5	21.6	68.5	71.2
10. Would you advise your son to work for this company?	Yes	2.7	7.4	67.0	1.8	29.7	45.1
	No	77.8	39.6	12.8	79.3	24.4	23.1
	Don't know	19.5	53.0	20.2	18.9	46.0	31.5
11. When management and union differ, which do you believe?	Management	0.7	0.7	8.1	1.8	11.7	11.7
	Union	67.7	34.2	7.4	52.3	14.4	16.2
	Sometimes one, sometimes other	31.6	65.1	84.5	46.0	73.9	72.1
12. Do you think this company is well managed?	Yes	6.1	21.5	89.3	5.4	66.7	77.5
	No	88.5	39.0	1.3	82.9	9.0	3.6
	Don't know	5.4	39.5	9.4	11.7	24.4	18.9

Since the detailed changes in the items have already been discussed on pages 164–167, we may confine ourselves to comparisons of the two audiences, which will test the influence of the order in which the attitude-change techniques were presented. Because some of the experiences used for attitude change describe specific changes that should influence some items directly, it is desirable to exclude these from the analysis. Thus items 1 and 7, which refer to conditions that were improved in connection with the supervisory changes, have been eliminated from this analysis. Likewise items 6 and 8, which refer to conditions that were clarified in the lecture, have been excluded. Table 9 summarizes the changes associated with the remaining items. In order to measure the changes in opinion resulting from these two types of experiences we have used the first response category in each item, except for items 9 and 11, where the third response category is used. This was done to make all rises in score indicate an improvement.

Table 9 shows that when the lecture preceded the change in supervision it resulted in a gain of a total of 83.4 points in the direction of improvement in opinion, but the description of the change in supervision which followed resulted in an additional improvement to the extent of 359.3 percentage points—more than four times as much as the lecture on finances.

TABLE 9

COMPARISON OF TWO METHODS FOR CHANGING ARTIFICIAL ATTITUDES

| | | Audience 1 | | | Audience 2 | | |
| | | Initial Opinion | After Lecture | After Change in Supervision | Initial Opinion | After Change in Supervision | After Lecture |
Item	Response Tabulated						
2	Yes	43.6	41.0	79.2	48.6	67.6	67.6
3	Yes	3.4	2.1	65.8	2.7	37.8	35.1
4	Excellent	1.3	4.0	69.8	2.7	29.7	44.1
5	More than 6%	18.8	11.4	23.5	18.9	20.7	15.3
9	About right	15.4	53.8	86.5	21.6	68.5	71.2
10	Yes	2.7	7.4	67.0	1.8	29.7	45.1
11	Sometimes one, sometimes other	31.6	65.1	84.5	46.0	73.9	72.1
12	Yes	6.1	21.5	89.3	5.4	66.7	77.5
	Total	122.9	206.3	565.6	147.7	394.6	428.0
	Gain in favorable responses		83.4	359.3		246.9	33.4

However, when the improvement in supervision preceded the lecture the opinion change was 246.9 percentage points, and the addition of the lecture contributed a further improvement of only 33.4 percentage points. In this case the improvement resulting from the change in supervision was more than seven times as great as that resulting from the lecture on company finances.

These findings show that the description of the change in supervision resulted in a much more widespread improvement in opinion than did a description of company finances and operations. Thus the order of presentation did not determine which of the two methods was superior. Furthermore, the change in supervision, when given without the lecture on company finances accomplished somewhat less (246.9) when given alone than when it was given after the lecture (359.3). In contrast, the value of the lecture on company finances was greater (83.4 points) when given alone than when given after the change in supervision (33.4 points). It seems that the lecture has its greatest value when attitudes are poor and there is plenty of room for improvement. After they have improved because of other reasons the addition of factual information contributes little more. The result of these two effects is that the procedure for Audience 1 resulted in a greater total improvement than the procedure for Audience 2.

An examination of the individual items clearly shows that the improvements resulting from the lecture were confined to items 9, 11, and 12, whereas all items showed an improvement after the description of improved supervisory practices.

It appears then that opinions are more generally influenced by personal experiences with supervision than by a knowledge of company finances. This is best explained by assuming that supervisory experiences influence attitudes toward the company, whereas the presentation of facts influence certain opinions only.

The difference in the effects here reported corresponds with what we know of conditions that affect changes in "real" attitudes, except that the lecture on company finances probably produced more favorable changes in our artificial attitudes than it would have in true attitudes. Our results show only a few adverse effects of the lecture. (Note the small declines in items 2, 3, and 5.) With true attitudes these adverse effects are more common and more marked.

The industrial group was made up of 175 male supervisors at all levels in the organization. The procedure was the same as that used for Audience 1, so that comparisons with this student group can be made. Table 10 presents the summarized results of this group.

It will be noted that the change in attitudes is again much greater after the discussion of the change in supervision than after the lecture on company finances. The major difference between the industrial

TABLE 10

COMPARISON OF TWO METHODS FOR CHANGING ARTIFICIAL
ATTITUDES IN AN INDUSTRIAL GROUP

Item	Response Tabulated	Initial Opinion	After Lecture	After Change in Supervision
2	Yes	63.5	66.3	89.1
3	Yes	12.5	14.3	77.1
4	Excellent	8.0	13.1	61.7
5	More than 6%	28.6	20.5	39.5
9	About right	28.0	57.8	86.4
10	Yes	14.9	28.1	74.3
11	Sometimes one, sometimes other	52.0	69.7	77.1
12	Yes	12.0	31.5	82.9
	Total	219.5	301.3	588.1
	Gain		81.8	286.8

group and the student group is in the initial attitude. For students
the initial score was 122.9, and for the industrial group it was 219.5.
This difference caused the industrial group to have more favorable
final attitudes (588.1) than the student group (565.6) and to show
less gain after the change in supervision (286.8) than the student
group (359.1). It cannot be learned from the data whether supervisors
in industry showed the initially more favorable reaction to the work
situation than did students because they had had experience in industry or because they were supervisors. It seems probable that supervisors were less able to role play the feelings of employees than were
students, and so reacted less unfavorably at the outset.

VALUES OF AUDIENCE ROLE PLAYING. Audience role playing has a number of values which may be summarized as follows:

1. Persons in an audience are given an opportunity to learn by
the method of participation.

2. The nature of attitudes and the way they influence opinions
are demonstrated by means of data obtained from the audience.

3. The way attitudes influence opinions and generalize their effect
is experienced both on an intellectual and on a feeling basis.

4. The ineffectiveness of facts and logic for changing attitudes is
demonstrated on an intellectual as well as on a feeling basis.

ARP may also be used to pretest materials designed to influence
opinion. Such materials include advertisements, public announcements, and employee-directed publications. In order to pretest such

material a group of persons could be given a variety of artificial attitudes. Thus the effectiveness of a given set of material could be tested on favorable as well as on unfavorable attitudes. Frequently training material designed to have a favorable effect creates instead an unfavorable impression. Such unexpected negative effects might be greatly reduced if the material were pretested on groups with artificially induced attitudes. The president of a company might pretest his speeches by having his subordinates listen to him while they played the role of hostile union stewards. The junior officers could then react with their artificial attitudes in a realistic way and in addition would not feel that they had to give him lip service. Although we have not tested this aspect of ARP, the fact that artificial attitudes follow the general principles of true attitudes is strong assurance that this method will have at least some pretest value.

6

Reactions to
Human Relations Training

Introduction

It goes without saying that a successful human relations program must be accepted by those exposed to the program, the company personnel responsible for initiating the program, and the company trainers. It is the evaluations of these persons who primarily determine whether a program will be continued. However, the crucial test of the value of a program is the reaction of persons whose supervisors received the training. A program which supervisors regard highly but which fails to upgrade their supervisory skills may be regarded as having questionable value.

We shall see that the latter type of evaluation raises some interesting problems and has not been systematically investigated. Canter (11) has shown that supervisory responses to test items reflect their training, but he has not shown how the employees of trained supervisors respond. Hariton (19), whose study will be described later in this chapter, concerned himself with changes in employee reactions before and after their foremen were trained, but his study, to date, has not included changes in employee job performance. A contribution to this aspect of employee behavior is included in the present book in the reports of case materials (Chapters 8 and 9), some of which are well enough controlled so that they approach experimental tests.

The results of the various evaluations reported in this chapter have been obtained from several companies and departments within companies. The content of the program, as outlined in Chapter 2 and as supplemented by some of the discussion and role-playing methods described in Chapters 3 and 4, has been adopted by three companies as a human relations program for supervisors. In each company the author presented the concepts, with limited time for discussion, to higher management, including officers and department heads. These were covered in groups of approximately 20 persons each. From this point downward the procedure included the free-discussion and participation methods, but the procedure for carrying the program downward differed. In Companies A and B, personnel from the various departments were first trained to present the program, and these trainers followed the plan outlined in Chapter 2, taking alternate half days for the informal presentation of new material and discussions utilizing various participation procedures. The training groups were usually limited to 12 persons.

In Company C the author presented the content material to groups of 100 to 200 supervisors. These presentations covered 2½ hours, with formal presentation procedures interspersed with group-participation methods, skits, or films. (Role playing in audiences had not been developed when these analyses were made.) These same supervisors also met in smaller groups for discussion and role-playing periods. The objective of these discussions was to discover on-the-job uses for principles presented, to motivate and encourage the tryout of methods discussed, and to develop insights through participation and free exchange of ideas and attitudes. The small-group discussions were conducted by supervisors in the line organization who received training in leading discussions as the program progressed. Thus the discussion leaders met with the lecturer and were able to report their experiences, to participate in planning discussion topics, and to develop added skills during the course of the program, which extended over 36 weeks. (Each group leader attended a lecture and a leader's discussion meeting and conducted a discussion once every 3 weeks.)

No attempt will be made to evaluate the relative merits of the procedures used in Companies A and B and in Company C, since the skill of the trainer is an important variable which was not controlled. Perhaps the most important consideration is to adapt the training objectives (content and discussion opportunities) to the existing practices and training philosophy of the company. Each company has a rather decided preference, and it is desirable that existing company interests be reflected in planning the program.

Evaluation of Topics Covered

In evaluating a training program one concern is to determine the relative merits of the various topics covered. Data on this question were secured from Company A, in which the training was entirely given by company personnel. These trainers were trained over a period of more than 40 days, and, as might be expected, there was considerable difference in skill. The figures obtained cover the reactions of 983 persons, who were trained by 20 trainers.

The five questions used were:

Question 1: Indicate the three topics in the list of subjects covered which you found most interesting to you personally. Write the names of the three of the ten topics listed in the order of their interest value.

Question 2: Indicate the three topics you found most useful or practical to you on your job by writing the names of these topics in their order of practical value.

Question 3: Indicate the three topics you found least practical by listing three topics in the order in which they were of least value.

Question 4: Indicate the three topics in which you feel you need or would like further training.

Question 5: If it was found necessary to shorten the program which three topics could be eliminated with least damage to the training program?

The responses to these questions are given in Table 11. In evaluating each topic, first choices were given a weight of 3, second choices a weight of 2, and third choices a weight of 1. Under each question the topics are listed in the order in which the weighted evaluations placed them, together with the weighted score. The numbers in parentheses indicate the number of first, second, and third choices, respectively.

It will be noted that the total number of first, second, and third choices are not identical. This results from the fact that all persons did not indicate three choices. Furthermore, the number of first choices is not the same for all questions because all persons did not feel that they could make a choice. This was particularly true of question 5. Many persons indicated that topics could not be deleted without spoiling the program, since the topics supplemented each other. Insofar as the question tended to force a choice by stating the condition of shortening the program, it was felt that some negative sentiment could be obtained without persons being made to feel critical or unappreciative. Despite this fact, only 522 out of over 900 persons voted a first choice on this question, and only 322 persons voted a third choice.

The fact that the number of persons expressing an opinion on questions allowing favorable opinions (such as questions 1, 2, and 4) exceeded the number of persons expressing opinions on questions allowing unfavorable opinions suggests that the general reaction to all subjects tended to be favorable. However, the degree of favorableness may be made the primary concern.

TABLE 11

EVALUATION OF TOPICS IN HUMAN RELATIONS PROGRAM

Question 1. Most Interesting		Question 2. Most Practical		Question 3. Least Practical		Question 4. Need More Training		Question 5. Material to Be Deleted	
Democratic technique (459-92-66)	1627	Democratic technique (612-70-44)	2020	Fatigue (215-164-99)	1072	Counseling (334-111-140)	1364	Fatigue (139-121-70)	729
Counseling (166-133-198)	962	Counseling (123-166-220)	921	Review session (126-78-119)	653	Democratic technique (168-94-39)	731	Review session (101-43-38)	427
Behavior causation (129-139-75)	740	Behavior causation (74-165-72)	630	Human abilities (127-82-63)	608	Human abilities (123-88-59)	594	Human abilities (77-48-35)	352
Frustration (72-139-115)	609	Attitudes (40-180-76)	456	Frustration (60-70-50)	370	Motivation (53-115-100)	489	Counseling (57-28-30)	257
Attitudes (42-134-73)	467	Frustration (45-75-73)	358	Behavior causation (57-58-45)	332	Behavior causation (67-77-69)	424	Frustration (31-46-52)	237
Motivation (26-76-143)	373	Motivation (28-113-146)	456	Counseling (49-45-31)	268	Attitudes (40-82-78)	362	Morale (30-48-21)	197
Human abilities (32-100-63)	359	Human abilities (35-95-59)	354	Morale (39-49-43)	258	Frustration (34-78-68)	326	Behavior causation (30-32-23)	177
Morale (14-64-50)	220	Morale (16-82-119)	331	Motivation (25-53-39)	220	Morale (27-70-64)	285	Attitudes (23-25-31)	150
Fatigue (5-15-27)	72	Fatigue (6-28-35)	109	Attitudes (28-35-36)	190	Fatigue (12-21-22)	100	Democratic technique (25-6-4)	91
Review session (0-4-13)	21	Review session (4-7-28)	54	Democratic technique (25-5-6)	91	Review session (10-6-21)	63	Motivation (9-20-18)	85
Totals 945 896 823		983 934 872		751 639 531		868 737 660		522 407 322	

It will be seen that democratic leadership was clearly found to be most interesting and most valuable and was second in creating a desire for more training. Since this topic was covered more thoroughly than any of the others, it may be supposed that a good selling job was done. Of importance, however, is the fact that this subject is most controversial and goes contrary to existing attitudes and methods.

The second most popular topic is nondirective counseling. Like the democratic method this subject is a procedure subject, and like democratic technique it goes contrary to existing attitudes and methods. But unlike the democratic technique it was given little time, and unlike the democratic technique it was given at the end rather than at the beginning of the program. Nevertheless it was voted the second most popular subject and was the one on which further training was most welcome. The fact that it was fourth from the top of the topics to be deleted and was the first choice for deletion by 57 persons indicates the presence of more opposition to counseling than to democratic leadership, which only received 25 first choices for deletion. This difference in acceptance is probably due to the lesser amount of time allocated to counseling than to democratic leadership.

The very fact that the two topics that go counter to existing attitudes and practices can be made the most popular topics indicates an existing need on the part of supervision for improved human relations methods. It also shows that proper training methods can successfully overcome resistance to change.

Two topics also stand out in being agreed upon as contributing the least to the program. Thus fatigue (including mental) and the review session obtained the least number of favorable votes and also were the top suggestions for deletion.

The review session introduced no new material and hence competed on a different basis than new topics. The low popularity of the discussion of fatigue may be due to the fact that it perhaps is seen as less important in the understanding of people or to the fact that it seems not to be a major problem in present-day industry. Perhaps the former is the major factor, since it was a difficult subject for trainers to present, and this may have caused it to be experienced as extraneous to the program.

It may be supposed that the popularity of democratic leadership and counseling is primarily a choice of lower supervision and that higher management may recognize them as definite deviations from present practices or even as threats to management's prerogatives. In a similar company (Company B) 20 officials also evaluated the topics.   Of these 18 gave democratic leadership one of their first three votes on question 1, and 16 gave democratic leadership their vote on question 2.   The subjects of motivation, attitude, and counseling received positions 2, 3, and 4, respectively, on these questions.

The fact that democratic leadership received first position indicates the receptivity of higher management to participation procedures, even to the degree that democratic supervision demands.   The fact that counseling was fourth in this company does not indicate opposition to the technique, since no votes were cast for deleting the subject.   The fact that this company had used counselors of the non-directive type, however, made the idea less new to them.   The subjects of frustration, attitudes, and motivation, however, had clarified this group's appreciation of the functions of counseling, and this seems to have made these subjects relatively more valuable.   This interpretation is supported by subsequent decisions of this group of officials which were in the direction of moving the counseling functions to the line organization.

The Response to the Program as a Whole

To test the reaction of supervisors to the training as a whole, a group of 371 supervisors in Company C were asked to fill out an appraisal form at the end of the training period.   Items 1, 9, and 10 were open end questions, whereas items 2 through 8 were rating questions.   Table 12 shows the layout of the appraisal form and gives the percentage of persons voting for each of the ratings.

Question 2 shows that over 60 per cent felt a personal gain, whereas less than 2 per cent felt that the program had not been helpful in contributing to their self-development.   The response to this item is particularly important, since a training program should offer something of personal value to the individual as well as to the company if trust and motivation are to be encouraged.

Item 3, which deals with the value of the training on the job, shows that over 44 per cent of the supervisors found the material more than merely helpful, whereas somewhat more than 5 per cent were willing to question the helpfulness of the training.   The fact that even those questioning the helpfulness of the program were not generally unappreciative of the value of the program is indicated by the fact that many made comments to the effect that they were already familiar with a good deal of the content.   Nevertheless, it is clear that the personal gains seemed to exceed the gains in job performance.

TABLE 12

HUMAN RELATIONS IN SUPERVISION

Appraisal Sheet

Your reactions to the course will be useful in estimating its effectiveness and planning its further use. Will you check items 2 to 8 and fill in blanks for the others? No name is necessary.

1. How do you feel about the course in general? _____

2. Has the course been helpful to your self-development?	43.3	17.2	37.6	1.3	0.5

1	2	3	4	5
Very helpful		Helpful		Little or no value

3. Has the course been helpful in the conduct of your job?

26.4	17.8	50.4	4.3	1.0
1	2	3	4	5
Very helpful		Helpful		Little or no value

4. Do you feel ready now to use the democratic method?

24.8	21.5	50.4	2.9	0.3
1	2	3	4	5
Very confident		Ready to try		Skeptical or not prepared

5. Do you feel ready now to try the counseling type of interview?

16.3	20.2	58.2	3.6	1.7
1	2	3	4	5
Very confident		Ready to try		Skeptical or not prepared

6. Has the course made any change in your job satisfaction as a supervisor?

29.8	40.1	28.0	1.7	0.3
1	2	3	4	5
Much greater satisfaction		Same		Much less satisfaction

7. Has the course made any change in your awareness of personnel problems?

55.0	31.3	12.9	0.8	0
1	2	3	4	5
Much greater awareness		Same		Much less awareness

8. From your observation, how many of the supervisors you know who are taking the course have benefited from it?

24.5	33.9	28.8	8.2	4.5
1	2	3	4	5
All		About half		None

The fact that responses to item 4 very nearly duplicate the responses to item 3, with about 46 per cent feeling quite ready to practice democratic leadership, suggests that question 3 was influenced by the supervisor's confidence in democratic leadership as a tool for supervision. The extent to which this confidence was based upon acceptance of the method as sound or upon a feeling of confidence in skill cannot be determined. It is clear, however, that nearly half the supervisors received sufficient training to make them express confidence in the method. Since this question does not require a favorable reply to indicate appreciation for the program but requires an indication of whether the training was sufficient, it seems that confidence in the responses given is justified.

Considerably less time was devoted to training in nondirective counseling than in democratic leadership, and this is reflected in the returns on item 5. Only 36 per cent of the supervisors felt more than ready to try the nondirective type of interview, and a little over 5 per cent expressed hesitation and skepticism. The returns for the open end questions contained a considerable number of requests for more training time on counseling methods.

That training in human relations was not looked upon as some sort of loss of prestige or an undesirable change is indicated by the fact that nearly 70 per cent indicated increased job satisfaction, as compared to 2 per cent who indicated less job satisfaction than formerly in their responses to item 6.

The training also seemed to increase the awareness of personnel problems. More than 86 per cent expressed increased awareness. The fact that a few, 0.8 per cent, indicated a decreased awareness perhaps reflects a few unfavorable attitudes produced by the training or to the inconvenience of attending the training sessions.

The returns from item 8 are especially interesting. Over 58 per cent believe that more than half of those attending benefited from it, and less than 9 per cent believe that less than half the group benefited. This judgment undoubtedly is influenced by each person's personal experience, but it also must be influenced by the exchange of opinions and observations of behavior, particularly of their immediate superiors. In permitting the expression of the opinion that no person benefited from the training we gave supervisors an opportunity to express an unfavorable reaction to the program without really involving themselves. Despite this fact, only 4.5 per cent registered this opinion. How many of this group disapproved of the program and how many were disillusioned by a failure to see a change in some particular individual cannot be determined.

Item 1 was a request for a reaction to the question, "How do you feel about the course in general?" A random sample of 114 responses to this question revealed 84 (73.7 per cent) enthusiastic responses, including such adjectives as *very, best, most, excellent,* etc., and containing no criticism. Another group of 18 (15.8 per cent) answered this question using terms such as *worthwhile, good, useful, valuable, helpful,* etc., without including criticism. In 4 returns (3.57 per cent) limiting terms such as *somewhat* (better able to handle personnel problems) and awareness of the *employees' side* of problems were used.

A total of 8 (7.0 per cent) reacted favorably to a greater or lesser degree, but they added criticisms about the length of the course (6) or expressed doubt whether others would profit (2).

Of the 114 appraisal sheets analyzed above, 76 (67 per cent) responded to item 9, which read, "Can you name one specific new practice on your job which you have begun as a result of this course?" Of these 76 responses, 40 (52.6 per cent) reported the use of group discussion as a means for solving a job problem, and 17 (22.4 per cent) mentioned the uses of listening as against advising.

Of the remaining 19 responses, 4 fall under the heading of increased tolerance and indicate more analysis of causes behind behavior with an appreciation of attitudes involved, 5 report trying to learn and understand the other person's side, 2 report reducing boredom by permitting employees to exchange jobs, 1 reports setting up periodic interviews, and 1 reports the consideration of off-the-job problems.

Item 10, which asked, "Can you name one specific *former* practice on your job which you have stopped as a result of the course because you now feel it is unsound?" was answered by 52 (45.6 per cent) of the 114 cases. However, 3 referred to others' (their bosses') improvement or other irrelevant facts, so that only 49 responses remained. Of these, 15 described reduced autocracy in connection with the group, and 10 others described avoidance of hasty decisions and transfers or assignments without consulting the individuals concerned. Increased consideration for the feelings of others was mentioned in various ways by 7. A total of 10 mentioned less talking and more listening. The remaining 7 mentioned the following: avoiding putting people on the defensive, being less critical of shortcomings, avoiding close supervision, dividing up unpleasant jobs, sparing the use of reprimand, and displaying more considerate attitudes toward minority groups and lessened tendency to become angry.

Responses of Discussion Leaders

The discussion leaders in Company C also were given an appraisal form. Table 13 presents the questions as well as the way the responses of 20 discussion leaders were distributed.

Question 1 indicates the degree to which the discussion leaders felt their activities contributed to the program. It will be seen that 17 (85 per cent) indicated that they felt they had made a real contribution.

The response to question 2 indicates that 18 (90 per cent) held regular meetings. This is a rather gratifying response, since the holding of meetings was primarily dependent on the leaders' initiative.

Item 3 reports on the length of the discussion meetings. The responses indicate that 15 (75 per cent) ran 2 hours or more.

The satisfaction with the discussion meetings is indicated by the responses to item 4. Fourteen (70 per cent) described their meetings on the favorable side of the ledger, indicating that meetings were more than "sometimes interesting."

The response to role playing was not very favorable. Half the leaders failed to try it, according to the responses to item 5.

Item 6 also indicates that not all the members of the group tried out procedures presented in the program. Only 11 (55 per cent) indicated that more than "some" of their participants practiced the procedures. However, all agreed that a few of their participants were influenced in their practices.

Item 7 indicates the need felt for more training. As many as 16 (80 per cent) believed that time for training follow-up should be arranged, and a like number indicated that help would be welcome (item 8).

Satisfaction with the aid supplied by the trainer for conducting their discussions is indicated in item 9. Sixteen (80 per cent) felt they had received training that was a distinct help in conducting discussions.

In the light of these findings the training for discussion leaders has been increased. Added emphasis on permissiveness of discussion leaders has been given, and time has been found to clarify the values of role playing. The general impression gained is that the quality of

TABLE 13

HUMAN RELATIONS IN SUPERVISION

Discussion Leaders' Appraisal Form

A large part of the human relations course (discussion and application to the job) has been in your hands as discussion leaders. We are anxious to get your estimate of this part of the work. In what ways has it been effective? In what ways has it not? How can it be improved? Your answers to these questions will help in evaluating the course. Additional comments and suggestions will be welcome.

1. Do you feel your discussions added to the training in human relations?	6	11	2	1	0
	1 Very much	2	3 Some	4	5 Little or none
2. How frequent were your meetings?	18	1	1	0	0
	1 Regular with each session	2	3 Occasional	4	5 Few or none
3. How long did your meetings last on an average?	3	4	8	5	0
	1 3 hours or more	2	3 2 hours	4	5 1 hour or less
4. How active were the discussions?	6	8	5	1	0
	1 Lively	2	3 Interesting sometimes	4	5 Dead
5. Did you try role playing?	0	0	6	4	10
	1 Frequently	2	3 Sometimes	4	5 Not at all
6. Did members of your group take the opportunity to try out things learned in the course?	4	7	9	0	0
	1 Many	2	3 Some	4	5 None
7. From the trend of your discussions, will you have need for follow-up meetings with your group on human relations problems?	5	11	3	0	1
	1 Very desirable	2	3 If time permits	4	5 Not needed
8. From the trend of your discussions, do you feel that your group could use opportunities for individual or group consultations in the future on human relations problems?	3	13	3	1	0
	1 Very desirable	2	3 If time permits	4	5 Not needed
9. How much help for your departmental sessions did you find the discussion-leader meetings with [name of individual in charge]?	10	6	4	0	0
	1 Very great help	2	3 Some help	4	5 No value

the discussions has improved. Certainly the number of instances of the use of the group-decision procedure has doubled.

The Effects of Training Supervisors on Employee Perceptions

Introduction. We have seen that the training program was rather enthusiastically received and that there was a belief among the supervisors that they would act differently on the job. Does this change in behavior actually occur? If it does, will employees recognize it and react favorably?

It is possible that a limited number of supervisors change after a single program, but in measuring a group as a whole a difference could be detected only if training were extensive enough to cause a change in a fair number of individuals. It is also possible that changes take place in a large number of supervisors but that it requires a certain amount of time before their changed behavior causes the employees to see them differently. This raises the question of the proper time to measure any improvements in employee perceptions of or attitudes toward supervisors. It is possible that an employee retains his attitude toward his supervisor until the supervisor has undergone a great improvement, and then his view of the supervisor changes suddenly. Thus the supervisor may improve gradually, but the employee may reverse his opinion of him abruptly.

Even if supervisors improve their methods of dealing with people, it may be a change that improves productivity without lowering morale or altering employee attitudes. In such case productivity would be a more sensitive measure than employee attitude changes.

Finally, one must distinguish between the value of what is taught and the degree to which the content of the training is practiced. To measure the value of the concepts and techniques taught one would have to train supervisors to the point of action on the job, and only measure results when there was reason to believe that the content of the program had been put into practice.

The answers to these and other questions require a whole program of research. In order to make a start in investigating these problems Hariton (19) conducted an experiment to determine the way foremen on a blue-collar job are perceived by their men before and after training. The training program used was the one described for Company C, in which large groups met in an auditorium for the content and then met in smaller groups with a line supervisor to discuss applications. A total of twelve $2\frac{1}{2}$-hour joint meetings were held at 3-week intervals. The schedule called for a similar number of discussion meetings. However, the length and the frequency of the discussion meetings were not under the experimenter's control, but the average was somewhat less than 2 hours, and most groups held regular meetings. The over-all program thus extended over a period of 36 weeks.

Experimental Design. Foremen in the overhead lines department of a public utility were used in this study, and an opinion survey of their employees was used to measure perceived changes in the foremen. The foremen and men belonged to 4 divisions. Each division had a division supervisor and his assistant and its own intermediate management (there were 8 general foremen in the 4 divisions), so that these units functioned independently of one another. A company-wide survey conducted the previous year revealed that Divisions 1 and 4 were similar, in that the employee attitudes and backgrounds matched, and Divisions 2 and 3, although having less favorable attitudes, were similar to each other. In order to make it possible to compare the results of trained and untrained groups that were alike at the outset, the foremen of Divisions 1 and 2 were given training and the foremen of Divisions 3 and 4 were not trained. The total number of foremen in Divisions 1 and 2 was 23, and the number of employees was 140. In Divisions 3 and 4 there were 18 foremen and 121 employees.

Previous to the experimental test all higher levels of supervision had been trained, so that the superiors of the foremen in each of the divisions were familiar with the content of the program and undoubtedly had opinions concerning its value. The employees of all foremen were informed of the experiment, and they knew whether or not their foremen were in the groups being trained.

The extent to which higher supervisors can influence the practices of foremen is not known. There was reason to believe that some of the training given to higher levels filtered down the line, since a number of illustrations of applications supplied by higher-level supervisors involved tests with rank-and-file employees. However, since this training was common to the supervisors in all divisions, its influence would be one of reducing rather than creating any differences that might be obtained.

Although Divisions 1 and 2 were similar, in that the foremen in these divisions were exposed to the same training principles, they differed somewhat in that each division supplied its own discussion leader.

Thus any difference obtained in the trained divisions could be a function of the discussion leader, initial morale differences, or differences in the way higher-management personnel supported and encouraged behavior changes in its foremen.

Kinds of Opinions Used to Measure Employees' Relations with Supervisors. All the employees in the four divisions filled out questionnaires just before foreman training in Divisions 1 and 2 was begun and again a year later, three months after the program had been completed. The items that dealt with the employees' reactions to the foreman referred to various forms of satisfaction with the supervisor and with their perceptions of his behaviors. In addition, some further items were added to the post-training measure in order to permit employees to register any observed changes in the supervisor's behavior in the past year.

From a list of 92 items dealing with employee reactions to supervision, 38 representative items were selected and made the basis for obtaining an index of change. An attempt was made to avoid similar items and to explore a wide range of opinion. The items selected are as follows:

1. Are problems brought up by members of the crew discussed at group meetings with the foreman?
2. Are suggestions for improving the job discussed at group meetings with the foreman?
3. Does everyone have a chance to say what he thinks at these meetings?
4. How much freedom does your foreman give you in running your job?
5. To what extent does your foreman praise you or give you credit for a job well done?
6. How often does your foreman take time out with you to talk over how you are doing on the job?
7. How sure are you of what your foreman thinks of you and the work you do?
8. How often does your foreman ask you to help in solving job problems that concern you both?
9. When a mistake is made on the job, does your foreman ask the crew for ideas and work it out with them?
10. Does your foreman have enough time to see you when you want to talk to him about something personal?
11. How much do you let your foreman know how you really feel when you're having a private talk with him?
12. When you are discussing a personal matter with your foreman, who usually does most of the talking?
13. Is your foreman easy to get along with?
14. Is he clear in his instructions?
15. Is he fair with the men?
16. Does he plan work well?

17. Is he open-minded?
18. Is he steady under pressure?
19. Does he admit his mistakes?
20. Is he considerate of the feelings of his men?
21. Is he reasonable in what he expects?
22. Does he encourage suggestions from the men?
23. Is he likeable?
24. Have any changes taken place in the past year in the way things are handled in your crew?
25. Has your foreman improved in the past year?

Items 26 through 38 were preceded by the question, "What changes, if any, took place in the following areas in the *past year?*"

26. How much you like the sort of work you're doing on your job.
27. How good your crew is in getting the job done.
28. Amount of cooperation you get from the rest of your crew.
29. How often your foreman holds group meetings with your crew.
30. How good these meetings are.
31. Amount of freedom your foreman gives you in running your job.
32. How often your foreman praises you or gives you credit for good work you do.
33. How often your foreman takes time out to let you know how you're doing on the job.
34. How sure you are of how you stand with your foreman.
35. How well your foreman handles suggestions made by the men.
36. How often your foreman asks your help in solving job problems that concern you both.
37. How free you feel to talk to your foreman about personal problems.
38. How satisfied you are with your foreman in general.

In order to aid employees in answering the above questions a number of categories were supplied, and the employee was asked to check the category that best represented his opinion. The types of categories used are illustrated in the following questions and indicate how the items appeared on the employee questionnaire.

What kinds of things are discussed at group meetings with the foreman?
Item 1. Problems brought up by members of the crew.

_____ Often _____ Seldom _____ Never

Item 2. Suggestions for improving the job.

_____ Often _____ Seldom _____ Never

Item 5. To what extent does your foreman praise you or give you credit for a job well done?

_____ He doesn't give credit for a job well done; he takes good work for granted.
_____ He occasionally lets me know how much he appreciates it.

_____ He sometimes praises me and sometimes just lets it pass.
_____ He usually lets me know how much he appreciates it.
_____ He always makes sure I get full credit for good work I do.

Item 35. How does your foreman handle suggestions now made by the men compared to a year ago?

_____ Much better now.
_____ Little better now.
_____ About the same.
_____ Little worse now.
_____ Much worse now.

Since the categories indicate different degrees of favorableness, values or weights were assigned to each category (e.g., values from 1 to 5), and in this manner it was possible to obtain group scores for each item and to combine items so as to assign a single over-all score or value.

Changes in Employee Reactions to Foremen. To obtain an over-all measure of changes in employees' opinions regarding their supervisors

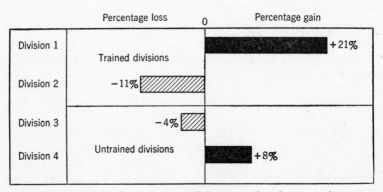

Fig. 14. Changes in employee opinion of foremen after foremen of Divisions 1 and 2 received training in human relations. The bars on the right side of the midline indicate the percentage of improvement in employee opinion after training, and the bars on the left side of the midline indicate the percentage of less favorable opinions.

the percentage of change from the before- to the after-training measures was computed for each division. The results obtained are shown in Fig. 14.

It will be seen that the most striking changes in employee opinions of their foreman occurred in the two groups that were trained. The important thing is that the changes were in opposite directions, so that if the two groups were combined the amount of change produced would be insignificant.

Similar trends also occurred in the two untrained divisions, and they likewise add up to no change. However, the changes in these untrained groups are slight.

Further analyses of the data revealed that the changes in the untrained divisions are to be expected by chance, but the changes produced in the trained divisions definitely exceed chance expectancy and reveal that they are due to something associated with the training.

The fact that the human relations training had strikingly different effects on the two divisions raises some important training problems. Hariton, therefore, analyzed his data in a variety of ways in an attempt to find the reason for the different ways in which the training affected the two divisions.

The first question raised was whether the training differences obtained might not be due to initial differences in supervisory practices. It is conceivable that in Division 1 supervisory practices are already superior and that such foremen are more receptive to training than those in Division 2.

To answer this question all 92 items dealing with supervisory practices were analyzed. It was found that, before training, employees in Division 1 answered 4 per cent of the items more favorably than employees of Division 2. However, after training this figure rose to 18 per cent. Thus the major difference between the behavior of the two groups of foremen occurred after rather than before training.

The same analysis of Divisions 3 and 4 revealed no difference on the pretraining measures (training was given to Divisions 1 and 2), and on the post-training measures Division 4 was favored over Division 3 on only 3 per cent of the items.

If previous relations between foremen and their crews are not sufficiently great to account for the effect of the training on foremen behavior, it is possible that the foremen in the two trained divisions viewed the training program and its value differently. Since the foremen also filled out questionnaires, certain of their items were analyzed to determine their perceptions of the program. Table 14 shows 4 relevant questions and the answers given by the foremen in Divisions 1 and 2.

The first striking fact in this table is that no foremen indicated that things would be worse if they practiced the principles. Thus it cannot be supposed that anticipated failure was a factor in a reluctance to use the principles. If we compare the two divisions on

TABLE 14

FOREMEN'S EXPECTATIONS OF CONSEQUENCES IF THEY USED THE
PRINCIPLES PRESENTED IN THE TRAINING COURSE

		Division 1		Division 2	
Question	Alternative	Num-ber	Per-centage	Num-ber	Per-centage
1. Foreman expects that relations between	Better	9	82	10	91
himself and his men would be	The same	2	18	1	9
	Worse	0	0	0	0
2. Foreman expects that relations between	Better	10	91	8	80
himself and his immediate supervi-	The same	1	9	2	20
sors would be	Worse	0	0	0	0
3. Foreman expects that the efficiency of	Better	9	90	6	67
his crew would be	The same	1	10	3	33
	Worse	0	0	0	0
4. Foreman expects that his own chances	Better	9	82	5	50
of getting ahead in the company	The same	2	18	5	50
would be	Worse	0	0	0	0

anticipation that things would be better if the principles were applied, we find Division 2 less optimistic, particularly on the last question, and this has to do with what effect the use of the principles would have on their own progress.

The major difference in the way the foremen in the two divisions viewed the program thus seems to throw attention on the line organization. Hariton's study of this question led him to further analyze the difference in management climates in the two divisions. He found that as compared to Division 2 the foremen of Division 1:

1. Were more receptive to the principles stressed in the course.

2. Perceived greater opportunity to try out their ideas on the job.

3. Were more satisfied with their superiors and received more encouragement from their superiors to use the principles of the course.

4. Indicated greater satisfaction with their jobs, progress, and chances for promotion.

5. Expected greater personal benefits if they used the principles presented in the course.

6. Felt more secure in their relationships with their superiors.

7. Were more adaptable.

Since most of these differences point to some aspect of the behavior of higher management, Hariton concludes that the value of a training program that requires a change in a supervisor's conduct is dependent upon the attitudes and behaviors of higher management. Without such active support training values become lost.

However, this reference to higher management includes the part played by the discussion leader. Although the discussion leader was selected by the division supervisor and may reflect the attitudes of the line organization, he cannot be entirely divorced from the training program. The particular program tested made the discussion leader an integral part of the training program, and, in the sense that he functioned as a trainer, he was an uncontrolled variable which could make the training different in the two trained divisions.*

Implications of Hariton's Study to Training

The Problem of Training Higher-Level Supervisors. Although it has long been believed that the values and thinking of the line organization influence the behavior of those below, it is important to have some experimental evidence that indicates how these line organization values can become forces that resist change. Many organizations adopt training programs for their supervisors and expect the training to do a job by itself. Supporters of such programs fail to appreciate the importance of the influence of the line organization. If Hariton's findings are accepted, they imply that a good training program must have the full support and continued encouragement of the line organization to be effective. It appears that a company cannot spend a year in training its supervisors and then expect the job to be completed. Thus, regardless of the motivation to change that a program may supply, this motivation in itself is not sufficient, since motivation from the line organization must be added.

This conclusion is supported by the author's general experiences with training. A repeated and persistent question is, "When is my boss going to get it?" Even department heads ask this question. The question is also asked frequently when the boss has had the training

---

* Since this report was written Divisions 3 and 4 have been trained, and final measurements of attitudes toward supervisors have been completed. In both these divisions the improvements were in the positive direction. Furthermore, in Division 2, where the previous data indicated a decline in attitudes toward supervision, the subsequent measure showed a sharp improvement. The analysis is still too incomplete to permit any detailed conclusions, but it is clear that the factors influencing measures of this kind are varied and elusive. (The author is indebted to Floyd C. Mann of the Survey Research Center, University of Michigan, for these additional data.)

and the supervisor who asks it knows he has had the training. Thus the question is often a loaded one. Supervisors have also reported that they have been reprimanded by their superiors for wasting time in group discussion, despite the fact that the supervisor in question has had a series of successes with the decisions reached. These experiences have led the author to emphasize the need for training higher levels more thoroughly than lower levels. With additional training, higher and intermediate management will include a larger number of converts, and they will be able to upgrade the skills of their subordinates.

Perhaps one of the reasons why higher and intermediate management generally has failed to support the training to the extent that is needed resides in the fact that management is more aware of the need for improving employee morale than for improving supervisory morale. Thus management personnel view a program as one for their first-line supervisors, and, as for participating in it themselves, they consider it as something to evaluate rather than as something to practice. The fact that higher management frequently requests a summarized version of the program suggests that this is a real problem. It cannot be considered the complete picture, however.

Reports about marked changes in higher-level supervisors are frequent, however, and perhaps the percentage who change because of the training is not very different for various levels in the organization. It is only human, however, that one recognizes the need for change in others before one recognizes it in himself. Thus supervisors recognize that their subordinates need training before they feel the need themselves, and so they approve new methods without adopting them themselves. The fact that a single second-line supervisor can discourage a number of first-line supervisors makes him stand out as an obstacle. The fact that other second-line supervisors have difficulty in getting some of their first-line supervisors to change their approaches is less likely to be raised as a serious problem, although it might occur just as frequently.

The Optimum Amount of Training Needed. When supervisory training demands a real change in conduct, an important problem is to determine the amount of training that will produce the desired results. Individual differences will make it impossible for all persons to profit equally from a given program, but one may still ask, "What is the proper length of training for a typical supervisor if one wishes him to change perceptibly on the job?"

Some persons have taken the full program on three successive occasions. Such individuals are obviously already favorably inclined toward the program, yet they report that they get more out of it each time. It is the author's belief that the program has been shortened too much for optimum effects and that the greatest gains will occur after more training, particularly with increased practice in role playing and participation in discussions. Principles by themselves have lim-

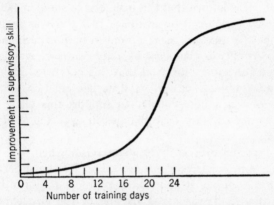

Fig. 15. Hypothetical curve of progress in supervisory skill. If the effect of training in human relations training followed the above curve it would mean that the last of 12 days of training would have much more value than the first 12 days. Only when the curve begins to flatten out would it be desirable to terminate training.

ited value, but with discussion and practice opportunities these principles can be made into tools that can be used with skill and without fear. A principle can be generalized and applied widely only when one feels thoroughly familiar with it. The values of training would probably increase for some time with continued training, and this improvement would occur at an increasingly rapid rate. Figure 15 presents this point of view graphically. What the actual curve would be like remains to be experimentally determined. The figure merely describes an impression gained after eight years of training with a program that has been fairly constant in length.

It is also apparent that the position of the sharp rises in the curves would vary for different individuals. The next two chapters present case material which will make it clear that certain individuals changed radically in their approaches to supervisory problems when they received no more training than others who changed imperceptibly.

Changes in Employee Expectations. When employees know that their supervisor is being trained in human relations, it is natural for them to become more conscious of his actions and perhaps somewhat more critical. It is possible that this factor explains the negative results Hariton found in Division 2.

It seemed at first that the negative results might have been due to the fact that some supervisors were irritated when their bosses did not give them support or treat them with the methods they were taught to use. It is known that this occurred in some instances. However, the survey uncovered no evidence that this was so in Hariton's study, since hostile reactions were absent in both experimental groups.

Another possibility is that lack of active support from above may have confused the supervisors and that this confusion in how to plan and handle job problems was reflected in their relations with the men. Although there was some evidence to support this view it does not exclude the real possibility that changes in expectancy of employees also may have been a real factor.

If employees react differently to a supervisor when they know he is being trained, some real problems are raised for the supervisor. One supervisor, for example, introduced a problem for group discussion for the first time and was asked by one of the employees whether this was one of the new doodads he had picked up in charm school. He never tried group decision again.

Many supervisors handle this problem of changing their methods by telling their employees about the course and frankly stating that they want to try out some of the ideas. Others point out that they want to change their approach and ask the employees to help them solve problems. These introductions seem to take care of situations arising whenever the supervisor feels uncomfortable about trying something out for the first time. There seems to be little point in trying to hide the existence of a training program from employees. The author has received mail from employees expressing interest in the program and asking whether the program will be extended to all employees.

It seems then that the fact that employees know about the program need not be a difficulty, but it is apparent that some supervisors have had to make references to the program in order to bridge the gap between the new and the old approaches.

The fact that the decline in favorable responses in Division 2 may be explained by a change in employee expectancies does not in any way affect the conclusion that a favorable management climate should accompany a supervisory training program. Even if Division 2 had shown no real loss, the fact that Division 1 gained much more remains.

However, it would be unsafe to conclude from the experiment that training may have adverse effects when the climate is not supportive. The change in expectancy has not been ruled out, and no evidence of hostility is present. Another unmeasured influence also remains. This is the fact that in Division 2 an unpopular management change was made while the experiment was in progress. Company officials feel this caused the negative results and that the training prevented a greater decline in morale than would otherwise have occurred. This conclusion, however, cannot be tested.

The Role of the Discussion Leader in Training. In describing human relations training stress has been placed upon the importance of discussions for producing attitude changes and for leading to specific actions in the applications of principles. In the sense that training in large groups limited these procedures, it was necessary to rely heavily on the discussion leader. Although it was desirable to have discussion leaders from the line organization, it was impossible to control the attitudes and the degree of skill of the discussion leaders in the two trained divisions. The extent to which a difference in the discussion leaders influenced the training results in Divisions 1 and 2 thus becomes an undetermined quantity in Hariton's study. There is every reason to believe, however, that some of the differences obtained reflect the influence of the discussion leader.

The initial hope was to have discussion leaders who received preliminary training in conducting discussions. However, this hope was not realized, and it was one of the concessions that had to be made in setting up the total program for the company. It seems that, if Hariton's study suggests to industry the need for having skilled discussion leaders, much will have been added to facilitate future training.

The conclusions reached here in connection with human relations training perhaps apply more to training in democratic leadership than to training in general, since such training requires a greater degree of change in supervision than most programs require. In Chapters 8 and 9 case material will be presented which will give the reader a more intimate picture of a supervisor's conduct on the job and, at the same time, will serve to emphasize the need for discussion and role-playing techniques in developing the attitudes and skills required. Although case material will not demonstrate the degree to which supervisors as a group change, it can indicate what happens when a particular supervisor applies the group-decision method.

7

Group-Decision
Procedure

Introduction

In order not to confuse supervisors with the complexities of the group-decision procedure it is desirable that they have some first-hand experience before details are added. Thus supervisors learn the general idea of putting a problem to the group for solution, and then are urged to try out the method on a problem that involves employee attitudes and at the same time is one in which the supervisor has no bias for a particular solution. Thus problems involving vacation schedules, who should get the new truck, distribution of overtime work, desk arrangements, wall decoration, lunch-hour or relief schedules, etc., frequently satisfy these conditions. Problems that are real headaches for the supervisor, in the sense that "he has tried everything he knows" without success, also satisfy these conditions.

After a supervisor has had some experience with group discussions he is ready to learn some refinements and to evaluate his experiences in terms of these refinements. At this stage a review period is effective, and at this time a detailed outline of the steps in the group-discussion process can be supplied without discouraging the members of a training group. The outline supplied is reproduced here, and its present form reflects the aid of Gilbert H. Selke and Howard F. Shout, who have worked with the program in industry.

The outline divides the procedure into four general areas or steps. The first step, *Studying the Problem*, is the preparation period and deals with analyzing the setting of the problem and the supervisor's attitude. The second step, *Sharing the Problem*, deals with the importance of stating the problem so as to obtain participation in solving the problem. This step deals with the manner in which the problem is presented and will greatly determine whether the employees react constructively or become defensive. Frequently mistakes are made; the supervisor presents a solution rather than a problem, and when this is done he finds that the group fails to react constructively. The third step, *Discussing the Problem*, is concerned with discussion procedures and the supervisor's responsibilities with respect to conducting a discussion. The fourth step, *Solving the Problem*, deals with the objectives for obtaining acceptance of a solution.

These steps should not be taken as a strict sequence in the procedure, although in general they do serve this purpose. However, one should also feel free to reverse the process. For example, the supervisor may discover that his attitude toward the group has been one of suspicion, or that the problem arose because of his attitude toward relief periods. After some discussion he may change his attitude, and this will be reflected in his procedure. By being sensitive to conditions a change in step 1 might occur during step 3. The same may be true of step 2. The nature of the resulting discussion might cause the supervisor to feel that he has presented the problem incorrectly or has been indicating his desire for a particular solution. If this occurs there is no reason why he should not summarize the discussion up to that point, indicate that he sees the problem more clearly now, and then proceed to restate the problem.

Of importance also is the desirability of adapting the procedures to one's own mannerisms and personality. The procedure is stated in a general way to point up principles. The vocabulary, the formal or informal way in which a person talks, etc., should be one's own. These little differences may be regarded as a person's style. As in writing, people may adopt different styles, yet each can be correct. Two baseball pitchers in throwing a ball may show differences by which each might be recognized, and at the same time each might be applying the proper principles of follow-through, coordination of arm, leg, and wrist movements, etc. In following principles people need not become alike; instead the principles should become a medium through which all can better express themselves. It is when we train people in the details of a technique, such as what to say when a customer seeks information or pays a compliment, that we groove or restrict their freedoms and develop stereotypes. Thus a person can change his attitude and consequently his behavior, but he need not show the change in the same way as another. It is for this reason that principles are emphasized in this program.

Outline of the Democratic Technique

I. Studying the Problem
  A. Check your responsibility.
    1. Consider each problem that arises to see how it involves your responsibility and authority.
      a. Is it a problem to be dealt with directly? Is it in your own area of freedom?
      b. Should it be discussed first with your supervisor?
      c. Is it something to be referred up the line?
    2. Wage matters and union agreements are limitations on the area of freedom which often need careful attention.
    3. Problems that you would have a right to handle autocratically should be given consideration for democratic handling. This may also give a clue on area of freedom.
    4. Check your responsibility toward units at the same level as yours.
  B. Analyze the situation.
    1. *How* to do the job—not *whether* it shall be done—may apply to a great many activities.
       (So often we assume that the job is specified from above. Note that the *how* extends the area of freedom. Many jobs are specified as *must* but there is generally leeway on *how* to do them.)
    2. Problems must concern the group.
      a. Reactions to work situation or anticipated reactions may make problems important to the group (work planning, assignments, schedules, etc.).
      b. Some problems may not appear to concern the group, and yet we later find strong attitudes about them.
      c. If the group is indifferent to a problem or its solution it is not a matter for the democratic technique.
    3. Attempts to solve some problems may reveal the presence of others. This is why free discussion is desirable.
  C. Check your attitude.
    1. Are you willing to encourage the group to solve the problem? You do this when you ask for help on a problem: "You are close to the work" or "I'd like the benefit of your experience."
    2. Will you have them consider long-range results as well as immediate results and have them look at the problem from various angles?
    3. Will you deal on a man-to-man basis, respecting the views of everyone and avoiding paternalism?
    4. Can you give a "yes" answer to these questions?
      a. Do you believe the group is capable of solving the problem?

   b. Will you be willing to accept their solution even though
    it differs from one you might have in mind?
  D. Plan your presentation.
   1. Finding a good way to present the problem will require
    study and preparation.
   2. It is essential to have the problem clearly in focus—know
    why it *is* a problem.
    a. Is production suffering?
    b. Are employees violating rules?
    c. Is our boss raising the problem?
    d. Is morale poor?
    e. Is there some other reason?
     (You might object to employees being tardy and find
     that their production is perfectly normal. The problem
     may arise from the fact that you are afraid of the effect
     on other groups. It would be unreasonable to approach
     such a problem in terms of production if production is
     normal.)
II. Sharing the Problem
  A. State the question.
   1. Present it in positive terms rather than in terms of object-
    ing to something.
    Example: "How can we improve our job so that we get a
    better start in the morning?" rather than, "What can we
    do about tardiness?"
   2. State the problem in such a manner that there is mutual
    interest.
    Example: "How can we take our relief period without feel-
    ing uncomfortable about it?"
   3. Make the statement so that it stimulates interest in solving
    the problem rather than giving rise to defense reactions.
    a. If you were presenting a mathematical problem or a
     puzzle there would be no defense on the part of the
     listeners, but rather a desire to find the solution.
    b. If the statement of the problem accuses them of some-
     thing there will be defense reactions. Watch for any
     defensive reactions and ask yourself why they found it
     necessary to defend themselves.
    c. Stating the problem in terms of the *nature of our situa-
     tion* rather than in terms of something *we do* helps to
     avoid defense reactions.
     Example: "Because of the fact that so many of our calls
     are on a rush basis we have a greater problem in pre-
     venting accidents than do some of our fellow employees."
   4. It may be possible to present the problem in a two-column
    approach, using the easel or blackboard.
    a. Develop with the group a number of the advantages of
     the situation under discussion. List these in one column
     on the easel.

Example: What are the advantages of taking short lunch periods?
b. Then develop a list of disadvantages.
c. Now our problem is how to reduce the disadvantages without losing too many advantages.
5. The problem may be presented in terms of fairness.
Example: How can we arrive at a solution to the problem of overtime work that will be fair to everyone concerned?
B. Furnish essential information.
1. Present facts. If opinions are important to an understanding of the situation state them but label them as opinions.
2. Look on information as ground rules for the game of problem solving.
a. Ground rules should not be used to eliminate free expression.
b. Basic information should be supplied at the outset and should not be used to discredit suggestions.
c. If a suggested solution is contradictory to some fact that you forgot to include in presenting the problem, list it as a possible solution and have the group search for other possibilities, or state frankly that you forgot to mention certain facts which the suggested solution does not recognize.
d. A supervisor does not lose face if he has to get certain facts from higher management during the meeting.
e. Exercise care that "your" ground rules do not stem from a preconceived solution you have in mind.
3. Share with the group the fact that you are trying to increase their participation in solving problems that concern them.
III. Discussing the Problem
A. Encourage free discussion.
1. Establish an atmosphere of permissiveness (interest in having everyone have his say without criticism).
a. A permissive atmosphere exists when the individual feels free to say whatever is on his mind.
b. Pay especial attention to the feeling part of any statement and respect this feeling.
c. An informal, relaxed spirit about the meeting will encourage free discussion.
d. Remember that the position a supervisor holds gives him prestige regardless of his personality.
e. Raising of eyebrows, a shrewd glance, and other expressions of blame or doubt can destroy the atmosphere of permissiveness.
f. Permissiveness does not mean a laissez-faire situation, in which the group is turned loose without a leader.
2. Let members of the group do most of the talking and answering of each other.
a. The leader can sense those who want to talk.

       b. Cross flow is a good indication of a permissive atmosphere.

   3. It may be hard to get discussion at first. The group may regard the leader with an attitude of suspicion: "What does he want us to say?"

   4. Members should be encouraged to assume a feeling of responsibility for the success of the solution.

   5. The supervisor should avoid stepping into the discussion and ruling out some idea that looks impossible to him. If there are flaws in the ideas let the group rule them out.

   6. The leader can get weak ideas eliminated by asking such questions as, "How would that be done?" "How would that work out?" "Let us analyze that from various angles."

   7. Write the various suggestions on the board. This gives a person recognition and permits the discussion to continue: "Now are there some other possibilities?"

B. Get everyone to participate.

   1. Participation means more than just getting a word of approval from every person. Encourage them to enter the discussion in an active way—to think and speak with the group.

   2. Ask quiet people for their views: "The group is interested in your views, Joe." But do not press for expression, particularly at first. It is best if group members ask a quiet person for his views.

   3. If some reticent member says he "doesn't care," be sure to give him a chance to voice interest later.

   4. Exert influence by getting everyone in the discussion, but avoid calling on them in consecutive order. Avoid putting anyone on the spot. Remember that he may have private reasons for not wanting to talk.

   5. The employee who says he "won't" talk may say so because he feels he does not belong to the group. As more meetings are held he will be helped to feel that he does belong.

   6. Try to develop an attitude in the group that each person has the responsibility for giving his views. Let the group discuss this phase of a member's responsibility.

   7. Getting everyone to participate is a way of preventing certain individuals from dominating the discussion.

C. Keep discussion on the point.

   1. This is the spot where the leader exerts control. A group of individuals if left entirely "on their own" will tend toward confusion rather than democratic operation. In such situations a member of the group may actually function as a leader to get the discussion back to the point.

   2. Individuals need to feel free to talk about many things, and this should be permitted within certain limits. This does not imply wide digression from the topic at hand. Remem-

ber that other members in the group will want to stay on the subject.

3. The group should experience progress; wide digressions prevent this.

4. Distinguish between this type of control and dominance. A dominating leader would rule out solutions that did not fit his preconceived notions by limiting discussions under the pretext of "keeping on the beam." This is an easy rut to get into.

5. If the group appears to be digressing discussion should still be allowed to go far enough to be sure it is not pertinent to the main topic.

6. If you feel that a contribution is unrelated to the problem ask the person if his idea relates to the problem. If he feels it does he is not off the subject. If he feels it is not related ask his permission to take up his problem on a later occasion.

7. If group members feel "responsible" they will tend to keep a discussion "on the beam." As participation increases, this feeling of responsibility grows. Thus discussions improve with experience. Both the leader and the group learn.

D. Respect minority opinions.

1. Failure to respect minority opinions may cause individual members to feel they "don't belong." Respect for minority opinions can pull back into the group those who feel they do not belong: "Your idea gives us a new slant on things, Sam" or "Let's get your idea down and see how it works in with the others."

2. If a supervisor aligns himself with the majority they may feel that they have his consent to rule out the minority.

3. Sometimes a minority opinion wins out. If group has a chance to hear what the minority has to say it may be sympathetic and decide in that direction. Good ideas are frequently minority ideas.

4. Respecting a minority idea permits a person to stop defending it.

5. Minority opinions often are hostile. Expressing hostility gives relief. Treat such an expression objectively: "That's what we're here for—to get all our ideas and feelings on this question" or "That's Ed's view on the problem, and if we have different slants that is all to the good. We are here to iron out differences."

IV. Solving the Problem

A. The solution is a meeting of the minds.

1. It contains some of each person's thinking. The solution thus grows out of the group. Some solutions, however, are compromises.

2. This differs from a voting process, where a majority rules. In that situation, ideas are not developed.

3. The democratic solution results from the interplay of forces in the group (social pressures) which produce a meeting of the minds. The solution may be one that no individual held at the outset.

4. A solution derived in this way involves the best interests of the group rather than the interest of any one individual.

B. The leader should summarize and check for group agreement.

1. As suggestions come out and are discussed by the group, the leader can sense when a conclusion has been reached.

2. Summarizing the points that have been made gives the group an experience of progress and clarifies the issues.

3. In checking for group agreement the leader permits individual attitudes to be expressed: "Is this what you all understand is the feeling of the group?" or "Am I interpreting this right?"

4. As points are summarized the group feels they have arrived at a basis for exploring the problem further.

5. Summarizing allows social pressure to act, since the group has a chance to learn who is *for* and who is *against* the suggestion. This points up the differences that remain as problems.

6. In summarizing, such remarks may be used as: "We have had such and such a suggestion. How do you feel about it?" or "We have had some discussion on this suggestion. Do you feel it is the answer to our problem?"

C. The solution should specify action.

1. The group may agree that something definite should be done, but the time for initiating the action should also be included.

2. If solution involves men taking turns the pattern of rotation should be specified.

3. Some discussion may be concerned with *what* should be done, but unless the *how* is included misunderstandings may occur.

D. The group should feel free to request a reopening of the subject.

1. The group may have set goals at the wrong level (too high or too low) or may not have fully considered the long-range results of its decisions. This may not be apparent until the solution is tried out.

2. An attitude of permissiveness allows for the fact that the group may not have hit on the ideal goal at their first try.

3. A democratic supervisor will understand that decisions are not made for all time. He will appreciate the need to rediscuss the problem if the group so desires.

4. The group should be told that the door is open to reconsider the problem if any member should feel it necessary.

5. The best solution is tailormade to fit the group and the circumstances existing at the time.

Problems Arising When Group Cannot Reach Agreement

A common reaction to group-decision methods is the belief that groups will not agree because each person is looking out for his own interests. Since many problems involve a conflict in interests, it is believed that great difficulty will be encountered if problems are not carefully screened before submitting them to a group.

The fact that agreement is reached a surprisingly great number of times in well-conducted group discussions indicates that failure to agree is not entirely a matter of the nature of the problem but is also dependent upon the conditions under which the group functions. When a discussion situation creates trust and when participants feel a sense of group rather than individual responsibility, the conflicting personal interests have an altogether different meaning. Thus each individual, instead of looking at the problem from his own point of view, sees it from the point of view of a group member. To agree on what is fair to the group is quite different from wanting what one feels he has coming to him (which feeling is largely influenced by what he feels others receive undeservedly). Group agreement thus involves seeing the rights of others, making reasonable concessions, protecting one's interests, and preventing others from taking an advantage, but it also means a willingness to do these things together, and hence it does not mean giving in or losing something. However, because of the fear that selfish interests may sometimes dominate, many leaders feel that democratic methods are only possible if the group is first trained in participation or if the group is made up of the right kind of people. Since the adequacy of a group seems to be so important to leaders, some of the investigations at the Research Center for Group Dynamics concern themselves with studying the structures of groups and finding training methods that create the right kind of groups. Although these are important problems, it seems that the leader must be trained to deal with groups regardless of their constitution and nature if the method is to be widely used in industry. This requires the developing of leadership skills and techniques that will meet group conditions as they exist. A group with an accomplished leader may form a responsible team and thereby reduce the time required for future discussions.

To aid the leader in obtaining this objective the following procedures may be used if a supervisor finds he is unable to obtain agreement in his group.

1. *Summarize the Points of Agreement and Disagreement.* In summarizing the points of agreement progress is experienced, and in summarizing the points of disagreement the problem is narrowed and the discussion may become more centered. This method can reduce or break a deadlock.

2. *Give Minorities an Opportunity to Explain Their Position.* Sometimes, after minorities have been given more time to clarify their position, they feel enough satisfaction to go along with the group. On some occasions the reasons given by the minority are so sound that the group changes. It may also be possible to concede something to the minority if they feel they lose by the wishes of the majority. Thus seniority rights might be given up in one situation if protected in other ways.

3. *State as a New Problem the Failure to Agree.* Suppose it is apparent, after considerable discussion and the use of procedures 1 and 2, that full agreement will not be reached. The supervisor may then state, "It seems that we are not able to solve our problem to everyone's satisfaction. This raises a new problem. What should we do in the light of our inability to get together?"

This is a method for putting the responsibility for agreement on the group. Up to this point it has been primarily a responsibility carried by the leader. In response to this new problem the group may agree to one of the following:

a. Ask the supervisor to make the decision. A supervisor must be hesitant in agreeing to this. Each faction may feel that the supervisor will side with it, so that in accepting the responsibility for the decision the leader places himself in the middle. He should not accept this recommendation unless he has reason to believe it is a true feeling.

b. Settle for the solution that is favored the most or disliked the least.

c. Try out the most favored solution for a stated period of time and meet again to discuss the issue.

d. Exempt some persons from participation in the plan until something better is worked out.

e. Alternate between plans that have strong support.

4. *Regard the Solution as the One Yielding Most Agreement.* Since the supervisor put the problem to the group for discussion, he can regard the group decision to be the plan that yielded the best meeting of minds. This procedure is particularly desirable when one or two persons seem to oppose all ideas except their own. A group containing one or two problem individuals cannot be kept in discussions indefinitely. Such individuals may be in need of counseling, and, although discussions and considerate treatment may be helpful, this consideration need not be extended to delaying the job.

5. *Regard Failure to Agree as Indecision and Withdraw the Problem.* Some discussions may lead to bickering over minor details. This condition may indicate that major issues are not involved or that the attitudes expressed are reflections of more important problems.

It may indicate a delaying action or even boredom. Although these conditions have not been reported in real-life situations they do sometimes occur in role playing. One might imagine such a situation arising if a discussion of the desired color of pencils were put to a group of office men. The supervisor may conclude the discussion by indicating that the attitudes were so varied that the problem does not seem to be one that can be settled through discussion. The leader may even ask the group whether the discussion is worth the time, and he should constantly be alert and sensitive to an evaluation of the worthwhileness of a discussion. People may argue on unimportant matters because they are bored with the discussion.

The above-mentioned procedures can be used as conditions seem to warrant. They should not be considered progressive steps that might be taken. Different leaders will have preferences for one procedure over another, and this seems desirable since it permits the development of leadership confidence. The important thing is for supervisors to increase their skills and to discover how constructively groups can behave and how effectively and frequently social pressure produces full agreement.

Problems Arising When Groups Cannot Meet

Some Practical Difficulties. The group-discussion and -decision method require that a group meet and interact, and it is desirable that all participate. Since these discussions are to be held on company time, what is to be done under the following conditions?

1. In an assembly line stopping work for discussion in one unit will shut down the work of all other dependent units. Although it may be argued that trouble in one unit may cause a walkout and that the plant is sometimes shut down anyway, this does not make a case for shutting down the plant in order to hold group discussions. Furthermore, it does not leave room for solving the many problems that fall short of becoming union grievances and yet contribute to poor morale.

2. A similar problem arises when all employees cannot be taken from a job without interfering with service. Thus department store clerks and telephone operators cannot delay customers while the employees are having a meeting.

3. In situations where one shift replaces another there may be problems common to the shifts, and yet these cannot meet together since the shifts have no common work period.

4. A group reporting to a supervisor may be too large to permit a good discussion. Although we have discussed methods for permitting participation in large groups (Chapter 3), these methods may not be satisfactory for problems involving considerable detail or the resolution of varied attitudes.

5. Sometimes a supervisor is unable to get all his employees together because they work at different locations, perhaps in different cities. This problem is even more frequent at higher levels in the organization, when communication with the supervisor is largely by telephone. Although these separated persons may meet occasionally for conferences, such meetings may be too infrequent to permit real participation on job matters.

6. Some work groups undergo constant change, so that a given supervisor may not have the same crew from week to week. This is likely to be true when men rotate on different shifts.

7. How can persons who were absent at the time of a group decision be made participants in an arrangement already agreed upon?

8. Some problems, if solved by the separate work units, will give rise to a variety of work practices. Sometimes the resulting discrepancies lead to a non-uniformity in practice which may interfere with efficiency. At other times the discrepancies may lead to dissatisfaction.

9. What is to be done with problems that overlap two or more lateral units, when a given decision in one unit may alter the routines and procedures on which the others depend?

10. Some problems overlap two or more levels of management, and as a consequence the solutions at different levels are in conflict.

The following procedures represent modifications of the group-decision method, and, although they all may not be as effective as the basic method, they retain most of the essential values.

Procedure A. Dividing Group into Smaller Sections. If for some reason or other all the employees concerned cannot meet for a discussion the supervisor may meet with a few employees at a time. Then each of the smaller groups would arrive at a tentative solution, with the understanding that the final solution would have to resolve differences. This procedure would require a minimum of two meetings with each group; the first meeting, to formulate the tentative solution, and a second (and perhaps a third), to resolve the differences. Usually the differences are not very great (sometimes the recommendations are identical), particularly if the conditions of work are similar

for each of the smaller groups. In such instances the supervisor can
be expected to be less intent on reaching full agreement, but the possibility of making changes or exceptions in the solution so as to adapt
it to satisfying a minority group should not be overlooked. An example
of a case of this kind is given on pages 247–249.

This modified procedure may satisfy some of the situations listed
under the first six conditions.

Procedure B. The Use of Group Representatives. This procedure
is designed to meet the same kind of conditions as procedure A, as
well as condition 7, and, although it is less time-consuming, it also
permits less participation. The general idea is to have some of the
members of a group meet and solve the problem through group discussion. By this method only some representative employees would
participate. General participation can be extended somewhat by
having the employees choose their representatives. Thus if 48 employees could not be moved from the job they could meet at different
times in groups of 6 or 8, as in the Phillips 66 pattern, and choose a
representative with the understanding that if the representatives
reached a meeting of minds their solution would be acceptable. The
problem to be solved would then be put to the representatives and
solved by the usual group-decision method. The evidence thus far
indicates that, in general, acceptance increases as the extent of participation increases. Thus, as the problem of resistance increases, the
desirability of extending participation becomes greater. When unfavorable attitudes are not too great, the use of representatives to solve
problems may give all the acceptance necessary for obtaining full
cooperation.

Procedure C. The Use of Questionnaires. When problems are relatively simple, in that a solution from several possible alternatives is to
be selected, employees may be asked to express their views by checking preferences on a short questionnaire. It is also desirable to permit
an expression of the least desirable alternatives, with a space to give
reasons. On the basis of the returns, alternatives that are both generally acceptable and not greatly disliked may emerge.

One may also include a choice on how the differences in opinion
should be resolved, indicating such possibilities as: (*a*) the alternative
receiving most votes; (*b*) alternative having the highest score when
votes against are subtracted from votes for it; (*c*) a meeting of representatives to select the best plan; and (*d*) a second vote on highest
three alternatives.

The questionnaire method may be combined with other procedures for the purpose of reducing discussion time. For example, on a new decorating job a questionnaire might be used to determine the color of paint desired, and group representatives might then meet to make the final decision. When used as a preliminary to other procedures, it permits some participation but no interaction between persons. However, it yields useful information which may be evaluated in discussion groups. For problems in which the emotional loading is relatively unimportant it may serve as the complete procedure.

Procedure D. Supervisor Serving as Clearinghouse of Opinions. In some instances the supervisor may contact individuals separately and obtain their views on a problem or proposed change. He can introduce the element of participation by relaying to successive individuals what others have contributed. By this method he obtains a variety of ideas, and, if he is permissive and accurately reflects the ideas of others, the elements of a discussion are present in that he reports and describes the various ideas to each as they accumulate. It is quite probable that, as he collects opinions and is receptive to the expressed criticisms of various ideas, he will have to contact some of the individuals more than once. This would allow minority individuals more time than others, and would be all to the good. This procedure, if used by an open-minded supervisor, can lead to a good deal of participation and to unanimous decisions.

Although this method is adaptable to all but the fourth of the first seven conditions, it requires a considerable amount of the supervisor's time. Its greatest value would be for condition 5, and it could easily be a supplement to conditions 6 and 7, with only the necessary individuals interviewed.

Procedure E. Group Discussions Leading to Conditional or Provisional Solutions Rather than to Decisions. Conditions 8 and 9 may be considered as variations of condition 10, since the need for uniformity and the proper integration of dependent units are matters of concern for the level of supervision one step higher up. If it is important, for example, that all units use the same forms when making job inspections or that all crews follow the same work practice, then the supervisor of no one unit can permit his group to make changes, even if the changes are improvements. Similarly, if two sections in a department must deal with one another it would not be permissible for a supervisor of one unit to permit his group to change their hours of work somewhat. In some instances the reason for not being able to accept a single unit's change in working hours, vacation schedule, or job procedure might be the effect its appearance would have on other units. In so far as restrictions on solutions to problems exist, because of the way certain solutions affect other groups, the problem of the area of freedom is involved. If a problem, wholly or in part, extends beyond the area of freedom of a given level of supervision, then it must be taken upward until the level of supervision whose area of freedom covers the point of issue is included. In this manner more than one level of supervision is involved, and we have the type of situation described under condition 10.

For the type of problems falling under conditions 8 and 9, when the sole consideration is uniformity and integration, it is possible for a second-line supervisor to hold a meeting with the first-line supervisors (which may be requested by the first-line supervisors), and agreement may be reached as to how each of them is to put the problem to his group. The first-line supervisors then put the problem, as agreed upon, to their groups, with the understanding that they are meeting to agree on a *conditional* solution and that the opinions of other units are also being considered. The question of how the provisional solutions from the various groups are to be reconciled into a final solution should also be raised.

After the foremen have held their separate meetings they again meet with the second-line supervisor for the purpose of considering the provisional solutions. Different foremen can then present the reasons and the attitudes that they have discovered in their meetings. If the groups have decided that the final solution should be based on the "best fit" of the recommendations, the final solution may be reached at this meeting and transmitted by the supervisors to their groups. If, however, the work groups have requested another meeting to study the differences, then the second-line supervisor should use his meeting with the foremen to formulate a summary of recommendations which points up the areas of agreement and disagreement. The points of difference then become the problem for the first-line supervisors' second meetings with their groups.

Most problems of this type are not so involved as might first be supposed. If they do become involved a difference in attitudes is definitely indicated, and the time spent becomes worthwhile in terms of returns in morale.

Where the number of individuals involved is not too great (40 or less) the process may be somewhat simplified. A group of supervisors at one level might agree to have their supervisor take the problem directly to their combined groups. This would permit the reaching of a final solution without going through the process of reconciling provisional solutions. This alternate procedure would be more adapted to higher levels in management because fewer individuals are involved. For example, a third-line supervisor might have to meet with only 20 first-line supervisors if his 4 second-line supervisors agreed to this plan, but a second-line supervisor might have to meet with more than 60 workmen if his 5 first-line supervisors agreed to his taking the problem directly to the men.

Procedure F. Group Discussions Leading to Recommendations Rather than to Solutions. This procedure is particularly adapted to problems in condition 10, in which each level in the organization has an interest, but the nature of the interest changes. For example, a first-line supervisor may be considerate of the attitudes of his men in his attempt to obtain an efficient and cooperating work group. The second-line supervisor to whom he reports, however, has an added problem. He may want to do what he can to support a given supervisor, but he cannot confine his problems to the interests of one crew. Several crews must integrate their functions so that, in addition to supporting each of his first-line supervisors, he must consider uniform practices and problems of coordinating work functions. Thus the second-line supervisor has a channel of influence in addition to the one exerted on the first-line supervisor, and it is easy for him to regard this added duty as his main one and to be inconsiderate of the problems arising at the first level. However, even if he is considerate of the problems of the first-line supervisor, he is likely to be misunderstood because he is influenced by this added source of influence to a greater degree than is the first-line supervisor.

The third-line supervisor has still an additional channel of influence. His problem may be to integrate sales and production. Thus the second-line supervisor in production, the sales manager, and staff men (experts in various specialties such as lighting, promotion, motion and time study, etc.) may each report to him with their unique problems. His major duty then becomes one of integrating these sources of influence, and he can readily be accused of giving too much weight to sales, production, or staff interests. Figure 16 diagrammatically describes the manner in which a problem changes in aspect from one level of management to another.

The increase in the spread of the channels of influence is characteristic of conditions in the upper levels in the management hierarchy. At each level in management the channels of information and influence increase in number, so that the problem of reconciling them becomes important to the person responsible. However, the supervisors in control of each of the channels tend to look at their problems as primary and so feel that their situations are not given due consideration. Frequently these channels of information are inaccurate or are actually

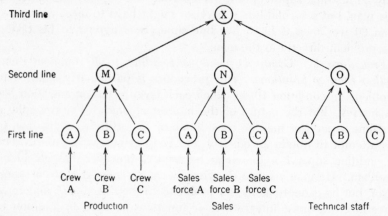

FIG. 16. Diagram showing channels of influence operating in a single problem situation. A, B, and C represent first-line supervisors in charge of groups of rank-and-file workers. These workers are affected by decisions made higher up. The arrows from the work groups indicate sources of influence the first-line supervisors may use. Arrows from first-line supervisors converge on the second-line supervisors, and these serve as sources of influence that he may use. The arrows from the second-line supervisors to the third-line supervisor represent the sources of influence available to him. It will be noted that the channels of influence show a spread as a problem involves higher levels, and as a consequence less influence from the bottom can pass through to the top. In order to obtain the greatest benefit from the converging channels a problem can be passed down the line, and recommendations rather than group decisions can be passed upward. The final decision then becomes the product of all sources of influence and is made at the level that initially had the authority to solve the problem. Problems that do not involve the reactions of employees at lower levels can be solved by group decision at the level at which the problem arises and need not go through this process to gain acceptance.

given undue importance (e.g., a second-line supervisor might assume that uniformity of practice is more important than morale), but, regardless of conditions, misunderstandings and problems of fairness will arise. How can a problem be solved so as to give each level its proper participation?

Let us suppose it is within the third-line supervisor's authority to modify a product to reduce its cost. He might turn this problem over to his staff of experts, but their solution might not be welcomed by salesmen and might cause production workers to feel that the change is resulting in an inferior product, or they may fear a change in job status. Thus a change in a product is a problem that affects the force as a whole.

Suppose the third-line supervisor presented his problem to the second-line men reporting to him and obtained some preliminary ideas of the implications of the problem to their forces. Suppose further that he showed an interest in their own feelings and was concerned with the feelings of the men down the line. Would not such a discussion lead to the idea of exploring the problem further, with each second-line supervisor taking a specific phase of the problem to his unit? Thus one second-line supervisor would be concerned with the production aspects, another with the sales problems, etc. Each could explore the attitudes and ideas that their first-line men would express, with the understanding that the attitudes of the rank and file would also have to be considered. Finally, the first-line supervisor would take the problem to his crew. The problem for a production crew might be to explore ways of improving their functions, their situation, or the details of a job to make their work more effective. They could be told that the company is interested in competing in a certain market and wants ideas from production, sales, and staff men.

In this instance the men in a crew would make recommendations, not reaching decisions, but agreement on recommendations should be sought. As a result of these discussions the first-line supervisor would learn what the men opposed and what they considered desirable. He would learn something of their fears, possible hostilities, and motivations. After each first-line supervisor held his meetings, the first-line supervisors would meet with the second-line supervisor, and in this meeting differences in the recommendations would be ironed out; these could be considered in the light of problems involving an integration of functions. The first-line supervisors, through the leadership of the second-line supervisor, could then reach agreement on a recommendation that included consideration of the attitudes of the rank-and-file workers as well as the attitudes and problems arising from the needed coordination between work units. A similar process would also be going on in the sales and staff groups. When all second-line supervisors had finished their meetings, the third-line supervisor would hold one or more meetings to solve the problem. The solution would involve a realistic consideration of a number of influences, including manufacturing, sales, and technical experts, as well as the attitudes of all the men who would have to make and market the product. In this

process each employee could participate in having a voice in the phase
of the problem that concerned him most, and each would become
aware of the phases outside his own unit which would have to be
considered.

The above illustration is a rather complex one, and it may be inaccurate or unrealistic in certain details. It, however, serves the purpose of illustrating how problems that extend through various levels
of an organization can be taken down and how the recommendations
can then move upward.

The method can be used in connection with promotions; one group
can make recommendations as to what they consider fair or acceptable,
and the next level can work from recommendations and compare these
with the job requirements, of which they may have special knowledge.

This method can also solve problems that overlap crews, when one
crew feels it should have certain considerations that others do not
deserve. For example, one crew feels it should have 15 minutes off
for showers because their work is dirty, and the first-line supervisor
considers the request reasonable. The second-line supervisor, however, feels that he cannot grant this request because other crews will
demand the same thing even if their work justifies the privilege to a
lesser degree.

Such a problem obviously involves the problem of fairness between
crews, because other crews see the privilege granted to one crew as
favoritism, and fail to react to the reasons for the privilege. If the
problem of working conditions were considered by various crews in
discussion with their foremen, and if the crews evaluated the undesirable features of certain jobs and what might be done to compensate,
it is possible that all crews would agree that a given crew was entitled
to shower privileges. Under such conditions the problem would be
solved at two levels, and the reason for the shower time for one crew
would be accepted by other crews.

The above two illustrations serve to describe the method of using
recommendations for solving problems that are not completely in a
given supervisor's area of freedom.

Problems that include several levels of management are relatively
more common at higher levels of supervision than at lower levels, and
for this reason skills in higher management positions are as necessary
as at lower levels. Higher management frequently feels that the number of factors that must be considered restricts their use of group-
decision methods. Lower management in turn feels that higher management, even when they do use the method, restrict its use to a single

level. It seems that if some problems were taken down to the rank and file by the method described a better understanding of the realities might be gained.

The Difference between Problems and Solutions

Reforms That Fail. In analyzing a number of situations in which committees of experts, commissions appointed by legislators, and organizations of citizens have failed to gain acceptance of reforms, it became apparent that all failed for the same reason. The conclusion reached was that the reform efforts failed primarily because the method of presenting the solution invariably led to hostility. In most instances the possibility of achieving reform was more remote after, rather than before, the reform plans were suggested. Consideration was given to the facts that destructive criticism was used to justify reform, that face-saving opportunities were not allowed, and that the reform group frequently acted as individuals rather than as members of a group, but one additional factor seemed even more important than these. This was that the reform committee recommended a solution and asked its acceptance. Each of the reform groups could have set as their objective the reaching of group agreement on how the problem was to be put to persons whose acceptance of reforms was needed, and facts could have been supplied to facilitate the problem solving. Instead, the participation of those expected to make the change was limited to accepting or rejecting the solutions furnished by the experts.

For example, if a commission is appointed by a state legislature to reorganize government functions, might it not as its report present the problem of overlapping functions, describe how such a state of affairs arose as time went on, present facts on the nature of functions, and raise questions about the direction in which improvement could be made, rather than come back with a series of recommendations? Thus general policy matters could be settled through participation, and their implementation would become the job for experts who had been thus instructed. Even if the commission had worked out remedies, should not these be withheld if the objective is to gain reform?

In one instance a state commission, which had the initial support of the legislature, the governor, the press, and the public, made 26 recommendations. Not one was accepted, and nothing resulted but hard feelings. Good solutions have little virtue if they are not ac-

cepted and put into practice. The commission might even have gone
to the state legislature with a set of reforms and permitted participation by asking the legislature to select any ideas for discussion that it
considered valuable. In this manner the most agreed-upon items
would have been considered first without pressure from the commission. The legislature would not be placed on the defensive and
could contribute to the solution by the process of selection. By expecting less and by respecting the fact that those who change must
do so voluntarily, the commission would have gained much more.

Accepting Solutions vs. Solving Problems in Industry. If we apply
some of this thinking to industrial problems we find that many problems in management are problems of getting a solution accepted.
Thus the supervisor in many instances is asking acceptance of his solution rather than presenting a problem. In a list of 33 problems submitted by a group of supervisors, 14 (42 per cent) were clearly statements of desired solutions rather than statements of problems. May
not some nonconstructive reactions in a group arise because the problem was not one for the group to solve?

Let us choose one of these "apparent" problems for further analysis.
A supervisor states, "My problem is that my girls make too many personal calls." Clearly the solution implied is "fewer personal calls."
With many groups a supervisor could put the problem of how to reduce the number of personal calls and receive a considered solution.
However, in so far as we are now seeking refinements and in so far
as such a problem might create resentment in some individuals, it is
worthy of further analysis.

Suppose we ask the supervisor why personal calls are a problem to
him. He may give a number of reasons. Suppose his main reason is
that the company is short on lines and that it will be some time before
better telephone facilities are available. If this is his reason for ob-
jecting to personal calls, then we have located the real problem. The
problem could thus be stated as follows: "In the light of our present
limited telephone facilities what can be done to improve our services
and make our office more readily available by phone?" Note that this
statement of the problem is not a criticism of individuals, but is put
in terms of a situation. The solution to this problem would certainly
introduce the question of personal calls if they were excessive, but
it might also introduce a number of other suggestions, such as more
prompt answering, more efficient service, shorter visits in connection
with business, etc., and these suggestions would come voluntarily
from the group.

Suppose, however, that the supervisor's concern over personal calls arose because of a criticism from his superior. Now the real problem takes on a different appearance. It might be stated as follows: "Our force is judged on the basis of its output, its housekeeping, businesslike manner, etc. We are average or above average on most phases, and so are doing a good job. I wonder if you would like to discuss ways in which we might improve a condition in which we are at a disadvantage. We have to be available for phone calls, and often there is a busy signal on our lines. In the light of our situation is there anything we can do to improve this condition?"

Again this problem is stated in situational terms, and a group is permitted to change without admitting faults.

A supervisor may maintain that the problem exists because the company feels that employees are under its jurisdiction for the time they work, whereas employees feel they should have certain freedoms. In other words, the supervisor's values do not seem to correspond with those of his group. Can he be sure his values are realistic? If he is exceptionally strict and has not changed with the times along with other supervisors he may find that an attempt to impose his values on the group may result in compliance with the regulations, but at the expense of morale and work output. Is his production low? If so, is it low because of personal calls? How can the supervisor learn the answer?

Suppose a supervisor who felt the group was making too many personal calls put the problem as follows: "There are always certain differences in point of view which may arise between a supervisor and his group. I would like to do the fair thing with all of you and not extend privileges to some and not to others. I wonder if the making of personal calls is fairly handled. Do you feel guilty if I observe you making such calls? Do some of you feel that others do more of it than necessary? I would like to know just how you as a group feel about it, and whether you think a better understanding could be reached by discussing the needs you have in this connection?"

Obviously the exact statement made would vary depending on conditions, but in no case should an individual be singled out by the statements made or the questions raised. If abuses are taking place some individuals in the group will reflect this because they feel cheated. The important thing is to make it a problem in the group and to emphasize fairness. As soon as individuals feel criticized they resort to excuses, and as a result they feel that they have been criticized for doing something that is beyond their control. A girl can't help it if her mother calls her, if someone is sick, or if she has to arrange for a ride home. The supervisor does not wish to eliminate valid reasons, and, unfortunately, only valid reasons are expressed when people are on the defensive. Thus selected reasons become excuses.

Analysis of this kind should permit other "apparent" problems to be put as situational problems rather than as solutions the supervisor wishes to have accepted. Often the problem exists only in the mind of the supervisor. Analysis may produce a change in his attitude, and then his problem disappears. Thus the supervisor who feels there are too many personal calls may discover that his problem is in his own attitude. If he does not discover it through analysis he may discover it when he puts the problem to his group in terms of fairness.

Some other examples of problems submitted by supervisors which in reality are solutions are as follows:

1. Too much tardiness.
2. Overstaying relief periods.
3. Horseplay in the group.
4. Getting trucks out on time.
5. Quitting early.
6. Talking on the job.
7. Wearing babushkas and hair in curlers in the office.
8. Overcrowding elevators.
9. Not calling in if not able to come to work.
10. Not getting job done.
11. Smoking in lounge.
12. Too many trips to washroom.

Obviously these are problems of concern to supervisors, but the question is one of putting them in situational terms and stating them in terms of what is behind the behavior.

Problems that are more truly situational in nature are:

1. How can we cover an undesirable shift that is coming up?
2. What are some of our problems in following safety instructions?
3. How should we schedule vacations?
4. How should we arrange the office after a move?
5. How should we schedule over the noon hour?
6. How can we get this rush job out?
7. How can we improve our housekeeping?
8. What is the best way to answer a phone?
9. What can we do in the direction of preventive maintenance?

Note how this list of problems reflects the situational condition instead of suggesting defensive reactions. Solutions to these problems would give rise to satisfaction.

There is no more effective way for destroying the effective value of participation than for the leader to have a bias for a solution. Evidence of bias makes a mockery of participation methods and degrades the group. Many leaders who believe they utilize participation have surrounded themselves with "yes" men. What is sometimes called consultative management is merely this type of participation. The basic reasons for a leader's preference for solutions seem to be fear that the group may take advantage, lack of respect for a group's thinking, and a tendency to put only problems to a group for which he can find a solution. It is good practice to try putting to a group problems for which one can find no solution. It will be a rewarding experience to discover that apparently insoluble problems frequently have simple solutions.

On one occasion a series of training meetings was scheduled for one day a week from 6:30 to 9:00 P.M. This time was set so that both the day-shift men, who left the job at 5:00 P.M., and the night-shift men, who began at 10:00 P.M., could attend. The hours were set so that each group would be inconvenienced somewhat. Before the first meeting, complaints began to come in because the night-shift men didn't want to wait around for an hour before going to work. The problem of how to deal with the complaints was discussed at three levels of management. It was assumed that the problem was insoluble because if the time were set to please the night-shift men the day-shift men would complain. There even was hesitation about bringing up the problem in the group because it would only produce disagreement.

However, at the first meeting the problem was put to the group in terms of whether a more satisfactory meeting time was possible. One man suggested a 7:30 time, and others approved. Exploration revealed no one was opposed to the plan, so that in 5 minutes approximately 50 men reached unanimous agreement. What management overlooked in this case was that the 7:30 meeting time permitted day-shift men to go home for dinner and return for the meeting rather than eat in the company cafeteria and wait around for the meeting.

8

Democratic Supervision
in Action:
Case Studies

Introduction

The training program so far described has been primarily directed toward the development of democratic supervision and management, and the group-decision procedure has been found to be the key skill area. In the preceding chapter the group-decision procedure was outlined for the reader so that he would have some conception of the process. In this chapter the objective is to further clarify this group-decision approach for management by translating it into action on the job. To accomplish this with the fewest number of cases the materials have been selected to illustrate a variety of problems so that the broad uses of the method may become apparent. In the next chapter some unselected cases will be briefly presented and some limitations described so that the reader may obtain a more typical picture of the way the group-decision method is used on the job.

In presenting case material it should be apparent that the results obtained are limited to supervisors who have practiced the group-decision method. Thus any values brought out by the cases represent the gains of particular supervisors in handling a specific job problem.

Although the group-decision method has previously been subjected to experimental tests (12, 23, 25, 35), a trained psychologist was always used as the discussion leader in these investigations. In the case material reported in these chapters a supervisor in industry utilized the procedure on his job. Further, the degree of skill utilized represents that gained by the amount of training given to Companies A, B, and C (see Chapter 6), and thus represents the minimum amount of training given. No cases are taken from supervisors who have had follow-up training.

Cases Selected to Illustrate Various Aspects of Group Decisions

CASE 1. AN OFFICE PROBLEM INVOLVING A CHANGE IN HABITS

This case was selected because it illustrates the attitudes that arise over small issues. Management is likely to be impatient when employees make a big fuss over "nothing." The group solution in this case is very simple and does not surpass that which a supervisor could have worked out, and yet the source of the solution seems to be a basic consideration.

The office in question contained 80 girls, who were divided into four groups or units and supervised by four managers. Mr. Jones managed the group at the front end of the office, whereas Mr. Smith managed a group at the rear of the office. Mr. Brown and Mr. Wilson managed groups in the middle part of the room. All groups did the same type of work. The district superintendent, Mr. Barr, was in charge of the whole unit and had an office just off the large general office, whereas the managers had desks near the groups they supervised. The work of the girls was such that it was necessary for some to leave their positions, whereas others were quite stationary and spent a good deal of their time in telephone contacts. However, in taking relief periods (scheduled or personal) and in leaving or returning to the office all girls had, on certain occasions, to move through the office. The office had one door which opened on the corridor. This door was located in the center of the front wall. To the left was a door into the district superintendent's office, and to the right a door opened into the mail room. The plan of the office is shown in Fig. 17.

A persistent problem in the office was the manner in which the girls moved through the office, particularly when entering or leaving the room. Instead of using the outer and center aisles they cut through various units, and this activity disturbed the work of girls who frequently had phone contacts. Furthermore, since it was the custom of girls to go in pairs or in larger groups, unnecessary confusion was caused when one girl went to another's position to join her in taking a relief period.

In other offices this problem had been met in the past by indicating that the aisles were to be used when going from one part of the room to another, rather than going "as the crow flies." Regulation of this kind, however, was not favorably received. Remarks about traffic lanes and stop lights as being the next innovations would be heard. The general reaction was that it was like school, and the girls resented regimentation. On occasion an office would become strict, but enforcement would only be effective for a week or so. Soon the girls would violate the regulation in large numbers, so that management had no choice but to overlook infraction.

Mr. Barr, the district superintendent, had decided he would live with whatever confusion the habits of these girls caused. He was not going to make an issue of so small a matter. On one occasion, however, he had tried a little experiment. He noted that girls frequently

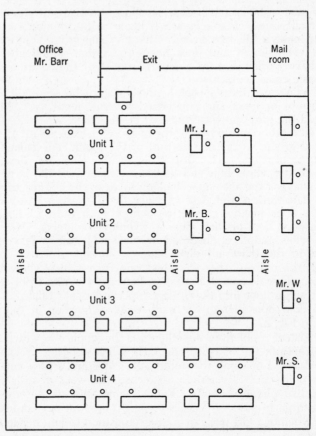

Fig. 17. Office plan for Case 1. The circles represent permanent work positions. Other girls (not shown) also use the space. The managers' desks and aisles are also indicated.

deposited mail in the mail box next to the door on their trips out of the office. He reasoned that if he removed the mail box from the position near the door and placed it in the left front corner near his office and then purchased another mail box and placed it in the right front corner (near the mail room) these mail boxes might serve to draw the girls toward the outer aisles and reduce the amount of diagonal traffic through the middle of the room. However, the results were disappointing. The girls continued to go directly to the door, then proceeded to the right or left to one of the mail boxes. Also, complaints were made about the unhandy positions of the mail boxes. With this personal experience and the failure to handle the problem in other offices as a background, Mr. Barr made no further attempts to correct this problem for a number of years.

However, the problem was reopened when Mr. Jones, who managed the group at the front of the room, came to Mr. Barr and said that Mr. Smith's girls (the unit at the back of the room) were disturbing the work of his girls by constantly cutting through the unit. He felt that Mr. Barr should do something about it.

Mr. Barr was participating in the human relations training conferences during this period and chose this problem for solution by the democratic method. He first had a conference with his managers, and among the problems discussed was the confusion in the office caused by girls cutting through units. Mr. Smith thought that perhaps his girls were the worst offenders and that he should give the problem attention. However, Mr. Jones commented that any greater problem among Smith's girls was due to their location in the room. This comment was particularly interesting in the light of Mr. Jones' earlier complaint. It was felt that the habits and attitudes of the girls were basic in the problem and that these might best be influenced by letting them work out a solution. Thus the decision at this meeting was for each manager to put the problem to his group.

On a Wednesday morning all four units held meetings. The office condition was stated as a problem, and no criticism was made. From the reactions of the girls it was apparent that they too were bothered by the interferences and interruptions. Suggestions for correcting the situation were soon made. In all groups the solution decided upon was to use the center and outer aisles in leaving their positions. The aisle to be used by each of the girls was worked out in detail.

One thing was not clearly understood, however. The original plan was to have the managers report their group's solution to Mr. Barr, and the managers were then to see whether the solutions could be integrated. However, one of the units immediately put its solution into practice. When this was done the other three units put their solutions into effect, so that by Wednesday noon 79 out of 80 girls were functioning in accordance with the new plan. The small differences in the solutions were unimportant and in no way interfered with the execution of the plan as a whole. Since there was general acceptance of the plan, good morale, and a high degree of execution of the decision reached, the experiment was considered a success.

However, consideration had to be given to the case of the individual who did not go along with the solution. At first it was felt that this one girl, Mary Comstock, might cause the plan to fail in the long run. Her behavior was of particular interest. Mr. Barr described Mary's exit as one of determination. He believed she clicked her heels harder on the floor and tilted her chin higher than formerly. When asked how he felt about her, he laughed and said he thought she was d—n cute. The fact that there was no feeling that Mary had shown insubordination indicated a further benefit in the use of the democratic procedure. Further investigation revealed that Mary had not participated in the discussion, and her manager believed that she was formerly one of the few girls who used the aisles.

It should also be noted that Mary's work had been under question. She did an excellent job in dealing with her phone contacts, but she was unsatisfactory in keeping her books. Because she was good on one phase of her work but weak on another phase, she had been the subject of discussion for transfers or discharge. However, her good qualities usually won out in these deliberations.

Anyway, the problem of Mary's exceptional behavior in the room was present and served as a source of concern. Discussion of the matter soon led to the belief that 79 girls would influence her more than she would influence them. It seemed that Mary's problem was now one of "saving face." It was hoped that after a weekend Mary might feel differently and go along with the group. Monday morning, therefore, was somewhat anxiously awaited. On Monday Mary continued to violate her group's decision on her first trip out of the office. However, on the next occasion she leisurely conversed with a couple of friends and then went out with them, their way. Thereafter, Mary followed the group decision. It was the belief of those who observed Mary's behavior that she had found a way of "saving face."

During the next few weeks all the girls practiced the solution. Now and then a girl would start to cut through a unit, stop, giggle in embarrassment, and then follow the route agreed upon. However, Mary came to Mr. Barr's office and requested a transfer. Mr. Barr was concerned because he feared that she might have been hurt by the social pressure. He asked her what type of job she wished, and she requested a specific job in the company—one that required dealings with people but that had no book work. Mr. Barr realized that this was exactly the job that Mary was fitted to do. He not only granted her request but asked her to choose the office in the city in which she preferred to work. He expected her to choose an office that had a higher prestige value than the present one, or one nearer her home. However, she asked to remain in the same building so that she could continue with the same friends. It seemed that Mary had no wish to escape from the group because of any shame she could have felt.

Because the solution to the office problem was worked out so easily Mr. Barr wondered whether the democratic technique should be given full credit. Maybe he had underestimated the cooperative spirit of his girls and had shied away from the problem unnecessarily. He therefore decided to make a test. After carefully considering the possibility of making a decision that no one could reasonably criticize he hit upon the idea of changing the glass in the door at the front of the room. This glass was opaque, and he had feared that some day someone would be hit with it, particularly since it swung both ways. One Saturday, therefore, he changed the opaque glass for transparent glass.

The next Monday he watched for reactions. He noted much looking in the direction of the door. Girls would speak to each other and then look in the direction of the door. By noon he had three complaints. One of them merely asked why the same kind of glass couldn't be put back if the window had been broken. Another pointed out that the new glass wasn't nice looking and bothered the girls. The third pointed out that the glare from the glass greatly interfered with her work. Interestingly enough, the third girl had to turn more than a 90-degree angle in order to face the glass.

On the basis of the complaints Mr. Barr put the problem to the group. He pointed out that he had replaced the glass not realizing that it made a difference. He was willing to make changes, but wondered what it was that bothered them. The criticisms given were unclear until one girl mentioned glare. Then all the girls set upon this as being very noticeable. He asked the group to help him find the best way to correct the matter. It was soon agreed that a shade be put on the window.

The shade was purchased and installed. Since then no one has taken the pains or the interest to see that the shade is drawn.

During the next two years we obtained reports on how the solution to the traffic problem in the office was holding up. Except for the deviations already reported, no violations have occurred. This record holds despite the fact that many new girls were hired during this period. Management people have not instructed the new girls, but in some way or other the new girls learn. The new manner of leaving the office has apparently become part of the culture in this office.

CASE 2. A PROBLEM OF EFFICIENCY IN A REPAIR CREW

This case is selected because it illustrates how a solution obtained from group discussion may be of high quality and, indeed, may be superior to one an expert might have devised. This characteristic of high quality in some group decisions is in addition to the benefits that arise because of the improved motivation and cooperative attitudes that invariably accompany group decision. The last two factors alone are sufficient to make group decisions effective, even when some of them may be of inferior quality from the point of view of experts. However, one must also appreciate the fact that in group decisions those who do the work frequently utilize and evaluate experiences in solving problems that higher levels of management may fail to know about or fully appreciate. Since management frequently fears that decisions of a lesser quality may be adopted by group decisions, it is desirable to highlight this feature.

This case was handled by a repair foreman in the telephone industry. Repairmen work individually and so have no direct supervision when on the job. The crew in this case involved 12 men.

The number of visits a repairman can make varies with the types of repairs he happens to be assigned, but over a period of a month the score in terms of the average number of visits per day gives a fairly accurate account of the efficiency of a crew or of a man. For the crew under consideration the number of repairs per man per day averaged between 8 and 9 visits over a period of 6 months. The foreman was asked by his boss to improve his record, since the company average was 10.8 visits per man per day.

The foreman had finished his training in democratic supervision and decided to apply the procedure to this problem. He, therefore, held a group meeting and asked his men if they had any ideas on how their work could be better coordinated. He wished to know whether there were obstacles and difficulties that they thought might be overcome and whether these might come to light if the group sat down and discussed various phases of the job. In his presentation of the problem he avoided any criticism of the relative standing of his crew. The group agreed that such a discussion would be worthwhile, and their attitude was one of a sincere desire to be helpful.

The group readily came up with criticisms on the way the job was organized. For example, the group agreed that there were too many *repeats*. A repeat is defined as a further report of trouble (second, third, etc., reports) from a station (customer) within 30 days after a repairman has visited the job. Repeats, therefore, indicate that the repair job was not properly done by a repairman or that the instrument went out of commission a second time for some new cause. A new cause cannot easily be prevented, but the first indicates poor workmanship. The proportion of repeats that is unavoidable is not known. The company practice for handling repeats is to send a more highly skilled workman on repeats, it being assumed that if the first man fails to correct the difficulty a more skilled man might. The group felt that this procedure was wrong. In the first place it did not permit a man to learn new things, and in the second place they were interested in knowing the outcome of their efforts. Thus the plan in force lacked motivation and deprived them of a sense of progress in developing skills, and it denied them experiences in success and failure which are useful in learning.

In order to solve this problem the group recommended that on all repeats the man who previously visited the station should be allowed to go back and that the foreman should go along with him in order to help him locate the difficulty. This suggestion was particularly interesting because the men were actually asking for training. Ordinarily men resist training, since it appears that when the foreman suggests training he is finding fault. Criticism leads to defensive reactions. When the difficulty is discussed as a problem, the men are in a situation conducive to constructive problem-solving behavior. Furthermore, by having the foreman visit the job with them they are protected from unfair evaluation and criticism.

Another item was then brought up for consideration. This was the time wasted in travel. The company practice was to send a man on a new assignment as soon as he became available. Thus the order in which jobs were assigned depended upon the order in which repair calls were received and the order in which the men completed their last jobs. The purpose of this practice was to keep the number of *subsequents* as low as possible. (A subsequent is a second or third call from a customer before a repairman arrives. The company believed that one of the ways of giving good customer service was to keep subsequents at a minimum. It was felt that when a repairman did not arrive as soon as a customer felt he should public relations suffered. For this reason the company kept accurate records on the percentage of calls that were in the nature of subsequents.)

The crew recommended that the district in which they worked be divided into 10 territories. A map was used to make up these divisions, so that about an equal amount of work would be required in each of the 10 territories. There were 12 men in the crew, and 10 men were to be given a territory. The remaining 2 men were to be *floaters*. The plan was that floaters would cover the whole district and that each of the 10 men was to do repairs in his own territory whenever possible. The floaters were to be used primarily to make up for irregular fluctuations in the repair load. The men were very particular about their territories and did not want other men working in them if it could be avoided. They also made a provision to guide the foreman in giving assignments to floaters in a territory. This was that any service call received should be honored within an hour.

In addition, provision was made for such marked changes in load as occur after storms, fires, etc. It was agreed that although the ten men were to work primarily in their own territories they could be moved into adjacent territories. By this procedure men could be pulled into trouble areas and leave single men to cover one (or even more) territories adjacent to their own. This plan allowed for the concentration of several men in any given section of the city and at the same time required the least amount of travel time. It was felt that by this plan more work would be accomplished and that the frequency of subsequents likewise would be reduced.

The remainder of the meeting was spent discussing which men were to function in each territory or capacity. Two men who liked driving elected to be floaters. At the end of the meeting the men expressed pride in the territories assigned them and acted as if they owned them.

All felt that a good job had been done to improve efficiency, and each felt pleased with his new responsibilities. The group did not set a "bogey," but all agreed they could beat the company average. The foreman regarded the plans to be far superior to any he could have worked out. Interesting also is the fact that a steward was a member of the crew and was one of the more creative participants in the discussion.

After the discussion there seemed to be an improved work interest. During the next 2½ years the effectiveness of the plan also reflected itself in the objective records. On the following items (which the company used to measure service) definite improvements were found.

1. Repeats, which previously averaged over 17 per cent of all service calls, now were held down to an average of 4 per cent.

2. Subsequents, which previously occurred about 20 per cent of the time, also fell to 4 per cent.

3. The number of visits per man per day rose from an average of 8.5 to an average of 12.5, while the company average remained below 11. Table 15 shows the individual performance of every man in the crew, both before and after the discussion. Before the group-decision method was used, the range in the number of visits was from 6 to 14. Since then the range in the average number of visits is from 9 to 18.

TABLE 15

PRODUCTION RECORD

| | Average Number of Visits per Day | |
Repairman	Before	After
A	14	18
B	12	17
C	10	15
D	10	14
E	8	13
F	8	13
G	8	11
H	7	12
I	7	11
J	7	9
K	6	9
L	6	9
Total	103	151
Average per man	8.5	12.5

The men are proud of their performance and take pride in having an outstanding record. They speak of having "licked" *repeats* and *subsequents* and are on the lookout for new problems.

This particular foreman has used the democratic technique to solve many of the day-to-day problems, and it is difficult to know how much of the above improvement to assign to the plan the men worked out and how much to assign to the morale he has achieved by his activities on other problems. That this foreman is highly popular is indicated by the fact that the company had difficulty in moving men out of his crew and that requests frequently are received from repairmen who wish to be transferred into his crew. On one occasion a union leader asked a member of his company, "What has that big Swede got on his men so that they won't cooperate with us in running some test cases? None of his men will give us a complaint so that we can get a good test on some of the grievances." This foreman did not have an unusual record before his training.

˙CASE 3. A PROBLEM OF ASSIGNING UNPLEASANT JOBS IN A REPAIR CREW

This case is selected because it is characteristic of the manner in which men solve problems involving prestige and seniority rights. At the same time it illustrates how the men on the job are aware of company objectives and do not take advantage of the company or of each other when allowed to solve problems in a constructive atmosphere.

The problem arose because a repair foreman in the telephone industry could not get men to clear *wet-weather drops*. A wet-weather drop is a defective line that runs from a pole to a building. These lines have to be replaced from time to time because water seeps through the insulation and creates a short. Thus after a rain there are reports of trouble, but since the trouble is present only when the line is wet the problem is purely temporary. During World War II, when replacement material was at a minimum, many lines suffered from this wet-weather difficulty. If a station is out of order for this reason the problem is not so serious as if the station were out for some other reason. Hence the company as well as the men regard wet-weather drops as less serious than emergency jobs. Furthermore, these men do not like to do this "unimportant" work, and they feel that anyone can do it without thinking. As a consequence, the men make little effort to get these jobs done. If the foreman decides to pressure men into bringing in a few wet-weather drops he finds himself at a disadvantage. The men may promise to pick up one or two and then fail to do so. When asked why, they can claim that they ran into extra difficulty on an emergency job and say, "You wanted me to do a good job on the others first, didn't you, boss?" Although the foreman may know the men are shirking, he never knows on what occasion the excuse is justified. It thus comes about that wet-weather drops are a headache to the foreman. When he gets far enough behind, he puts one man on the job full time and lets him clear wet-weather drops. The man in question feels degraded and wonders why he is picked on. To be as fair as possible, this job is usually given to the man with least seniority. He may complain that he has had the least seniority for the past five years, but among supervisory groups this is considered the fairest way to handle the situation. The company invokes seniority on such jobs, believing that is what the men want, and, anyway, only one man has the least seniority.

In a particular crew of 12 men the number of wet-weather drops was gradually accumulating, and the time was approaching when something would have to be done about the matter. The foreman decided that this was a good problem for group decision. He told his men that he realized no one liked to clear wet-weather drops and that he wanted to have their reactions on how the problem should be handled.

Of interest is the fact that no one in the group felt that a man with the least seniority should always do the job. A man with most seniority talked against the idea of picking on the fellow with least seniority, saying that he hated being stuck with the job when he had the least seniority, and that he couldn't see why everybody shouldn't do a share of it. It was soon agreed that the job should be evenly divided among the crew. This crew divided up the job by area. (Other groups have divided a pool of wet-weather drops.) Each man was to be responsible for wet-weather drops in his area, and he was to be given a list of those in his area. Each morning the local test desk was to assign a particular drop for each man, and he was to clear this one, if at all possible. This condition took care of clearing up the drops that were most essential from the point of view of the office. In addition, all agreed that each man should clear as many additional drops as his load permitted. However, when a man had cleared up all the wet-weather drops in his area, it was specifically understood that he should not be asked to help out another. This last condition clearly reveals an attitude built up over the years. It is evident that the reluctance to clear wet-weather drops hinged on the idea that, when a man was conscientious, advantage was taken of him. Soon he got to be the "sucker" in the group, or perhaps the foreman's pet. It was evident that all men were willing to do their part, but they did not wish to run the risk of being made a "sucker." Other foremen have testified that this defensive reaction made sense from the manner in which the job is frequently handled. The foreman wants to get the job done, and soon he begins to rely on those individuals who have cooperated in the past. Soon these men find they are doing all the undesirable jobs. It is just a matter of how long it takes a man to find out that he is losing out with the group.

The results of the discussion were immediately apparent. Over a 3-month period previous to the discussion a total of 80 wet-weather drops had been cleared. The week after the discussion 78 wet-weather drops were cleared without any let-up on the rest of the work, and within a few months the problem was practically non-existent. The reaction of the men also bore out the effectiveness of the decision. Men discussed the number of drops they had cleared and showed a friendly competitive spirit. They discussed the dates when they expected to be caught up and would only have to take care of wet-weather drops as they arose. All agreed that they had solved the problem in the only possible manner.

This solution is typical of all cases that involve an unpleasant assignment and temporary transfers to undesirable locations. The group solution is never one of choosing an individual, but one of sharing equally. The group argues that if everybody does a piece of the unpleasant work or does it for a while the job can be done without its being a burden to anyone. Now and then certain individuals are exempted from taking turns, but this usually happens when certain individuals are needed elsewhere, or when their skills are superior. Then it is agreed that these individuals cannot be spared from more important work, and the remainder of the group divides up the unpleasant assignment. On one occasion a stubborn individual held out and said he would not take turns. The group excused him from the rotation plan. The next day he asked to be included.

CASE 4. PROBLEM OF ALLOTTING A NEW TRUCK TO INSTALLATION CREW

This problem is of interest primarily because the group discussion was initially reported as a failure. The nature of the final solution is typical in that group values are considered whenever a problem is presented to the group, and hence this phase of the problem merely supplements Case 3 in this regard. However, the large number of values that had to be integrated poses interesting possibilities.

The problem and the values associated with it arose primarily because of the difficulty of purchasing trucks during automobile shortage of World War II and afterwards. As a consequence, the average truck in use was older than normal, and the acquisition of a new truck by a crew was a special event. One of the foremen in a training class had just received word that he was getting a new truck, and, since hard feelings and charges of favoritism invariably arose whenever the foreman determined who should get the new truck, he decided to let the group make the decision.

The following week he reported his results to the training class. He said that he called the crew together, informed them of the good fortune of receiving a new truck, remarked that he didn't have any opinions on who should get it, and said that he would leave the matter entirely up to them. After an hour he returned and found that the men were still wrangling. He felt that the group-discussion method had failed because the men were unable to arrive at group agreement. He asked what to do in such a case. Was he to make the decision? The class discussed his problem and immediately put its finger on the difficulty. He had used the laissez-faire technique, since he was not present to lead the discussion. He readily agreed to try it again and to remain with the group.

The following week he reported his findings. He put the problem in terms of what would be the fair thing to do. The following group values were brought to light during the discussion.

1. The man with most seniority is entitled to consideration.
2. The man that has most driving to do should have a good truck.
3. The man with the poorest truck should get a break.
4. The man with the best accident record should receive some consideration.
5. The best producer should be rewarded in some way.

Each of these items can be seen as important by a disinterested party, and it will be apparent that each item would be of particular importance to some member of the group. Thus differences in values come to the surface, and if the members fail to function as a group a clash in selfish interests is inevitable. However, if the differences in values are considered to be the crux of the problem the question becomes one of resolving conflicting forces, rather than one of finding out who will win.

The proper method of weighting the importance of each of the values would be a challenge to any expert, and few foremen would welcome such an assignment. However, the group resolved the problem in 30 minutes. The details of the solution are too complex to report. Suffice it to say that every man in the crew got a different truck. There was a complete reshuffling of trucks, and each man felt that he had gained. Thus one new truck meant something pleasant in the work of all, rather than a large gain for one.

When the new truck arrived, the garage was the center of holiday spirits. Equipment was hurriedly shifted from truck to truck; there was much whistling, and the talk was gay. The foreman reported that he had never seen such enthusiasm before. The time lost in arriving at a solution and putting the solution into effect was not apparent from the production records.

CASE 5.   PROBLEM OF MAKING UP A LOST DAY IN A CUSTOMER BILLING UNIT

This case was selected because it involved a group decision in a large group. It illustrates that agreements can successfully be reached in large groups and shows how the respecting of group values may cause the group to rise to an emergency. Generally motivation is high under emergency conditions because the group feels important and so accepts responsibility. Responsibility, however, cannot be imposed on a group. The key factor in such conditions is a *willingness to accept* responsibility. To achieve this willingness one must know the values that employees place upon their roles in the task.

On the last day of the month Mr. Roberts, the supervisor in one of the offices of the accounting department, realized that something would have to be done about the fact that the billing of customers was a full day behind schedule. This condition arose because earlier in the month there had been a company-wide work stoppage for one day. On subsequent days the work had not been such as to make up the ground lost. On previous occasions overtime work was the solution to problems arising when, for one reason or another, something occurred that prevented the maintaining of a fixed schedule. Since this was a Friday morning and it was obvious that the job could not be finished, Mr. Roberts assumed that the girls would have to work all day on Saturday. However, he had not announced this decision. The girls, either through the grapevine or because of the previous way the problem had been handled, seemed disturbed on Friday morning because of a rumor about Saturday work. Several told Mr. Roberts' deputy supervisors that they could not work on Saturday. Consequently Mr. Roberts, who had previously used the group-decision procedure on other problems, realized that he had a problem on his hands. He had assumed that the girls would be willing to work on Saturday, but he now feared that there might be widespread opposition to the idea.

Mr. Roberts was in charge of the work of 110 girls, and all of them were involved in this problem. He decided to use the group procedure and to meet them in two separate groups.

At each meeting he stated his problem in terms of the necessity of getting the job out on time and getting back on schedule. No reference was made to the reason for being off schedule. The problem, as he put it, was to determine the best way of handling the situation. He made it clear that he was obligated to get the bills out on time and wondered if the girls had any ideas on how this might best be accomplished.

In the meeting with the first of the two groups of girls there was general opposition to working Saturday, but there was no objection to working overtime on Friday. Mr. Roberts pointed out that by law girls were limited to a 10-hour day, and that permitted only 2½ hours overtime. Nevertheless, the girls felt this was adequate. When Mr. Roberts pointed out that, according to his records, they were a full day behind and that this could hardly be made up in 2½ hours, the girls replied that by putting in extra effort all day they could accomplish a good deal. If they could get a little extra help, they felt, they could do the whole job. He agreed that extra help was a possibility worth considering, but even with it he still had his doubts. He asked, "What will we do if we do not finish with overtime Friday night?" To this the girls responded, "If we don't finish, then we will work Saturday." But several added, "Don't worry, we won't have to work Saturday." Gaining some confidence himself, Mr. Roberts explored further the kind of added help that was needed. With little difficulty it was settled that two extra comptometer operators would be adequate. These he promised to attempt to obtain. It was agreed also that the final solution would be contingent upon the opinions of the other group of girls, and that, if they agreed, the plan would be followed. It was also agreed that he would stay with them and do his end of the job. The meeting required a little over half an hour.

The second group of girls met almost immediately after the first. Apparently some communication between members of the two sections occurred. Anyway, the second group was of a similar opinion about working overtime on Friday. When Mr. Roberts mentioned the fact that two comptometer operators could be borrowed, the second group agreed to the plan already decided upon by the first group. This meeting took less than a half hour, and there was a general good feeling among the members of this group, similar to that found in the first group.

By 10:00 A.M. all the girls were back on the job. Their spirits were high, and there was more talk and laughter than usual. When the two comptometer operators arrived, members of the teams to which they had been assigned during the discussion took charge of them and planned their work. Inter-team spirit was displayed in the way various groups of girls helped out others. Each kept track of the progress of the others, and, if one group fell behind, those who had finished came over to help.

It should also be mentioned that a previously planned "shower" was also held. Usually a shower pretty much destroys the latter part of an afternoon. On this occasion Mr. Roberts witnessed the snappiest shower he had ever seen. It took exactly 5 minutes. Everyone was excited and joined in the fun, but the party started and stopped as if signals had been called.

The girls took a half hour to eat at the company cafeteria. Mr. Roberts joined the groups and gathered from their conversation that they intended to set a record. He enjoyed the groups and felt that he was welcome in their midst as never before.

The job was finished at 7:30 P.M., one-half hour ahead of the deadline. There was no evidence of fatigue, and he agreed that he had never seen the equal of such enthusiasm. Nor had he ever had a day when so little supervision was demanded of him.

On Monday Mr. Roberts reported this experience of making up a lost day to his supervisor, Mr. Jones. Mr. Jones was skeptical. He suggested that certain blocks of work probably were overlooked. Mr. Roberts immediately checked and reported that there had been no oversights. Mr. Jones then suggested that there must be many errors. A subsequent check showed that the errors for the month were distinctly lower than for previous months.

Of great satisfaction was the fact that no one in the organization familiar with the job suggested that the reason for the remarkable accomplishments was poor performance on other days. All agreed that the job of doing two days' work in one was the result of effort definitely beyond the call of duty.

Mr. Roberts' ability to use the democratic group technique was exceptional, and it should not be supposed that large numbers of persons can always be as readily brought to as satisfactory a group decision as in this case. By consistently using the democratic technique Mr. Roberts, although in charge of a very large unit, was able to keep close to his group, and as a consequence he became one of the most popular supervisors. Whereas formerly the girls had sometimes referred to him as "sourpuss," they now talked about his "dry" sense of humor and loved this characteristic. When he was transferred to a new location, the girls in his unit were ready to raise an objection. However, when they found that the new job was a distinct promotion, they were highly pleased with his success.

CASE 6. CUSTOMER CONSIDERATION IN GROUP DECISION

This case has been selected both because it illustrates how group discussion may serve a training function and because it shows that employees will think much like management when they are given responsibility.

A common fear among management personnel is that if employees make decisions regarding production problems they will tend to consider only their own attitudes and overlook the customers. This fear is related to another closely associated with it. It is that employees will not take a long-range viewpoint but will consider only the more immediate objectives. A common belief is that management alone will do long-range planning. It is quite likely that these fears are well founded. Nevertheless, the basis of these fears may be overcome if management supplies the problems and the proper questions.

In one of the companies concerned with this problem it was an important policy to give the customer high-quality service so as to maintain public goodwill. Girls, therefore, were trained to give the most courteous treatment to customers over the telephone. At some stages in the training even the proper words and phrases to use in answering queries were supplied, to produce the most favorable effect. Pains were taken to organize the job so that the customer was kept waiting the least possible amount of time. Careful measures were also developed to evaluate this service. Even after a girl was trained to do a perfect job in answering questions, dispensing information, and using considerate phrases the company was not satisfied. Training programs were started to improve the way the remarks were made, to teach the girls to use words that were adapted to the customer as well as the situation, and to eliminate stereotypy and coolness. Thus the new kind of training was instituted to teach the girls to be "warm" in their contacts with customers.

The company was seeking very high standards. A great demand was now made upon the girls' attitudes and personalities. Could these things be taught? Difficulties were encountered because the girls accused management personnel of being inconsistent in their teaching. They complained that one supervisor told them they should have said, "You're welcome," on a given occasion, but another told them they were overdoing the phrase. Under these conditions how could the girls tell what a given supervisor wanted? Frequently the girls felt "picked on" and began to accuse the company of protecting customers regardless of how unreasonable they were. Sometimes there were tears and anger over problems of this sort.

One supervisor decided to put the problem to the girls in terms of, "What kind of service do you think we should give customers?" He wanted to know what the girls thought about the problem. "You have been drilled and trained from above up to this point. What does the situation look like after experience with customers?"

This discussion revealed that the girls were confused as to what the company wanted, that they felt spied upon, that they were trained to the point where they could not be themselves or talk like normal people. They talked about how they thought customers should be treated and believed that if they themselves were freer they could talk to customers more naturally. They compared themselves to recording machines. It was their view that the customer was not always right, but that he should always be treated as if he were right, since he may have misunderstood. Soon the girls talked about how the job should be done. The standards they began to set for service were higher than the company had set. The girls suggested ways of giving faster service, ways for the company to avoid injuring customers' feelings (such as better reminders to customers for unpaid bills), and little ways of pleasing customers. And, as they discussed the problem, their attitude toward unreasonable customers began to improve so that they became very constructive in their attitudes toward difficult customers.

Since no objective or solution was demanded from the problem as stated, the meeting ended after the various issues had been fully discussed.

The following month the service in the office improved on all counts, whereas other offices showed no similar change. Most improvement was shown in the service measure, which dealt with the "warmth" of the customer contact. The very aspect that seemed to escape training procedures became the aspect of the job that improved most.

A change in the attitude of the girls was also noticeable. One expressed it this way: "Before, when we talked to a customer, we had to think about what the supervisor would want us to say. Now, we are able to pay full attention to the customer." This remark is very illuminating. It represents a shift in attention to the customer, where it rightly belongs. Too rigid training requires attention of the supervisor, who in effect stands in the background as a critic, or it requires too much attention to the medium of expression rather than to the person receiving the message. This difference in attention is very important. In acts of skill one must eventually learn to attend to the end rather than the means to the end. Thus we can play better tennis when we can forget our footwork and pay attention to the spot where we wish to place the ball. So it is in all performance. Attention must be properly placed to obtain the most out of the degree of skill we possess, and in dealings with people the person we are dealing with demands our full attention.

Thus we find that employees do take a considerate view toward customers when they have the opportunity to tell their side of the story and are given the responsibility of dealing with the problem. As long as management assumes the responsibility it is not fully accepted by the employee. Responsible behavior is dependent upon being given responsibility. It is psychologically sound to say that human beings are more likely to accept responsibility when it is given to them than when it is demanded of them. One may regulate behavior from the outside, but a sense of responsibility must be stimulated from within.

CASE 7. GROUP DECISIONS IN SETTING GOALS

One of the more common types of group-decision discussions is that of setting production goals or job-completion dates. In such instances it is particularly important that the supervisor refrain from criticizing present production. Rather, his interests should be in discovering what goals the group considers fair and in determining whether the group would be interested in setting goals. Would having specific goals make the job more interesting, and would the group feel freer from supervisory criticism?

The common experience is one of finding such interests in the group and of discovering that the group frequently sets goals in excess of those the supervisor would demand if he set the goals himself. Most surprising, however, is the accuracy with which a group can set goals. In one instance the company had set December 31 as the deadline for terminal cleaning work, a routine inspection job that had to be done in all locations throughout the city once each year. This was an unpleasant job and was carried in addition to the usual load. In one crew the men not only decided how the job should be done but they set a new deadline for December 20. The job was completed December 19, ahead of all other groups, some of which were unable to make the company deadline.

This accuracy of achieving the goals that are set, even when they are high, applies also to situations in which there are factors beyond the control of the individuals. One group of girls in training as service representatives set a goal of one *delay* in 15 calls. (A delay is a customer contact in which the customer must wait more than a minute before the service representative can obtain the needed information.) It is regarded as poor service to keep a customer waiting more than one minute. Since the difficulty of obtaining information from records varies with the type of situation, some delays are inevitable. The objective, however, is to keep these delays at a minimum, and the company measures service in terms of the frequency of delays. This group of trainees had a record of 1 delay in 6 calls for a 2-week period before setting the goal. For the 2 weeks after the goal was set the delays numbered 1 in 21 calls. During the same periods two experienced groups of service representatives averaged 1 delay in 12 calls. That inexperienced girls could set a goal higher than the record that prevailed in the regular office and then set about to surpass the goal is a startling experience. And one cannot assume that the goal was achieved at the expense of other service measurements, since these did not suffer.

In order to describe the process of setting and achieving goals that seem so accurate, even when they appear to be, in part, beyond the direct control of the individuals, we have selected the case of tardiness in an accounting department office for more detailed discussion. In this unit, in which 27 girls worked, tardiness had been high for some time, and previous efforts to correct the condition had failed. As a consequence, the problem had not been approached for some time. Mr. Green, the supervisor, decided that this might be a good problem to test the group-decision method.

At the time, tardiness for this group regularly exceeded 7.5 per cent each month. The departmental average was 3.6 per cent and was based on the records of over 400 girls.

In putting the problem to the group Mr. Green pointed out that work could more easily be scheduled and there would be less inconvenience to others if he had some idea of the extent of tardiness to expect. He wanted to be fair about it, however, realizing that there were good reasons for being tardy. Would the group be willing to discuss the problem and set some kind of objective?

The girls were a bit puzzled at first by the approach, and so he had to encourage discussion. Mr. Green pointed out that he thought that the group's discussion was important, since management frequently looks at these problems from its own point of view. The girls became interested and wanted to know what was done in other units; whether their own record was worse than that of other units; how their record compared, etc. Mr. Green supplied information as it was requested. He then turned the discussion to the various types of reasons for tardiness. This led to a rather free and frank discussion during which the girls interacted with each other. The usual reasons, such as oversleeping, missing a particular bus, a bus being late, having to do an errand, being delayed here and there, a slow watch, forgetting to watch the time, poor elevator service, etc., were mentioned and evaluated. The girls felt that recognition should be given to many of these causes, but they also felt that many of the reasons could be overcome if they didn't try to get to work exactly on the dot. More and more the feeling was expressed that they might try to arrive a few minutes early, and if Mr. Green recognized when they got there early he might not mind their being late occasionally. He agreed that he wanted to be fair about the whole thing and that the purpose of the discussion was to make for more tolerance.

The subject was then turned to setting some reasonable figure. To Mr. Green's surprise, figures such as 2, 2.5, and 3 per cent were mentioned. He told them that these figures seemed to be low and that they were being too strict. The group felt that its record should be better than average and put Mr. Green's objections aside.

Soon the girls were divided quite evenly between the 2 and 3 per cent figures, so that a compromise at 2.5 per cent was unanimously agreed upon as the goal.

During the following two months this unit attained a record of 2.1 per cent. However, during the second month Mr. Green became aware of certain undesirable features. As a matter of fact, he feared that in correcting one problem he might have created a worse one. The girls in the unit began making disparaging remarks about girls in other units who frequently were late. He noticed that in the elevators and during working hours the girls were acting as though their unit was better than other units.

When a solution does not produce the desired results, the procedure recommended is to face the new situation as a new problem. As a matter of fact, it is desirable to re-examine any solution after it has been put into practice and determine whether or not the group is satisfied. Mr. Green, therefore, had a second group meeting on the subject of tardiness.

In this meeting he wanted to find out whether or not the group had been too strict with themselves. He was proud of the record the girls had set, but thought it was too hard to maintain and told them so. Would they not like to relax the goal a bit? The response was negative. They had not been inconvenienced; rather they liked it much better than before because everybody got to work on time. One girl pointed out that she merely moved her alarm clock ahead 5 minutes and didn't miss the difference in sleep. As a matter of fact, she was less hurried in the morning and had a happier breakfast. Another pointed out that she got up earlier and didn't have to race a couple of blocks for fear of missing her bus. Others agreed that there were no reasons for changing.

Mr. Green next raised the question of whether their excellent record might not make them critical of other units that could not boast of such a record. Several thought this was a possibility. They also thought that their own decision should not be used to influence others. The girls agreed that any attempt to influence others would lead to hard feelings. After some discussion along these lines Mr. Green wondered whether they would not like to make their goal a bit more elastic. The best he was able to obtain from the group was a goal between 2.5 and 3 per cent.

A year and a half later the writer obtained the subsequent results of this unit's record. The adverse effects seemed to have entirely disappeared. The girls ceased all evidence of a critical attitude after the second meeting, and the question of tardiness has never again been discussed. During these 18 months this unit has had the best tardiness record of all the units. In no month did it exceed 3 per cent, although the departmental average never went below 3.6 per cent and other units continued to exert efforts to keep their tardiness within the limits considered reasonable by management.

Factory Situations

CASE 8.   UNLOADING FREIGHT CARS IN A FACTORY

A natural question arises about the limitations of the group-decision technique. Can it be used only where employees are fairly well educated or where the morale is already very high? The author's experience in factories is limited, but in one industry a group of foremen and higher management personnel has been trained, and a few of their cases are cited. The trained group of men were members of a department whose duty it was to keep production lines stocked. The men were known as material handlers. The group trained was not selected either because of superior or inferior ability to handle people. Rather they represented a cross section of the factory's first and intermediate levels of management.

The first of these cases is of particular interest because the question of a good day's work is involved. Whenever added activities are introduced into a job, men become suspicious and tend to develop protective attitudes. Thus human relations problems arise whenever changes are introduced into the work situation.

When the company changed to a different vendor of car doors, the method of shipping the doors was changed from truck to railroad boxcars. Unloading of boxcars had been tried for about 10 days with very low production. With trucks the crew had been able to unload an average of 3328 doors per day, but with boxcars the number had dropped to approximately 2000 doors per day.

To hold the doors in place in the boxcars long dunnage bars, weighing about 55 pounds each, were fitted into slots along the sides of the car. It was necessary to remove the bars before unloading the doors and to replace them in the cars after the doors were unloaded. When doors were shipped by truck, dunnage bars were not used. Each boxcar held 720 rear doors or 432 front doors; for either type 120 dunnage bars were needed to hold the doors in place. The rear doors weighed 43 pounds each, and the front doors approximately 50 pounds each. It was necessary to unload an average of 1664 doors, or 3 carloads, on each of two shifts in order to keep up with production. This volume might vary between the two shifts, provided the total output equaled 3328 doors per day.

Three classifications of workers were involved in the unloading of doors. These were material handlers, material handler leaders, and powered-truck drivers. Sixteen men and 2 drivers were needed on the evening shift, and 12 men and 2 drivers on the day shift. Due to the congestion in the unloading area on the day shift, fewer men could be used than on the evening shift.

The job involved removing the bars from the boxcar and carrying or sliding the doors to the conveyor, which ran parallel to and about 6 feet away from the side of the boxcar. The conveyor carried the doors inside the plant, where they were removed by hand and stacked into racks. A PT truck moved the loaded racks from the conveyor to the door inspection and finishing area and set the racks beside the roller conveyor or stored them nearby. The doors were removed from the racks and placed on the conveyor, which moved them to the inspectors.

Because the change in carrier from truck to boxcar had involved the extra work of handling the bars, the men felt that additional help should be supplied. Since each bar weighed approximately the same as a door, the men reasoned that every bar moved was equivalent to moving a door. Since there were 120 bars per car and each bar had to be moved twice, 240 fewer doors were moved with the same amount of work. This resulted in approximately 2 less cars unloaded per day. The change from truck to boxcar was made without any preliminary warning or build-up on the part of supervision.

During working hours on the day shift Mr. Brown, the assistant superintendent, called a meeting of the men, their job and regional stewards, and the foreman and general foreman of the crew. He believed that any meeting of this nature required the presence of the union representatives in order to show the good faith and intentions of supervision. He, therefore, contacted the stewards a few minutes before the meeting, explained its purpose, and asked them to attend. In this way they could voice any objections at the meeting.

The meeting was held in the conference room near the material handling department. The assistant superintendent asked the job and regional stewards to sit at the head of the table. He opened the meeting by stating, "First of all, this is not a meeting but a discussion, and I want you all to feel free to say anything you want." He presented the problem to the group in this way: "We have to have an average of 6 carloads of doors unloaded per day. This is roughly 1664 doors per shift. What do you want or need, that we can give you, in order to get this much work done? You are the ones who are doing the work. You are closer to the job than we are, so we are asking you for your help, your suggestions and ideas, for getting this problem solved."

The meeting was then thrown open for free discussion in which Mr. Brown acted mostly as a listener but would occasionally bring the discussion back to the problem of unloading doors. Many constructive suggestions and ideas were aired, such as: "If we had a relief man for this crew the flow of doors would be steadier and faster. Could we get a relief man?" "Is it possible to have a few more racks available, so the men who unload the doors won't have to wait for a truck to return with an empty rack?" "How about getting some kind of weather protection for us men on the outside?" Mr. Brown assured them that he would do everything possible for them if it would help get the doors unloaded. The discussion was quite free, and everyone participated.

After about an hour the group asked for a restatement of the problem. The members of supervision were then asked to leave the room by the regional steward. After about 5 minutes they were called back, and the regional steward announced that the group agreed to unload the 6 carloads of doors a day, provided they got the relief man, more racks, and some sort of weather protection.

The total time for the meeting was about 1½ hours.

Since the discussion there has been no trouble in getting the 6 cars per day unloaded on two shifts. Competition has developed to see which shift can unload the most doors. Men of each shift ask the foreman for the number of doors unloaded by the previous shift, and then try to better the record. Consequently, instead of unloading 4 carloads per day in two 9-hour shifts, they now easily unload 6 cars on two 8-hour shifts, with the evening shift often starting on the seventh and occasionally the eighth car. No attempt has been made by the foreman to get more work done, nor has he pulled the men off the job and given them other work. Occasionally, towards the end of the shift, however, he has asked them to do other work, and the men have willingly cooperated. If the cars are not available for unloading, the men have also willingly accepted other work. If the last car is unloaded within one-half hour to an hour before quitting time the men are not assigned other jobs.

Since the meeting Mr. Brown believes that the company has won the confidence of the men and the union. He also believes that relations between the men and supervision has improved. When asked what they thought of meetings such as this, the group was unanimous in its approval and wanted similar meetings held more frequently. In fact, several men have approached the foreman about holding meetings *daily* to talk over job problems and other important subjects as they arise. Suggestions have become more frequent.

With an increase of only 6 per cent in working force, as a result of the meeting, production has been increased an average of 60 per cent to 75 per cent and has occasionally increased 90 per cent, and the volume of work formerly requiring 9 hours per shift is now being done in 8 hours or less. This is a reduction from 288 man-hours of labor per day to 264 man-hours of labor per day.

CASE 9. FACTORY HOUSEKEEPING PROBLEM

A problem in some departments is keeping materials, equipment, and surroundings in order. Management sometimes becomes so disturbed that the importance of housekeeping becomes exaggerated.

The foreman of a crew of over 21 men put the problem of "how to arrange our stockpiles so that all materials are easier to find and at the same time more accessible." The crew was very much interested in this problem, since the men thought the present arrangement was bad because (1) it made things hard to get to with a truck; (2) some piles were too high and created an accident hazard; (3) the most used materials were not the most accessible; and (4) the disorder resulting from the arrangements created a fire hazard.

The group then developed a plan that involved a complete rearrangement of the stock. The foreman accepted the plan and made the necessary arrangements with neighboring foremen. The crew then went to work and in two days completely rearranged the materials and stockpiles. Everyone worked hard and, without raising a question, many worked outside their job classification in order to be helpful. With all this extra work they carried on their regular job, so that no complaints of stock shortage were received from the production line. Neighboring foremen witnessed the process in amazement.

CASE 10. STOCKPILING COAL DURING AN EMERGENCY

A yard crew had the job of unloading coal from boats and railroad cars. They operated the equipment that unloaded coal and transferred it to bunkers that supplied the furnaces. They also operated company railroad cars and engines that hauled the coal to stockpiles. In order to keep the furnaces supplied for 24 hours the men had to transport 38 cars to the bunkers. When coal was available at the dock, 12 additional cars were stocked. When not available, coal was transported from stockpiles to bunkers. Ordinarily this crew handled 50 cars in a day. Thus, with coal coming in, 12 cars could be stocked.

The crew was made up of 30 men. They worked a 40-hour week, and their days off were staggered so that the job was covered 7 days a week.

A problem arose when a coal strike was threatened. The company had 3 months to stockpile coal. To reach the desired stockpile the company was willing to pay overtime, hire additional men, and do whatever else was needed to build up the stockpile. The company estimated that, if the men could handle 55 cars in an 8-hour day, overtime and some extra hands would create the desired stockpile. However, the problem was how to achieve this objective without disrupting morale. Long hours, temporary upgrading, jealousies, and friction were inevitable in a crew that was already having problems.

It was decided to put the problem to the crew. The company stated its needs in terms of the amount of coal necessary for the stockpile. The supervisor in charge of the meeting pointed out that overtime and extra help would be required and asked the men to aid in planning the job. In the discussion the production of an 8-hour day was used as the figure from which to determine the need for extra time. The men set 60 cars per day (22 for stockpiling) as a goal for the 8-hour day. They expressed their desire to work a 6-day week and to work overtime rather than hire extra men. The duties, involving job changes, temporary upgrading, and extra train crews, etc., were carefully planned so that all men would share in the extra pay and inconveniences in an equal manner. Men whose vacations fell during this period decided to give up vacation plans until the emergency was over.

The results were most gratifying. The company achieved the desired stockpile, and morale improved rather than declined. The supervisors involved all agreed that the cooperation was unusually good. There is evidence that morale is continuing to improve with subsequent use of the method of group decision.

The objective data reveal that an average of 31 cars were stocked during the 73-day period covering the emergency situation. This average takes into account the fact that on one day no coal was available for stocking, and that on other days the coal supply for stocking was limited. The highest record for stocking was 42 cars. Previously when the men worked an 8-hour day the coal handled was 11.73 tons per man-hour. During the emergency the coal handled was 11.99 tons per man-hour.

When one considers the fact that a 6-day week and long hours were worked, it is indicative of good morale to find that productivity per man-hour maintained itself. It is apparent that the crew did not take advantage of the fact that the company needed a stockpile and was willing to pay a high price in order to get it.

Problems Involving Promotions

The question of promotion is of particular interest in a human relations program, since the group values of favoritism and discrimination are so closely related to it. In so far as group values are involved it seems that group-decision methods might be helpful. However, the question of qualifications is also an important aspect of a promotion, and this source of information may involve confidential items and may be facilitated by tests, job analysis, and the judgment of experts. Thus in some respects the problem of promotion involves an area of freedom that belongs to a higher level, and at the same time concerns the attitudes of the group from which the promotion is made.

One way of reconciling this difference in the levels to which the problem belongs is to post the job and its qualifications, thus giving opportunity to those who wish to try for the job (interview, tests, etc.), but to leave the final selection to higher levels. The author has found this to be an effective procedure in the three known instances that it has been tried. Unqualified employees with greatest seniority do not apply, and at the same time do not feel that they have been by-passed. Frequently employees feel hurt, not because they wished the job, but because they have been by-passed.

Another method is to put the problem directly to the group and ask for recommendations. Those recommended will then have to compete. Will employees choose wisely under such conditions, or will they play politics?

We have had some opportunity to test the wisdom of groups in choosing an employee for promotion to group leader positions which are not management positions but nevertheless require some leadership ability. Since previously these promotions had been based largely upon seniority and since problems arose when a senior man sometimes was by-passed or when unqualified senior men were selected, management was willing to permit a test of group decision. The following case is typical of several such instances which have been reported.

CASE 11.   TEMPORARY UPGRADING PROBLEM

A material handler foreman was faced with the problem of selecting a member of his crew to fill in for his two inventory control men when they left on their vacations. In his crew were 22 men who were eligible for this opening. In the past the policy had been to promote the senior man, but the foreman knew that the best man did not always get the job when this procedure was followed. In his present crew, for example, he felt that the several men who had the most seniority would not be able to handle the job as well as some of the others who had less seniority.

He called his men together and explained that the second inventory control man would take his vacation after the first one returned. The man who would substitute for them while they were gone would be upgraded for about 5 weeks. He would first be trained for 2 weeks and would then take over the jobs when the regular men left. The foreman stressed the responsible nature of the job to the group and then asked them who they thought should get it. After a short discussion the man with the most seniority suggested that if anyone wanted a crack at the job he should speak up. The group thought that this was a good idea. After three men had volunteered the rest of the men decided that was sufficient. The top seniority men were *not* among those who volunteered. It was decided that the new temporary inventory control man would be selected from among three workers. Two of these men had much more seniority than the third.

The foreman later spoke to the volunteer with the most seniority and asked him if he thought he could handle the job. The worker replied that he had changed his mind, that he didn't feel it was worth all the trouble for a 5-week period. He also told the foreman which of the remaining two he thought should get the job. His choice was the man who was next in line in seniority. The foreman then spoke to the middle seniority worker and found that he wanted the job. When the third volunteer worker was told that the older man wanted the job, he readily accepted the decision. The choice was made and O.K.'d by the whole crew. Incidentally, this man was the worker that the foreman had had in mind from the beginning as the best man for the job. However, he did not believe that he would be able to make this arrangement because of the strong emphasis the union placed on seniority.

Reactions of Union Representatives

Although it would be desirable to obtain the participation of union leaders in planning a training program in group-decision methods, it has not yet been feasible to include them. A major problem is to obtain the support of top-management, and once this support is given there is a general desire to get the program to all supervisory levels as quickly as possible. This is highly commendable, since isolated supervisors, using methods that deviate from the accustomed procedures, are influenced by the opinions and social pressures of those not yet trained. During the training period the pressures in the group are in the direction of change, and all participants gradually change together. The degree of change becomes apparent after the supervisors return to the job and receive no further stimulation from the training conferences. The problems arising in having trained and untrained supervisors can best be reduced by hastening the training program as much as possible.

If union leaders were exposed to the program before all levels of supervision were covered, it is apparent that the union would be better versed in management policies than supervision itself, and, as a consequence, the union leaders might expect untrained supervisors, or even inadequately trained supervisors, to conduct themselves according to the new procedures. Companies feel a first obligation to their own supervisors.

This does not mean that participation of the union leaders might not be possible. Rather, the methods for obtaining such participation have not yet been satisfactorily worked out. The question for the present, therefore, becomes one of determining the union's reaction when it has not been given an opportunity to participate.

Naturally, the type of reaction from the union will depend upon the relationship that previously existed, the personalities of the industrial and union leaders, and the type of industry. It is impossible to introduce the training without the union's knowledge. Any member who is trained fails to hide the fact from the group that reports to him. He frequently mentions the training to this group and uses the fact that he is being trained as a way of introducing new procedures. There seems to be no reason for companies to wish to hide the fact that they are training supervisors. They frequently publicize the human relations training in the company magazines and regard it as a good policy to keep employees informed.

The author's experience with training programs extends to four unionized industries, three of them utilities and the fourth a factory. Only the factory situation has raised problems, which will be discussed later. The other three companies have raised no real problems thus far. In one of the three, following a prolonged strike, the problem in one unit was one of hard feelings apparent after the strike. Not all employees of this unit had stayed out on strike, so that after the strike there was friction in the group between those who had stayed out and those who had worked. A union stewardess was a member of the faction that had struck, and she apparently was a leader in maintaining the split in the group. The supervisor in charge finally put the problem to the group. He pointed out that he was aware that things weren't so congenial as formerly and that the strike had created hard feelings. He also thought that no one was happy when hard feelings existed. He wondered whether the group felt that a frank discussion might help things out. The group was interested in ironing out the problem, and an active discussion was held. The supervisor tried to reflect and interpret the opposing attitudes, and he found a definite decline in hostile remarks as the discussion progressed. Soon the group was ready to talk about what might be done. Those who had not been out on strike were more readily accepted when it was found that they had financial problems, problems with parents, etc. They reacted as they did after the strike because of guilt feelings. The group that had been out on strike were belligerent on their return because they expected discrimination. Their reactions were less hostile when through discussion they were made to feel that the supervisor did not consider them less loyal than others and that nonstriking employees were not attempting to gain an advantage. During the discussion the supervisor found the steward to be the most constructive and resourceful person in the group. The discussion finally terminated in a willingness on the part of all to drop the whole matter, and there was complete acceptance of the belief that the problem arose because of misunderstanding and distrust. After the meeting the group behavior was as good as or better than formerly.

In the three companies a number of stewards have been involved in group solutions of job problems. Five such instances have come to the author's attention, and in none of them has the steward raised a question about the technique; in three instances the steward was regarded as better than average in his cooperation. In no instance has a supervisor reported to trainers the appearance of a special problem or difficulty with a union steward. This obviously is no proof that problems may not arise. However, returned questionnaires show that management's fear that the union may object to the training program is entirely absent in the groups that have completed training. In all training groups this fear is expressed by a majority of the members at the outset. (See discussion of risks in Chapter 3.)

CASE 12.   UNION STEWARDS AND THE SENIORITY ISSUE

In the fourth company (factory) the union places great emphasis on seniority and seemingly regards the union contract to mean that seniority is more important than ability to do a job. The union issue arose in this company primarily because the foremen, in a training conference, decided not only to put to their groups a problem that involved the interpretation of seniority and adequate ability but also to put it to several groups at the same time, thus giving the problem publicity. The problem involved the selection of group leaders, a nonmanagement job classification which pays the individual 10 cents an hour over the wages of the team he leads. The group leader performs the same work as other individuals, but he has the added responsibility of keeping his team busy. At the time the problem was raised, group leaders were supposedly chosen from the job classification on the basis of seniority and competence. Vagueness, however, existed about what constituted a job classification in that it could be narrowly or broadly interpreted. In actual practice, group leaders were chosen primarily on a seniority basis, but the job classification was variously interpreted. Apparently no crucial case had arisen which pointed up the difficulty of determining the accepted definition of job classification. However, some grievances and work stoppages had occurred when occasionally group leaders were chosen that the group found unacceptable, even when seniority was practiced. In other instances problems arose because the company had by-passed individuals that it regarded as wholly incompetent. It seemed that problems might be simplified if the group decided on how the group leader should be chosen.

Six foremen, with the consent of management, agreed to put the problem of choosing group leaders to their respective groups, with the understanding that adjustments would be made if the different groups came up with different solutions. The groups were told by their respective foremen that all groups involved would have to agree on the same plan. The following questions were asked: Would they like to discuss how group leaders were to be chosen? Would they like to make the recommendation in each instance for permanent and temporary group leaders? Would they like to express their views on the size of the group from which he should be selected?

A total of approximately 100 men were involved. Four foremen with the large crews (having several group leaders) found that the men wanted a "say-so," that they wanted group leaders chosen from the crew in which the vacancy occurred, and that they thought seniority should be followed whenever the senior man was able to fill the job. These four groups felt capable of determining competence. The union steward was a member of one of these groups. He maintained that the problem could not be discussed because it was covered by union contract. Other members of the group disagreed, feeling that if it had a say-so it could still use seniority when it applied. The steward finally admitted that he personally liked the idea but would have to take the matter to the regional steward.

The fifth foreman found that his crew, which was small (five men) and had no group leader, felt it was not involved in the question, but the members thought that they should have a chance to become group leaders. If leaders were chosen from the immediate crew in which they worked they would not have a chance. If the other crews preferred to choose leaders from their own groups, would a concession be made? They wondered whether the foreman would arrange to get a man transferred to a crew that had group leaders if the man wished to become a group leader. The request made by this crew was later accepted by the other crews, with the understanding that a

man should not be transferred for the express purpose of making him
a group leader, but that he would have to prove himself acceptable
and take his chances along with the others.

The sixth foreman found agreement between five men, with one dissenting. This dissenting individual had previously been rejected by
the group, and he pointed out that his only chance to get ahead was
to force seniority. This individual was only partially reconciled, at
best.

With this degree of agreement the plan was put into practice, and
several appointments were made.

In one instance the man who had the most seniority but who was
regarded as incompetent by the company was chosen by the group as
a temporary group leader. The recommendation was put into practice. Surprisingly enough, the job was well done. Other members of
the group did the senior man's work, since he was unable to do the
simple arithmetic and writing necessary. Later he was by-passed
when a permanent choice for a group leader was made, and he raised
no objections. Several other selections for group leaders also were
made about this time, but all followed seniority, and so no problems
arose.

In the meantime the regional steward, together with two other
stewards, met with the department head. The plan for choosing
group leaders was explained. Only one of the stewards was suspicious
and held out for straight seniority. The others agreed that an incompetent group leader caused trouble with the men. The dissenting
steward insisted that the men be forced to get on with the group
leader, regardless. The final decision, acceptable to all, was to wait
to see how the plan worked out; if grievances arose they would be
processed as formerly. Several stewards agreed that the idea might
be good. One found the foremen to be better to deal with than
formerly. It was also agreed that the foremen would go no further
in approaching controversial subjects, but would limit the use of the
group-discussion techniques to problems that were clearly within
management's area of jurisdiction.

Subsequent to this discussion two group leaders were selected. In
one instance the steward refused to accept a group's recommendation,
but did accept it when he found that the persons by-passed had no
grievance. In the other instance the company conceded to the union
and followed seniority because the union insisted upon it. Whether
this was a mistake is an open question.

Of interest also is the fact that, in at least two instances, stewards
have raised questions about men doing work outside their job classifications. In both instances the work the men were doing was the
result of group decisions. The men had decided to make some changes
in the work. One problem had to do with housecleaning, and the
other with switching jobs to make work more interesting. The steward

raised questions in both instances but dropped the matter when he found that the men wanted to do what they were doing.

The program has not progressed to the point of giving a final answer to the problems a union might raise. Certainly, group decisions should not violate union contracts. However, consideration must be given to the possibility that certain aspects of union contracts may be for the purpose of protecting men from the company rather than for selfish gain at the expense of the company. The unions may feel more inclined to have fewer specific protective regulations when they find that there are opportunities in a company to tailor conditions to fit the needs of specific occasions than when such opportunities do not exist. Certainly, it is reasonable to hope that, even though companies, foremen, stewards, and unions vary in their cooperativeness, a company's willingness to settle problems on the job will eventually lead to more constructive cooperation.

Problems Arising When Area of Freedom is Limited

At any level of management a supervisor frequently feels that his area of freedom is too limited to correct certain conditions in the work situation, even those that he himself may recognize as unsatisfactory. Frequently problems are created by the decisions of higher management, so that a supervisor at a lower level feels there is nothing he can do about them. Sometimes this restriction of freedom is more imagined than real; nevertheless, such situations can and do arise, and this raises the question of whether or not democratic supervision has something to offer.

Obviously a group decision opposed to a higher-management decision is excluded; however, group discussion of the problem may be of value. Group discussion permits attitudes to be expressed, and this expression not only relieves frustration but also leads to better understanding. Furthermore, the supervisor learns about attitudes of his subordinates, and this gives him information that he may communicate upward when the opportunity affords itself.

Naturally it would be desirable if such situations did not arise, and they would be kept at a minimum if democratic supervision were practiced at all levels in the organization. However, democratic leadership practiced by all men at all levels of an organization is an ideal toward which a company may strive, but in the meantime one must face the practical fact that ideal situations are the exception.

Let us examine, therefore, a few cases in order to illustrate the function of democratic leadership as a discussion procedure when limitations in the area of freedom do not permit a group decision. The cases to be reported are typical of those that have come to our attention.

CASE 13.   THE INTRODUCTION OF NEW BILLING MACHINES

Three billing machines of a new type were introduced into an office, and it was planned that such new machines would be added periodically to gradually replace all of the old type. The unfavorable reaction to the change was a surprise to Mr. Watts, the manager in charge of the group, and he reported this reaction to his immediate superior, Mr. Hill.

In seems that after the three girls operated the new machines for a few days they formed the opinion that the new machines were more fatiguing on the eyes than the old ones. They wanted the old machines back. Not only were the three girls upset by the change, but other girls in the office were complaining about the fact that they too would be required to use the new machines in the future, and they wanted the orders for them canceled. Several of the girls threatened to quit if they were forced to use the new machines.

Mr. Hill was keenly aware of the need for correcting the situation, and so he informed his superior, Mr. Brode, about the reaction and asked if the order for the additional new machines could be canceled. Mr. Brode pointed out that the new machines were better; they cut down on eye movement and reduced eye fatigue. He was very insistent that the new machines be introduced and pointed out to Mr. Hill that it was not his job to determine the merits of the machine but rather to get the girls to like the new machines.

Mr. Hill then sought technical advice. He wanted to know whether fatigue was greater for maintaining eyes in a fixed position or for moving them from one point to another. Not knowing anything about the background of the case his advisor told him that under some conditions eye movement might be less fatiguing than holding the eyes steady, because in a fixed position the eye muscles might pull against each other and introduce unnecessary fatigue. However, the true facts would have to be determined experimentally.

When Mr. Hill found that there was a possibility that the opinion of the girls might be right, he felt very much bottled up. "My boss insists that we use the machines regardless of the reaction of the girls, and there is nothing I can do." Thus it seemed to Mr. Hill that his area of freedom was so limited that the problem could not be solved.

In this instance the problem really became, "How to make the girls like the new machines." Up to this point the girls had not participated. What might be accomplished by a discussion of the things that are wrong with the new machines? Might this not lead to a discussion of how to reduce these undesirable features?

Mr. Hill decided that he would have a discussion with the girls after he had cleared the idea with Mr. Watts, the immediate supervisor. It was agreed that Mr. Watts was also to be present in these discussions, and he wholeheartedly cooperated with the plan.

During the first meeting the girls freely criticized the new machines and at no point did Mr. Watts or Mr. Hill reject or criticize opinions. Eye fatigue was the major complaint. When the question arose as to how eye fatigue could be reduced a number of plans were suggested. The girls were asked if they would like to try out some of the plans— to do some experiments in testing the plans. This idea met with hearty agreement. It was decided that weekly meetings would be held to discuss the experiences with the various procedures.

The procedures tested had to do mostly with inserting short rest pauses at certain points in the work. There were such plans as: (a) looking out of the window for one minute after doing ⅓ of a page; (b) looking out of the window for two minutes after doing a whole page; (c) shifting positions after doing a specific amount of work, etc. These eye rest pauses, of course, were in addition to the general office relief periods. On some of the combination tests the time spent resting the eyes exceeded the actual working period.

The immediate reaction to the experimental approach was favorable. The girls were interested in trying things out, and there was no talk of getting rid of the new machines. This interest continued as the conferences were held, and all suggestions were of a constructive nature. Other girls in the office began to ask how long it would be before their new machines arrived.

With regard to productivity, it is of interest to note that all combinations tested yielded practically the same results. Thus spacing the rest pauses differently or greatly increasing their frequency or length had no effect on production. The decline in production due to introducing the new machines was wiped out, and production became as good or slightly better than formerly. The final choice of the procedure to follow was left to the girls and was decided upon in terms of comfort. Thus, Mr. Hill solved the problem of getting employees to accept the new machines and no one lost face.

CASE 14. THE NO-SMOKING RULE

Because towels and toilet seats in the girls' washroom had sometimes been burned, higher management passed a rule forbidding smoking in the washrooms. Since smoking was not allowed for women in the office, this left the women's lounge as the only smoking place.

Mr. Harrower, the supervisor in charge of one of the units affected by the ruling, felt that some of the critical attitudes and the lack of cooperation following the ruling was a direct result of the ruling. Some of the girls had vocalized their reactions, but Mr. Harrower was not sure of the extent of the unfavorable attitude it might have caused. Since he was not involved in the ruling and was in no position to rescind the ruling, the solution to the problem appeared to be out of his area of freedom.

Mr. Harrower decided to discuss the problem with his group, his intention being merely to learn the nature and extent of the attitudes the ruling had stimulated.

He called the girls together and told them that he felt that some of them had been hurt by the ruling. He asked if they would be willing to talk about it, even though he doubted whether there was much he could do. With a little encouragement the girls began to talk out their feelings. The following opinions were expressed with emotional loadings: the ruling was an insult; no one in their group had done anything wrong; there seemed to be no good reason for the ruling; any damage caused by smoking had been exaggerated; and inconveniencing everyone because of a few was unfair.

After considerable feeling had been released, Mr. Harrower asked why they preferred smoking in the washroom rather than in the lounge. The answer to this was quite clear cut. The washroom had a mirror, and the lounge did not. Since the mirror seemed to be so essential to the girls during their relief, Mr. Harrower asked whether a mirror in the lounge might solve the problem. The girls thought it would. Mr. Harrower was able to obtain an attractive mirror for the lounge and believes it has solved the problem.

CASE 15. TAKING AWAY COFFEE PRIVILEGES

During an economy drive a large company circulated a memorandum informing all supervisors to refrain from taking out time for coffee during working hours. The ruling did not apply to nonmanagement personnel, who regularly were allowed 15 minutes' relief both morning and afternoon.

This ruling produced violent resentment in management personnel. It was freely discussed, and many talked about getting their coffee off the premises. A slump in the company restaurant's noontime business, which occurred about the same time, was explained by some as due to the fact that supervisors were boycotting the cafeteria.

Higher management personnel felt that, although the unfavorable reaction might have been averted, it was not serious and would gradually subside. When, however, after several months, the reactions to the memorandum were still apparent, some of the offices held gripe sessions. In these sessions the men freely expressed their opinions. As a result of these meetings the men reported that they felt better and now could pass off the memorandum as just one of those things that happens and that it really didn't seem so serious any more. Thus the memorandum changed from a big to a little thing.

Although no solution or change occurred, the discussion seemed to change the appearance of things. This change in appearance thus became the corrective measure in a situation that could not be changed.

General Characteristics of Solutions Reached by Group Decision

The above cases illustrate some of the outstanding characteristics of solutions worked out through group decisions. The characteristics of these solutions and others resulting from the same approach may be summarized as follows:

1. Group discussion eliminates self-centered solutions in that each individual is forced to consider the rights of others. Thus what is *fair* takes on a group meaning. Individuals may agree that an imposed solution is unfair, but this is quite different from agreeing on what is fair. The discrepancy between what management considers fair and what a group of employees considers fair is less than the discrepancy between what management considers fair and what individuals consider fair.

2. Goals set by group decision tend to be high, and frequently they are higher than goals that management would dare to impose.

3. The quality of group decisions is surprisingly good, and frequently sources of information of which management personnel are unaware are utilized. In some instances the solutions are actually ingenious.

4. Groups develop constructive solutions when a problem is presented to them in such a way that they do not feel criticized or inadequate. Anticipated self-centered solutions are eliminated in discussions, and the final trend tends to be a cooperative product.

5. Goals developed by a group are highly realistic. When a production or quality figure is set it is met, even when management considers the goal out of reach. This tendency to set a high goal, and to meet it almost exactly, occurs even when there seem to be factors beyond the group's control. Thus tardiness, errors, and even accident figures, which involve conditions beyond an individual's control, seem to be accurately predictable and frequently are superior to managements' prediction when management has access to records. A group of men who are on the job seem to be well aware of the factors within their control.

6. The behavior of employees in discussions is one of frankness and true interest, once doubts as to the supervisor's motives are clarified. The group enters extensively into the discussion of the problem, and union stewards as well as other employees participate.

7. The solutions are characterized by a high degree of acceptance and pride. Employees become more cooperative, and a team spirit develops.

8. Solutions tend to reflect and protect against sources of fear or countermotivation that previously existed. Frequently the fears are based on imagined motives attributed to management or on misunderstandings within the group. These factors are clarified, and the solution often makes provisions to protect against them.

9. Solutions tend to be generous in that they do not impose unreasonable demands on less capable and less experienced members. Furthermore, the solutions do not take advantage of seniority rights. When pleasant or unpleasant duties are to be assigned, the general tendency is to devise a plan that permits all to share equally.

10. Group decisions include superior communication between the parties concerned. The degree of understanding of the solution, of the reasons for it, and of the implications involved is superior to that existing when solutions are passed down from above.

11. Responsibility for executing the solution is assumed by the group. The supervisor is not placed in the position of enforcing a plan agreed upon. Rather the group is motivated to make the plan work.

12. Once a plan is accepted it has a surprising "staying" quality. It seems to become part of the group's culture. Whereas plans that are autocratically imposed deteriorate when discipline is withdrawn, plans reached by group decision seem to hold up over long periods.

13. A surprising feature is the quickness and completeness with which agreements are reached. It is our impression that these characteristics improve with the use of the method. Of course, a variable in this success is the nature of the problem. Nevertheless, it is apparent that the interests of a group of employees are not as divided as most supervisors initially suppose.

14. Group solutions are tailor-made to fit the nature of the membership and the existing conditions. When necessary, they can be modified or improved. The need for setting up practices and customs is greatly reduced, and face-saving problems are avoided when changes seem desirable.

15. Group discussions of problems permit raising of issues of which management may be unaware. Thus employees can raise complaints, and grievances can be avoided by treating complaints as problems.

16. Supervisors tend to like the group-solution approach. They feel that their job is a more pleasant one and that they get a better understanding of the group's previous behavior and point of view. No

supervisor who has tried the method indicates on questioning that he felt that he has lost or given up something.

In considering the above qualities of group decision, one should not gain the impression that it is a method by which employees can be pressed into exerting themselves unduly. Used as a speed-up procedure, the method will lose its basic value and the concept of fairness will be violated. Employees are willing to do a "good day's work" if they feel they are not risking their jobs or their rights and privileges. At present the higher production observed when the method is used seems to be due to the removal of some of the counter-motivating factors. These include job insecurity, poor morale, hostility, boredom, and distrust. If a company is willing to settle for a removal of these countermotivating forces and does not attempt to obtain motivation of a degree that makes a job highly and unpleasantly fatiguing or stressful, the group-decision method should be effective. Efficiency in labor should be viewed as a method for removing energy-consuming interferences, and not as a way of increasing production by the expenditure of more energy.

Why the Democratic Approach Works

At first glance it may be surprising to some that the democratic method is as effective as it is. Yet it is a psychologically sound approach in that it utilizes a number of generally accepted behavior principles. Some of these have been discussed in previous chapters, but for summary purposes it may be well to list them again. The following are perhaps the most obvious and generally acceptable ones.

1. *A group derives ego satisfaction and pleasure from solving a problem.* All people are challenged by a problem, and frequently we stay up nights to solve a problem or puzzle, even though no external gain is apparent. We obtain pleasure and satisfaction just from reaching the solution.

2. *Participation is effectively used.* Participation is not only a pleasant social experience, but it gives one a feeling of belonging—of being wanted. By using it in a work situation employees are made to feel that they are a part of the company. Thus the distinction between employees and management is reduced. When this occurs the tendency to react as separate groups with different values and special interests declines, and mutual interests can be discovered.

3. *Attitudes and objections can be voiced and receive recognition.* The mere expression of hostile attitudes and the mere acceptance of the individual who voices them have a therapeutic value. Since a democratic supervisor is permissive, encourages expression, and reacts understandingly to feelings, he is reducing fears and hostilities. With these factors reduced the discussion situation becomes more constructive, and the real problems can be attacked.

4. *Each individual must recognize the rights of others.* When a meeting of minds is required individuals must interact, and through this process a variety of values becomes apparent. The problem thus becomes one of resolving the differences rather than of determining who is right. When there are many conflicting values in a problem, there is less likelihood that opposed camps will form than when only a few alternatives exist. Even the minority individuals become important in a group decision and hence feel some group membership. Hostility to a group usually occurs when an individual feels he is being excluded from the group or is not welcome. Thus recognition of the importance of each individual develops a group spirit rather than a number of cliques.

5. *Social pressure is constructively used.* Social pressure is an extremely strong motivating force. It may be used to cause people to restrict production, or it may be used to cause them to carry their share of a load. Thus social pressure may cause individuals to line up in terms of their group membership, and they may do this with constructive or destructive accomplishments. The supervisor, in protecting minority individuals, stating a problem in situational terms, accepting hostile attitudes, showing a desire to obtain a solution acceptable to all, and not pressing for his own solution, brings out the constructive abilities of people. It is this ability which solves problems and engenders cooperation. Thus social pressure acts to make people want to go along for the good of the group rather than fear not to go along, or to go along with a group bent on revenge.

6. *Individuals do not feel ordered about.* People do not necessarily object to having their freedoms restricted. All of us experience restrictions in our freedoms whenever we are in a social situation. It is *how* our freedoms are restricted which creates resentment. Thus persons willingly do unpleasant things when they feel it is necessary, or when it is a reasonable choice. Group decisions are choice reactions to situations, and when choices and situations force unpleasant activities people accept them. Being forced to do something is de-

grading, and hence one is both motivated to do something through fear and motivated not to do it through pride.

7. *Goals are specified by the group.* When a group sets a goal, this goal is real and is a goal for each individual; when a supervisor sets a goal, it is his and has no direct effect on the group. For a supervisor to make his goal effective, indirect motivation must be added. This indirect motivation may be fear, a desire to please the boss, or a monetary reward. It is apparent that a group's productional goal functions as a motivating factor which is inherent in the situation and not something added from the outside.

8. *Job interest increases because progress is experienced.* Experience of progress is the experience of approaching a goal. When the goal is set by a group, it becomes the point of orientation for experiencing progress. Nonacceptable goals or goals set by others are less realistic and hence permit a lesser experience of progress. What is called *ego involvement* largely describes the degree to which a goal is personalized. Interest and motivation increase rapidly with ego involvement.

9. *Responsibility is experienced.* Responsible behavior requires the assumption of responsibility. People are more likely to assume responsibility for their own decisions than for the decisions of others. Thus, when a group decides something, the responsibility is placed in the group. So long as supervisors set goals and make decisions they behave as responsible individuals and often cannot understand why their employees fail to accept a similar responsibility.

10. *Working in cooperating groups is pleasant.* Since group decisions bring individuals together with a common goal, morale or team spirit is high. Individuals help each other out because they are working on a group project, and each becomes responsible for the group product. Working for a common goal gives people common interests, and this common set of objectives permits them to behave as the social beings they naturally are when fears and jealousies are reduced. Thus group decision permits our relations with others to become a pleasant experience.

It will be noted in the above points that a variety of effective motivational factors, both individual and social, are incorporated and utilized. In addition, obstructing influences, due to misunderstandings and frustration, are reduced. A single procedure that harnesses so many basic principles and apparently does violence to none may not be the ultimate, but it must lie in the right direction.

9

Case Studies (Continued)

Unselected Cases

Although the emphasis in training is to make democratic supervision a day-to-day matter on the job, so that employee participation is increased and employee attitudes are treated permissively, the group-decision method has been presented as the democratic approach to problems and, therefore, is a specific technique within democratic supervision. For this reason case histories of the use of group decision have become the most clear-cut examples of democratic supervision in action. In the preceding chapter cases were selected to illustrate: (a) the variety of problems to which the group-decision method lends itself; (b) the manner in which various attitudes become introduced and reconciled in discussion; and (c) the characteristics of solutions reached by group decision. In order that the reader may obtain a better perspective of the ways in which supervisors use democratic supervision, it seems desirable to present a cross section of cases. The cases in this chapter represent the first examples which were received in the use of democratic supervision for handling day-to-day problems on the job. They were obtained from the company in which training in large groups was attempted. Thus the lecture presentation method, supplemented with discussions in the line organization, was used. The unselected cases are of value in giving the reader an idea of problems supervisors select in attempting to become democratic leaders.

The cases are grouped according to departments of a company but, with the exception of a few that were too sketchy to be clarified through editing, no cases have been excluded. It will be noted that some of the cases are somewhat imperfect illustrations of the group-decision method, and instead reflect the supervisor's interpretation of the method. This is a second value in presenting an unselected group of cases. Our training problem was not only one of testing a procedure, but also one of testing what supervisors would do with the training.

The third reason for presenting unselected cases is to destroy any feeling that might have been gained from the selected cases that group decision is primarily an efficiency method or a way of manipulating people. Instead, democratic supervision should be viewed primarily as a way to increase job satisfaction. The unselected cases should reflect the supervisor's attitude in this regard, and they should also reflect his attitude toward his position.

In obtaining cases supervisors were asked to fill out a form which had a space to describe each of the following: (a) statement of problem; (b) method of handling the problem; (c) solution reached; and (d) results. This method encouraged a brief report, and we have presented the cases verbatim, with minor editorial changes only. In some instances higher levels of supervision were in the training program and, instead of describing a problem at their own level, have worked with one of their supervisors and have reported his problem. The reader may desire more details in some instances, but it has seemed best to report a large number of cases and to sacrifice detail for the purposes of this chapter.

CASE 1

Statement of Problem: Confusion frequently resulted because first one man and then another made coffee for the morning coffee period and the noon lunch. This caused arguments as to who made it last time. Also, the coffee pot often was not cleaned and was left on the stove until it was time to make coffee again. I made coffee for a period of time, then ordered the men to take weekly turns. Soon, however, arguments developed again as to whose turn it was.

Handling of Problem: I called the group together on the job location and explained that we had a problem in making coffee and keeping the coffee pot clean. I asked the group if they had any ideas as to how they would handle the situation.

Solution: All agreed to try to solve the problem by handling it as before, but with a penalty attached for those who reneged. An initial fine of 15 cents and 5 cents additional for each successive failure to make coffee when a turn came was set. The men agreed that they would see to it that the fines were paid. One man who did not feel like making coffee agreed that he would take his turn when the men promised to relieve him on the job.

Results: The first man neglected to make coffee, and, when after three days he did not pay his fine, the group exerted pressure. He paid the fine. The second man performed the job perfectly. The third man missed once but paid the fine without any trouble when requested and also paid a fine for not cleaning the coffee pot. After that all did as they had agreed to do.

CASE 2

Statement of Problem: Each month before steam bills are mailed to customers, the steam consumption is copied onto cards provided for this purpose. Each customer's monthly consumption is then analyzed on a degree-day basis to determine whether there has been an error in the billing procedure. (Steam is metered by use of a condensate meter, and, if condensate escapes before reaching the meter, an under-registration would result; likewise, if city water should get into the steam system by some manner, an over-registration would result.) After the consumption is recorded, the cards are passed out to engineers familiar with the customer's piping, and from the degree-day analysis he is able to determine whether the billing is correct. This procedure must be completed before bills are mailed to customers.

The problem that caused trouble in the office routine was that cards which showed unusual consumption were kept in the engineers' desks until they were able to determine the cause of the trouble. Sometimes this investigation required a week or more, and during this time the cards were not in the file and were not available for the use of others in the office. The question was how the cards could be kept available for everybody concerned?

This situation had existed for many years. Various efforts had been made to solve the problem. Most of them were simply requests to the engineers to try to be more prompt in returning cards to the file. Regardless of the efforts put forth there were always many cards in individual desks. Sometimes they were almost impossible to find.

Handling of Problem: The office group was called together to discuss general departmental matters. This particular problem was brought up, and its seriousness was stressed. It was pointed out, for example, that delays in billing, errors, and confusion resulted from this practice. The group discussed the matter from all points of view. Everyone seemed to recognize the problem as important and wanted to find an answer.

Solution: The group decided that the engineers would not keep the cards in their desks at all. They would instead make a pencil record of all bills needing further investigation. The cards themselves would be returned immediately to the file, and only the pencil record would be kept at the desk. This solution was acceptable to all and was put into effect immediately.

Results: The new method has been in operation for several months, and no difficulties have been experienced. Everyone seems satisfied.

CASE 3

Statement of Problem: Because of a change in our operating procedure, we had more men working on the day shift. This brought up the problem of enough room for all the men to have a place to eat their lunch.

Handling of Problem: The men were called together and a very informal meeting was held. The problem was to find a suitable place for the men to eat their lunch and play cards during the lunch period. Suggestions were requested.

Solution: After some discussion the suggestion was made that, by rearranging the tools and furnishings of the instrument room and laboratory, sufficient space could be gained to make a fair-sized dining room. All the suggestions for rearranging these rooms were made by someone in the gang.

Results: All the work was done on company time. However, most of it was done between jobs by some of our own men. The whole job will be completed with very little cost. Although the dining room is not yet completed, we feel sure that it will be well received by everyone.

The democratic method seems to be very suitable for this type of problem.

CASE 4

Statement of Problem: A summer maintenance job had to be done under very hot and disagreeable working conditions. Some of the men had crabbed about doing it, and no one was very enthusiastic about this particular assignment.

Handling of Problem: On a recent cool day, while the maintenance men were working on other assignments, the foreman approached them about this hot job and asked them, "How about getting it over with?"

Solution: Everyone agreed that this was a fine idea, and plans were made as to which men should do the job.

Results: As many as could be used worked together and completed the task in a short time. It all worked out in complete harmony, since there was no sign of discord in the group who worked willingly on this disagreeable job.

CASE 5

Statement of Problem: The problem arose because the group asked if they could have coffee in the morning, since they were working out of doors in all kinds of weather. Up to that time there was a lunch truck at the plant next door, and the men would go there and buy coffee, etc.

Handling of Problem: I called the group together. After they talked over the problem it seemed as if it would be a benefit to them and would help the job along if coffee was made available.

Solution: It was decided to have the group make their own coffee. One man was to make the coffee, and after he had it made he would drink his coffee. Then he would replace one of the others on the job so that another man could have his coffee. Thus the men would take turns until all had coffee. It was also agreed that they would take as short a time as possible, and the last man would clean up the locker room.

Results: The plan has worked out very satisfactorily during the cold weather, and with the warm weather coming on the men have stopped making coffee.

CASE 6

Statement of Problem: Our team patrol room was dirty and cluttered up. Trucks were also dirty inside, and there was considerable junk and refuse in them. Uniforms were sometimes not clean.

Handling of Problem: I told the group about the problem and asked for suggestions regarding improvements in the housekeeping. There was much discussion on the matter.

Solution: The group agreed to try to clean up the room and trucks. They suggested that the foreman have a new locker and that trucks be equipped with a whisk broom. A new locker was purchased, and whisk brooms were furnished for each truck.

Results: The patrol room is cleaner. Trucks are also kept cleaner on the inside. Most of the men are much more particular about their uniforms.

CASE 7

Statement of Problem: The proper location for the telephone caused disagreement between three supervisors, two electricians, two maintenance men, and one instrument man.

Handling of Problem: All involved were gathered together to discuss the problem. Discussion revealed that there seemed to be three possible locations, and there was plenty of argument for each of the three locations, but only one of them was a logical place for the telephone.

Solution: The final decision was the one logical place, and everyone in the group was satisfied. It happened to be the place where the supervisor wanted the phone. (The location preferred by the supervisor was not known by anyone in the group.)

Results: Everyone is well pleased with the location of the telephone.

CASE 8

Statement of Problem: Daily balance records were composed of seven distribution sheets. The objection to this type of record was that there was too much paper handling. I consulted the company auditor, but he offered no solution.

Handling of Problem: The group head presented the problem to the senior clerk, and she agreed that these distribution sheets should be condensed.

Solution: The senior clerk suggested using general report sheets, and all details of daily deposit balance, received and refunded, could be transcribed to four sheets instead of the original seven.

Results: Solution has been in effect for a 2-month period and to date has proved satisfactory. The clerk is still somewhat skeptical as to its being a permanent improvement, but has been assured that the problem can be reopened for further discussion.

CASE 9

Statement of Problem: First attempt to use democratic technique with group of 11 members. Problem 1: Leaving for lunch ahead of schedule. Problem 2: Friction between two members of the group, well known to others.

Handling of Problem: Presented background of new technique, importance of individuals in group, responsibility of supervisors, etc. Then presented problem 1 and, after its solution, problem 2.

Solution: Problem 1: Those who had been going to lunch at 11:50 should be allowed to go at 11:45 to avoid rush and line-up at restaurant. Problem 2: The past would be forgotten and friction removed.

Results: Too early to know.

CASE 10

Statement of Problem: We had 54 control panels for the new machines in our powerhouse and also cutovers on the old machines to be drilled, painted, and wired by a certain date. Fourteen people were involved.

Handling of Problem: We went to the men and stated our problem. We asked if they would back us up in our estimate of time involved and not take any time off that was not absolutely necessary.

Solution: The men agreed that they would do everything in their power to help us out. They also suggested working every night for a reasonable time.

Results: The panels were completed within the specified time, and I don't believe any time was lost during this period.

CASE 11

Statement of Problem: A job had to be at a certain powerhouse by 7:00 A.M. The bearing weighed 550 pounds. The job could be done either in the lathe or the boring mill and would involve three men and overtime work.

Handling the Problem: I called the group of five men together and told them of the importance of the job. I explained that the job had to be completed by 7:00 A.M. The men were asked for their opinions about the possibility of getting the job done on time, which machine would be most suitable, and who would work overtime.

All wanted to do the job that involved overtime, and so there was an initial tendency for each to favor the machine on which he worked.

In discussing the details the following points were made: (a) the job could be done in the lathe by bolting it to the chuck and making a plate and bolts for it; (b) if the job was going to be done on the boring mill a steel ring would have to be made; (c) if the job was to be done on the lathe the bearing would have an overhang, and the operation would be much slower; (d) if the job was done on the boring mill it could be fastened to the table.

Solution: All agreed that the boring mill would be the machine to use.

Results: The job was done on the boring mill. The men worked faster than usual to show it was the proper machine on which to do the work. The men who did not work overtime agreed the next morning that the boring mill was the right machine to do the work.

The job was at the powerhouse at the required time, and all the men were satisfied.

CASE 12

Statement of Problem: The problem arose because of the claim of unequal distribution of work among five janitors. Some of them thought that they had more work to do and more difficult tasks to perform than the others. Each one had been previously told individually that this was not so, but they were not convinced.

Handling of Problem: The group was called together, presented with the problem, and asked for their opinions and advice on how to correct the situation. Each one was encouraged by the leader to state his duties and make comparisons with the work that others had to perform. It was found that the difficulty being experienced was not due to too much work but to the fact that the duties were not being performed in the most efficient sequence.

Solution: It was decided that the workers affected would perform their duties in a scheduled manner, which gradually would work into an efficient routine, and they would find that they could do all their work much easier and in the required length of time.

Results: All the men now seem satisfied.

CASE 13

Statement of Problem: The men frequently complained about not having a place to eat their lunches.

Handling of Problem: The men met in a group and were asked for suggestions to improve the conditions under which they had to eat their lunches. The men could see we were attempting to improve the condition of not having a definite place to eat their lunch. It was suggested having a lunch counter, but it was pointed out that the cost would be too great. It was then suggested that a hot meal be brought from the general office restaurant. It was pointed out, however, that there would be too much confusion, since all the shop men ate during the same period. It was then suggested that if they could have milk or hot coffee and a table and benches for lunch the situation would be cleared up.

Solution: The men agreed that the last suggestion was a practical one. One man was selected to make coffee for those who wanted it, and milk was made available to others. A table and benches were furnished.

Results: The men are using table for lunch and are, or appear to be, satisfied with this solution.

CASE 14

Statement of Problem: A portable bench drill press was always being left in someone's way on a bench. We had previously tried to have each man put the drill press back in a place provided which was out of the way, but the men did not follow this rule. Eight men were involved.

Handling of Problem: I called the men together and stated the problem. The following suggestions were voiced: (*a*) I want it near so I won't have to walk so far; (*b*) it should be made portable on a rolling bench, since this would make it easy to use and to roll back to a fixed location; and (*c*) put it on a bench about to be vacated.

Solution: The accepted solution was to put the drill press on the vacated bench until a portable rolling bench could be made.

Results: Everybody is satisfied with the solution.

CASE 15

Statement of Problem: We had the problem of keeping machines clean in a department where each man in the group operates each and all of the machines frequently. A total of 18 men were involved. Previously I had talked to each man individually, and all had promised that they would clean each machine after they were done. Everything would be fine for a short time, and then the machines would be left in dirty condition again. I went through this procedure several times.

Handling of Problem: I decided to call group together and try to find a solution. I pointed out to the group that we had an understanding in the department that each man would clean up his machine after each operation. However, the machines were still being left in a dirty condition. Perhaps they could suggest some better way of keeping the machines clean. Points brought up were: some did clean the machines, others did not; why should we do it? Why not clean them at night? One man refused to clean any machine or *anything*. The general opinion was that if each man did his share the present method would be all right. The man who refused to clean left the meeting.

Solution: It was decided to ignore the one man and go ahead as before and clean machines after each man's operation.

Results: Everything worked out fine, and before long (a week, to be exact) the man who said he would not clean any machine was doing his part with the rest of the group.

CASE 16

Statement of Problem: There are nine employees in the group, some receiving three weeks' vacation and the others two weeks. Scheduling was complicated because too many persons could not be away at the same time. Each individual picked out his own dates, but this resulted in too many duplications.

Handling of Problem: The group was brought together and the matter discussed. Length of service, dates of vacation in previous years, marital status of employee, and previous arrangements that had been made were discussed.

Solution: It was decided that those persons with families would have the preference of the school vacation periods. Others would take their vacations earlier or later in the year. In the following years these dates, where possible, would be reversed.

Results: Vacation scheduling was accepted. It did not fully satisfy everyone, but everyone agreed that it was the only solution.

CASE 17

Statement of Problem: Quite frequently six or eight out of twelve persons in the office would be away from their desks at the same time, making it impossible for those left to properly take care of the incoming telephone calls.

Handling of Problem: In discussing this situation with the entire group it was found that some left the office to consult with persons in other departments, some were at lunch, and others just left their desks, paying no particular attention as to how many and who were still in the office.

Solution: It was agreed by all concerned that when it was necessary for anyone to leave the office, he would let someone in his group know where he could be located and about how long he would be gone, and he would also satisfy himself that there was a sufficient number of persons remaining at their desks to properly take care of the work, including the handling of incoming telephone calls.

Results: The arrangement has worked out satisfactorily. There has been no further difficulty in locating a person who is away from his desk and is wanted for an important telephone call or other business.

CASE 18

Statement of Problem: The coffee hour brought about a problem when it became the social hour for the division. Several people would go out at the same time. I mentioned to individuals who seemed to be the leaders that they should not arrange to go in groups. After that they left one at a time, but the result was the same: too many away for too long a time.

Handling of Problem: I arranged to talk to the group as a whole and explained to them that it was not intended, when the coffee time was set up, that the department would close down for that hour. I told them some in our group were taking advantage of those who remained at their desks either because they did not care for coffee or were aware of the necessity of at least a very small part of the group being present.

Solution: They seemed surprised at first, but it was evident that they really had not thought about the rest of the group or the fact that so many absences created a bad impression on anyone having occasion to be in our division during that hour. They all decided that once a day was sufficient for coffee and that they would go one at a time.

Results: The results were amazing. At this writing there is only one in the department who now goes up for coffee every day, and then only in the morning. The others have told me that the lines are too long and that too much time is lost waiting. It is a rare day when one other girl leaves the office for that purpose.

CASE 19

Statement of Problem: Errors in work-order numbers on bills of material created a serious problem.

Handling of Problem: Work orders were being assigned by one man, who checked with the estimator in doubtful cases. The group thought this procedure led to errors.

Solution: It was decided after discussion that all work-order assignments would be checked and initialed by the estimator for each job.

Results: Errors were reduced greatly, but sometimes this checking becomes too routine and checking up is necessary.

CASE 20

Statement of Problem: Should personal tool boxes be taken back to shop every night? The men did not like carrying tool boxes back to shop. Five men were involved.

Handling of Problem: All five involved were contacted and their opinions heard. They all wanted a place to lock up tool boxes at the place of work and thought this should be done.

Solution: A place to lock up tool boxes at each work location was provided.

Results: Everybody is happy about the solution.

CASE 21

Statement of Problem: The method for sending out periodic follow-up reports on division field employees seemed to be inadequate because it was difficult to keep up to date. Some pressure had been put on employees responsible for sending out reports to field foremen, but still we were lagging behind. Foremen were complaining that it was difficult for them to make out reports on men because too much time had elapsed.

Handling of Problem: I discussed the problem with the two employees responsible for sending out periodic reports. They realized that something had to be done to eliminate sorting out cards on 230 employees each time it was necessary to find which reports were due. Several points were raised about making lists for each month, showing employees' names and the dates that reports were due.

Solution: It was agreed that we would make a card file of division employees and file the cards according to dates. Each week cards would be checked and reports made out for follow-up reports due. The cards were then to be noted with date of next report due and filed accordingly.

Results: To date it appears that the problem has been solved. The work has been made easier, and both the employees responsible for issuing reports and their supervisors are satisfied that collectively they have come to a good decision on the matter.

CASE 22

Statement of Problem: Why do the men wash up before the bell rings to go home from work? There are eleven men in my department. Most plants outside the company give 5 minutes before the bell rings for quitting. The men seem to think that the company cannot do much about the problem of washing up before quitting time and that it is not strict enough in enforcing the rules it makes.

Handling of Problem: I called the group together, and a discussion was started. I asked questions such as the following: "If you were in charge what would you do?" "Do you wash up early because you saw someone else do it first?" "After you wash do you wait for the bell to ring?" The group freely discussed these questions.

Solution: The company should give 5 minutes for washing up, and we will stick to it. Each man is to stay in the washroom or on his floor until the bell rings and not be around the time clock 5 minutes before it is time to quit.

Results: The plan has worked very well.

CASE 23

Statement of Problem: The work allowed only two clerks to be away on vacation at the same time. A junior clerk planned to be married and take two choice weeks for his vacation. Three other clerks with greater seniority desired the same two weeks and refused to change when contacted individually.

Handling of Problem: The four clerks were called together, and the problem was presented to them. During the discussion a great deal of jovial advice was given to the clerk about getting married. One clerk with greater seniority had definite plans and reservations made for his two weeks of vacation. The other two clerks had made no definite plans for theirs.

Solution: The clerks having no definite vacation plans agreed to let the other two clerks with definite plans have the weeks of their choice.

Results: All four clerks involved were pleased with the decision.

CASE 24

Statement of Problem: Some new men working under a rather conservative work leader felt that their ideas were not receiving proper attention. The "grapevine" had magnified the seriousness of the situation. Explanation and a little practice had eased the original difficulty a little, but the "grapevine" was still active. The first-line supervisor suggested to the division head that a formal question box might be established. In the past suggestions had been welcomed but were handled informally. This often resulted in suggestions that were not well thought out.

About 30 engineers were affected. All expected to take a part in a formulation of practices.

Handling of Problem: At a regular monthly meeting of the division the division head mentioned that a question box had been suggested. He stated some of the factors involved in having a question box and then turned the discussion over to the men. After quite a lot of talk, mostly from the older men, a committee was appointed to work up a proposition. A plan was submitted a month later which decided against a question box, but instead proposed a form on which questions could be submitted. It also proposed rules making it mandatory that prompt answers to questions be given.

Solution: The committee's recommendations were unanimously approved and immediately put into effect.

Results: The plan is working fine. There have been no complaints; one formal suggestion was submitted the first year, but there have been plenty of informal suggestions which were more carefully worked out. There has been good two-way cooperation.

CASE 25

Statement of Problem: A group of 28 substations covers a large rural area of three counties. Six maintenance operators handle these substations, working in teams of two in each of the three counties. Each team normally is responsible for the maintenance and operation of eight to ten stations.

Because of the location of the stations it was considered impossible to divide the routine work equally. Two of the men felt that they were shouldering much more than their share of the routine work. The other men generally agreed that these two had the most work, so much so that they attempted to help them out whenever it was at all possible. This one team normally maintained eight 40-kv and four 4.8-kv breakers, while the other teams each had three 40-kv and three 4.8-kv breakers.

Because of this difference in work load there was some dissatisfaction with the set-up.

Handling of Problem: The group was brought together and the problem discussed. It was agreed that the first step was to find out how much difference there was between the work load at the one location and those at the others. The men decided to approach the problem by breaking down the routine jobs, for each station and for each major piece of equipment, into units of work; then they would attempt to measure the number of units in the various jobs.

Solution: Each of the two-man crews was contacted at the work locations for discussions on breaking down the various jobs into units. The supervisor with the crews worked out values which were agreed on by all the crews before they went to work on the project. The values agreed upon were as follows:

Conventional-type station	10 units
40-kv oil circuit breakers	$2\frac{1}{2}$ units
40-kv transformer banks	1 unit
40-kv automatic pole top switches	$2\frac{1}{2}$ units
4.8-kv oil circuit breakers	1 unit
Machine oil circuit breakers	1 unit
4.8-kv capacitor banks	$2\frac{1}{2}$ units
Operation of machines	$2\frac{1}{2}$ units
Key station duties	5 units

Results: When the analysis of the jobs was completed and the figures totaled, the groups compared closely. The team that had previously thought themselves to have the least work of the three had a total of 137 work units. A second team, which had little or nothing to say on the subject previously, had a total of 126½ units. The third group, who had felt that they were shouldering too much of the burden, had a total of 124 units. All members were surprised at the closeness of the work balance and agreed that it would be impossible to bring it any closer. The complaining team was completely satisfied, and all groups have worked in harmony since.

CASE 26

Statement of Problem: Three or more "B" crews (small crews who work independently) used the same electrical measuring instruments at different times. Storage space for these instruments was not very

convenient. Tools and equipment of other kinds were stored with
them in floor bins not properly marked. There was no real system
of storage. The problem involved not only storage but also maintaining the instruments in working order with all necessary connections and leads. In the past several sets of leads had been ordered
and attached to the instruments so that there would be spares. However, when an instrument was taken out, it was almost always short of
something.

Handling of Problem: Shelving space for test instruments recently
was obtained, and a meeting was called for all persons involved.
The problem was stated as follows: "We have moved into a new warehouse and now have a permanent place for our instruments. In the
past it has been very difficult for you to know where the instrument
you wanted was, and, when you found it, it was not ready for use.
From time to time we have put leads on these instruments, but something happens to them. I know it has been very difficult for you, and
I too have been concerned about this condition. That is the reason
I would like to have you solve the problem. What are your ideas,
and how shall we go about this?"

The first reactions of the group were that something certainly needed
to be done. Such remarks as these were made: "Anything would be
better than what we had." "I wondered if we were always going to
have to fish for these things." "If we did this at home we would get
in trouble."

The group then settled down to the problem of how they could
straighten things out and keep them that way.

Solution: The group decided that one of the crews would install
the lockers, put the parts in, and label each bin as to kind and number of instruments. After that each man who took out an instrument
would return it only if in good condition. If it weren't in good condition he would not put it in the bin, but would turn it in at the office.

Results: The handling of the instruments has been satisfactory since
this date. The bins are well marked and instruments properly cared
for. Members of the group have expressed pride in the way they have
organized this part of their job.

CASE 27

Statement of Problem: The problem involved the number of employees who could take vacations during the first week of the deer
hunting season. It was necessary to have a large enough force on
duty to take care of maintenance and construction satisfactorily.

Three employees had not gone deer hunting in the past. This year
they decided to take the first week of their vacation during the first
week of the hunting season. These men had seniority and therefore
were entitled to their choice of vacation time. Three other employees, who had been deer hunting in past years but who had less
seniority, also asked for the first week of the hunting season. This

meant that six men would be off at the same time, and this would not leave a sufficient force for maintenance and construction.

Handling of Problem: A meeting was called of all the employees at the warehouse. The problem of vacations during the first week of the hunting season was presented. The need for a certain number of men on duty was explained, so that everyone understood the nature of the problem. All agreed that the coverage requested was necessary.

Solution: After discussing the seniority set-up in relation to vacations, the group agreed that men with the most seniority should still have first choice of vacation time. Two of the three men with the greatest seniority decided to withdraw their request for vacations during the first week of the hunting season. Two other men agreed to take their vacation during the second week of the deer hunting season. Doing this gave them a gain of one day in their vacation, since a holiday (Thanksgiving) fell during that week. This left three of the former deer hunters with their vacations in the first week of the deer hunting season.

Results: Company maintenance and construction forces were ample in the district for the deer hunting period. Vacation arrangements were satisfactory to all men in the group.

CASE 28

Statement of Problem: Arranging an on-call schedule with four two-man crews to cover seven days a week after regular working hours. (No previous efforts made.)

Handling of Problem: I held group discussion with the eight men and asked them how they wanted to divide the time each would have to stand call. Some wanted the same days all the time, and others did not.

Solution: The two men who work regularly on Saturday and Sunday took those days on call because they are the only crew to work regularly on the weekend. The other three crews work by the schedule they decided on, which is to alternate two days a week for two crews and one day a week for one crew. Each month these three crews change their on-call days.

Results: Everyone is satisfied.

CASE 29

Statement of Problem: Some men did not like the idea of working every Saturday with the off day on Monday. This involved about 16 men. No previous efforts to solve the problem had been made.

Handling of Problem: It was put before the men that the crews could rotate, deciding how long a period they wanted to work before changing off days. As some preferred to have Mondays off all the time, it was suggested that the men could change off days individually with one another rather than by crews.

Solution: The men decided against rotating the crews, but anyone who wanted a Saturday off now and then could make his own arrangements to change off days with someone else.

Results: Very little changes of off days have been made, but the privilege has been used.

CASE 30

Statement of Problem: Arranging a work schedule for the temporary transfer of one clerk to cover an 8- to 12-week period in another office about 35 miles distant, but in the same division. The problem arose because one of the regular clerks had to go to the hospital for an operation, and another of the clerks had previously been granted a 7-week leave of absence to take a trip to Europe.

Handling of Problem: The problem was presented to three clerks, and they were told what the company would do in the way of paying for room, board, transportation, etc. They were asked what their ideas would be, as a clerk would have to be furnished for the 8- to 12-week period.

Solution: It was decided that, rather than have one clerk go to the office in question for the whole period of time, they would alternate between the three of them, viz.: each girl would cover the schedule every third week. Owing to previous commitments, such as weddings and social functions, there was one week that the three of them all preferred staying at their regular work location. It was decided that, for this one week only, the office that required the clerical assistance would send any typing work they could to the office where the three clerks in question would be.

Results: The plan is working out satisfactorily.

CASE 31

Statement of Problem: Four men were within two weeks of completing their first year of apprentice training as linemen. The set-up is that trainees alternate between the training center and their respective line crews, one month in each. The foreman and instructor are required to turn in individual written reports on their progress.

Two of these men were with Foreman A, and the other two with Foreman B.

After one year of training, it has been agreed by the company and the union, a man should be qualified and is expected to start working "primary" (4800 volts).

Official reports of the men from the foremen and instructor were satisfactory, but the job steward reported that the linemen on Foreman A's crew were going to refuse to work primary with the two apprentices assigned to him.

The general foreman had heard through the grapevine that the two men in question were not doing so well as had been officially reported. Any questioning of the foremen or instructor resulted in reassuring statements to the effect that these men were not quite so good as the others, but that they would make out all right if given enough time.

Handling of Problem: A meeting was called by the general foreman and was attended by the division supervisor, the other general foreman in the district, all the foremen involved, the job steward, and the assistant business manager of the local union.

The problem was stated, and the following questions were raised: "If these men are not ready to work primary, why had it taken us so long to find out?" "Was there some misunderstanding about the qualifications?" "What should be done to correct the situation?"

Although the two men in question had spent most of their time in the field with Foreman A, they had worked with the other foremen a little, so that each of them had an opinion. All the foremen agreed that, although these two men did not seem to have the ability possessed by the others, they should be allowed to continue their apprenticeship and would eventually make satisfactory linemen.

The job steward said that he understood these men were incapable of working low voltage correctly, and, until they could demonstrate that they could, they should not work primary.

The question was also raised as to the opportunities presented by the jobs that Foreman A had been assigned; whether he had allowed the apprentices to work when he did have an opening or whether he had held them back in preference to faster and more experienced men.

Foreman A finally asked that the linemen on his crew, who had reputedly said they would refuse to work primary with these apprentices, be brought into the meeting. This was done on the same afternoon. It was agreed, however, that the other foremen and the second general foreman would not be needed in the afternoon session.

When the linemen were asked for their opinion they practically repeated what had been said by the job steward. However, another point was brought up, which was that they had understood that, once they accepted these apprentices to start working primary, they would be stuck with them, and that nothing would ever be done regardless of what kind of workmen they turned out to be. They were assured by the general foreman and the division supervisor that this was not true, and that they wanted the linemen's cooperation in training new men. They said they realized that a lineman should have quite a bit to say about the work habits of an apprentice who was going to work alongside of him.

Solution: After a thorough discussion it was decided that these apprentices would go ahead as originally planned and would do the work on primary that was expected of a beginner, but if the lineman felt that the job was too complicated for an apprentice to help him he would ask the foreman for more experienced help. It was also decided that the general foreman would check with the linemen each month to see how the apprentices were doing.

Results: I have had nothing but good reports from everyone concerned. The linemen feel that they are being considered and are a part of the apprentice training program. The apprentices have a new lease on life and, of course, that helps them do a better job. They had felt for some time that they were being railroaded, as it was getting to them that these linemen were going to refuse to work with them.

NOTE: This meeting was also a forerunner of a new procedure in grading the apprentices. The foremen didn't feel that they wanted to commit themselves on paper as to whether a man was doing all right, so we now have agreed to meet every two months and discuss the apprentices' qualifications and progress. Also, the apprentices will change from one foreman to another, so that their experience will be broadened and more foremen's opinions will be available.

CASE 32

Statement of Problem: On weekends, when no cleaning women were on duty, the room became quite dirty because two or three individuals in a group of eight people were rather careless about wastepaper, cigarette ashes, etc. This condition was called to the attention of the group several times, but very little improvement resulted.

Handling of Problem: A meeting was arranged with the entire group. The problem was stated, and the group was asked for opinions on how conditions could be improved. The first suggestions were that (a) the boss be held responsible for enforcing housekeeping rules, and (b) one person be appointed to watch over the others. One person thought the problem wasn't serious enough to bother about.

Solution: The group finally decided that the best solution would be that each person be responsible for his own position; and if anyone got careless he would be reminded by his neighbor and would then clean up.

Results: Solution has worked very well. The room is as clean on weekends as at any other time.

CASE 33

Statement of Problem: Joe, who has worked on the line board for quite a few years, became ill and was off the job for about 5 weeks. On returning to work he was in quite a nervous state because he thought he had a heart ailment. This upset him so that he became frightened when using the radio, so that he froze up and was unable to talk on the radio. He told me of this feeling. I told him to forget about using the radio for the present.

Handling of Problem: I talked to the rest of our group (excluding Joe) and told them about Joe's feeling, and they agreed to take Joe's turn at operating the radio until he was feeling better. After about a month Joe began to feel like his old self again, and so I arranged another meeting with the group (again excluding Joe).

Solution: It was agreed that when a crew was reporting on a job on the radio they would make themselves busy, so that Joe would have to take the crew's report on the radio.

Results: The above arrangements worked out very well, and it wasn't long before Joe was dispatching crews on the radio and taking his regular turn.

CASE 34

Statement of Problem: Sixty per cent of the group was abusing rest period (for coffee) by taking too much time. I previously tried to solve this problem by dropping hints and setting an example. Twelve people were involved.

Handling of Problem: I arranged for a group meeting. The problem was presented by asking what the group thought was a reasonable time for a rest period. This created quite a discussion. The major points raised were the difficulty in being waited on, and the fact that members of the group sometimes stopped at other offices on business after the coffee period.

Solution: Fifteen minutes was agreed upon as a fair amount of time needed.

Results: The plan has worked very well.

CASE 35

Statement of Problem: The boiler maintenance group is made up of three job classifications: boiler repairmen, 1st; boiler repairmen, 2nd; and boiler repair helpers. Overtime assignments, for a long while, have been distributed separately within each of these three classifications. For example, the boiler repairmen, 1st, rotated work among themselves without involving the boiler repairmen, 2nd.

Handling of Problem: At a regular meeting of the boiler maintenance group the question of the overtime distribution came up for consideration. Two conflicting viewpoints were expressed by the group: (*a*) overtime should be balanced among the whole group as a unit; (*b*) overtime should be kept balanced within the three classifications, as it had been in the past. The group as a whole thought the past plan was acceptable, but that the method of overtime distribution needed to be clarified.

Solution: Keep the present system, but operate it on this basis:

1. Helpers will have first call on cleaning furnaces and turbining boiler tubes.

2. On jobs requiring boiler repairmen, 1st, the necessary first-class men should be called in and the assistance will come from the boiler repairmen, 2nd.

3. If the required number of helpers to do a job cannot be obtained from the helper group, the remainder required will be called from the boiler repairmen, 2nd.

4. If the required number of boiler repairmen, 1st, cannot be obtained to do a job, the boiler repairmen, 2nd, will be called.

5. In each classification the man with the lowest amount of overtime will be called first.

6. The group will start out as of June 7 with a zero balance on the overtime book.

7. The men starting out on a job which runs into overtime will have first choice on this overtime.

A final question brought out by one of the helpers was, "What would happen if the weekend cleaning of furnaces should be discontinued?" The problem was whether the helpers would then have a chance to share the overtime of the boiler repairmen, 2nd. It was agreed that the present method, as clarified, would be continued until the men in any one classification felt that they were not getting a fair share of the overtime. At that time another meeting would be held to make any changes thought desirable by the group as a whole.

Results: This plan has been operating satisfactorily. Recently the boiler repair helpers have asked for another meeting to talk over the situation.

CASE 36

Statement of Problem: Four men who worked as pipe fitters were dissatisfied because of poor opportunities to learn advanced work and because of the tiresome routine of some of their jobs. The jobs included work on a dump truck and on a drip truck. (Liquid by-products of the gas collect in small chambers along the mains. These chambers are called "drips." A tank truck collects the liquid periodically.) In the past the senior men had the best jobs, and the junior men had all the worst jobs. The drip truck usually was the assignment of the junior men.

Handling of Problem: The four men and the supervisors concerned were called together. The problem, as presented, was that there had been feelings of dissatisfaction with the jobs by almost everybody who had been on the work at various times; that the supervisor didn't know what was the best way to tackle the problem; and that their help and suggestions would be welcome. At first the men did not understand this opportunity to help plan the job. After discussion got under way, however, they expressed their ideas freely. The discussion brought out clearly the two possible ways of carrying on the work: (*a*) assigning jobs according to seniority, and (*b*) rotating jobs without regard for seniority. All sides of the problem were considered.

Solution: The group came to complete agreement to rotate the jobs on a four-week basis. It was felt that this would give each man

1. A better idea of all duties required.
2. An opportunity to work under different foremen.
3. More opportunity for training on service work.
4. An equal chance for overtime.

Results: This plan has been working well for four months. All the men are well satisfied with the job as it now operates. Numerous practical safety suggestions have been made by the members of the group, and these have been followed through.

Some changes have been made in the situation. One man has been advanced out of the group to a serviceman's classification. He has been replaced with another man, who follows in rotation the one who had been the junior man. Each man is also spending two months in a row on the main repair crew.

CASE 37

Statement of Problem: There was dissatisfaction among a group who had the job of cleaning fires on gas generators. The past method assigned a gas maker, a pump man, and a utility man to specific doors. The sub gas maker was allowed to help at all three doors. The gas makers felt that men on lower jobs should be assigned so they themselves would be free to check all doors.

Handling of Problem: We got the group together at fire-cleaning time and told them we were aware of the dissatisfaction, and we asked if they had any suggestions to improve conditions. The group felt some plan of alternating on all doors should be worked out.

Solution: All men decided to try rotating as follows: three men would be assigned to specific doors, and a fourth man would help on all doors for a period of one week; the next week all would change places, with a different man allowed to work on all doors; the third and fourth weeks, the procedure followed, progressively. Relief men were to take the position of the man being relieved.

Results: We started this job last week, and so far everyone in the group is satisfied.

CASE 38

Statement of Problem: A job required the installation of wires and weights in precipitators of high-pressure boilers.

Handling of Problem: The men had ideas of how to do the job which differed from ours. They said that if they could do the job their way time and money would be saved.

Solution: We decided to do the job the men's way.

Results: Time and money are being saved.

CASE 39

Statement of Problem: The department was in need of additional office space. None was available in the building where the department was located. One thousand square feet was made available in another building. The question was, which of the six groups should move. The conditions were as follows:

(a) Groups 1, 5, and 6 could not be moved.
(b) Group 6 needed space more than any other.
(c) Group 2 could most easily be quartered at a detached location.
(d) Group 2 and group 4 did much the same kind of work.
(e) Group 6 had to have ready access to records, safes, and typing services.
(f) Group 3 had no special problems.
(g) The number of employees in the groups varied considerably.

Handling of Problem: The supervisors of the groups were called together and presented with the problem. They examined the available space in both buildings, made trial desk layouts, and felt out the attitude of their employees on the possibility of moving. The supervisors as a group decided that it would create great inconvenience for group 4 to move away from group 6. They agreed that groups 2 and 3 could best be housed in a detached location. Since this would require more space than the 1000 square feet, inquiries were made about the possibility of getting a larger area. It was found that an additional 1000 square feet could be obtained.

Solution: Supervisors of groups 2 and 3 accepted the supervisory group decision that they should move. They discussed the matter with their employees and took them to the new location to survey its advantages. Details such as partitions, safes, typing service, and desk arrangements were worked out cooperatively.

Working together, the employees developed a moving plan that was agreeable to all and involved several changes that the general supervisor might not have considered.

Results: The move has taken place, and adjustments are being made. So far, the solution appears to be very satisfactory.

CASE 40

Statement of Problem: The distribution of two new chairs to members of a group of cost estimators.

Handling of Problem: I called the group together and informed them that two new chairs had been received and were to be assigned to the two members that the group decided should deserve them. I pointed out to them several ways that the decisions could be made; seniority in the department, seniority in the company, type of job, etc. The group discussed the problem, and several persons with low seniority urged that they be passed out by lot; those with most seniority seemed agreeable. One individual, who was not in the work group but who happened to be present, said it was the supervisor's problem and that he was trying to "pass the buck." The group didn't agree, however, and continued to discuss the problem despite heckling by the outsider.

Solution: The group decided to draw lots for chairs, but two of the younger members, with least seniority in the group, refused to draw, asserting that they didn't believe they were entitled to the chairs.

Results: The result of the draw was that a member with the most seniority in the company got one chair, and the other was drawn by the member with second longest seniority in the group. The oldest member in years and with most seniority in the group did not get a new chair. All members expressed satisfaction with the result.

CASE 41

Statement of Problem: Four passes were available for the meetings of an accounting conference. Included were four luncheon tickets for one day and four dinner tickets for the second day. These were to be distributed among ten employees.

Handling of Problem: The employees were told of the above situation, and it was explained that those who attended on the dinner date would get the dinner tickets, and those who attended on the other date would get the luncheon tickets.

Solution: Two employees said they could not attend either day; four employees said they could not attend the first day; and four employees said they could not attend the second day.

Passes and tickets were distributed on this basis.

Results: Everyone appeared satisfied.

CASE 42

Statement of Problem: We had to determine who should prepare relief refreshment. The problem was created when the girl who previously did this extracurricular work, by personal choice, left the department. The subsequent indefinite volunteer procedure was unsatisfactory; there was some bickering and considerable criticism. The refreshment was enjoyed by most of the people in the department, 75 per cent of whom were males and the other 25 per cent females, mostly stenographers.

Handling of Problem: An informal discussion meeting of the stenographic group and the supervisor was held in the stenographers' room. Although the group was acquainted with the problem, all pertinent facts and details were reviewed. There was a very lively and interesting discussion during which each member of the group had something useful to say. The following issues were raised and settled:

Should all who enjoyed refreshment take turns at preparation? No. Men should be excused—not dependable, away from headquarters too often, don't have "know how," etc.

Should all girls in the department take turns? No. The few girls in other divisions should be excused, as their work location was too remote from preparation location. Too much lost time and motion.

Should all girls in the stenographic group take their turn? No. Girls who did not avail themselves of the refreshment should be excused.

Solution: Girls in stenographic group who enjoyed refreshment would take turns at preparation. A team of two girls was to be "on duty" for a period of one week, one of the girls to prepare refreshment in morning, the other in afternoon, and to change about each day. This plan was to continue until each girl had taken her turn, and the established sequence would be repeated. It so happened that there was an even number of "qualified" girls.

Results: Excellent so far (after about five weeks).

CASE 43

Statement of Problem: We wanted to change the salutation to customers (telephone contact) when asking a customer to wait on the line. Six clerks were involved.

Handling of Problem: As it is difficult to get the group together because of the nature of the business, we gave each clerk a slip asking her to put down what she thought would be a good salutation.

Solution: The slips were examined by the supervisor, and each clerk was contacted and shown the results. Since the answers made by the clerks were quite similar, it was not difficult to arrive at a salutation agreeable to all.

BEFORE: "Just a minute, please."

Now: "Billing information—just a minute, please."

The customer still has to wait, but he now knows that he is waiting for the person he wants to talk to.

Results: I checked again with the clerks, and they feel that the new salutation is working out well.

CASE 44

Statement of Problem: Should we specify copperweld ground rods to replace galvanized steel pipes for primary installation grounds on customers' property? The national code prohibits the use of solder, which had been the method used with galvanized pipes. Efforts to use some mechanical connection between the pipe and the copper conductor have met with grave resistance from contractors and customers. Nearly two years have been spent in the search for a solution. A substitute must be inexpensive, use less labor in field, and have high electrical conductivity for long periods of time.

Handling of Problem: The group understood that a good ground was necessary to protect life, that a ground was necessary at each transformer location and each primary house, and that $6\frac{3}{4}$-inch pipes 6 to 8 feet long driven full length is our present standard. They reacted constructively, in that each agreed we should follow the code. They questioned (1) the wisdom of brazing pigtails as a field job, owing to nonuniformity; (2) the possibility of purchasing rods with a lead already brazed on; and (3) the possible use of mechanical clamps to fasten a lead to the rod. The group also considered the actual material cost of copperweld rods compared to galvanized pipe with soldered lead; the acceptance by contractors and workmen; the difficulty of enforcing the present standards (since the workmen do not like the present method); and the nonuniformity in the field.

Solution: The group decided that copperweld ground rods or a substitute should be used with a suitable clamp for connecting pigtails.

Results: A test is underway in a particularly bad location where the earth is vibrating. It is found that the copperweld rod is more expensive, and a search for a suitable, less costly substitute is being made.

CASE 45

Statement of Problem: Should major appliance field men continue carrying Knickerbocker kits for small parts and repair tools for customers' service, or would a standardized small kit containing the most commonly used tools be more desirable and convenient? The larger kit could be left in the car for use as needed.

Handling of Problem: The group was called together, and the problem was stated. Opinions were asked of each individual, and discussion encouraged. The disadvantages of each type of kit brought out were: (1) Knickerbocker kit: bulky and difficult to carry through close quarters without bumping customer property; hard to find space for in a crowded, cluttered kitchen out of the way of housewife and out of reach of children; can be overloaded until too heavy. (2) Small kit: may not have proper tool; would require more running back to the car; might cause slighting of job rather than going to car; and does not present as good an appearance.

Solution: The group decided by oral vote of seven to four to continue to use the Knickerbocker kit.

Results: No further mention has been made of tool boxes as of this date.

CASE 46

Statement of Problem: Among a group of three dispatchers and six senior telephone clerks there was a feeling that favoritism or discrimination was being shown because one of the dispatchers received more overtime than anyone else in the group. This appears to have been caused by the practice of calling the nearest available man when additional help was required.

Handling of Problem: All of the group involved were invited to make suggestions for a solution. During the discussion it was pointed out that the employee having a day off during the week would be far more likely to have a chance to work on his day off than would those having Saturday for a day off, because of the lack of work on Saturday.

Solution: After all suggestions had been discussed, it was decided that a chart should be made, showing each employee's name and the last date he worked overtime. This chart was to be posted in the department. Whenever overtime is necessary, the chart is to be checked and the employee with the least overtime asked to work. If he is not available, then the employee with the next least overtime should be asked, etc.

Results: The results are not definite. The plan is still on trial, although all employees involved believe that this is the best possible solution.

CASE 47

Statement of Problem: Stock handlers fill a large number of requisitions and bills of material each day. In transposing stock numbers from the bin labels to the orders, errors were frequently made. This was sometimes due to speed in handling, sometimes to illegible writing, and sometimes to blurred bin labels.

If the errors were not detected and corrected before the papers were mailed to the general offices for tabulation, the wrong stock numbers would appear on the checking tape. When the check was made and the error discovered, the office clerk would have to fill in a form and mail it to the accounting service department to get the matter corrected. This involved extra work for the warehouse office, the tabulation division, and the accounting service department. Of course, if the incorrect stock numbers were discovered in the warehouse office the papers were taken out for correction by the man making the error.

Previous efforts had been made to solve the problem by reminding the group of the need for care. These efforts had resulted only in slight and temporary improvement.

Handling of Problem: The supervisor called the stock handlers together and explained the problem to them. He described the extra work involved in correcting these errors. He asked the group for suggestions on how the trouble could be eliminated or the number of errors cut down. The group talked freely about the problem and reacted favorably toward working out a solution. Reasons for the errors were listed; another list was made of ways to meet the difficulty.

Solution: The group agreed on the following plan:

1. They would copy the number carefully from the stock bin label onto the requisition or bill of material.

2. After they had copied it they would verify it against the stock number on the bin label.

3. If there were any cause to question the stock bin label, they would check the number against a stock tape kept in the warehouse.

Results: Errors have been reduced from three or four a week to one in two weeks.

CASE 48

Statement of Problem: At previous meetings with cable-pulling foremen it was agreed that a pulling crew should consist of 11 men including the foreman, and that crews would work short-handed when men were absent because of sickness or vacation.

Handling of Problem: At a recent meeting the foremen were asked if they wanted to continue the present practice or be guaranteed a 10-man crew, with men from a manhole-cleaning crew to replace those absent (manhole-cleaning crew to act as a pool).

Solution: Foremen unanimously agreed on the guaranteed ten-man crew, with necessary replacements to be furnished from manhole-cleaning crew.

Results: Solution will be tried later this year.

General Conclusions from Unselected Cases

The above cases illustrate the use of group discussion for handling a variety of day-to-day job problems. Most of them reflect a good degree of awareness for personnel problems and represent a sincere attempt to correct some dissatisfaction. There is little evidence that great difficulty was encountered in obtaining free discussion in the first attempts. In some instances the supervisor has exerted a controlling influence by suggesting solutions, and, instead of raising a problem, has presented the group with choices. Even in these cases, however, a considerable degree of permissiveness has been evidenced.

The cases also show that the supervisor has made a sincere attempt to change his previous approach and in some reports has mentioned that the group reacted to his change in procedure. Nevertheless, the process of changing the approach for solving a problem seems not to have been an unpleasant experience.

None of the cases reflect an unsatisfactory result, and some of the results are strikingly satisfactory. In practically all instances mention is made of the group's satisfaction, and it is this satisfaction, rather than increased production, with which the supervisor seems most concerned. A reading of the cases makes one feel that employee morale is one of the great concerns of a present-day supervisor. It is also apparent that employees show a willingness to tackle efficiency problems even when the problems are sometimes put rather bluntly.

A surprising thing has been the fact that in actual situations employees work more cooperatively than they do in the role playing of cases. When role playing is used, the leader usually has difficulty because the persons who play the parts of employees reflect a considerable degree of hostility or suspicion. It appears that when supervisors play the parts of employees they read into the employees' roles a rather strong desire to protect themselves and avoid efficiency. It would seem that previous experiences with employees have not given them an opportunity to see their constructive abilities. Thus an actual experience with group discussion sometimes gives the supervisor a rather pleasant surprise.

With a changed view of employees, the supervisor can become more permissive and more and more he can see how conditions in the situation, rather than unconstructive attitudes in people, are the starting point of personnel problems. Human relations training must accomplish such an attitude change in supervisors if the group-decision approach is to perpetuate itself.

Failures in the Use of Group Decisions

General Considerations. No discussion of cases is complete without a study of failures. One can learn as much from failures as from successes. However, a record of case failures has been very difficult to obtain, and supervisors tend not to report them. There is perhaps much truth in the contention of many supervisors that they have no failures to report.

There are a number of possible reasons for the democratic method to fail to produce desirable results. Some of these are as follows:

1. The supervisor failed to present all the necessary information.
2. The supervisor confused his attempt to sell a solution with the true group-decision method.
3. The supervisor, rather than permitting the group to develop a solution, gave employees a choice between two procedures, and they chose poorly.
4. The supervisor did not respect the limits of his area of freedom.
5. The group was uncooperative and evolved a solution that was unreasonable.
6. The group saw an opportunity to remedy past grievances at the company's expense.
7. The group was incapable of solving the problem.
8. The group's solution did not work out.
9. The group could not agree.
10. The solution is of lower quality than the supervisor desired.

It can readily be seen that failure is not always an objective fact but may be an opinion, as implied in item 10 above. Is someone merely disagreeing with a solution, or is the solution of truly poor quality? A failure may also be due to faulty understanding on the part of the leader, so that the failure is not due to the method but to the supervisor's failure to use it effectively. The first 4 items seem to fall into this category. Finally, failure may be attributed to the method, when alternative methods might have also failed, perhaps to an even greater degree. To expect the method to solve all problems or to deliver to its user all the things he desires is too exacting. True failure would be evidenced when the method was less effective than an alternative known method. It is conceivable that the method might be successful more often than the autocratic method and be a success as an over-all procedure. Yet if the autocratic method were more successful under a certain few conditions than the democratic method, it would be well to know these conditions. Only in this manner can the limitations of a method be determined. If such determinations are made it then becomes possible to seek for improvements that might prevent these failures.

In order to accomplish this end it was important to collect cases of failure of the group-decision method. The following constitute the cases that have been reported as failures. In each instance an attempt will be made to determine the reason for the failure.

CASE 1. PROBLEM INVOLVING TIME OFF

During hunting season many men wish time off and often take their vacations then. One crew of 12 men had a good percentage of hunters, so this created quite a problem. The second level of supervision had agreed that it was reasonable to spare two men at a time for this purpose. The problem put to the group was how the schedule should be arranged so that everyone would get the most out of the hunting season.

The discussion revealed that four men wanted to go hunting, and each of them had a week's vacation coming. However, each wished an extra week off without pay. The best of the schedules discussed, with each man given two weeks off, left the crew with four men short for a period of 10 days. Finally, one of the men not requesting time off suggested that they adopt the schedule under consideration and that the crew work extra hard to cover the job completely when four men were off. The rest of the men agreed that this was a good idea and that they would all bear down if this solution was acceptable. The foreman thought that the request was reasonable, and he was satisfied from his other experiences with group meetings that the job would be covered if the men said so. He, therefore, took the liberty of accepting the solution, although it went beyond the limits specified by his superior. He thought that he could straighten it out and took this chance. He, however, failed to convince his superior and was mildly reprimanded. In the sense that a violation of the area of freedom did occur this solution must be considered a failure to solve the problem.

However, the results of the solution should also be considered. During the questionable period when four men were off the eight men covered the job and kept up their end of the arrangement. In addition, a storm, which lasted a week, began a couple of days after four men were off the job. Nevertheless, this crew kept their bargain and did the extra load without complaint. They showed a high degree of initiative and judgment in some of their activities. Where possible, they arranged temporary connections and so were able to give all customers uninterrupted telephone service during the emergency. Furthermore, in the midst of the heavy load, two men returned three days ahead of time. When the crew asked, "Don't you fellows think we are able to cover the job?" the two men gave as their excuse the fact that each had gotten his deer and had hurried home to help out if things got tough. Without their help the job would have been covered, but their aid was, nevertheless, welcomed. Evidence of the high morale maintained was the men's boasting and pride and the way they jokingly told the hunters that they could have stayed away longer.

The fact that the men were able to cover the job reveals the cooperation that group solutions engender. Nevertheless, it must be recognized that supervisors have responsibility only in their area of freedom. In this instance the violation can be explained away in that the supervisor was trained in the procedure and had confidence in it, whereas his superior was not trained. Had both been trained it is possible that the area of freedom would not have been made so specific and binding.

CASE 2. CARRYING THE MAIL

The messenger job is the lowest-rated job in a large department. When the messenger is absent, it is difficult to obtain a substitute from among the office force. Any girl requested to do the job feels degraded. The problem of obtaining a substitute for the messenger, therefore, raises a problem in which group values and status are involved. The problem of how to obtain a substitute when the messenger is absent or is not obtainable at the required time because of a long errand was put to the group. The number of girls (typists) involved and available for this duty was five.

After a brief discussion the group unanimously agreed that the job should be rotated among them. This is the typical group solution when unpleasant jobs must be assigned, and it can be seen that this solution removes any stigma that might be attached to the tour of duty. At the time, this solution struck the supervisor as perfectly satisfactory, and it was put into practice.

The girls performed their substitute duties and executed the agreed-upon plan very well. However, the supervisor reported the solution as a failure. She said there were many complaints arising from the fact that it was difficult to trace or check certain things. Different girls distributed the mail on various hours, so that no one knew what had been carried on the preceding trip. However, the supervisor didn't know what to do about this difficulty because she said, "The girls think it is working fine and are perfectly satisfied, whereas the fact is that it is not working out. How can I now tell them they are all wrong when they are so pleased with the arrangement?"

> Is the solution of the problem really a failure, or was the morale problem solved and a new problem created? If the latter is true, can the new problem be put to the girls without their losing trust in the supervisor's willingness to use the democratic procedure?

After discussing the failure the supervisor agreed that the difficulty could be considered as a new problem, and she decided to put this new problem to her group.

In taking the new problem to the group she pointed out that difficulties arose because mail could not be traced, and she wondered how the matter might be corrected.

Instead of abandoning the solution, as the supervisor thought would be necessary, the girls merely modified and extended their solution. It was agreed that written records of tours should be made on a form and kept at a central point. The record would show when each girl substituted and the places she visited.

As a consequence the ability to trace mail was improved, since it no longer was necessary to rely on the memory of the messenger or anyone who substituted for her.

In this instance a true failure arose, but it was the type of mistake that the supervisor likewise might have made. Furthermore, in recognizing the failure as an inadequate solution additional facts were supplied to the group so that improvements could be made.

CASE 3.   JOBS INVOLVING DIFFERENT LEVELS OF SKILL

In electrical repair work it is customary to recognize that certain repair jobs require more skill and knowledge than others. Repairing an electric stove obviously is more difficult than replacing a fuse. New men are usually assigned the more simple house calls, whereas the men with more experience and seniority are given the more difficult assignments. Invariably this condition leads to some dissatisfaction. The new men want to do more difficult assignments even though their pay would not be affected. They want variety and *new experiences*.

Recognizing this as a problem, one supervisor put the issue to his group. Should we continue as we now operate, or should we give assignments in the order that they are received? The group voted for the latter, which was what the supervisor feared. He tried it and found that he was right. Some men were going out on jobs that they could not handle.

In discussing this solution in the training group it soon became apparent that giving men a choice was not quite the same as having the men solve a problem. The supervisor in question believed these to be the only two possibilities. Other members believed that a variety of other solutions would have been possible. What this group would have done had they been given the problem rather than a choice between two solutions is a matter of speculation. However, it seems reasonable to suppose that if there is opposition to a plan in operation and men are given an alternative they may vote against what they dislike rather than for an alternative. A choice situation of this kind does not permit the necessary analysis which ordinarily occurs when a problem is presented, but tends to close the issue too quickly. It also gives the group an opportunity to vote against management rather than solve a problem.

CASE 4.   THE INEFFECTIVE GROUP LEADER

The job in this case is supervised by a foreman, but the men who report to him are divided into small work groups or crews, each of which has a group leader, who is usually chosen on the basis of seniority. A group leader organizes the work of his crew and also works himself. Thus he lacks the status of a supervisor, but nevertheless has certain leadership responsibilities.

A group leader of a particular material handling group was unable to organize the work of his crew and was unable to get all his men to do their share of the work. As a consequence the foreman was forced to spend much of his time in this area in order to keep the supplies moving and the lines supplied.

The group leader was colored. The crew was composed of 11 men: 10 white and 1 colored. Some of the crew would cooperate, but others would not. The foreman had talked to the group leader many times about his duties and responsibilities, but the group leader was still unable to handle his crew effectively. There were two merry-go-round assembly lines in this area which had to be supplied with material. A stock conveyor from outside had to be emptied and the supplies stored.

The foreman called the crew together for a discussion. He summarized the job, discussed how it was running, said that something had been wrong in the past, and asked the men for their ideas on how the job could be done better in the future. (The men themselves knew that things were not running smoothly.)

The group responded immediately and began making suggestions and presenting their ideas. Only three men had to be asked by name for their opinions. The group insisted upon hearing what these three had to say and told them to speak up. The group leader, however, was reticent and said little. One man started to make wisecracks and "sound off"; the rest of the group turned on him and told him to "shut up."

The suggestions of the group were as follows: They wanted the group broken up into smaller units. Four men were to be assigned to each production line, and two were to supply cotton pads to the lines. The cotton pad job was felt to be the worst one because it was dirty and hot work. All were to take turns working with the cotton pads. They were to rotate each day, so that each would work one day with the pads. The men should not rotate by twos, but individually. The group leader was to appoint two men each morning for the cotton pad job.

The group leader was also requested to fill in for absentees and to help out any of the units in rush periods. Further, the groups were to be flexible enough so that the group leader could assign men to different groups when one group fell behind or had more work to do than the others. The purpose of the above plan was to make each man more responsible for some part of the work. The group felt that several men were not doing their share, and the solution would make the division of work more nearly equal.

The foreman then asked the group what had been wrong in the past. Before they answered he asked the group leader what he thought his duties were. The group leader merely said, "To keep the stock on the line." The foreman then asked the group what the group leader's duties were. They said: (1) to keep the line bins full of stock; (2) to keep the stock moving; and (3) to see to it that the men did their work. The group leader agreed that these were his duties. The foreman then asked the group how they would feel if the group leader reported to him any refusals to work. The men agreed that the group leader *should* report these refusals to the foreman.

The foreman asked the group leader how he felt about the men's decision. The leader felt that they were right. He agreed with the group, but, when asked why he hadn't been doing this, he dodged the issue.

The foreman feels that most of the trouble lies in the fact that the leader is colored and all but one of his men are white. He had noticed that the leader would rather do the work himself than ask anyone else to do it. Later, when the foreman spoke to the men individually, they said that the leader had improved, but still mumbled when giving orders. They had no objections to his remaining their leader.

Before the group discussion, one of the men had asked for a transfer. His reason was that the fumes in the work area were bad for his health. Shortly after the group discussion he withdrew his request, stating that "conditions around here have improved lately."

The reason for reporting this case as a failure is that the group leader still was not so effective as desired. It is true that the men worked better and there was less shirking of responsibility, probably because of the social pressure created in the discussion. Nevertheless, the group leader still remained reticent. In so far as this leader is concerned more improvement is needed, and it seems that this is an individual problem. The desirable thing to do would be to supplement the group discussion with a counseling type of interview. Apparently the Negro leader is afraid to give orders, and the willingness of the group to receive them has not been sufficient to overcome his timidity. It is also possible that additional group discussion might further improve his relationship with the group.

CASE 5.   SETTING A POLICY

One of the clearest cases of the failure of group decision arose in connection with the problem of setting a departmental policy regarding the giving of presents. It had been customary for employees to contribute money for gifts whenever one of their members had a special occasion in his life. Thus, marriage, sickness, leaving the company, and the like were occasions when sections within a department contributed to a fund for purchasing an appropriate gift. Under this procedure some of the employees benefited, whereas others were consistently giving out money. The extent of the group contributing varied, and there was no clear-cut custom regarding the number of units or individuals who would be expected to contribute on a given occasion.

The supervisors of the various units meeting with the department head agreed that the problem should be put to each of the units and discussed. Then representatives of the units would meet with the department head and attempt to establish a uniform plan for the department.

This procedure was followed, and in all of the unit meetings the feeling was generally expressed that the business of giving presents had gotten out of hand. When the representatives of the units met with the department head, it was soon agreed that the custom of giving presents should be discontinued.

Shortly after this agreement was reached, a popular man on a staff job accepted a position in South America. He had been with the company a long time. The employees of the unit in which he worked collected money and presented him with a handsome going-away present. Thus, the group decision was violated on the first test case.

When others pointed out to the unit that they had violated an agreement reached, the reply was that the unit had not agreed that the group decision covered this situation. They had not agreed to any blanket rule. This fellow was going to South America and had freely contributed to gifts in the past. It wouldn't be fair to let him go without some expression of appreciation.

It is possible that a misunderstanding on the group agreement existed, and if this is so it means that group decisions and their implications must be clearly stated. It is also possible that the discussions were not sufficiently free, so that many individuals gave only passive agreement. If this is so, it means that leaders of group discussions must be sufficiently sensitive to distinguish between passive acceptance and a meeting of minds.

In this instance, however, we feel that the defensive reactions of the unit that violated the agreement were due to the fact that the original decision had not taken all eventualities into account. The unit in question, it seems, did not feel it was fair to practice the decision in an instance that perhaps was more deserving than any that had previously come up. Such a group decision would seem like rank discrimination.

If this interpretation is correct an interesting group-decision problem is raised regarding the setting up of guides to future action. It is frequently true that practices and rules are made to fit all situations and, hence, are not perfectly suited to each individual situation. How seriously should we take violations or a disregarding of such group agreements? When a group agrees to violate its own solution, there must be something wrong with the solution. Should the problem in such instances be examined in the light of the new values that have come to the group's attention, or are these instances in which a group decision is inadequate? It seems only reasonable that, in questions concerning a company or group practice, accumulated experience may be necessary before the problem is finally solved to the desired degree of satisfaction, and this would require repeated re-examinations of the question. Too often such problems are solved on the basis of certain existing conditions, and, hence, such solutions are tailored to fit a given situation, but at the same time lack the universal application that a policy or practice must serve.

CASE 6. PLANS FOR COVERAGE DURING VACATIONS

In a large office involving several units it was customary to hire sufficient temporary help to keep the job running smoothly during the period when many employees were on vacation. Supervisors reporting to the second level of management reached a group decision that the problem of the need for extra help be put to each of their units.

This was done, and it was found that there were a variety of solutions. About half the units agreed that they needed no temporary assistance. These groups agreed on the maximum number that should be gone at any one time. Other units felt that help was needed, and it was agreed by the supervisors that the requests were reasonable. The fact that different units presented different recommendations created no problems between the groups.

Subsequently, however, a problem did arise. In one unit it had been agreed that only two persons should be on vacation at a given time and that extra help was not needed. However, in arranging schedules, it was found that three employees wanted vacations at the same time. A girl with the least seniority found it very important to take her vacation when two girls with considerable seniority wanted theirs. Although this conflict in schedules was later solved, an important problem still remains to be considered. Had this unit not agreed to cover the job without extra help, a rearrangement of vacation schedules would not have been necessary. At least that is the way the supervisors reasoned. Thus the groups that might be considered the most cooperative, since they did not request temporary help, found themselves in an unfavorable position with respect to other groups. Would this eventually lead to dissatisfaction and cause all groups to request help, whether they needed it or not? Suppose the discrepancy in vacation time between the three girls could not have been straightened out. Should the group be held to its decision, or should the decision be changed in the light of the new problem? These were issues considered in the discussion when this problem was reported, and the question was raised as to whether this type of problem should be solved on a departmental basis rather than a unit basis. If the departmental plan were to be used the procedure would be one of getting preliminary suggestions from the units and then building a single plan from the suggestions.

It seems likely that the problem in question is not important enough to make it the basis for a departmental practice. Even if this were done, the next issue would be the question of a company-wide plan. One of the virtues of the democratic procedure is that it tailors solutions to the needs of the time and the individuals concerned. All groups are not alike in their needs for help to cover vacation plans, and to set a rigid practice which fails to take the existing differences into consideration would seem to miss an important virtue in the democratic procedure. Rather, it seems that group solutions should be permissive and allow for modification when unforeseen events occur. Thus the discrepancy in vacation plans could be handled by the unit if the first solution was not regarded as a rigid commitment.

Conclusions. The above cases describe a variety of conditions or new problems that arise as a result of practicing group decisions. None of them seems to indicate clearly a failure of the method as such or to suggest a serious difficulty that arose because of an error on the part of the supervisor. In all instances it seems that by following the spirit of democratic leadership and attempting to adapt it to the situation, rather than depending on rigid procedures, the difficulties encountered can be overcome or corrected by taking them back to the group. If supervisors get the spirit of the method and understand its major objectives they adequately adapt themselves to exceptional conditions. In analyzing their own successes and difficulties they continue to develop skills. It is apparent, however, that counsel and guidance should be available in the early stages, so that failures do not produce discouragement but instead may be used to increase skills.

However, the above cases should not be taken as evidence that more disturbing failures may not occur. The list of reasons for failures given on page 286 must still be taken seriously, and guidance should be given to reduce them. The types of failures we have reported are based on the degree of training we have used in companies that already have good supervision and good morale. The degree to which these experiences can be generalized is an open question.

It is satisfying to observe that supervisors who have practiced group decisions on their jobs for some time find their groups very outspoken and sometimes hypercritical, and yet they seldom regard this critical attitude as a bad sign. Their reaction is, "Now they let us know how they really feel." Even the criticism of not being democratic enough fails to strike supervisors as unreasonable. Some think the group may be right, while others regard it as a sign of frankness. Yet it is quite possible for members of a work group to really become hypercritical. Some individuals who first experience group decisions expect to have their own way and expect special privileges. However, the pressure from other group members soon reduces this view in individualists, and a "we" attitude replaces it. It would be desirable to have experimental measures of these reactions and changes as democratic supervision is introduced. At the present time one must depend on the views expressed by supervisors when this subject is raised in group discussion with them.

An Experimental Test of Group Decision in an Unorganized Group

Introduction. Can the method of group decision be used in situations in which the group is unorganized and represents more an aggregation of individuals than a social group? It is apparent that in an organized group social pressure becomes a much more vital influence than in an unorganized group. Since persons in industrial groups work together day after day they invariably are organized, and the group takes on a definite social structure. However, students in a classroom of a large university may be assumed to lack this degree of structuring, since the specific group of individuals is present in a given class only for a short period in a week. Many do not even know each other. It is for this reason that a university student body presents a good opportunity to investigate the above question.

The author's course in psychology of management has an enrollment of approximately 300 students (range 285–347) each semester, and this group is broken into 7 to 10 laboratory sections of 25 to 35 students each. The laboratory offers a number of projects in human relations. For one of these projects a problem with which the students themselves are vitally concerned and in which they are emotionally involved was selected to test group decision. This was the problem of grades. The question to be answered was, "What do you consider to be a fair way to distribute A's, B's, C's, D's, and E's in the course?"

Each laboratory section was presented with the problem, with the understanding that the results of the various sections would be integrated in the lecture section. The solution put into practice would be the one reached by this procedure.

In order to test the effect of large and small groups in answering the question, each laboratory section was divided into two groups. One group, called a committee, had a chairman appointed (from the student body) by the instructor, and with 5 to 8 other students the chairman was to go to another location and lead a group discussion. He was requested to return in an hour with a unanimous group decision. The rest of the class of 18 to 28 students remained, and the instructor conducted the group meeting.

These discussions, in general, revealed a high degree of hostility toward the grading policies of the university and of various professors, as well as hostility toward other conditions in the university, but when it came to putting specific values on the various grades, the opinions expressed were surprisingly constructive. The problem of the questionable justification of grading on the basis of a distribution curve, rather than on some absolute scale, was vital to the students, but it was felt that this question did not apply to large populations, so that after a little discussion the groups were willing to assign percentages.

The Goals Set by Various Discussion Groups. The results of the first attempt are given in Table 16, which shows the group decisions

TABLE 16

GROUP DECISIONS ON GRADES

Distri-bution of Grades	Class Decision on Percentage for Each Grade					Committee Decision on Percentage for Each Grade				
	A	B	C	D	E	A	B	C	D	E
Sec. 1	10	35	45	9	1	10	30	50	10	0
Sec. 2	10	25	50	10	5	10	25	50	10	5
Sec. 3	11.5	21	48	15.5	4	12	21	48	15	4
Sec. 4	10	25	45	15	5	10	20	50	15	5
Sec. 5	10	25	50	10	5	10	15	65	10	0
Sec. 6	10	25	50	10	5	15	30	40	10	5
Sec. 7	15	25	45	10	5	13.5	35	41.5	10	0
Av.	10.9	25.8	47.6	11.4	4.3	11.5	25.1	49.2	11.4	2.7

reached by the committees as well as by the classes. It will be seen that the various laboratory sections and the committees showed striking similarity in their recommendations. For the classes the recommended percentage of A's and B's combined ranged from 35 to 45, and the D's and E's combined ranged from 10 to 19.5. The committees show slightly greater range; the combined A's and B's recommended varied from 25 to 45 per cent, whereas the combined D's and E's varied from 10 to 20 per cent. However, the average of the committees is only slightly more lenient than the classes. Thus the absence of the instructor as a discussion leader had little effect on the outcome.

In this instance the lecture group as a whole decided that the class and committee recommendations should be combined by weighting the class and committee recommendations 3 and 1, respectively. The results of the combined class and committee decisions, weighted on a 3 to 1 basis, is shown in the first line of Table 17. The second line of

TABLE 17

DISTRIBUTION OF GRADES BY AUTOCRATIC AND BY GROUP-DECISION
METHODS

	Percentage				
Distribution of Grades	A	B	C	D	E
1947 group decision	11.1	25.6	48.0	11.4	3.9
1946 autocratic decision	12.6	34.0	38.9	13.8	0.8

this table shows the distribution of grades given in the same course in the previous semester when the decision was made by the writer. It will be seen that the instructor previously gave a total of 46.6 per cent A's and B's, whereas the students' decision requested 36.7 per cent. With respect to D and E grades, the two distributions are similar. The instructor gave a total of 14.6 per cent D's and E's, whereas the students requested a total of 15.3 per cent.

Since this procedure has been used for five successive semesters, it is of interest to note the changes that have occurred. For this comparison only the combined results of the sections and committees have been used. These figures are shown in Table 18. It will be

TABLE 18

DISTRIBUTION OF GRADES REQUESTED BY SUCCESSIVE GROUPS

	Percentage				
Distribution of Grades	A	B	C	D	E
Spring, 1947, group decision	11.1	25.6	48.0	11.4	3.9
Fall, 1947, group decision	14.8	34.9	41.8	7.5	1.0
Spring, 1948, group decision	14.8	29.8	45.1	8.1	2.2
Fall, 1948, group decision	12.3	26.9	48.2	10.4	2.2
Spring, 1949, group decision	16.9	30.7	40.5	9.3	2.7

noted that all the succeeding groups have been more lenient with themselves. At first the author supposed that a repetition of the procedure may have been the cause of the increased leniency. However, the whole college has shown a similar trend. The university policy has been one of increased strictness, and as a consequence there has been an increased leniency on the part of the faculty. (This condition also results when supervisors are required to rate employees and when discharge is associated with certain ratings. Supervisors seem to be willing to give low ratings, but they do not wish to be held responsible for a discharge. When low ratings are directly associated with discharge, there is increased hesitation to give them.)

Even the last column, which shows the most lenient group decision, however, is not lenient with respect to the college or the department, and in this instance a modified procedure (to be discussed later) was used. Although a great deal of variation exists, these are typical of the grades given by the college as a whole, except for the percentage of E's. Here, the student decision is somewhat more strict. (Because of the confidential nature of grade distributions, specific figures from the college have not been included for comparable courses.)

Thus it appears that when students make a group decision on grades, they do not become excessively lenient. Rather, there is a surprising degree of insight into the actual situation that prevails on the campus as a whole, despite the fact that grade distributions are not available to students. Nor does the presence of the instructor play a determining part in keeping the decisions realistic, since the committees, with an appointed student leader, arrive at results similar to those of classes led by an instructor. This was true not only for the first group described, but also for the committees used on three succeeding semesters. However, this does not mean that the leader is unimportant. Rather it means that the leader need not be an instructor to keep the situation realistic.

To test the importance of the leader a further test was made, utilizing a modified form of the Phillips 66 (see Chapter 3) method. During the last semester groups of six were asked to make preliminary recommendations before the problem was put up for group discussion as a whole. In this instance a leader was not appointed but was chosen by the group. A total of 40 such groups were used.

On the whole, these committees made quite representative recommendations, such as those already described. However, there were three marked deviations. One group recommended 98⅔ per cent A's and ⅓ per cent grades in each of the other categories; the other two groups recommended 60 per cent A's and more B's than C's. Some of the others also were very lenient. A total of 14 groups (35 per cent) recommended 50 or more per cent A's and B's combined, and 8 groups (20 per cent) recommended 5 or less per cent D's and E's combined.

When the laboratory groups as a whole discussed the problem, the extreme groups were less influential than the others in that the whole group's decision tended to be more strict than the average of the committees of six. The combined results of each of the laboratory groups are given in the last line of Table 18, and show the influence of social pressure exerted by majority groups.

It was evident that some of the committees did not consider the interests of the group as a whole. It became apparent from the discussion that certain committees, or dominant individuals in them, were not considering the problem of fair grading but instead were attempting to satisfy other interests and were taking advantage of the opportunity. Some talked about rectifying previous injustices, and others felt the need of being excessively lenient in order to offset some group that might be strict. Here and there a person wanted to test whether or not we were serious in presenting the problem to them.

The results of the committees without appointed leaders indicate that the method of determining the leader may be important in effective group decisions. Official leaders accept the responsibility of keeping the group problem-centered. This does not mean that duly elected leaders might not do as well or better than appointed ones. But leaders chosen on the spur of the moment can hardly consider their office as a responsible one. In any case, it appears that the responsible leader is an essential factor in preventing certain factions and atypical influences from dominating. These factions may argue that the others have nothing to lose and thereby stifle discussion, but, under proper leadership, discrepancies in values can more easily be voiced. As a matter of fact, it is the leader's duty, under group-decision technique, to see to it that there is full and free discussion.

The effects on morale of the group-decision method for arriving at fair grades seem to be favorable. There is universal agreement among the students that they like it and consider it fair. Furthermore, it has almost completely eliminated charges of unfairness and of excessive strictness. Thus the number of visits to the office is limited to requests for information about grades, possible errors, and less than 1 per cent hardship cases. The latter are requests for help because of failing grades, but even these are less than half those heard from formerly.

It is difficult to give an objective answer to the question of the quality of work done. Year after year, similar examinations are used, and it can be stated that the absolute scores remain at least as high as formerly. There certainly is no indication that a poorer quality of student has been attracted to the course or that students have reduced their efforts, realizing that no objective standards will have to be met to obtain an A. This is not surprising, since most large courses use some sort of percentage in distributing grades.

Significance of Findings. Considering all the experiments on group decisions in determining grades, it appears that, although standards set by students themselves have not been higher than those of the faculty, it cannot be said that they were lower. Rather, the decisions reached were reasonable judgments and were based on values derived from the general mass of student experience. Thus it is evident that students do not have low standards, but it is also evident that the group-decision method, when applied to them, does not make for higher standards than the autocratic method. This means either that the superiority of the group-decision method does not apply as well under the conditions of unorganized groups or that the standards already are very high.

A comparison of the student discussions on grades and employee discussions on work standards gives one the distinct impression that social pressure and respect for other members of the group are less functional in student discussions than in the employee discussion groups. These differences seem to be a direct outgrowth of the fact that the student groups were not true social groups, such as exist in a work situation. Nevertheless, the surprising thing is that standards, even under these conditions, were as high as they were. One might even wonder that group decisions were achieved at all. The mere fact that a discussion is being held seems to cause a group to take on a social structure, and from this structure a "we" feeling emerges.

It is this feeling of belonging to a group that permits fair and responsible values to emerge and to become dominant. However, these values must grow out of the perceptions of the group and cannot come from the leader, since his perceptions may differ. Discussion causes perceptions to square with external realities, and this fact tends to cause group decisions to be realistic. Perhaps this is why the group decisions on grades were so close to the actual practices existing on the campus despite the fact that before discussion the grading practices were considered unfair.

10

The Quality of Group Decisions
as Influenced by
the Discussion Leader*

Introduction

The experimental evidence on group decision thus far indicates that a solution worked out by a group is more acceptable to the group than one imposed on the group by an authority (9, 12, 22, 23, 26, 35, 36, 50). Thus, if acceptance is desired, this method can be depended upon to produce results. However, industry needs more than acceptance of decisions. It needs good decisions, too. Must we forego good decisions in order to obtain acceptable decisions?

Group thinking may be regarded as superior to that of an individual, since the thinking of a number of individuals is pooled. The evidence available tends to support this view, but certain special questions might be raised. Watson (59) found that groups did better than individuals in a problem requiring the building of as many words as possible out of a given set of letters. However, the pooled results of several isolated individuals were superior to those of the same number working together as a group. This is not surprising, since the task required merely involved the addition of individual contributions. Thus, one would expect a group of 5 to do better than the most superior individual working alone, but not better than the combined effort of 5 working alone. Shaw's study (56) is more to the point of our problem. She compared groups in ability to solve what might be called reasoning problems for which one correct solution was possible. Since the solution's value could be objectively determined and did not require acceptance or approval by the group, attitudes were not greatly involved. Her findings support the contention that a group interacting does a better job of solving a problem than a single person. With

* This chapter originally appeared under the same title in *Human Relations* (39). Only minor alterations and additions have been made in the text.

21 persons working alone on 3 different problems, 5 solutions were produced out of a possible 63, or 7.9 per cent. However, 5 groups of 4 each working on the same 3 problems produced 8 out of a possible 15 solutions, or 53 per cent. Even assuming that the number of individuals involved is about the same, 21 working individually and 20 working in groups, one must recognize that 5 solutions were produced by the lone workers, and 8 by the groups. Shaw's further analysis of results indicates that a group's superiority over that of isolated individuals is partly one of evaluating suggestions and rejecting false ideas.

Findings of this type suggest that group thinking is superior to individual thinking. Such a conclusion would have profound practical implications. It would mean that the use of conferences should be extended in business and government and that these conferences should be used not only to disseminate information and achieve cooperation but to solve complex problems. It would mean that even a first-line supervisor, using the democratic approach, should have higher-quality solutions to problems than a supervisor making autocratic decisions. However, the fact that groups are superior in thinking to individuals of like knowledge and ability does not preclude the possibility that the thinking of certain individuals working alone may be superior to that of a group. The supervisor, because he is highly selected and because he has a rich background of experience, may reasonably be regarded as such an individual, and management might be expected to make such a contention. Certainly one would not wish to overlook the possibility of sacrificing high-quality or creative solutions, even though they may occur rarely, in order to get group acceptance. It is quite possible that highly creative ideas are made mediocre through group discussion with less creative persons. What can a creative individual do when he needs the support of others in order to put his creative efforts to work?

If the supervisor is the most superior individual in the group can he be permitted to present his views to the group and so influence the group thinking, or will his views tend to be resisted because he, in effect, will be functioning largely as an autocrat? Is there a way for the supervisor, who is capable of high-quality thinking, to influence the group without producing resistance?

Before treating this problem in greater detail it is well to clarify some other matters. In the first place, all problems do not raise the issue of solution quality *per se*, since the fact of cooperation and support of a plan may be more important than the nature of the plan.

The important thing is to get a plan that is acceptable. Thus, if an office is being moved to a new building, it is more important to have an arrangement that is satisfying than to have a particular plan that may be objectively slightly superior to another in that, let us say, fewer steps to a filing cabinet are required. Good morale may easily compensate for a few extra steps. When the reaction of the group is considered, therefore, the satisfying plan may be more efficient than one that a time-and-motion expert might evolve but which is not so satisfying to the group.

In the second place, many problems that require technical knowledge and seem to demand the services of an expert may also involve facts that the expert may not have at his disposal. A safety engineer may design what appears to be a very good safety practice but one which involves extra effort, and later find that such a safety procedure tends to be violated. An example of this type of safety procedure is that of requiring a lineman to take a trip up a telephone pole to fasten a pulley in place so that a drop line can be used. This procedure is followed so that the workman will not have to carry the line up the pole and run the danger of being pulled down by traffic hitting the cable. The safety engineer, however, may have been unaware of the fact that a foreman has put pressure on the men to increase production. Thus the men are motivated by the foreman to increase production and incidentally to taking shortcuts, and are also motivated by management to practice safety at the expense of production. Can the expert by himself be expected to take all such conflicts in motivation into account when designing safety measures, or must he and the foreman solve problems with a knowledge of the worker's reactions? The democratic procedure would tend to supply the workers' side of the picture and add valuable factual information. In this case we are not dealing merely with obtaining the workers' acceptance of a solution, but rather with obtaining for them the freedom to practice a safe solution even when they approve of safety methods.

In the third place, some solutions may be improved through group discussion because the men who actually do the work become aware of facts and conditions about which management is likely to be unfamiliar. To compensate for this fact some companies believe it is essential to select all management personnel from the ranks. However, this may not be adequate because (a) conditions change from year to year; (b) it may be unsafe to generalize from one's own experience; and (c) the experience of a worker may vary from one section of the city to another. Thus management objects to the fact that men from a sales department, who make deliveries of electrical products, should stop for coffee before even beginning deliveries. If such stops occurred at midmorning they would make more sense to management. A local factor that is overlooked is that customers do not answer visits made the first thing in the morning, but if a coffee stop is made such useless calls can be reduced. Management might also overlook the value to morale of visits over coffee. By stopping on the way just after leaving the garage the men can meet in small groups, whereas later in the morning they would be scattered.

A common problem with commercial drivers is that they tend to return to the garage at or before 4:45 rather than 5:00 o'clock. If the foreman criticizes this behavior of early quitting he finds that the men hide behind billboards. When this problem was discussed in one company, it was found that the following factors were involved:

(a) Men did not want to start big jobs after 4:00 o'clock.

(b) Some of the men ran out of work.

(c) When problems occurred in late afternoon the men couldn't reach anyone at the office for further instructions.

(d) Each man didn't want to be the last man in the garage and get unfavorable parking space.

All these problems were soluble when the employee's side became known, and a solution satisfactory to all was reached by group discussion.

Finally, it must be recognized that some problems are purely problems of attitudes, so that practically the whole subject matter for the solution is in the group. On one occasion it was necessary for a supervisor to get two out of three girls to work on Sunday. All of them had dates, so none volunteered. The supervisor might have set himself the problem of selecting two girls, and he might have tried to be fair by flipping coins or following seniority privileges. In this instance, however, a group discussion was held. The discussion revealed that one girl had a date with some other girls. All three girls agreed that this was not a real date, and so the girl in question volunteered. The other two girls had dates with men, but one of them was engaged to her date, whereas the other had a date with a new man. All three agreed that the only real *date* was the one involving a new conquest. This girl was excused from work by agreement of all, despite the fact that she had the least seniority and had worked less frequently on Sundays than the others. It is clear that the virtue of this solution resides in the fact that it reconciled values and attitudes, not that it had universal application or perfection in its own right.

Problems of attitude clearly fall into the category for solution by group discussion, whereas some of the other types might seem to profit in varying degrees by cooperation with experts.

Preliminary Experiment

To highlight the possible value of the expert in solving at least some problems, a problem has been selected for analysis to which there is one solution that is definitely superior to others. When a single solution has elegance or the quality of an invention, the question of *solution quality* is clearly apparent. In such cases we may rightfully raise the question of how a supervisor or an expert might lead the group to this superior solution.

In factories doing assembly work, the speed of an assembly line is paced by the slowest worker, unless arrangements are made to budget the size of the job to fit the personal abilities of each man involved. This can be achieved in a variety of ways, all of which are specific to the particular situation and the varied abilities of the individuals involved. In subassembly work certain special conditions are present which permit specialized solutions. Can a group of persons solve the problem of increasing production in a subassembly job, sometimes called a *parasol* assembly because the work is laid out in a circle?

To test the problem-solving achievements of groups as compared to individuals we presented such a problem to groups of college students, all of whom had received some training in group-decision methods. The problem as given is as follows:

Visualize a subassembly situation in which 7 men work in a circle and assemble part of a car (carburetor or instrument panel, for example). The basic unit enters the circle at one point, and each person adds his pieces and pushes the unit to the next worker, who adds his elements. When the unit leaves the circle, it is a completed unit. This work arrangement is diagrammed in Fig. 18.

Suppose there are 4 such parasol subassembly stations, each one supervised by a foreman. Suppose further that station A assembles 85 units per day; station B, 80 per day; station C, 60 units per day, and station D, 50 units. It is a fact that station D previously assembled 60 units. The foreman was dissatisfied with the production and reprimanded the group. Following the reprimand production fell to 50 units per day.

The assembly work is simple and requires a minimum of training for each step. The aptitude requirement is primarily good finger dexterity. The materials for each assembly position are located in bins which are kept supplied by material handlers. Thus each worker has his essential material at his elbow. The job has been analyzed by time-and-motion experts so that the positions are of equal difficulty.

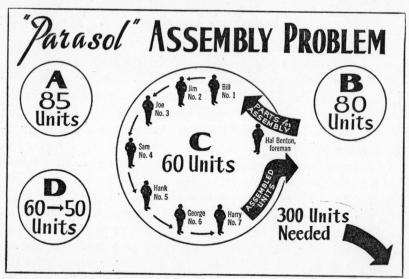

FIG. 18.   Diagram of four subassembly stations. The stations represent four groups of men who work in teams and assemble a part of a car. All groups do the same work, and the combined assembled units are used to supply the production line. The combined output is 275 units, just 25 short of what is needed. The foreman of station C wishes to raise his group's production. He has a bottleneck in Joe at the No. 3 position. Work piles up at this position, and Joe seems unable to keep up the pace. How can the problem of low production at station C be solved?

Pay is based on hourly rates. The total factory production is dependent upon receiving the required number of assembled units from these four stations. The production is now so low that the factory production as a whole has had to slow down. The desired quota is 300 parts per shift for the four stations combined. We are concerned with station C, which is producing at the rate of 60 units. The work piles up at the position of Joe Brown. The unit must pass through him (position 3), and he always has several units piled up waiting for him. Foremen on nonproduction jobs are not willing to accept Joe as a transfer. Joe is a man of 60 with 30 years of service in the company. Emphasis on improving production has brought his deficiencies to light.

One of the following two descriptions of Joe was given to each group of persons assigned the task of solving the production problem.

1. Joe is a nice congenial fellow. He is liked by the group of workers, but is slow and unhandy. However, he tries. Joe has to work for a living.
2. The group blames Joe. When men try to hurry him, he argues that they are falling for a speed-up. From time to time there are hard feelings. Joe does not eat with the group but stays alone. He has never been a good worker. His coordination is poor, but on previous jobs he got along well with others. In this situation the first evidence of Joe's poor attitude has become apparent.

Twenty groups of 4 to 6 college students were asked to play roles of workers in this situation. The groups were obtained from 6 classes, each of which was divided into 3 or 4 such groups. In each group one member was added to play the part of the foreman, and one of the group members was given the role of one of the Joes. The others were asked to assume their own roles. The foreman was asked to solve the problem by the method of group discussion. Forty other individuals were asked to solve the problem by themselves, half with the "good" Joe and half with the "bad" Joe.

The solution regarded as having the quality of inventiveness or elegance was that of periodically having the men exchange places, progressing from one position to the next in a counterclockwise direction. In this manner the fast workers would reduce work piled up in positions occupied by slower workers, and at the same time variety would be introduced into the job and would make the work less monotonous. Such progressive changes would make production dependent upon the ability of the average man rather than on that of the slowest man. This is an objective fact if we assume there are no adverse attitudes. The special condition that permits this rotation is the fact that the work is simple, requires a minimum of learning, and demands similar aptitudes. The only problem that seems necessary to put the solution into practice is the willingness of the group to adopt it. This willingness, of course, will depend somewhat on the type of Joe that is present, but this is not necessarily important, since the poor attitude on Joe's part might be due to his inability to keep up with the group.

An added feature of insight, which conceivably might accompany the solution, is the fact that the solution applies to all the other groups. Each one is paced by the slowest worker.

The argument against discharging the slowest worker is that it merely creates another "slowest" worker. If discharge is practiced it will either lead to insecurity or a protection of the slow workers. When all members of a team slow down, management is merely not aware that the pace is set by the slowest worker.

Apparently this inventive solution is difficult to achieve or to fully appreciate, and this might be due to the fact that the actual work situation was not present.   The usual solutions obtained from our groups and independent subjects were as follows:

Transfer Joe to another unit.
Give Joe a talking-to and warn him.
Transfer Joe to a nonproduction job.
Retire Joe.
Let the group work it out.
Give part of Joe's work to others.
Divide the men into various units according to ability.
Put Joe in an easier position.
Discharge Joe.

The groups differed in that those with the more pleasant Joe were less inclined to discharge or transfer him.   Most groups gave a variety of possibilities, many of which were not solutions but descriptions of how they would go about solving the problem.   As can be seen from the above list, many of the solutions supplied did not respect the following facts that were given: (1) the foreman is in charge of one unit and cannot influence other units; (2) Joe cannot be transferred; (3) Joe's primary difficulty is low aptitude in finger dexterity; and (4) the positions are equal and require the same aptitude.

None of the groups and none of the individuals produced the desired solution or its equivalent.   In three instances an individual in a group mentioned rotating the men, but each was talked out of this line of thinking by other members.   These individuals did not appreciate the possibilities of their ideas enough to follow through on their own suggestions.   It is apparent from these findings that the rotation solution is not an obvious one.

It was also found that when the instructor presented the solution to 3 of the classes after the groups had reassembled, the solution was accepted by less than 50 per cent of the persons.   Arguments against it are illustrated by the following examples: "It's impractical."   "If it's good why isn't it used in industry?"   "No group would go for it."   "It's no better than ours."   "That's what we meant when we recommended giving Joe less to do."

Students that accepted the solution, in a few instances saw that the same solution applied to the other stations, but mild acceptance rather than a recognition of elegance was the general trend. Thus under the conditions tested the inventive solution was neither found nor acceptable when given to the group.

Major Experiment with the Parasol Assembly Problem

Relevant Aspects of Problem-Solving Behavior. Can this solution be stimulated in a group by proper leadership, and at the same time produce general acceptance? Experimental work on the nature of thinking and the factors that block the development of new ideas may supply some of the answers.

This writer found (31, 32, 33, 34, 40) that an individual's ability to solve reasoning problems is blocked by habitual or first ideas which tend to perpetuate themselves. Suppose one was presented with the problem of building a hatrack in the center of an ordinary room and was given two poles (each 7 feet long and about ¾ inches square) and one 3-inch table clamp for this purpose. The first or habitual idea would be to attempt to use one pole as a support and to use the other as a leg. This is the obvious first idea because ordinary hatracks are uprights with three legs. The most one could accomplish with the material given would be a two-legged affair, and, at best, an ingenious person might attempt to use the clamp to furnish minor support on the third side. This type of construction would be a most inadequate hatrack. If this solution is rejected by the experimenter as unsatisfactory, further attempts become varied improvements on this basic idea. Thus a characteristic aspect of problem-solving behavior is to persist in working along the line of the first idea, regardless of how fruitless it may be. In so doing the person is kept from exploring further and finding the less obvious idea, that of building a hatrack by wedging a stick between the floor and the ceiling. By clamping the two sticks together at the proper length the combination will fit snugly between the floor and the ceiling, and the clamp becomes a hook for the hatrack. This solution becomes a creative invention and is new.

It does not follow that all persons will come upon this unique solution, but the point remains that those who are capable of solving the problem may be prevented from doing so because they are busy trying to devise legs for the type of hatrack first conceived.

In thinking, one's explorations follow particular lines or *directions*. For example, if doctors had the problem of preventing yellow fever, two contrasting lines of thinking would be (a) seeking methods of making man immune to germs, and (b) finding ways for preventing germs from reaching man.

A direction in thinking is more than a first idea in that it incorporates a number of related ideas. Thus the direction in thinking serves a selective or screening function. One's mind is open to ideas that correspond with the direction and closed to those that do not. In the yellow-fever problem any ideas that are consistent with making man immune to the germ will receive a favorable reception if that is the direction of the thinking of a given investigator, whereas ideas relating to the way germs are carried about will seem silly to him. The author's experiments showed that persons who tried to construct a hatrack by supporting it with legs were unresponsive to interruptions that drew attention to the ceiling, or activities that required them to make the stick longer. Thus when a person, who for two hours had tried different ways of building legs, was asked to sit in a chair and obtain a package of cigarettes 12 feet away, he did so by clamping the two sticks together, but he resented the interruption. However, persons who tried different ways of wedging the stick between the floor and the ceiling, using blocks, chairs, etc., immediately solved the problem when asked to get the cigarettes. These persons had failed to solve the problem because they had found no way of producing a tight fit with the stick between the floor and the ceiling, and for them the suggestion was relevant and welcome.

Ideas are constantly suggested by chance events, by the remarks of others, and by the things we look at. However, the ideas that are used or selected depend upon our direction. Thus our failure to solve problems often is due to our inability to react to suggestions when we have a false or fruitless direction. Such directions are far worse than none at all, and this is the reason why many problems are solved when we are engaged in recreational activities or when we make fresh starts. The direction in thinking has momentum and tends to perpetuate itself. If we are to influence or aid the thinking of others this can be achieved more readily by recognizing and influencing the direction their thinking is taking. A given idea is plausible only when it is consistent with a direction. Since one approach is likely to be more fruitful than another on a given problem, much depends on the direction the thinking takes.

It was experimentally found (34) that problem-solving success was greatly increased by training individuals in (a) the inadequacies of first ideas, which are usually obvious and false when difficult problems are presented and, therefore, should be rejected; (*b*) the meanings of different directions and how they function in selecting ideas; and (*c*) the importance of keeping the mind receptive to these variations. It seemed reasonable to suppose, therefore, that the leader might improve a group's thinking by furnishing these types of aids to a group.

One of the blocks to a solution of our group problem is the strong tendency to get rid of Joe. He is the obvious stumbling block, and removing him represents an habitual first idea. If this is the case the leader can accept such a suggestion by writing it down and adding, "That's one possibility, but before we settle on any one approach let's explore some other possibilities." This should permit the problem to be analyzed further and become the first step toward finding a better solution in a different direction.

The leader may further function to protect Joe. In doing so he lends security to the group and induces constructive approaches. He demonstrates that he is concerned with solving a problem and not with blaming someone. Tendencies to find someone to blame are likewise false and ineffective habitual approaches.

This function of the leader is highly important, since he can determine to a considerable degree whether the behavior of individuals will be dominated by frustration or whether the individuals will proceed to approach problems as motivated individuals. Experimental evidence reported elsewhere (38) and the analysis of discussion methods in Chapter 3 highlighted the point that problem solving proceeds only during a state of motivation, whereas in a frustrated condition people are hostile, childish, and stubborn.

As suggestions are given, the leader may stimulate further analysis. Thus if someone suggests giving Joe less to do he might ask, "What are the different ways in which this can be done?" By listing the suggestions made he can stimulate further thought in the direction of the solution and prevent the dismissal of good ideas without proper consideration. By asking, "Are there any arguments against this?" he can recognize a poor lead and perhaps have it eliminated by the very person who suggested it.

The leader should also be able to bring about increased congeniality in the group. In protecting Joe; in stating the problem as a production obstacle rather than as one having to do with persons (who do and do not do their share); and in recognizing that differences in work output are always present, that even the same person feels more like working on some days than others, he can keep the discussion away from blame and fault-finding and direct it into constructive channels.

The use of this technique in leadership implies, of course, that the leader has the ability to distinguish good from poor solutions. This is not always the case. However, when he does have this ability or when he knows of an elegant solution it seems that he should not be handicapped by being unable to influence the quality of a group's thinking. If, however, he cannot obtain acceptance of his influence then even an elegant solution remains ineffective.

Introduction of Roles and a Trained Leader. In order to determine the conditions essential to obtaining the solution to the parasol assembly problem it was decided to introduce two new factors that were lacking in the first experiment. One of these was to use a leader skilled in practicing the procedures discussed above and familiar with the rotation solution, so that he could properly utilize the reasoning principles. However, the leader's function was to conduct the discussion but not to participate in making suggestions. A second factor was to make the problem more realistic by giving each individual a specific role to play. Thus the group members would approach the problem from the point of view of specific individuals on the assembly line and would be less inclined to work on the problem from the way each member of the group thought workmen might react.

The roles for the seven men in the production team were as follows:

1. *Bill:* You find you can easily do more work but have to slow down because Joe gets behind. In order not to make him feel bad you hold back. You don't want to get Joe into trouble.

2. *Jim:* You and Bill work closely together, and you usually are waiting for your part from Bill. This waiting for the work is more prevalent in the later part of the day than in the beginning. To keep busy you often help out Joe, who can't keep up. However, you are careful not to let the foreman catch you helping Joe because he might let Joe go.

3. *Joe:* You work hard but just aren't as fast as the others. You know you are holding things up, but no matter how you try you get behind. The rest of the fellows are fine boys and have more energy than you do at your age.

4. *Sam:* Joe has trouble keeping up, and you sometimes grab Joe's part and finish it for him when the boss isn't looking. Joe is a bit old for the pace set, and he feels the strain. For you the job is easy, and you feel the whole job is slowed down too much because of Joe. "Why couldn't Joe be given less to do?" you ask yourself.

5. *Hank:* You feel a bit uneasy on this job. There isn't enough to do so you have to act busy. If only Joe could speed up a bit. Why don't they move him out of the group? Is the company so blind that they can't see where the production trouble is?

6. *George:* You are able to keep up with the pace but on the last assembly job you were pressed. Fortunately Joe is slower than you are, so he keeps the pressure off of you. You are determined that Joe is not going to be moved off the job. Somebody has to protect people from speed-up tactics.

7. *Harry:* You get bored doing the same operations over and over. On some jobs you get variety by working fast for a while and then slowly. On this job you can't work at a good pace because the work isn't fed to you fast enough. It gets you down to keep doing exactly the same thing over and over in a slow motion. You are considering getting a job some place where they can keep a man busy.

Experimental Procedure for Group Discussion. Before beginning the experiment the same objective facts in the assembly situation previously described were presented. The group was told that these were the things that anyone would know from being on the job. Each person was then given a slip of paper on which one of the above roles was described, and requested to play the part assigned to him as accurately as possible. The group was told, "These roles describe how each of you feels about the job situation. Naturally, what you say and how you interact with each other will depend on how the situation develops. Your comments and feelings are to be guided both by your roles and by what ensues in the conference."

The stage was then set for acting out the situation. A diagram of the assembly operation was set up in the foreground (see Fig. 18, p. 306), and the members were seated in the order in which each worked on the line. The performance was witnessed by an audience in which no member was familiar with the solution, but in which all were made familiar with the problem. The presence of the audience gave each person in the experiment a sense of responsibility, but it seemed to have no influence on the effectiveness with which the persons played their roles.

The writer acted as the foreman in six such role-playing demonstrations, which were given in connection with a program of human relations training. He introduced the problem by remarks such as, "Boys, I stopped the assembly line this morning because I thought it would be a good idea if we had an opportunity to talk things over from time to time. You fellows are closer to the job than I am, and there may be some things that you have ideas and feelings about that might make things more pleasant if we have a chance to iron them out. Do you think talks like this are worth having?" The response, of course, was agreement.

The next step was to inquire into the job routines by asking such questions as, "How is the material coming through?" "Are the parts O.K.?" "Do the material handlers keep you supplied?" These questions usually brought out the answer that these things were satisfactory. When some problems were raised, these were discussed.

After the general exploration of the situation the group was asked, "How is the line being paced?" "Do you feel we are driving you too hard?" These questions aroused disagreement, and the point of issue was, therefore, set up on the blackboard as a problem. The situation was further explored to determine whether there were other problems. The question of monotony then arose, and this was recorded as another problem. From this point on the procedure changed to one of solving problems.

In the six groups of industrial personnel in which this procedure was used five of them reached a unanimous agreement on the systematic rotation plan as a solution to the problem. In the sixth group the unanimous solution was to determine whether positions were equally difficult by rotating at daily intervals. After this was tried and if no difference were found, the rotation was to be at intervals (the frequency to be determined by experience), so as to distribute the load. Thus this group supplied two solutions, the first of which was to test the positions and the second of which was the inventive rotation solution. The reason why this group held off on the daily rotation plan was that Joe insisted that his position was difficult. This was an obvious face-saving reaction.

In no instance did one single individual supply the desired final solution. Rather, it developed out of the variety of suggestions made for giving men an opportunity to work at a pace that suited them. Except for the one group, the agreement was always to give the rotation plan a try for a week and to start immediately. The frequency of changing positions varied from once per hour to once every two hours. It was agreed to reconsider the problem after a week in order to improve the plan.

Observers agreed that the leader did not furnish the solution in any instance. Rather, his contributions were in the form of summarizing, encouraging analysis, interpreting, supplying information, and preventing hurt feelings. Observers familiar with the solution felt that there was some guidance in the manner of questioning and the rewording of suggestions of others, but observers unfamiliar with the solution could not determine the solution the leader favored. In no instance were these observers able to anticipate the solution or point to the leader's bias. Thus it seems that a knowledge of the solution is necessary if the observer is to detect the leader's specific contribution. To what extent did the leader's skill promote the solution, and to what extent did the nature of the roles assigned make the solution inevitable?

Setting up an Experimental Plan. To determine the part played by each of these two modifications, college students again were used. Groups of eight were created, with each of the seven roles being played by a member of the group and the eighth member being the foreman. The foreman's role as assigned to him was as follows:

The foreman, Hal Benton: You are the new foreman in station C and have been instructed to get production up. The job has been analyzed by time-and-motion study men, and the amount of work at each position is practically the same. The number 3 position (Joe's position) is, however, slightly easier than the others in that one less motion is required. Undoubtedly the previous foreman put him there to reduce the bottleneck. You have received training in group-decision methods and are going to try to work out your problem by this method. You therefore have stopped the production line for a discussion. You understand that what you do is your problem. You cannot pass Joe off to another foreman. You find Joe a likeable person, and it is your impression that Joe gets along well with the other men in the group.

Since this experiment was performed during the beginning of the course in psychology of management, the foremen conducted themselves according to their limited knowledge of the group-decision procedure. In being assigned the foreman's role the person was merely asked to sit down and talk the problem over with his men to see if an agreeable solution could be found.

As controls, two other groups of persons were to work alone and conduct themselves as experts. They were to present the instructor with a recommendation of the action that should be taken. A specific request was that they were to report a solution, and not a procedure that they would use to find the solution.

One of these groups had only the problem to work from. The other group was given the roles and was told that these would furnish an idea of the way the different men felt about things on the job.

The condition of the trained leader was also repeated. Five leaders previously trained in democratic leadership conducted 11 group discussions with groups of 7 students each. They duplicated the situation of the trained leader already described, but their groups consisted of students rather than men in industry. It is also important to note that the trained-leader condition included not only some conference skills but also a knowledge of the rotation solution to aid him in his use of the reasoning principles. In tabulating results we have combined these 11 groups with the 6 previously described, making a total of 17 groups led by trained leaders.

In order that these trained leaders would duplicate as much as possible the author's preliminary tests certain procedures were outlined. The major points emphasized in these instructions were as follows:

1. Present the problem not as a production problem, but instead determine from the group whether they have problems.

2. Recognize all suggestions but influence direction in thinking by asking for further suggestions.

3. Protect individuals from criticism of other group members by interpreting all remarks in a favorable light.

4. Keep the discussion problem-centered and see that no one is blamed or criticized by you.

5. Make a list of all suggestions, so that methods of fitting the pace of work to individuals, methods for reducing monotony, methods for increasing pride in work, etc., are included.

6. When the list is fairly complete, probing questions may be asked. "How can we change things to combine some of these features?"

7. Good leads may be kept in the discussion by asking, "How would that work out?" "How can we avoid confusion?"

8. Do not hasten the solution by capitalizing on the first good lead, or in any other way reflect your preferences.

9. Always work toward the ideal of removing undesirable features from the job. Make your objective one of resolving differences in the group.

This phase of the experiment thus contained four groups: two groups of persons who solved the problem as individuals working alone (one set without a knowledge of the roles, and another set with a knowledge of the roles) and two groups of persons divided into problem-solving teams (one set of teams led by untrained leaders, and another set of teams led by trained leaders). In both sets of teams the individuals played the roles assigned to them.

The Results and Their Meaning. Table 19 summarizes the solutions obtained under the four experimental conditions. The solutions are divided into seven groups: (A) the inventive solution, which involves systematic rotation in order to spread the work so that differences in

TABLE 19

TYPES OF SOLUTIONS PRESENTED

Conditions for Solving	*Individual (without Roles)*	*Individual (with Roles)*	*Group (Untrained Leader)*	*Group (Trained Leader)*
Number of cases	31	41	29	17
A. Inventive solution (rotation).	0	1	1	111111½111111
Total	0	1	1	12½
B. Give less capable less to do:				
1. Reorganize job so that some positions will have less work.	1½	111½11½	11111	1
2. Put fast workers next to slow ones so that they can help out.	1111	111½111	111½111	0
3. Hire additional man.	0	1	0	0
4. Have Joe periodically change places with a faster man.	1	111	11	11
5. Exchange Joe and Harry periodically.	0	0	11	0
6. Have others help Joe (and George).	1½	111	1111	0
7. Other ways for doing some of Joe's work.	0	11½½½	1½	0
Total	8	23	21	3
C. Change Joe's make-up:				
1. Train Joe.	½	0	0	0
2. Put pressure on Joe.	½	0	0	0
3. Improve Joe's attitude.	½	0	0	0
Total	1½	0	0	0
D. Promote Joe to foreman.	1½	1½½	½	0
Total	1½	2	½	0
E. Get rid of Joe:				
1. Dismiss Joe.	1	1	1	0
2. Retire Joe.	1111½	½½	0	0
3. Transfer Joe.	11111½1111½	1½½	0	0
Total	15½	4	1	0
F. George mentioned in solution:				
1. Dismiss George.	0	1½½½	0	0
2. Transfer George.	0	1½½½½¼	½	0
3. Put pressure on George.	0	½¼	0	0
4. Exchange George and Harry.	0	½	0	0
5. Put George in Joe's position.	0	½	½	0
Total	0	7½	1	0
G. Solutions violating stated conditions:				
1. Put Joe in No. 1 Position to take off pressure.	11	0	11	0
2. Put Joe in No. 7 Position (no help).	1½	11	1	0
3. All help Joe in No. 1 Position to build stockpile.	1	0	0	0
4. Have each do full assembly.	0	0	1	0
5. Introduce piece rate.	0	½	0	0
6. Let men solve problem themselves.	0	1	0	0
7. Rotate until each finds best position.	0	0	½	½
8. Match ability in all 4 assembly units.	0	1	0	0
9. Leave situation unaltered.	0	0	0	1
Total	4½	4½	4½	1½

ability will not interfere with production; (B) solutions that recognize differences in ability and arrange for some way of permitting the more capable workers to aid the less capable; (C) solutions that are directed at Joe and suggest improving him; (D) solutions that suggest promoting Joe, the slow worker; (E) solutions that recommend removing Joe other than through promotion; (F) solutions that recognize the next poorest man (George) as a problem; and (G) solutions that violate the stated conditions of the problem or that seem inconsistent to these stated conditions. Classified under these categories are the specific solutions that were suggested.

In classifying the solutions it was frequently found that more than one plan or change was suggested. Thus one solution might be to promote Joe and to discharge George; another, to give Joe help and to warn George; and still another might be to train Joe and, if this does not work, to discharge him. In classifying these two-step solutions we have scored each part of the solution as ½ in the table. In one instance two recommendations about George and one about Joe were made, and these were scored as ¼, ¼, and ½, respectively. A 1 in the table indicates that the solution can be classified as a unit. Thus a solution might suggest putting various men in different positions and would still be classified as "putting fast workers next to slow workers."

In considering these classifications it is apparent that, next to the rotation solution, the most feasible group of solutions is that in which the more superior individuals in some way help out the others. Probably the least effective solutions are those violating the conditions of the problem (class G), and we may consider these as instances of failures.

For purposes of comparing the results of the different groups it is well to examine Table 20, in which only the major groupings are used. This table shows the percentage of instances that each type of solution was recommended under the four experimental conditions.

The inventive solution is primarily confined to the condition in which the trained leader is used and was obtained in 73.5 per cent of the groups. (The instructed leaders obtained this solution in 7 out of 11 instances.) This solution was never recommended by individuals without a knowledge of the roles, and it occurred only once in each of the other two conditions.

The other cooperative solution, which suggested that the less capable workers receive help from the more capable ones, was recommended by 25.8 per cent of the individuals having only the problem to work

TABLE 20

RELATIVE FREQUENCY OF EACH TYPE OF SOLUTION

Conditions for Solving	Individual (without Roles) Percentage	Individual (with Roles) Percentage	Group (Untrained Leader) Percentage	Group (Trained Leader) Percentage
Number of cases	31	42	29	17
A. Inventive solution	0.0	2.3	3.4	73.5
B. Give less capable less to do	25.8	54.8	72.4	17.7
C. Change Joe's make-up	4.8	0.0	0.0	0.0
D. Promote Joe to foreman	4.8	4.7	1.7	0.0
E. Get rid of Joe	50.0	9.5	3.4	0.0
F. George mentioned in solution	0.0	17.5	3.4	0.0
G. Solutions violating stated conditions	14.5	10.7	15.5	8.8
Total	99.9	99.9	99.8	100.0

from. However, with a knowledge of the roles this solution was recommended by 54.8 per cent of the group members, or more than twice as many. Thus, with some insight into the human side of the problem, cooperative solutions seemed more feasible.

When, however, the roles were played out and the individuals could interact, this cooperative solution was suggested by 72.4 per cent of the teams, even when the leader was untrained. Thus mere discussion with the members of the group evolved a solution requiring cooperation. When the leader was skilled, nearly all the groups that did not find the elegant solution of cooperation found the other cooperative solution. Thus the reason that only 17.7 per cent of these groups recommended the second cooperative solution was that most of them had discovered the superior inventive solution.

Individuals working alone and without roles concentrated their solutions on some way of removing Joe. Joe was a bottleneck, and the problem was to attack the location of the bottleneck. Thus 50 per cent of their solutions took this form, some being generous in their treatment of Joe, others less generous. Undoubtedly the degree of generosity was due to the fact that the situation was not one loaded with emotion.

Individuals working alone, but with roles, recommended removing Joe only 9.5 per cent of the time. The nature of Joe's role made them generous and lenient, and, instead of hurting him, they attacked George as a problem to be dealt with. Usually the mention of George in the solution was combined with other recommendations, and yet the total proportion of such solutions was 17.5 per cent. From Table 19 it can be seen that George was mentioned in a solution 14 times (totaling 7½ solutions) by this group, not at all by individuals working without roles (which is not surprising, since the nature of the individuals had to be assumed), and only twice by 46 groups working as teams, to which George was able to express his views.

Impractical solutions occurred infrequently in all groups. Individuals working without roles violated the conditions of the problem only 14.5 per cent of the time; individuals working with a knowledge of the roles did so in 10.7 per cent of their solutions; groups working with an untrained leader violated the conditions 15.5 per cent of the time; and groups working with a trained leader did so only in 8.8 per cent of their solutions.

The fact that a group working with an untrained leader violated the conditions of the problem hardly more often than did an individual working alone is of particular interest. It shows that the condition of divided responsibility, even if not controlled by a trained leader, seems about as effective as the full responsibility given to an individual as an expert.

In general the results show that the skill of the leader plays a large part in determining the appearance of the creative solution. Certainly it cannot be claimed that the roles contained the solution, since the individuals working with a knowledge of the roles and the groups playing the roles with an untrained discussion leader failed to produce the desired solution. However, this does not mean that the roles supplied were not an aid. It seems that they gave the leader the setting upon which to build a group discussion. When individuals in the preliminary experiment had no roles to play but were asked merely to assume their own attitudes, they tended to behave in accordance with their own conception of uncooperative workers and thus opposed cooperation or any increase in efficiency. Under these conditions constructive discussion was precluded. In assigning roles this attitude was removed from several of the roles, and a constructive discussion was thus made possible.

It may be assumed, of course, that the roles assigned were not characteristic of workers. However, in a real-life situation the problem was actually solved. Furthermore, Dr. Joan U. Longhurst set up a real production problem and assigned students in a summer school class to work on the job for two hours at a time, once a week for several weeks. Sure enough, a "slow Joe" turned up in the group. When the problem of solving the bottleneck was finally raised, the inventive rotation solution was found, and with it production and job satisfaction rose. With a skilled discussion leader and with the group on a monotonous production job the solution occurred without the assignment of roles.

Implications of Results. It is apparent that a skilled leader can greatly improve the quality of a group's thinking. This is shown by the fact that only with the trained leader does the inventive solution occur with any dependable degree of frequency. Thus a leader with creative ideas can cause a group to be creative if he has skill in conference procedures. However, even when the leader lacks skill and has no knowledge of a creative solution, he does better with a group than when working alone. The fact that people are different in ability and cannot work at the same pace is most likely to be recognized when there is group discussion. The solution of helping out the slower workers is practical only if the faster workers are willing to do this. The roles make this willingness apparent, and yet a mere knowledge of the roles does not bring out this solution as frequently as does a discussion between the individuals.

The individual who works without a knowledge of the roles and attitudes seldom assumes that employees are willing to help out each other, and hence he seldom recommends the idea. In a sense he is correct in this opinion since, if he asked employees to help each other, they would very likely oppose the idea. Without the benefit of this form of cooperation this type of solution is not often entertained or analyzed further by a person, and hence most of his efforts are directed toward techniques that do not recognize the fact that people are different. He tends to overlook, therefore, the fact that a new bottleneck will be created when one is removed.

Since any solution involving cooperation between human beings requires acceptance and since even solutions of less quality, with acceptance, might be more effective than solutions of higher quality without acceptance, we must inquire further into the problem of the leader's ability to achieve acceptance. Does the leader who is skilled in obtaining the elegant solution pay a price by obtaining less acceptance of the solution?

The Problem of Acceptance. Table 21 shows the frequency with which the solution reached by a group was unanimously accepted as the best solution. In this analysis the groups led by trained leaders are divided into two subgroups: (*a*) those led by instructors trained by the author and made up of student personnel, and (*b*) those led by

TABLE 21

ACCEPTANCE OF SOLUTION UNDER DIFFERENT LEADERS

Type of Leader	Number of Groups Listed	Percentage in Which Unanimous Agreement Was Obtained
Untrained leader	29	62.1
Instructed leader	11	72.7
Most highly trained leader	6	100.0

the author and made up of industrial rather than student personnel. This separation is made because the results differ somewhat.

It will be seen from the first line of the table that even the untrained leaders obtained full agreement in 62.1 per cent of their attempts. The groups led by trained leaders, in which the inventive solution was obtained in 7 out of 11 instances, reached unanimous agreement in 72.7 per cent of the tests. In 6 of the 7 instances (85.7 per cent) in which the inventive solution was obtained, unanimous agreement was reached. As already reported, the writer obtained unanimous agreement in all instances.

The trend in results is clear. Acceptance is not sacrificed for quality, but rather, with the rise in frequency of higher-quality solutions, acceptance also increases. This does not mean that one depends on the other, but rather that both are influenced by the leader.

Of interest also is the fact that in most instances in which unanimous agreement was not reached Joe was the obstacle. This seems surprising at first, since Joe stood to gain the most from the rotation solution. George, who also would be protected by the solution, also objected, but he was somewhat less likely to hold out. In analyzing the actual process of the conferences the reason for Joe's opposition becomes apparent, however. Frequently he was mentioned as slow, old, a bottleneck, or an obstacle. He then defended himself, and, if the leader was unable to prevent such statements or gloss them over, Joe remained hostile and uncooperative. Thus the obstacle in reaching unanimous agreement is not primarily one of unwillingness to help out others, but rather one of hurt pride.

Summary and Conclusions

In summary, these experiments show that a leader, if skilled and possessing ideas, can conduct a discussion so as to obtain a quality of problem solving that surpasses that of a group working with a less skilled leader and without creative ideas. Furthermore, he can obtain a higher degree of acceptance than can a less skilled person. However, even an unskilled leader can achieve good-quality solutions and a high degree of acceptance. The democratic leadership technique is, therefore, a useful procedure not only for obtaining acceptance and cooperation but also for improving solution quality. Even when the leader possesses exceptional ability in solving technical problems, he need not sacrifice this ability in order to maintain group goodwill. Rather, he can learn to conduct conferences in such a manner as to stimulate thinking and thereby have his ideas rediscovered and accepted. Frequently it is felt that one must impose new ideas on groups because groups tend to resist change. Our experiments indicate that this can be circumvented by proper conference procedures. However, if a group resists reaching a solution that a leader regards as of high quality he can assume that if he imposed the solution upon the group it would not be given a fair test.

It also seems likely that if a group failed to reach a solution after considerable discussion the leader might suggest one. How his suggestions will be received will of course depend upon his relation to the group. The nature of the conference and the attitudes displayed will give him a clue as to whether this can be done. However, the motivation will always be improved if the solution can be elicited from the group.

The question unanswered by these experiments is whether a leader can achieve a creative solution when he has no knowledge of the solution. We found it necessary to supply him with the solution so as to guide him in the use of leading questions and in taking the group out of false lines of thought. However, if he lacked the knowledge of the solution one can assume that the solution reached would, at least, be as good as the one obtained from unskilled leaders.

In testing one's own attitudes on the question of solution quality one may imagine for himself a problem situation in which he could not get his own views recognized. For example, suppose you were the president of a company and were told by the board of directors that you would have to show better results or give up the position. Soon thereafter you are confronted with a major decision, such as, "Should the company expand by purchasing a new plant, or should it hold the line?" You discuss the issue with the officers reporting to you, and the group, after full discussion, unanimously agrees that expansion is unwise, whereas you strongly feel that expansion would be wise. Since the board of directors will hold you responsible for the decision, would you act on your own decision or would you accept the group's decision?

Naturally one feels that if one is to be held responsible he must have the final "say-so." But is the final "say-so" a protection and a desirable privilege? How can one know when one is being stubborn? All of us think of others as stubborn, but when are we stubborn? Is failure to make one's own case a sign of stubbornness? Is disrespect for others, who also know the situation, a sign of stubbornness?

Suppose in the above instance that the president's decision were of high quality? Would his associates help make it appear so? Suppose he succeeded—would he have the support of his officers? In the event that his decision turned out poorly, would he blame himself or the poor support he received? How would the board of directors view the decision? Would they view his behavior differently if he acted in accordance with his associates than if he acted contrary to them? What support would his associates give him in case of success or failure?

A group discussion of this problem soon reveals attitudes associated with the right to decide when the chips are down. May it not be that it is in exactly such instances that a group decision would have its greatest value?

Improving Solution Quality vs. Manipulation. Haiman (18) has pointed out that in increasing the skill of a discussion leader one is making it possible for him to pervert subtly the group-discussion method. He indicated that the procedure described in this chapter is a powerful one because the group lays its thoughts bare, and the leader can take advantage of the group. In expressing this danger it seems that Haiman has failed to distinguish between a leader's function of upgrading a group's thinking and his possible desire to manipulate people to gain his own ends. The quality of thinking is something quite apart from the leader's wishes or desires, since solution quality must have some objective criterion. A leader who wishes to develop a poor-quality solution will find himself definitely handicapped in a group discussion.

In order to test for quality in group discussion it has been necessary in the foregoing experiment to supply the leader with an objectively superior solution so that he could ask stimulating questions. It has been pointed out that a creative leader can upgrade the thinking of a group by his questions. However, this does not imply that a group can be led to accept an inferior solution by this method. In some incompleted experiments on group thinking with mathematical problems the author has found that when a minority individual has an incorrect answer he fails to persuade the majority, but when he has the correct answer he often can persuade the majority to accept his answer.*

The next chapter will throw further light on the limited extent to which a leader can impose his favored solution on the group and, at the same time, win the acceptance of the participants. The danger of using leadership skills to manipulate people is one that bears watching, but this danger seems to be at a minimum when the leader truly desires acceptance. Certainly a leader who influences people to achieve greater satisfaction cannot be regarded as a manipulator, unless one makes manipulation and influence synonymous. It is the influencing of people to do things contrary to their own interests that should be avoided, and this seems to be Haiman's objective also.

* These experiments have been completed since this book went to press. They show that groups holding problem-solving discussions led by leaders who merely encouraged others to talk obtained better solutions than groups holding discussions without a leader. The cause of the difference obtained was found to be the presence of a discussion leader. A discussion leader gives persons with views that differ from those of the strong majority an opportunity to express themselves. However, these minority views carry an influence only when they are supported by external realities. Ungrounded opinions of persons in the minority had little influence in either type of discussion.

11

Transcriptions of
Two Problem-Solving
Conferences

Introduction

In the early chapters the principles of group discussion and group-decision procedures were described. It was pointed out that a group's participation in the reaching of decisions makes such decisions acceptable and hence more effectively executed.

In describing the leader's role in achieving good discussions the permissive character of the leader was emphasized. However, in the last chapter some additional concepts were added in the form of active things the leader might do in order to improve or upgrade the quality of a group's thinking. The problem of blending the type of leader whose function it is to bring a group's thinking together and the type whose function it is to stimulate better thinking by asking probing questions and influencing the direction of thinking is a delicate one and cannot be described by simple rules.

Some actual cases of group problem solving, with descriptive comments regarding what the leader is doing, may be the most helpful way to supplement what has already been said. This chapter, therefore, is devoted to a presentation of transcriptions of cases phonographically recorded and supplemented with stenographers' notes. These transcriptions are unrehearsed and have been edited only to clarify meanings. They should not be regarded as perfect demonstrations but merely as a leader's performance under unrehearsed circumstances.

In order to have a problem in which both ideas and conflicting attitudes would be present the conferees were given roles to play as well as a problem to solve. In this manner the conference leader was placed in a situation in which he would have to distinguish clearly between stages in which resistance was involved and stages during which ideas might be stimulated. Thus he would be required to work both for acceptance and quality of thinking.

Since the parasol assembly problem, discussed in the previous chapter, has an inventive solution and involves the problem of acceptance when set up in role playing, it seemed ideal for this purpose. In preparing the groups for their roles the procedure was the same as described in the preceding chapter. The objective of the leader was to see if he could get the group to arrive at the inventive rotation solution. The time limit was 50 minutes, and this amount of time is usually adequate.

The descriptive comments are presented in two styles of type. Comments referring to the functions of the democratic leader, in which acceptance is the primary objective, are presented in small roman type; whereas comments which refer to the function of the leader as he influences the direction of thinking are given in small italic type. It will be recalled that in influencing the direction of thinking the leader does not supply solutions. The suggestions of solutions or parts of solutions must be distinguished from influences that take persons away from unproductive lines of thought or steer thinking into new channels. Thus when one asks, "Have you tried some other combinations?" or "Is there any way in which we can make use of that obstacle?" one is directing thinking away or toward something, but one is not offering a solution. Thus by influencing directions in thinking one may make insights easier but still leave the experience of discovery to the other fellow.

The first transcription is the report of a successful case. It will be noted that in this instance a considerable degree of direction was supplied by the leader. In some cases discoveries come readily from certain group members, and the leader's task is a relatively easy one. This case is especially instructive because group members were not too inventive, and the leader was required to exert considerable direction.

The second transcription is of special value and interest because it represents a group's failure to achieve the inventive solution. In it the leader first supplied directing influences, but without success. He then went beyond influencing direction and began supplying the solution in stages, often using questions but going beyond what we have called influencing direction in thinking. The result was that the group refused to accept his suggestions. It is quite possible that the forces that caused the group members to reject the leader's suggestion also operated to prevent them from discovering the solution themselves. This would mean that if a group is unable to discover a solution with proper help from the leader they are not ready to accept ideas beyond their own stage of development. Then it becomes the leader's function to permit further development at a later meeting. Pushing things too fast may retard progress.

The fact that the group accepted the solution in the first instance and rejected it in the second does not prove that the difference lies in the leader's method. Groups behave differently, regardless of the conduct of the leader, and it is the leader's job to adjust to his specific group. The purpose of presenting the transcription, therefore, is merely to demonstrate and describe different conference methods, not to use them as evidence to support principles.

Case 1. Inventive Solution Develops

HAL BENTON: Good morning, fellows.
EVERYONE: Good morning.
BENTON: I hope you all feel free to smoke in here. (*Several men light up.*) (*After a pause*) I pulled you off the line this morning because I'd like to talk to you and learn from you about the way things are going on the job. As a matter of fact, I'd like to take the time to do that every so often. You fellows are close to the job, and you undoubtedly have experiences on the job that I don't know about. I thought it might be desirable if I knew something about them and in that way got closer to things. I'd like to have meetings with you regularly—once every two weeks or something like that—just to talk over the job. How do you feel about it? (*Men nod approval.*) Do you think that there would be anything to gain by discussions of that kind?

> Here Benton tries to create a congenial situation and establish mutual interests. Meetings that lead to better relations would benefit both Benton and the men.

SAM: Why, I don't know. Could be.
BILL: We have problems that we might appreciate talking over if we were assured something would result from the talk.
BENTON: I think that if we did talk them over and if there are things that we can do something about, why, I'd certainly be very happy to make any changes that I had the authority to make. How is the job going? Just how do you feel about the job? You find it satisfying? What are some of the angles you have? (*Pause*)

> Here Benton shows a willingness to improve things and is permissive. He follows his acceptant statements with general questions. The use of general questions permits people to talk about anything that is foremost in their minds, provided they feel that the situation is permissive.

HARRY: We could use some more work. I get tired of doing nothing all day long. I have to keep waiting and waiting for the units to get up to my end here. On some other jobs that I had I could work a little faster and I felt better, but here I have to work the same old slow-motion pace all day long.

BENTON: Well, Harry isn't too well satisfied with the pace. (*Benton writes "pace slow" under the heading "Problems" on the easel.*) Is there anyone who feels that the pace is too fast already?

> Although Harry gives a lead that might test the foreman's interest in low production, Benton does not capitalize on it. Instead, he turns to explore the possible opposed views. This brings others into the discussion.

HANK: I feel the same as Harry does.

BENTON: You think it's too slow.

> In this instance, Benton merely reflects Hank's expression, neither approving nor disapproving.

JOE: Why, I would say it's just about right.

BENTON: Joe, you feel the pace is just about right. (*Benton writes "pace about right" on the easel.*)

> Similarly, he reflects Joe's contribution and registers interest in the difference in opinion.

JOE: Just about right.

BENTON: Anyone else feel it's just about right?

> Next, Benton explores for more support for Joe. Joe has put out his neck and needs support.

SAM: Why couldn't Joe be given less to do—some other job? I have to help him out. Oh, I shouldn't say that because I don't want you to know about it, but that's the only way we can keep the line going.

BENTON: Well, I see no reason why you shouldn't be allowed to help him out if you want to, provided Joe doesn't object. Do you object to it, Joe?

> Although Sam does not agree with Joe, he gives him support. And when he slips and gives away a secret, Benton approves of his action. This approval adds to the permissiveness Benton is attempting to create. He then turns to explore whether Joe has been hurt.

JOE: Well, no, I'll admit at times he does give me a hand there, but I'll admit that I have to kind of stretch the point a little bit once in a while. But I thought I was holding my end up.

BENTON: Well, it's perfectly all right if Sam wants to do it, if you don't mind.

> Joe indicates some discomfort, and Benton adds further assurance that no one has been betrayed by Sam's remark.

JIM: We have been talking this over among us. Some of us feel the same as Harry does—that work is just too slow. But we'd want to be pretty sure, too, that we don't pick out any one man—that there'd be no drawbacks on this, such as having to let anyone go. We're responsible as a group for our production, aren't we? We can work any way we like to get that production out.

BENTON: Why, I'd like you to feel that way, Jim. People are different, and what is a good pace for one person might be fast for another and slow for still another. In other words, we just happen to be made different, and I think that's just one of those things we have to face. There are also days when one man feels better or feels like doing more than on other days.

> Benton adds assurance that he is not trying to blame someone, and in this way is removing defense reactions. This sets the stage for solving problems constructively.

JIM: Well, you don't care then how we get the production out as long as we get her out as a group?

BENTON: I am very concerned that no one feels he has to pressure himself to get production. You all want to work at a pace that is satisfying. Now, Harry and Jim feel that too slow a pace is hard because they have to move slower than is a natural pace for them, but others might have quite a different natural pace. Each of us has a pace that's right. When we walk, we all walk a certain pace—if we walk faster it's more tiring—and if we walk slower it's more tiring. So, there are differences in the way a pace makes us feel. Let's just get a general idea of how you feel about the work pace. How many feel that the pace we have right now is too slow to be most satisfying? (*Pause*) How many feel it's too slow at present?

> Is Jim's question a trap? Benton proceeds to clarify his position to assure the group that he is not trying to take advantage of anyone. He returns to the problem, and in asking for a show of hands, he is extending participation.

> *Benton here is clearly exerting control over the discussion, but he is doing it primarily by being permissive and clarifying a problem—that of a difference of opinion in the group on the question of pace. He further exerts a control when he brings others into the discussion. At this point a dialogue might have developed between Jim and Benton.*

(*Bill, Sam, Harry, and Hank raise their hands.*)

SAM: That's right, it's too slow.

HARRY: It's too slow.

BENTON: Then several of you feel the pace of the line is too slow. Now, how many are there of you who feel our present pace is too fast? (*Writes "too fast" on the easel beside the other items dealing with the pace.*)

> Benton summarizes the responses without attempting to press for affirmative responses, but instead explores the other side of the

issue. Thus, before anyone can be made to feel that he is taking
sides, he asks for expression from the others.

GEORGE: Yes, I feel it's too fast. I think it should be slowed down.
I feel that Joe is giving an honest day's work.

BENTON: Well, I'm sure he is. Does anyone feel that Joe is trying
to hold back? (*No one indicates disagreement. Pause.*)

> George has come to Joe's rescue and has clearly sided with him.
> Benton recognizes this and accepts George's view. Then he turns
> to the group and gives them an opportunity to demonstrate that
> they are not critical of Joe.

JIM: No, Joe is working just as fast as he can go there.
SAM: Joe is a bit old on the job.

> Jim assures Benton that Joe is trying, and Sam tries (rather
> bluntly) to explain Joe's slowness away.

BENTON: So everybody is doing a good day's work—what's a good
day's work for him.

> Benton here merely summarizes the group's good feeling toward
> one another.

HARRY: I think it's a management problem. I think the company
should do something about it.

BILL: I'd go along with that. The job calls for limber fingers, and, if
the company allows Joe to remain on the job, then the fact is that
they consider that he is the man for the job. If things don't go so good
why put—

> Harry and Bill, however, are not satisfied. They seem to fear
> that things won't be corrected without doing something about Joe.
> Maybe they have talked to each other. In any case, hostility to-
> ward management is indicated.

JIM: I don't know, Bill, we've been working together for most of five
or six years in the same group, and there's been no complaint about
our production. Maybe there's some other solution.

> Benton lets the members interact to permit the expression and
> clarification of the hostility. Soon Jim comes to the rescue and
> exerts social pressure by talking about group membership.

BILL: Possibly the production scheme. Is the scheme all wrong?
Has the company considered that?

BENTON: Well, I think that's just one of those realities that enter into
the picture when we do group work. What we find here in this group
is that some say the line moves too fast (*points to easel*); some of you
say it's about right (*referring to easel*); and some of you feel it's too
slow. (*Points to "slow" on easel.*) See, we have differences in opinion on just that subject of pace, and we have it right in this group.
Now I'd like to explore some more to see whether there are any other

problems. (*Pause*) (*Benton at easel*) The pace, as such, is a problem that we have already located, isn't it? Do you have any other problems? (*Pause*) Now, some of you feel that something should be done about the pace—that it's a company problem. Well, if you can help solve the problem, isn't that all to the good?

> Bill has put a question to Benton and has indicated that management hasn't done all it should. Benton does not go on the defensive. He accepts the criticism and brings the group back to problem solving. He attempts to drop the question of pace and explore for other items, but the group does not respond. He senses that the group is not going with him and returns to the pace and to Bill's point. Note that instead of putting the finger on Bill he makes a general reference to the feeling that the pace is a company problem.

BILL: Well, our remarks certainly shouldn't be thought of as putting the finger on Joe. We respect him—we've worked with him for a long time, and, if there is any solution, I believe, and I think that the others will agree, that it should be one that shows proper consideration for Joe.

> Bill's remark clarifies the difficulty. Bill apparently has been too hard on Joe and now protects him. Others join in.

BENTON: Is that the way—
HANK: Maybe Joe just doesn't feel good.
BENTON: In other words, all of you feel that we're not here to point the finger at anyone or put the pressure on anyone. Is that right?

> Here Benton reflects the group feeling in a permissive manner and receives assurance that the problem must be solved to everyone's satisfaction.

> *The recognition that no one is to suffer from a change serves to get the group away from a defensive position. This move is the prerequisite to constructive problem solving, and in making it the leader is exerting an important control over the discussion.*

EVERYONE: That's right.
BENTON: I think that's a good attitude to have. We are a crew. We want to work together. We want to be congenial. In other words, if the work is satisfying, then we're going to have a happier crew. And we're in disagreement on the pace. If we could do something to make that more satisfying, then it would be all to the good, provided we could do it without in any way putting the finger on anybody. Now if we just tried to take care of those that want to slow the production line down, then those who think it too slow already would be inconvenienced; and if we speeded it up to take care of those who think it's too slow, then those who find it too fast already would be pressured. That makes a nice problem, doesn't it? (*Refers to easel where problem is indicated.*) Let's see if there are some other problems.

After the group has agreed on its interests Benton takes a stand, too. Thus he and the crew have a mutual interest. Then he again states the problem having to do with pace.

Having clarified the old problem and having accepted it, he attempts to get the group out of the rut so that they will broaden their perspective. In doing this Benton is influencing the direction of the group's thinking.

BILL: I wonder if we shouldn't establish first what is the pace that satisfies the main line's requirements. We'll have to conform to that as a group eventually anyway.

BENTON: Well, if we are doing the best we can I think it's a company worry.

The group members persist in talking about pace, but the leader is accepting what is said without criticism and at the same time turning attention away from the problem.

Here he is again exerting an influence over direction in thinking in that he is weakening a persistent line of thought, thus permitting a broader perspective.

BILL: In analyzing what is satisfactory to the company, I think we should consider that there is another group doing a much worse job than we are.

BENTON: That's right.

BILL: I wonder if we are so bad then.

HARRY: I think we are doing the best we can under the circumstances, and, as I said before, I think it is partly a management problem.

BENTON: Well, if we are doing the best we can, then it is a management problem. Now, if there is any way in which we can make changes or make adjustments, that you want to make and that we have the authority to make, there wouldn't be any harm in that, would there?

The leader continues to be acceptant.

In addition to being acceptant Benton also is influencing the direction of thinking. He is actually pointing to thinking in a larger area when he speaks of "adjustments that you want to make."

JIM: Well, I talked to Harry before, and he feels like I do, that there isn't just enough to keep us busy all the time. I wonder if it'd be all right—most of these operations we know or can learn pretty fast—if when we finished up our work, kind of rotated around—jumped in where we were needed. He is like I am—wants to keep busy.

Benton's influence on direction bears fruit. Jim makes a suggestion which is definitely a step forward.

BENTON: Why do you want to keep busy?

Here rotation is suggested, and it might be regarded as a real lead to the solution. However, Benton is not overanxious. To turn it into something that Jim did not have in mind would be resented. However, he doesn't let the suggestion drop. Instead, he probes.

In probing for further analysis and clarification of feeling, the leader is keeping alive a good direction in thinking and permitting it to grow.

JIM: It is harder to make work than it is to go ahead and do it.
BENTON: In other words, you feel that it's difficult to look busy at times. Do any of you have a problem of boredom with this job?

Here Benton is not only reflecting feeling but also enriching the direction by using the word "boredom." In addition he is bringing other members of the group around to express feelings in this area. Bill responds.

BILL: It's very boring. That's another answer as to why we want to keep busy.
BENTON: Um-hum.

Benton accepts Bill's contribution by a mere nod. He wants more members to come in. Hank responds.

HANK: How about moving us around?
BENTON: So another problem is boredom. (*Writes "boredom" on the easel, so that both pace and boredom appear under the heading "problems."*) Now if we could do anything to make the job less boring—that would be something that you'd be happy about. Is that right?

With support from Jim, Bill, and Hank, Benton is ready to state boredom as a group problem. He suggests that this problem may have a solution.

Thus Benton is again influencing the direction of thinking.

HARRY: Hank just suggested that we rotate around within the job unit itself. Maybe that'll help. Maybe we could put Joe somewhere where he wouldn't hold us up too much.

Harry responds with a suggested solution—that of rotation. However, he weakens the idea by bringing Joe back into the issue, so that rotation has a further meaning—that of swapping jobs.

JOE: Well, now, after all I've been around here 30 years. I've been doing this job a long time.

Note how Joe goes to his own defense, and the thinking in a constructive direction is lost.

SAM: Yes, but you're getting a little old, friend.
JOE: A lot more thumbs than I had before, with 30 years behind.
BENTON: We agreed that we weren't going to put the finger on anybody; that what we wanted to do is see if we could solve the problem in a way that would be satisfactory to everyone. Now I want you to clearly understand that I'm not here to put the finger on anybody.

What I would like to do is to see if I can take some of the boredom out of the situation and see if there's any way of doing something with the job that would permit this pace to fit all of us better without putting any pressure on anybody. See, we've got some people who feel that they'd like to do more; we've got some people who feel it's about right; and we've got some people who feel they're already doing too much. Now, is there anything we can do? One suggestion has come up—that of boredom. Apparently tied in with the boredom is also the pace. Harry feels that he'd like to change around a bit. In what connection was that, Harry?

> Benton allows some exchange and then restates the problem issues. Note how closely he brings together the questions of pace and boredom. Up to this point they have been quite separate issues. In putting them next to each other he is permitting some insights, in the form of new relationships, to occur. He goes further and puts the solution of changing around close to pace and boredom problems. Is the group following him? He gives Harry, who suggested the idea first, an opening. Can he get the solution out of Harry?

> *In this speech Benton has clearly applied the principles of reasoning to problem solving. He is turning the thinking in a general direction, and he is making insights easier by putting the ideas that are to be combined closer to each other. However, he has not supplied ideas or made the combination. He wants these to come from the group members.*

HARRY: Within our own unit—just rotate jobs within the unit.
BENTON: In other words, the suggestion of rotating jobs. Now what would that accomplish—what would we accomplish by rotating jobs?

> *Harry is moving in the right direction but isn't there yet. Benton reflects Harry's speech and highlights "rotating." He probes further.*

BILL: Wouldn't accomplish anything on the pace problem. All our jobs require finger dexterity, and apparently that is where Joe is lost.

> Bill hasn't experienced insight and dismisses the idea.

BENTON: Would it help the boredom?

> *Benton doesn't allow it to be dismissed. His question keeps the rotation idea alive.*

JIM: I think it would.
BENTON: In other words, you think that if you worked on different positions the job wouldn't be as boring.

> Benton reflects Jim's views so that he can gain some responses from others, but Jim makes some reservations.

JIM: Not unless the pace was stepped up; it would be about the same. It would relieve boredom at the outset, but after a week or so I think we'd just have a variety of boring jobs rather than one single boring job.

JOE: Well, it seems that everything hinges around my particular position here. I've been putting that same little oil gauge on there for a long time, and I've gotten kinda used to it. I take a lot of satisfaction doing a good job at that one thing. I'm not bored a bit.

Joe is defensive and doesn't help things.

SAM: Well, you do a good job, Joe, but you're awful slow. (*Turns to Benton.*) I think he should be given less work to do—maybe a different job.

HANK: Maybe Joe's job is tougher than it used to be for some reason that we don't know about. Give someone else a chance at it.

BENTON: Joe, granted that you like what you're doing now, but suppose the other fellows wanted a change. Would you mind if they changed with you and you did something else, providing we didn't put any pressure on you?

Benton lets the group members influence Joe. After the members have been generous with Joe, Benton gives Joe a chance to be generous.

JOE: Sure, I'd be willing to try it. But if it's a question of the pace, why, changing to another job that I'm not familiar with is going to slow things down even more.

Joe goes along, but notice how he protects himself against criticism for his slowness.

BENTON: Well, there are two things—you see, we have two problems; we've got the pace problem and the boredom problem. Now the rotation might help the boredom, at least for a while. We can explore this idea and see if we agree that rotating jobs would cut down on the boredom. If it did it would make a job more satisfying. I think that anything we can do in the direction of making the job satisfying would be to the benefit of all of us, wouldn't it?

In order to prevent resistance from Joe, who is somewhat on the defensive, Benton is separating the problem of reducing boredom from the problem of pace. He is expressing a willingness to solve the boredom problem on the basis of a general benefit to all. Then if rotation reduces Joe's production it will not be held against Joe. Will the group agree to this? He is exploring the group's acceptance of this idea.

Benton is also improving the quality of thinking by differentiating between the two problems.

BILL: I'm certainly willing to try the rotation. (*Some of the others nod agreement.*)

BENTON: Well, what would be accomplished—is there anything else that we might accomplish with the rotation that might give us some idea as to *how* we might rotate?

Having obtained some acceptance of the rotation idea, Benton is now encouraging further analysis.

This is the probing type of influence which keeps the idea in front of the group. The idea has some merit which is meeting with acceptance, but the full value of the idea has not been appreciated. Then too, more time is needed, and the leader in influencing the group by asking for more analysis. In adding the question of how they might rotate, he is leading them away from their present direction of thinking.

SAM: Well, maybe Joe will find out that he can do one of the other operations faster than he can put on those oil gauges. He hasn't tried it.

Sam sees one new value of rotation, finding a job that suits Joe better.

BENTON: We might discover jobs that fit us better. (*Writes the idea on easel.*) Anything else we might accomplish?

In writing Sam's idea down he accepts it and at the same time moves the thinking along when he asks for other things.

This procedure permits the leader to move away from suggestions that are not productive, without being ungrateful.

JIM: It would teach us all the jobs over a period of time, so if we did have a lag on the line later on, any one of us could jump in and help.

BENTON: You would learn more jobs. (*Writes "Learn more jobs" on easel.*) Is that an important one? (*Jim nods.*) You feel you've got an awful lot to learn on each of these jobs?

Jim suggests a contribution which rotation might make. Benton reflects the idea, but he also causes the idea to be examined and evaluated. As a result of closer examination, the idea is dismissed.

Benton is here influencing the quality of thinking by asking questions that provoke an examination of the idea. Thus unproductive ideas can be eliminated so that room is made for productive ideas in new directions. It is important that this idea of differences in the job be eliminated because it stands in the way of rotation. Although the objective facts do not support the notion that the jobs differ, there is a tendency to emphasize differences because the group is still trying to find something for Joe. Thus the thinking is still influenced by the initial view of the problem: that of Joe's being an obstacle.

Note that the procedure bears fruit. Harry and Bill discount the importance of learning new jobs so that Benton does not have to pass judgment.

HARRY: I think we could all do each other's job right now.
BILL: I agree with that. These jobs are of equal skill.
BENTON: So the learning part would be just a matter of half an hour or so, and then you'd have it.

Benton here reflects the remarks of Bill and Harry, but he goes a bit further. He protects Jim by indicating that some learning may be needed, but that it would be of short duration and hence, would not be a concern to management.

BILL: Probably won't enlarge our job description at all.

Bill accepts Benton's interpretation.

BENTON: So that isn't an important consideration. Are there other angles?

Benton then disposes of this line of thought and reopens the issue.

HANK: This shifting around could be done for a definite period of time, and, if it doesn't work out to an advantage, try some other combination.

BENTON: Now many of you seem to like the idea of shifting positions. (*Most men indicate acceptance, but Joe seems uneasy.*) Joe, do you feel that you're under pressure on the present arrangement?

Hank has renewed his earlier suggestion and has made a bid for action. Since the suggested action may be premature, Benton explores the degree of acceptance. He feels that Joe may not be ready for the idea and shows concern for Joe's feelings. Perhaps Joe feels a change in jobs will put him at a further disadvantage. Benton therefore gives Joe an opportunity to express his present disadvantage.

JOE: Well, granted that I have a couple more thumbs than I used to have, but it takes me a little bit longer than it does the others.

BENTON: Do you feel under pressure?

JOE: Oh, to a certain extent.

BENTON: You feel as if you're hurried?

JOE: Yes, I have to keep right at it all the time. I don't get any chance to smoke or run out and get a drink or anything like that.

BENTON: By being in that position you feel that they're pushing you a little bit.

JOE: That's right.

BENTON (*thoughtfully, and with consideration and understanding*): Does that make you nervous?

JOE: Well, as I say, I've been doing it for 30 years and have gotten used to the pace but realize it is pretty fast. These other fellows are hopping around and they aren't working when I am still plugging away at it, but— (*shrugs his shoulders*)

The exchange has revealed that Joe is trying his best and feels his disadvantage. Benton then turns to George, who has also been reluctant, and seeks his support for Joe's feelings.

BENTON: How about you, George? Do you feel hurried?

GEORGE: Yes, I'm pressed at times, but I could maintain the pace if there was one which could be worked out to keep Joe in the unit.

BENTON: Well now, a couple of the fellows feel a bit hurried, and some of you feel that you haven't enough to do. While we're talking about that rotation, what would happen, Joe, suppose you've gotten a little bit behind—suppose now we all changed jobs, Joe to go in Jim's position—all of you shifted positions on this rotation—what would that do? You'd get out of that difficulty, wouldn't you?

> Since George has supported Joe, Benton reflects the clear-cut difference in the group on the question of pace. He now places this problem next to the rotation idea. The group had failed to see a connection between the rotation suggestion and the pace problem, but now Benton raises the question of whether or not there is a connection. He asks specifically how the rotation plan would affect Joe and his problem.

This question clearly points up a direction in thinking, and yet it cannot be called a suggested solution.

JOE: Well, I'd be out of the hole. I'd be stepping over to a job that was all caught up, I suppose, and my friend over here would be stuck with a couple of jobs that I hadn't quite finished.

> Notice that Joe gets an insight into the situation but shows consideration for Sam. Considerate treatment for Joe has paid off.

SAM: Well (*reassuringly*), I've been doing it right along.
JOE: Well, after all, you're a young fellow. You're able to stand up under that a little better.

> Despite Sam's reassurance, Joe tries to save face.

SAM: You're good, Joe, all right (*kindly*), but you're getting old.

> Sam tries to help him save face but isn't too expert at it.

BENTON: Now what would happen to you, Harry? You've had the stuff coming to you. If you shifted down a notch what would that do to you? George, would that put you on the spot?

> Joe having been appeased, Benton tests George and finds him agreeable, even if not quite comprehending the outcome.

GEORGE: I think the pace on the two jobs would be about the same. I am willing to try it.
BENTON: Now suppose, Sam, when you take Joe's place, that some work has piled up in Joe's position. You would obviously have more to do with work piled in front of you. Would you feel that you had to make that all up?

> Benton here is continuing to stimulate an analysis of the effect the rotation plan would have on different individuals. He wants to make sure that the individual next to Joe will not have to carry him. Sam could easily become the goat, and so might have the wrong insight. He anticipates any such fear by putting his question.

In so far as Benton is exploring the effect the rotation plan will have on the work of others, he is clearly influencing the direction of the group's thinking so that various angles receive constructive consideration.   This prevents fears and defensive reactions from arising.

SAM: No, I don't think I should have to make it up.   I'd be willing to go part way.

BENTON: In other words, if you wanted to work faster, you could.

SAM: That's right.

BENTON: Then if you didn't want to work faster, you could leave it. And then, if that went on awhile and everybody shifted again, what would happen?

JOE: Same thing.

Benton continues his exploratory questions and at the same time reveals that he is not trying to take advantage of superior workers. Note that Joe is going along with the thinking.

HANK: How often would this shift take place?

BENTON: I think that's something we want to work out.   We're trying to explore what it would do to us if we shifted positions.   Suppose we shifted every so often; I don't know what the right period would be, but let's think about that later if this looks like a good solution. In any case, where would the work pile up if we made some more shifts?

Hank is beginning to wonder about the outcome.   Benton accepts his question and sets it aside for later consideration so that he can proceed with his exploration.

Here he is definitely controlling the direction of thinking, and perhaps he is pressing too hard.

BILL: Well, that's what troubles me.   These jobs are of equal skill, and they all demand the same kind of skill.   I'm afraid that the unfortunate thing is that wherever we place Joe there's going to be a pile-up.

BENTON: But where would the pile-up be if you shifted—in what position?

BILL AND JOE: Piles all over.

BENTON: In other words, you'd have a pile-up in different places, so instead of work being piled up in one position, there would be pile-ups all the way around the line, wouldn't there?

Benton summarizes, but is he thinking ahead of the group?

HANK: Well, that would probably be the solution to our problem right there.   Maybe there's someone in the group who should be given some other type of work—put in some other group.

The second part of Hank's remark indicates he has missed something and is back on the bottleneck line of thinking.

BENTON (*smiling*): I think we agreed in the beginning that we weren't going to pick on anyone.

> Benton tries to get the thinking away from Hank's suggestion and to protect Joe at the same time.

HANK: Yes, I know we did.

JIM: I think this whole thing, this rotation, is just an accordion action; that is, as soon as jobs pile up, you rotate. I think if Harry wants to pitch in one day and Bill or myself the next, and we jump in on those spots where Joe might be, or even in George's place, it should be O.K. If they're a little bit pressed for time, and as long as the whole production gets out, you don't have any objection to our helping, do you? (*Benton indicates agreement.*) I can't see anything wrong with that, or what difference it makes how Harry or the rest of us want to work.

BILL: I think that is too uncertain a standard for management to rely on. I am usually awfully nasty on Mondays and Thursdays and don't want to help anyone.

BENTON: Well, if you didn't want to help out and even if no one else wanted to help out, then I suppose we'd eventually have little piles all around the circle, wouldn't we?

> Benton lets group members interact until Bill indicates that management might object. Benton then, in a matter-of-fact way, describes the results Bill fears without showing any concern.

HANK: Well, I think that would give us the answer to our problem.

BENTON: How?

> Is Hank getting the idea or is he still in the "bottleneck" rut? Benton checks to see.

HANK: If we shift around, why, this piling up is going to shift around according to the way we do our shifting. It's going to indicate that there is a weak link somewhere in the chain, and that's the link that something should be done about.

> It appears that Hank is still trying to blame someone.

BENTON: We also have the problem that some people think the pace is too slow and that they can't work any faster because of present conditions. Now if you happened to get into a position where there was a pile-up and if you wanted to work faster, you could, couldn't you?

HARRY: That's right. I hope that's going to help things. I've been looking around for another job. They gotta do something pretty quick around here. I'm getting tired of sitting around doing nothing half the day.

BENTON: So Harry definitely feels he wants more to do. Now the question with this rotation solution is whether Joe will be helped if he could get from behind the pile, and whether Harry will be helped if he could move into a place where there was a pile-up of work so that he could do more if he wanted to. Is that the kind of thing you'd like to see, Harry?

Benton is quick to seize on Harry's discontent and use it to help both Joe and Harry.

HARRY: That's right.
JIM: What if George moved into it?
GEORGE: Well, there would still be a pile there.
BENTON: What would be wrong with George leaving the pile?

Jim has asked a good question and George has been quick to answer it, perhaps to protect himself. Hence Benton assures the group that George's answer is acceptable.

BILL: What if I moved into it on Mondays or Thursdays?
BENTON: Then there would still be a pile at your position. Right? (*Bill and others nod.*) In other words, if there were a pile-up in all places and nobody cleared it up, then the piles would gradually get smaller. Right? (*Various members nod.*) Because no one would be expected to work at a pace other than that which he thought was just about right for him. In other words, if you people got into positions where there was a pile-up, then if you wanted to, you could do more; if it so happened that none of you wanted to do more, then we'd be in the same situation that we're in now.

Bill checks to see that he has no obligations, and is assured that he has none. Benton then proceeds to summarize the effect that rotation would have on each of the men.

HARRY: In other words, you mean this rotating should take place every so often so that, whenever we feel that we want to accomplish some more work, we can do it.

Harry begins to get the idea of rotation as it affects the pace of the job.

BENTON: We could rotate if we wanted to spread the piles all over. Then each of us could get in a position where there was a pile, and this would permit us to work faster if we wanted to.

Benton again reflects the ideas as developed so far and again emphasizes the voluntary features of doing extra work.

SAM: Yes, but Joe would have twice the size in his pile.
BILL: Would management let us tie up that much stock?
JIM: These are pretty big pieces, these dashboards.

Sam, Bill, and Jim aren't quite clear; they see some potential difficulties and anticipate that they might have assumed obligations.

BENTON: Well, they get piled up now. If the piles were spread over all positions, would there be more of a piling up than we have now?

Benton at this point begins to answer the question raised and, realizing he is defending a solution, turns the answer into a question.

SAM: Joe can't increase the pace—it'll pile right up.

Sam can't see how the plan will work with Joe present. He still is bothered with the bottleneck idea.

JOE: Well, Hal, I like all of these fellows; I've worked with a lot of them quite a few years. Now this idea of the pace being too fast, well, some of them say they want to work faster and most of them are willing to go along on a plan that's going to spread the work out so they'll have an opportunity of working faster, but, as I think about it right now, I don't believe that they think it's too fast after all. They don't seem to want to increase the production. If things are fixed so that the work is there if they want to do it, they don't seem to be willing to do it. I don't think it's too fast for them either.

Joe goes to his own defense. It is apparent that he has grasped a good deal of the significance of rotation, and he assumes that the failure of others to go along with the plan is unwillingness to do extra work. Although the resistance to the plan is largely due to a reluctance to assume an obligation to make up for the deficiencies of others, it is well to have this other interpretation clarified. Would the men rather work at a monotonous pace than do more work by helping Joe? Benton could not have raised this issue because he would then be expecting others to do Joe's work.

BENTON: Yes. How do the rest of you feel?

Benton merely accepts Joe's statement and puts the responsibility of answering Joe up to the group. At this point the men can agree that the present pace is satisfactory, or they can move on to a suggested change.

BILL: I am not sure, under that rotating system, whether or not I wouldn't resent being branded with the pile in front of me. I know I can work a lot faster. In Russia they give awards to the man that turns out the impossible production, and then they expect everyone else to meet it. We certainly shouldn't do that here.

Bill reveals another source of resistance. Would not the rotation plan make some of the good workers appear, to outsiders, unable to keep up? He also fears a speed-up plan.

BENTON: I agree with you.

Benton is acceptant of Bill's feeling and likewise opposes a speed-up plan.

BILL: But if you're going to make this reduction of the pile purely a matter of choice I believe that we, as individuals, and possibly management, are faced with this situation. We have before us our own pile, and the inherited pile which we are diminishing when we work.

If we leave a pile, are we leaving what we inherited or are we leaving what we should have done?

> Bill sees the significance of rotation and definitely is raising the question of obligations assumed when a man moves into a position where work is piled up.

BENTON: I don't think that we should look at this rotation as a means for imposing responsibility on anyone. I would definitely be opposed to making a person feel that he's got to do more because he has inherited a pile of work. But if the rotation would relieve boredom, would that be all right? (*Several nod their heads.*) Suppose the rotation would permit Harry to work at a faster pace, if he feels like it on occasions when he has some work that could be made up, would that be all right? (*Several nod again.*) Then if he felt like it, he could not only do the work that's coming through, but he could also catch up some of the other work. If that would make him happy, would not rotation be giving him an opportunity to do what he wants to do? Now how about some of the others of you who also express the feeling that the pace is too slow? At present, you can't work faster than you do because the work isn't coming through, but, if work piles were spread around and if you could inherit some piles of work, would that give you the opportunity of working faster when you felt like it? Of course it is understood that no one is expected to diminish a pile unless he wants to.

> Benton clarifies his position that no obligation would be assumed. He again summarizes the effects of rotation and how it relates to the problem of those who think the pace is slow. He has added no new thoughts, but he is emphasizing the constructive features of the plan. He is assuming that the fears have been removed.

BILL: Well, I think you put that very fairly and, on those terms, I'd be willing to acept it if inspecting managers realize the pile in front of us doesn't indicate that we're not working.

BENTON: In other words, no one is to be held responsible for the pile that's in front of him.

BILL: Absolutely.

JIM: I will go along with that—give it a try.

> Apparently Benton was right in supposing that the barrier to accepting the rotation plan was a fear that good workers would get blamed for the deficiencies of the others. Both Bill and Jim accept the plan, and Joe has previously argued for it.

BENTON: Would you like to try it?

> With this approval Benton explores for the degree of acceptance, but notice that in asking for acceptance he has not asked for a commitment. Rather, he has asked whether the men would like to try out the plan. If the idea really is a good one, its execution will introduce new insights.

In raising the problem of action Benton is moving the discussion forward and is thus directing the group's thinking.

HANK AND SAM: O.K.

HARRY: Sure. Give it a try.

GEORGE: Fine. Sounds good to me.

The rest of the group indicate approval.

BENTON: And what we're concerned with is to watch whether the plan gives each of us a pace that is more satisfying; that is, whether the job is made more interesting because of the fact that you are permitted to change speeds in your work and also to change the kind of work you are doing. (*Men show interest and nod agreement.*) It is also agreed that, if a change in position in any way slowed you down, Joe, no one could point the finger at you. It is understood that you may have trouble because you're moving around to new positions. I think we also agreed that everyone will work at a pace that he wants to work at if the work is there, and that if anyone doesn't feel like reducing the pile he inherits, well, he just won't do it. So, eventually, you see, he moves away from it. No place can pile up too much if no piles are reduced.

> Benton summarizes how the plan is intended to solve the pace and the monotony problem and in doing this is clarifying the relationship between the solution and the problems raised at the outset. In asking the men to evaluate the plan with respect to these problems, he is extending their participation throughout the trial period and is emphasizing its provisional nature. He then turns to check whether or not the group agrees to accept Joe's inadequacies and summarizes the previously accepted attitude toward Joe. Then he summarizes the position agreed upon that no member of the group has assumed obligations. This summary, then, includes the statement of the plan as well as the major feelings expressed.
>
> *This summary statement may have introduced some new insights. Although no new details were added, the mere fact of putting them together may have enriched the meanings in the solution. If this occurred the leader definitely increased the quality of thinking in that he stimulated the experience of new relationships. However, he did this by working from the facts which grew out of the discussion. Thus he influenced direction in thinking.*

JOE (*jokingly*): Can't tell—maybe I'll find a job that I can do a little faster.

BENTON: You might. I think that would be another thing to watch for, Joe. (*Goes to easel and writes as he enumerates the points he then summarizes.*) Watch the pace, watch the boredom, and watch for jobs we like. Of course, if everybody likes the same job, what would we do then?

> Joe's remark may indicate some defense. Perhaps Benton overprotected him. However, his feeling is not serious. As a matter

of fact, he seems to be feeling his oats and is hopeful that he can make a good showing.

SEVERAL: Have another meeting.

The reaction of the group is good. New problems would call for another meeting.

JOE (*in a gay mood*): If they all like the same one, I'm liable to inherit the same pile I left, of course.
BENTON: Then we would all just have to slow down until that pile got caught up. If we all like the same job, would you be willing to have everybody "divvy" it up? (*Group nod agreement.*) In other words, we would continue rotating if this happened, wouldn't we? Would you like to give the plan a try?

Benton answers Joe's question. Time is running short, and Joe is distracting the discussion. Benton then moves to see if the group would go along with rotation in the event that certain positions were favored. He moves fast and accepts nods from the group as answers to the questions raised.

The degree to which a leader may influence the thinking of a group increases as the group reduces its defensive reactions and reaches a problem-solving mood. Benton has sensed this change in the group and therefore feels free to hasten the pace of the conference. However, if he makes a mistake and starts pushing too fast he may create a defensive condition. He checks to see if the group still likes the plan.

BILL: How does that sound to you, Harry?
HARRY: I think that it might work out. I'd be willing to give it a try for a few days anyway, or a week or so. I think that it might help us out a little bit.

Note that Bill checked with Harry. They have been the most vocal individuals. The fact that they check with each other indicates that they feel quite free.

BENTON: When would you like to start?

Having obtained acceptance, Benton raises the question of action.

In raising new aspects of problems for consideration the leader is exerting a control over the group's thinking. This is the usual type of control, since the problem of action is part of most decisions.

JIM: Sooner the better—start tomorrow.
BENTON: How often do you think we ought to rotate? Of course, we might want to experiment with that a bit.

Benton accepts the response of Jim because others seem in agreement. He goes on to raise the question of the frequency of changing positions, but at the same time leaves it subject to change.

HANK: I think that would depend on results.

BENTON: How they pile up, eh? What should we start on?

JIM: Every half hour.

HANK: Every two hours.

SAM: Every half day ought to do it.

BENTON: If we did it every half day, would that permit your pile to spread?

> Benton is favoring frequent shifts. With the half-day suggestion he raises a question.

> *In raising questions the leader can influence the degree of thought given to various suggestions. However, in order not to press for his interpretation too much, he leaves the discussion rather free so that a variety of ideas will be expressed.*

HARRY: I think a better plan would be whenever it begins to pile up, let's just move around. See if we can't spread it out a little bit. Let's not have any set time on it.

BENTON: Well, what do you notice now? How does it work out now? After how long do you notice it piling up in some positions?

> Harry's suggestion, though good, tends to interfere with putting the plan into action, and so Benton encourages further analysis. At the same time, he recognizes Harry's suggestion of letting experience determine the frequency of rotation, but he uses it to have the group explore their past experience.

> *In having the group explore their past experience, the leader is guiding the group to a source of information.*

JIM: There isn't much piling now, not particularly. We just slow down.

BENTON: Well, isn't there a pile before you slow down?

BILL: Piles in front of Joe.

BENTON: How soon do you notice evidence of it piling up?

JIM: When Joe has a good day, it takes about two hours or so.

JOE: That's right. Say along about the middle of the morning. Then I kinda slow down a bit. At ten o'clock or so, why, I get a little bit slower and things begin piling up.

BENTON: Now for the boredom part of it. Would it be better to rotate, say, in the middle of every half a day, or more often than that?

> This exploration favors a two-hour plan, but Benton does not settle for it. He probes further to see if the suggestion suits the boredom factor.

> *This represents further guidance on Benton's part. By the use of questions he is determining the group's range of exploration.*

HARRY: I'll go along with the every-two-hour plan. Every two hours might be a good way to start out.

> Harry has been most vocal on the boredom issue, and he accepts the two-hour suggestion.

BENTON: We could try out the two-hour idea, and then if we wanted to change the time of rotation we could change it. So the idea is to experiment with it, start immediately, and—let's see—it's now ten o'clock—then at noon everybody shifts forward a position, is that the idea?

> Having Harry's acceptance, Benton reflects the acceptance, giving special attention to the point that the two-hour interval is provisional. He then summarizes the action part of the solution and clarifies the direction of rotation.

> *Since the direction of rotation has not been discussed, Benton adds it to the summary. In doing this he is definitely adding a detail to the solution. Here he is again speeding up the conference, and he can do this because he has the confidence of the group. No one seems to object to this added detail, and it is possible that its addition was unnoticed.*

HANK: That's it.

JIM: Yes.

GEORGE AND SAM: O.K.

BENTON: And now, how long do you think it would be before we get a feeling of how things are going?

> Having obtained general acceptance, Benton plans for the time of the next meeting.

BILL: We certainly should try it for a few days—three or four or five.

BENTON: What do the rest of you think?

EVERYONE (*mixed voices*): At least a week I think—a week would be about right.

BENTON: Try it for a week and then make any other changes that we feel are called for from this trial run. So it would be O.K. if we met next week at the same time and discussed how the thing's working out, and then we'll talk about it from the boredom point of view; and whether we like the pace better with the change or whether we feel we can improve the pace. And, let's see, in a week we will have tried out all jobs. There are seven of us. Well, you would have tried each of the jobs two or three times, wouldn't you? If we rotated more often, we'd have tried out more of them. Will a week give you enough experience, with a few trials on each job?

> The group readily agrees on a trial run of a week. Benton summarizes the problems to be worked out at the next meeting and leaves the door open for questions or unfavorable reactions.

HANK: I think so.

JOE: Yup.

BENTON: So we'll see if it has solved any of these problems and whether we should make any adjustments as to a change of the rotation. Is that right now? Have I got it straight? (*Group members nod agreement.*)

> Benton double-checks for acceptance.

JIM: Fine.

BENTON: O.K., then, after lunch everybody shifts; at three o'clock, shift again; and the next day everybody shifts still another position, and so on. Is that right? (*Pauses for nods of agreement.*) Thank you very much, fellows, and we'll give it a try and meet next week at the same time.

Case 2. Inventive Solution Not Accepted

HAL BENTON: Fellows, I asked you to come in this morning because I thought it might be a good idea if we stopped the production line from time to time and had a little chat about how things were going. If you want to smoke it's perfectly all right. (*Several men light up.*)

HARRY: How about chewing?

HAL BENTON: Perfectly all right too. (*Pause*) You fellows are closer to the job than I am; you are right out there doing the assembly work, and there may be things that you run into that I don't know about. I thought that if from time to time we could just talk things over to see how things are going we might make the job more satisfying to you fellows. Do you think it would be a good idea to try the plan of stopping the work for a while every so often and having a chat like this?

HANK: It would give me a rest.

HARRY: Oh, I think it's all right. It's pretty near stopped, anyhow. Things are going so slow that you get sick and tired just doing the same thing over and over, and there is no variety to it.

HAL BENTON: A little stop now and then would give you a change then. If it's O.K., I'd like to try the idea of having discussions for a while and see whether we might not make it a happier situation.

> Harry raises a problem at the outset, but Benton doesn't pick it up. He wants to explore the group feeling first.

GEORGE: Now listen, Harry, what's this remark about the line being too slow? What do you mean by that?

> It is well that Benton didn't pick up Harry's point. George reacts defensively to Harry's remark.

HARRY: Well, your material doesn't come through; if you want to speed up a bit you run out of stuff.

> Harry dodges and makes his original complaint a vague issue.

BENTON: How is the material coming through?

> Benton ignores the incident, so that George is not made to feel that Harry gave anything away. Instead he raises a general question, so that Harry's criticism may be directed toward persons outside the group.

GEORGE: It's O.K. for me.

HARRY: Not too good.

BENTON: Are the material handlers keeping our bins filled? (*Writes "supply problem" on easel.*)

HANK: Yes, the material handlers are doing all right.

JOE: I'll say.

HANK: Well, Joe is the guy that holds things up.

BENTON: Well, if the material handlers are keeping us stocked we don't have any worries in that direction. (*Goes to easel and crosses out "supply problem."*)

> Hank makes a reference to Joe's slowness, but Benton does not make an issue of it. Instead he summarizes the remarks about the supply question and disposes of it as a problem. He is trying to demonstrate that he is not looking for someone to blame.

HANK: That's O.K.

BENTON: How is the stuff coming through? Are the parts fitting O.K.? Do you have difficulty in sometimes jamming them in? (*Writes "problem with parts" on easel.*) How is that part of it?

> Benton raises another question. In his preliminary exploration he is raising issues on which there is likely to be agreement, and at the same time is keeping the discussion centered on the situation rather than on people.

HANK: No trouble at all.

HARRY: They are working all right.

JOE: I don't know, it's kind of hard sometimes getting enough of them done.

BENTON (*understandingly*): You don't have any objection to the material itself, do you, Joe?

> Joe uses Benton's question as an opportunity to state a problem he has, and Benton asks him another question so as to separate Joe's problem from the problem of materials. He doesn't want the issue to remain vague. However, his attitude is friendly, so that Joe is not made to feel that he must find excuses.

JOE: Oh, those boys do what they are supposed to.

BENTON: Part manufacturers are making the stuff all right?

GEORGE (*slowly and assuringly*): What do you mean by that, Joe? Isn't yours all right?

> George apparently doesn't want this potential excuse eliminated. In asking Joe a question he is giving Joe a chance to protect himself if he feels like it.

BENTON: A couple of years ago, you remember—some of you were around here then—we got a batch of material that just didn't fit and we had to drill some extra holes to make the holes larger, in order to get the screws in. But we haven't any problems along that line now, do we? (*Goes to easel and points to "problem with parts" written on easel.*)

> Benton responds by clarifying the issue of what defective parts means so that the discussion may move along.

This is Benton's first control over the course of the group's thinking.

BILL: Not on my end.

HARRY: The parts may be coming in fast enough up at that end of the line, but when they get down here it's just a bottleneck.

BENTON: But your parts and your bin supplies are O.K. (*Crosses out "problem with parts" on easel.*)

Harry has given Benton another opportunity to recognize the bottleneck problem in the group. However, Benton does not appear anxious. To register interest would indicate a critical attitude and show that he has ulterior motives.

HARRY: Yes, they are O.K., but the work doesn't come through fast enough.

BENTON: Well, that might be another problem. Now how about the speed of the production line? (*Writes "problem of pace of production line" on easel.*) You see, the pace might be right for some of us; it might not be right for others. It is sometimes difficult for us to tell just what the proper pace should be.

Harry persists in his criticism of Joe and states the problem clearly. Benton now recognizes Harry's statement as a problem, and he accepts it as a problem rather than as a complaint. He then restates Harry's point as the problem of the pace of the production line. In stating it he recognizes the likelihood of differences in opinion and encourages the expression of such differences.

GEORGE: I think the pace is all right the way we are going now.

HANK: Oh, it's too easy. Nothing to it.

BENTON: You think it's O.K., George? (*Writes "pace about right" on easel.*)

GEORGE: I think it's O.K.

HARRY: Oh, we can all work faster.

HANK: It's too slow.

BENTON: Some of you think it's too slow. (*Benton writes "pace too slow" on easel.*) Does anyone feel it is moving a little too fast?

Benton accepts in a matter-of-fact manner the fact that Hank and Harry disagree with George, and uses the difference of opinion to demonstrate the existence of a problem. He then explores for a third possible point of view.

JOE: Yeah, a little fast for me.

HANK: I think it should be a little bit of both, so you have a little bit of variety because sometimes you feel like working a little harder than you do other times.

BENTON: That's another angle. Now if you consider the over-all pace we have a little problem there, in that it doesn't fit all of us, which isn't too surprising because everybody isn't exactly the same. As a matter of fact, I wouldn't be a bit surprised if on some days (*turning to Hank*) you feel like doing more than on other days.

Hank has suggested a little variety in pace, and Benton has accepted the suggestion as "another angle." He can fall back on this idea to raise the boredom problem, but at this stage the group may not be prepared. The pace issue has to be recognized as a problem rather than a criticism in order to insure constructive thinking.

In persisting in the discussion of the pace problem Benton is influencing the thinking in that he is determining the order in which things will be discussed.

Benton then attempts to get Hank's acceptance of the slow pace by indicating that he might approve of the slow pace on certain days, and in doing this he keeps alive the variety suggestion of Hank's. Note how Hank goes along with the idea.

HANK: Sure do.

BENTON: Well, it seems that some say the line seems to drag, then others say it's too fast—

Benton summarizes, but George interrupts by taking sides.

GEORGE: Personally, I think Joe is right there.

BENTON: Some say it's O.K., others, that it's too slow, and some say it's too fast. We all don't feel the same about it. We don't all feel the same about the pace, so we have a little problem in that. (*Points to easel where problem has been indicated.*) Now Harry said the job is monotonous. Do the rest of you get kind of bored with the job?

Benton again summarizes and makes the difference of opinion a problem to be solved, not an issue to be debated. Thus the question of *who is right* need not be debated, since the existence of a difference of opinion is accepted. Having located one problem Benton turns the discussion elsewhere. He is exploring for problems, and so he returns to the monotony problem raised by Harry at the outset.

In turning the exploration elsewhere Benton is influencing the group's thinking by having them all consider the same issue at the same time. This is only possible if the group is not resistant. By recognizing the pace problem without placing anyone on the defensive he feels that the group will go along.

HANK: I do.

BILL: I think we all do. It's the same old thing every day. You put on the same piece all day long, and come in the next day and put on the same old piece all day long.

BENTON: In other words, if we could do anything to the job to make it less monotonous that would be all to the good, wouldn't it? (*Writes "problem of reducing monotony" on the easel.*)

Benton not only reflects the feelings of Hank and Bill, but turns their feelings into a problem that might be solved.

In turning a complaint into a statement of a problem Benton is influencing the direction of thinking, although he is not supplying or even suggesting solutions. Solutions should emerge from the group.

BILL: It would be very desirable. I think it would give everybody a little more interest in their work. Maybe that's one reason why those people that slow it down don't do the work a little bit faster. They get tired of looking at the same old speedometer all day.

BENTON (*nods acceptance to Bill, and then turns to the group*): If we could do anything to get the pace so that it fit all of us a little bit better that would be fine, eh? We have disagreement there. We really have two problems. One of the problems is to get a pace that we can feel better about, and the other one is to do something to the job to take the monotony out of it. Those are two interesting problems.

Benton accepts Bill's point as an expression of opinion. Since Bill is in full agreement with the monotony problem, Benton feels he has general group acceptance. He, therefore, places it next to the pace problem in the minds of the group. Will the nearness of the two ideas stimulate insights?

New ideas occur when people put certain things together in the right way. Sometimes it helps if the thoughts that must be combined are highlighted or made the center of attention at the same time. Benton is making problem solving easier by this process, but the problem may still be too difficult.

HARRY: If you could only get something fixed up here. I've thought of getting another job because there is no incentive to do any good work, with the monotony and everything. You get fed up on it.

GEORGE: We can't all be as fast as you, Harry.

HANK: Some of those fellows down there, Bill and Jim, I suspect that they feel the same way; if they turn out the stuff and it jams up when it gets along down somewhere else in the line, why, they don't like that either.

HARRY: Why can't Joe speed up a bit?

GEORGE: Joe is doing all right.

JOE: Hal, can anybody show me how to do this job faster and easier? Maybe I don't know how to do it very well. I've been working here a long time, but I know I'm holding them up.

BENTON: I think that what we are doing is talking about some differences. You always find certain differences in people, and those differences become problems. Now the time-and-motion men worked out this job, and they tried to make all these positions equal. On the other hand, people are different and they feel differently about things. I think it would be a good idea if we talked about some of these problems to see whether we could make some adjustments—do things to the job that might solve those problems—and that's why I like to talk to you fellows.

Benton has permitted a free discussion to bring out different attitudes. The slowness of the pace has been a source of irritation for some of the men, and he has let them voice their feelings. Furthermore, the discussion reveals that Joe is not on the defensive but that George is. At this point Benton summarizes the differences as a problem and demonstrates a permissive attitude by speaking of the value of such discussions. This should encourage other views to be expressed, so that all of the feelings in the group can be explored. Such exploration might lead to views that reconcile differences.

Benton is influencing the thinking of the group by keeping the opposed views in balance. In doing this the thinking tends to be directed into the area of resolving conflicting views. Thus Benton is not suggesting solutions, but he is causing the group to move away from lining up on opposite sides and is directing the thinking toward resolving a conflict.

BILL: Everybody seems to be picking on Joe here. I think that if Joe didn't put clocks on all day long and instead put on speedometers for a while, he would do a little bit better.

SAM: That's what I say. Joe is always busy. He's always at it, and if we can help him out a little bit by distributing the load maybe that's what we can do.

BENTON: What I'd like you fellows to know is that this kind of thing, these kinds of feelings are the kind of feelings that any group of people might have. I'd like to look at such differences as problems. We don't want to lose Harry, we don't want to lose Joe. In other words, we are a group of people, and we have a problem. Now some of you have suggested some things that we might do in the direction of solving that problem. What was yours again, Bill?

Bill and Sam have helped the discussion to progress and have come up with constructive suggestions. Sam's suggestion is very much to the point, since it involves helping others. Will the group accept this? Benton feels he must explore. He therefore reflects and accepts the group's feelings, indicating that such differences are expected. He then returns to Bill's suggestion by asking him to restate it. Will Bill combine his idea with Sam's?

Benton is in a position to refer either to Bill's or Sam's suggestion. Sam's suggestion contains the important idea of helping out others, whereas Bill's suggestion contains the idea of exchanging jobs. There would probably be more resistance to Sam's idea, so that it is desirable to have this idea suggested again. In asking Bill to restate his idea Benton is giving him a chance to incorporate Sam's suggestion, and in creating this opportunity he is exerting an influence on the quality of the thinking. Perhaps he should have selected Sam's idea for restatement. Might this influence have given the thinking a better direction?

BILL: Well, I think that these jobs are all relatively simple. I feel that everybody here can do my job, and I feel pretty sure I can do everybody else's job just as fast as I'm doing my own. I think it might be a good idea if once an hour we just shift over a position,

or once every two hours, or maybe just every other day or so. Just
something to give you a change. Say Joe gets working on something
different and everybody can see this whole unit progress through the
assembly line, and you sort of grow with it and you feel a little bit
better about what you are making.

> *Notice that Bill has actually suggested the rotation solution, but
> he has not appreciated its full significance. Shifting hourly would
> tend to solve both the pace and the monotony problems, but shift-
> ing every other day would not help the pace problem at all. In
> suggesting that all forms of rotation will help, Bill seems to have
> failed to see how Joe could be helped by others.*

BENTON: You are suggesting that one thing we might do is change
positions from time to time. (*Writes "exchanging jobs" under "Suggested solutions" on the easel.*) Now what are some other suggestions?

> Benton picks up Bill's rotation idea but reflects the rotation part
> and makes the frequency aspect vague. He then calls on others
> for suggestions but does not yet request acceptance of the rotation
> idea.

> *In asking for further suggestions Benton is opening the door for
> further contributions. Thus he may influence the quality of think-
> ing if others have gained some insights.*

HANK: It seems to me that we ought to attack the problem where it
is, right with Joe. He's the one that is slowing things up. Find out
what's the matter with him.

SAM: Now listen, Joe is a swell fellow. We can fix this up some way
so that he can have a job that he can do and the rest of us take some
of his load. Why not redistribute it?

BENTON: That's another suggestion. Sam, your suggestion was to—

> Hank digresses and points the finger at Joe. As a result Sam
> defends Joe by restating the "helping out" suggestion. Benton
> then labels Sam's defense of Joe as a new suggestion.

> *In making Sam's defense of Joe a suggestion Benton is not only
> preventing an argument but is also turning it into a constructive
> idea. Will his placing of the idea of helping out others next to
> the rotation idea produce some insights? In any case Benton's
> behavior illustrates a kind of influence a leader might have in up-
> grading the thinking. In asking Sam to repeat his idea he is also
> giving Sam an opportunity to become still more constructive.*

SAM: Redistribute the load.

BENTON: Redistribute the load, yes. (*Writes "redistribute load" under "Suggested solutions."*)

SAM: Yes, so everybody is busy.

BENTON: How would you redistribute the load? Do you have any
ideas along that line, Sam?

> *Sam has improved his idea by including the suggestion of helping
> out others in the plan of redistributing the load. This idea has
> two possible meanings: (a) it might mean changing the amount*

of work on certain positions; and (b) *it might mean exchanging positions so as to be able to help those who are behind. Benton might have put the question to the group as a problem; however, he turns it back to Sam. In doing this he has reduced the possibility of getting the idea analyzed and has required Sam to answer his question. It seems that Benton, at this point, has failed to grasp an opportunity to improve the quality of thinking.*

SAM: Well, several. Some of these processes don't take quite as much time as some of the others, although the time-and-motion men have divided it up. Get them in again. Let them take a look at it.

Sam comes through with a possibility other than the two indicated. He is implying that the load is unequal at different positions, and hence is introducing a factor which is contrary to the facts given.

BENTON: Um-hum. In other words, the problem of redistributing the work would be in the direction of tailoring it, not to make the jobs equal but to make them—

Benton attempts to salvage as much as he can. He tries to supplement Sam's thinking by including it as a variation of the load-redistribution idea, so that it will fit in with the idea of giving some men less to do. To have another time-and-motion study would not solve the problem of differences in ability. In making this change in Sam's contribution Benton is directing the thinking of the group away from a new job study. Will Sam recognize the influence as consistent with his views or as a misrepresentation? Benton is taking a chance in this attempt to upgrade Sam's thinking.

SAM: To make some of them take a little less time.

BILL: Well, that's a good argument there. In the case of Joe, he is 60 years old. He's probably getting stiff fingers and that sort of thing. This is delicate work. Maybe we could find another place for him.

BENTON: Find another place for Joe. That's another suggestion. (*Writes "find another place for Joe" on easel.*) Are there some other suggestions? (*Pause*) Let's take a look at the variety of possibilities there are. (*Indicates items on easel.*) I think you see we are already working in the direction of doing something about our problem, aren't we? Let's get some more ideas up there.

Sam and Bill accept Benton's modification, so that the idea of having the job restudied is lost. Bill has offered another suggestion. It is not in the direction of the solution, and so Benton accepts the idea and moves along by asking for further suggestions. When suggestions are not offered, he refers to the previous suggestions and indicates that progress is being made.

Benton's control of group thinking in this case is purely one of influencing the group to explore other areas.

BILL: If you want to redistribute the load I don't think you want to do it in an arbitrary sort of a way. Why don't you give Joe a chance at all of our jobs and let him decide which one is going to be the best one for him? The one he can work best at and the fastest at is the one he should keep. I can certainly put out more work down here.

BENTON: Now you are arguing for this suggestion (*points to item "exchanging jobs" on easel*) of yours?

> Bill has been the most vocal, and so Benton indicates that his idea has already been accepted and thus leaves the discussion open for additional ideas. Benton is attempting to get more uniform participation.

BILL: Somewhat, yes.

HARRY: I kind of agree with Bill on that. To help to correct any monotony situation, why not try to shift around a little bit?

BENTON: You feel that this suggestion would have the virtue of solving both problems at the same time?

> Since Bill suggests moving Joe to different jobs and Harry suggests shifting places to reduce monotony, Benton reflects Harry's remarks by indicating that changing jobs may solve both the pace and the monotony problems.

> *He again is attempting to influence insights by indicating that a single solution might solve both problems.*

HANK: I don't think so. I think that would please most of us all right. We would like a change. It seems to me we still have to go back and get this bottleneck cleared up. It isn't a case of getting bored with the job; it's just a lack of ability to do it. There might be another way. Maybe we can develop some gadget to hold these nuts so we won't drop them and be able to slip them on easier.

> Hank fails to see any connection between changing jobs and work load, and raises the problem of Joe's pace.

BENTON: In other words, you would like to work more specifically with the bottleneck.

> Benton reflects and therefore highlights Hank's disagreement. Since Hank has pretty much continued to voice the bottleneck problem, it seems necessary to clear this up.

GEORGE: Hal, that sounds like speeding up to me. That's all speed-up stuff.

BENTON: I can see how you feel about that, George.

> When George expresses fear of a speed-up Benton is acceptant. For Benton to argue would tend to keep the fear active and would actually give some basis for the fear.

HARRY: You haven't been working too hard.

BENTON: If we start picking on bottlenecks then there always would be somebody that would be getting the heat, wouldn't there? Now what we've got is a different feeling about what the pace should be.

> Benton again protects Joe and attempts to get the discussion problem centered.

SAM: Well, let's fix up some way so we can give Joe a little less to do; then we can all be busy.

BILL: Why should he have a little less to do?

JOE: You fellows are all young punks and I'm an old guy, and if you moved around to every job you'd like that. I don't know how it would be for me. I'd slow you up more than ever if I had a new job every day.

Bill is not in favor of Sam's suggestion and antagonizes Joe. As a result Joe becomes critical of the plan of changing positions.

HANK: I agree with him on that. He wants a steady job, but I think he needs a job where he can either be handling bigger stuff that he can grab hold of easier or develop some gadget so that he can handle things without dropping them.

JOE: Who says that? Maybe I've got the toughest job. The oldest guy with the toughest job. I don't know what Hank is doing down there. Maybe he isn't doing much anyhow.

Hank also hurts Joe's feelings when he finds fault with Joe's work, even though this appears not to be his intent. However, with Hank and Bill both seeming to be critical Joe becomes touchy.

GEORGE: You're doing all right, Joe.

BENTON: Putting Joe in another place and changing positions from time to time have been suggested. Those two ideas have something in common, don't they? If we change from time to time that would give Joe a chance to try some other spots. If he liked the idea of changing he might find a spot that he likes. Understand, Joe, that there is a pace that you can work at comfortably, and we would like to solve the problem in such a way that we would take the pressure off you. Do you feel any pressure on you now?

Benton attempts to rescue the situation by suggesting that putting Joe on a different job (Hank's suggestion) and changing positions (the idea that Joe criticized) might be examined further. He then proceeds to protect Joe, who has been made to feel like the underdog.

In so far as Benton has suggested that finding a good spot for Joe and changing positions have something in common he is influencing the group's thinking, not in the sense of supplying a new factor but in directing attention to their relationship.

The fact that Benton terminates by turning to Joe indicates that he feels Joe may be the real obstacle to a rotation solution. Will Joe admit that present conditions could be improved and hence be willing to consider changes?

JOE: No. Well, I have to work hard all day long.

BENTON: If we could do anything to take the pressure off you, you'd like that?

JOE: Oh, sure.

BENTON: Now if we don't think in terms of trying to speed things up but of trying to solve the problem in such a way that we can work at the speed that we feel like working, that would be a nice solution, wouldn't it? In other words, it would be nice if we could find a pace that would be most comfortable for Harry, and another pace that would be most comfortable for George, and so on.

> Having apparently satisfied Joe, Benton again introduces the pace problem.

BILL: Things are a little slow down here. I don't like to keep piling them up in the middle. I work next to Joe, and maybe once in a while I'd pick up one of his clocks and put it on his panel if I were sure not to get a dirty look from the foreman.

> Bill, however, talks first and doesn't follow Benton's lead. However, he has ceased blaming Joe and indicates he would help him if he were not criticized by Benton.

BENTON: Well, I can understand that you might be concerned, and I suppose you also feel that if I don't pick on you, maybe the superintendent might go through and he will.

> Benton accepts Bill's criticism and permits him to air other fears.

BILL: Somebody might.
HANK: Look busy. I can get this through in about half the time the stuff is coming through now.

> Hank belittles Bill's fears, and Bill seems willing to drop the issue.

BENTON: Let's take a look at this business of changing from time to time and putting Joe in another place. Might there be some way of combining them? And then we have this other suggestion of redistributing the load. I wonder if there is some way in which we could incorporate all of those ideas.

> Benton is again attempting to get the men back on the problem and is suggesting that the various ideas mentioned so far might be reconciled. However, one may question whether he has allowed sufficient opportunity for the expression of hostility and mistrust.

> *In making this positive suggestion Benton is attempting to direct the thinking along constructive lines and is also trying to get the group to re-examine the recommended ideas in a new light. His leads are in the form of directing thinking without supplying solutions.*

JOE: I'd like to try Hank's job for a couple of days. He runs around a lot, and he doesn't do much. He's always running around and smoking cigarettes, drinks more water, and loafs. Maybe his job is easier. Maybe I could try his job.

> Joe, however, has become defensive and tends to neutralize any favorable effect Benton may have had on the group.

HANK: That's O.K. with me. I have to do something in my spare time.

BENTON: Then (*turning to Joe*) you'd like to try some of the others. Maybe there is another job that is easier.

> Benton picks up Joe's lead that some jobs may be easier. Although the idea that there may be easy jobs in the line is contrary to the facts as presented, it has developed into a persistent idea and so it must be considered.

JOE: Maybe there is—could be.

GEORGE: I go along with that too, Hal.

BILL: It would only take a week—there are only seven jobs here. Let him try everybody's job for a day. I think we could put up with that for a week.

> Several men pick up Joe's lead as a possibility. Benton knows the idea is unsound. Should he attempt to alter the direction of thinking?

BENTON: Well, now, let's take a look at what we've got. One way of exploring it would be to see whether some jobs are easier to do than others. Now these positions have been worked out so that they are about equal. If there was an attempt to make certain positions easier that would still stick each of us on a single job, wouldn't it? This other suggestion, changing jobs from time to time, would not only give us a chance to find out whether the jobs are really equal, but it would also give us a variety. Now does that in any way redistribute the load? Here (*draws diagram of production line on the easel and points to Joe's position*), let's suppose, Joe, that you're behind for the time being. Now you feel that you've got to catch up that work. Let's suppose now that we made a change and you moved to a different position. In that case you wouldn't have to worry about catching up that work. If somebody who took your place felt like catching up the work he could; if he didn't feel like it, why, then, the work would be left. Anybody that followed, who happened to feel like catching it up, could do it. In other words, if we changed, and you come to a position that has some stuff piled up, you should not feel that you have to do the work just because you were unlucky enough to get into that position. If you wanted to do more, then you could catch it up. Would that be combining some of these ideas?

> Benton summarizes and then tries to change the group's trend of thinking. He actually goes so far as to describe a solution built from suggestions previously made.

> *Here Benton is going beyond the point of influencing the direction of thinking and is supplying a solution. However, he is supplying the solution in a permissive way and is making no unreasonable demands. Will his suggestion be accepted?*

HARRY: I think the trend would be in that direction, yes.

BENTON: In other words, could we take Bill's idea of changing from time to time and work out a plan in such a way that we would actually be accomplishing all the things we have been talking about?

JOE: Well, you mean if you see work piling up in one position and you think that Hank could do it faster than one of the boys that's in there, you're going to change them around, thinking maybe Hank can go in there and catch it up for him? Is that it?

Note that Joe refers to the plan as Benton's.

BENTON: That would kind of be putting the heat on Hank, wouldn't it?

JOE: Well, yes, you wouldn't want to do it that way, would you?

HANK: I don't want to do it that way.

BENTON: What would be a good way to do it?

BILL: Why don't we arrange it so that, when we change, everybody has to have his work done up?

SAM: That isn't going to help any.

HANK: Could we work in pairs? Could we divide the work up so that two people could be doing a particular job instead of each one doing something alone?

BENTON: Wouldn't it be crowded while you're working there?

SAM: Just have certain things that two people are responsible for instead of just one.

HARRY: I don't know how two people can work on a small instrument at the same time.

JOE: Well, two pieces out of the same bin keeps the bin empty. Get a larger bin with two people taking parts out of it.

HANK: Harry can help Joe out.

JOE: Put a young fellow with an old fellow, that's a way you could train. You could find out who is going to do this work when I get out of here. Put a man in here and I'll train him in the routine, and between the two of us we could get the work done and he learns. You could do something like that.

HANK: We'd have nine men then.

HARRY: That wouldn't correct this monotony situation, though, would it? Give us a radio, give us music.

BENTON: Well, I hear they have been considering tuning in on some of the music. Muzak gives a service like that, and I hear there has been some talk upstairs about getting some of that down in the shop. So we may get it, but you still feel you'd like to do some different things?

HANK: Yeah, like shifting around.

BENTON: Sam, do you also feel that you would like to help out some of the positions where there is some difficulty?

Benton has let the group exchange views freely to see if anyone might support his suggestions. Finally Hank suggests shifting around, and Benton explores for support. In letting the group freely explore an idea he emphasizes that he is attempting to regain the permissive condition he may have lost by making suggestions.

SAM: Sure, just anything to lighten Joe's load a little bit so he doesn't have to keep up quite as fast as the rest of us.

JIM: Well, I think if it makes things run more smoothly I see no reason why, if somebody wants to help out, he shouldn't. If you (*turning to Benton*) wouldn't object to it.

HANK: How is that going to cure it? We don't stay put here all the time. We keep changing around from department to department. Joe here has been here a long time. Next fellow in probably won't want to do that; then we got the same bottleneck all over again.

JOE: These are good lads. If they want to help me out let them.

BENTON: Any others of you feel that you'd like to help out if somebody got behind?

> Benton also explores for support of the idea of helping each other, since the rotation plan depends on a willingness to do this.

JIM: We work as a group, and it would seem to be a good idea for anyone who is ahead to help a man out who is behind because it is a group output.

BENTON: That's another idea I believe. Help those who are behind and not feel compelled, but if you get the time and if you feel like it, help somebody who gets behind.

BILL: I think that some people take advantage of you that way.

HANK: I think so, too. They are all getting the same rate of pay here; why should they do that?

GEORGE: That sounds like a speed-up to me.

SAM: Listen, I've been helping Joe out when the foreman wasn't looking. I think that's all right.

BILL: I don't know. It seems to me that anybody with the tendency to loaf is going to loaf harder that way. He's going to expect the guy next to him to do all his work.

JOE: Who's loafing?

BILL: Well, you don't get the material out that you should get out.

JOE: You young lads here, you are younger than I am. I work hard all day, but I just don't get it done.

BENTON: I've watched Joe, and I think he is conscientious all the time, and I think all of you really feel that way.

> The helping-out notion has developed suspicion, and again Joe has become defensive. Benton supports Joe to show he does not favor a speed-up.

HANK: Oh, I think Joe works all right.

HARRY: Why not put Joe over in another department?

SAM: No. Joe is all right. Let's just help him out.

BILL: A little bit, anyway, because if we don't, it clutters up the line a little farther on. Now it seems to stop there. I can put out more work down here at this end, if we can keep it going faster.

BENTON: I think we have quite a number of possible ideas. If some of you feel that you would like to help out and some of you don't feel that way, we can arrange things so that both things are possible. Harry would like to change his speed from time to time. In other

words, sometimes you like to go a little faster, and then you like to
lean on it and take it easy for a while.

Benton shows understanding and acceptance of different feelings.

He is also pointing up aspects of the situation which may be
soluble and thus is directing the thinking.

HARRY: That's right.

BENTON: You get a little variety in that way. Now changing would
give us variety in doing different jobs.

HANK: That doesn't get the stuff out.

BENTON: If we change positions from time to time, if we got into a
position where there was some work piled up, then that would be the
time to work faster if you felt like it.

Benton supports his own solution to meet Hank's criticism. Harry
sees a virtue in Benton's suggestion, but note that George becomes
suspicious.

HARRY: There is also the thing of days when somebody doesn't show
up. If we are changing from time to time, then everybody is able to
fill in on any part of the job.

GEORGE: I think you should have some more Joes in this line, not so
many Hanks.

BENTON: I think we got to take the people we have. We have a
good gang around here, and I'd like to make the gang happier.

HANK: Well, Hal, we got to make the same pace as the other departments—we've got these panels going out with the instruments assembled—we've got to meet the rate of the other departments. They can't
be expected to wait for us, so we can't hold the line up. These panels
have got to be down there to meet the chassis that come through. We
are behind, now, as I understand it, and it seems to me that we have
simply got to get up to the speed where we belong. This idea of
sometimes working fast and sometimes slow doesn't seem right to me
at all.

BENTON: Well, I was just wondering if we might not accomplish
some of those things with some of the ideas we have here. We have
quite a number of ideas that are related to the problem of adjusting
the pace so that it's satisfactory to each of us. We have some ideas
of solving the monotony problem too, haven't we? Now if we could
combine those or get together on some kind of a plan— Bill, do you
see how that might work out?

Benton has been put on the defensive. He obviously favors a plan,
and the plan is being criticized by men who feel the pace is too
slow and by men who feel the pace is too fast. Notice that he
discovers that he has become defensive and attempts to turn back
and draw another member into the discussion.

BILL: Only by following some of these suggestions. There have
only been two things mentioned so far that seem to have any merit
according to the way I think; one is to change jobs every hour or two,

and the other one is to do something about Hank's idea here of getting some gadgets that might remove some of the finger work that you have to do, and so speed things up. At least some thought ought to be put on that. Maybe we can turn it over to some of these bright young engineers to figure out.

BENTON: In other words, the last idea is a problem that we would have to refer elsewhere, but the one of changing from time to time would be something that we could do in the meantime.

Despite Benton's leads, there seems to be little tendency to follow his direction of thinking. Whether the difficulty arises because the group members have failed to gain essential insights or whether conflicting interests in the group cannot be reconciled is unclear. If lack of insight is the difficulty the group is in need of more guidance; if conflicting interests are the difficulty more free expression is needed in order to clear the way for acceptance of the idea of helping each other.

Benton conducts himself according to the belief that insight is lacking. He therefore accepts both of Bill's contributions but sets the second one aside for the time being and directs the thinking on the idea that has possibilities. In doing this he is attempting to upgrade the thinking, but he is not removing emotional resistance.

BILL: Sure, Joe would like that.

BENTON: Now let's see what would happen. Bill, you are out here (*referring to a position on the diagram*) pouring the work out and passing it to the other fellows, and your suggestion is that you would stay there for a while. Now Harry is over here (*pointing to Harry's place on the diagram*). Suppose, after an hour, you move to the second position (*pointing to diagram*), and Jim moves to the third position, Joe moves to the next position, and so on.

BILL: That seems to have merit.

Note that Bill does not take credit for the suggestion, but he does indicate reserved approval.

BENTON: What would happen if we did that? Let's suppose Joe is behind. He has four panels piled up here in the third position. Then he would be followed by Jim. If Jim felt like it, he might catch up one of those panels that was behind. If he didn't feel like it, he might leave the three there and just do the new work. If you felt like working fast when you got to that position the next hour, you might catch them up if you felt like it, or you might not. So if anybody didn't feel good on a particular day, his work would pile up, but it wouldn't pile up in one spot. It would be in all different spots. Is that right?

Having obtained some approval, he goes on. Note that he tries to get participation in that he asks the group to help him analyze. He is making it clear that he is making no demands on the men but that the plan merely permits the men to do what they wish to do. However, he has found that it is necessary for him to point out all the merits of the plan.

*In analyzing the plan Benton is still selling a plan, not having the
group develop one.   The group seemed to be unable to come up
with what he wanted, and so he is offering a solution which, at
best, might be his answer to the problems the group raised.*

JIM: Yes.

BENTON: Now if anybody wanted to work harder there would be
work to make up in various positions from time to time, is that right?

JOE: Maybe we could get a bin for everybody and then when they
pile up and you have to move you could put them into another bin.

This remark indicates that Joe has missed the point of the plan.

HANK: I don't think everybody is going to be charitable enough to
do that.

Hank may understand the plan, but he is not accepting it.

BILL: Isn't that one way to redistribute the load?   It divides the pile
up among everybody.   If I move into Joe's position and find three
behind, why, I'd make them up.

Bill seems to understand the plan.

JOE: Maybe.   Pass them along, we all know how to do the work.
Take the pile-ups and redistribute the pile-ups and then let everybody
catch up again.

HARRY: Well, Jim would have to be working fast all the time because
every time he moves he would have to be making up Joe's work.

Harry does not see the complete effects of the plan and sees only
the effects on the man that follows Joe.   The bottleneck aspect
still is prominent in his mind.

BENTON: Suppose he made up one of them?

HARRY: If Joe is slow all the time and every time we move ahead
he left some—then what?

BENTON: Suppose the next man made up one of them each time, or
one on every other position?   You see, the next man wouldn't *have*
to make them up.   What difference does it make if some parts are
piled up in the third position or in the fourth position or in the fifth?

Benton attempts to clarify for Harry.

JOE: They wouldn't pile up in the first position.

BENTON: They wouldn't pile up in the first position—that's right, and
sometimes Joe would be in the first position.

Joe's failure to comprehend distracts, and Benton accepts his
contribution.

*He also adds an angle which suggests periods of relief from pres-
sures and thereby made Joe's distraction constructive.*

HARRY: Then everybody else would be slowed down.

JOE: They'd all catch up on what I left behind.

JIM: Maybe Joe wouldn't be slow in all these positions.
HARRY: Well, maybe that's right.
BENTON: That's another thing we could learn.

Again the discussion is reflecting a lack of insight. The possibility that the positions may be unequal has been revived, and Benton accepts it as a possibility.

When Benton accepts the idea that the positions may be unequal and sets this problem aside for future consideration, he is attempting to influence the quality of the thinking by keeping the discussion on the point.

JOE: I'll go along. I'll see what I can do. Maybe there is a place where I can put the stuff out. If I find that place maybe I could stay there.
HARRY: We'll anchor him there.
BENTON: Would that make the work more interesting, Harry?

Benton is again attempting to tie the boredom problem to the rotation and thereby gain acceptance of the plan by the superior workers. Joe is willing to accept the plan even if he doesn't understand it, because he feels he will be helped out.

Benton's question is a good one for influencing direction of thinking. It is exploratory and does not suggest a bias for a solution, although it might stimulate new insight with regard to the solution.

HARRY: I think so.
BENTON: It would give you different positions to work with and somewhat different tools, not too different, but, you see, it would give you a chance to change your pace.

Benton here reflects what Harry may see in the solution. If he is right he may hasten the process, but if he is wrong he may be pushing too fast and so create resistance.

SAM: I think we ought to try it. I think it's worth a try.
HARRY: You aren't going to criticize us if you catch us helping Joe either, are you?
BENTON: Wouldn't it be more easy if, instead of helping Joe, there were positions that you took over that were behind. If you catch up some work it would be an easier way to help out than reaching over to Joe's position, wouldn't it?
HARRY: That's right.
BENTON: I'm not interested in picking on anybody or blaming somebody or saying he should do a certain amount. Maybe we can get a plan whereby each of us can do more of what he wants to do.
SAM: Let's try it for a week.
BENTON: Would you like to try it for a week, Joe? See how it works out?

Benton feels he has Harry and Sam understanding and accepting the plan. With fast workers in favor of the plan, he checks back on Joe.

JOE: Sure.

HANK: I don't see that that's going to do any good for a week. New jobs for all of us every day and at the end of the week—why, production is liable to be lower than it is now.

SAM: We'll talk it over again then.

BILL: Do you want to do my job, Hank? Don't you think you could do my job?

HANK: Perhaps.

BENTON: Maybe we can see what these differences are. During the first week we will be learning these jobs and see what they are like.

> Hank thinks rotation will slow things down and hasn't shown any inclination to accept the plan. Benton realizes that the rotation solution, as a way of spreading the work and reducing boredom, is not acceptable. Can he salvage the rotation idea as something to try out for comparing jobs? Perhaps if he can make rotation acceptable he can build periodic rotation into it later on.

> *Benton at this point is attempting to locate a stage in the development in the group's thinking on which there is agreement. If he can get the group together, perhaps they can move forward. The leader here is influencing thinking by having them meet at a certain point and agree on something.*

BILL: Not much to learn.

BENTON: Suppose it did slow us down.

BILL: It isn't a question of learning. All this stuff is a matter of natural ability. Take that speedometer. It's way up there in the corner and in the center of a lot of other instruments. The next guy who comes on that, it takes him probably an hour before he gets the idea of getting that in there and slapping in the bolts that come through there.

BENTON: How do some of the others feel? Jim? You haven't said much.

> Benton is exploring to see if the group is willing to try changing or exploring different positions under any circumstances. He has also finally decided to use Jim, who has not been an active participant.

JIM: Well, we'll have to take it gradually for the next week, and each one of us kind of take a look at the fellow ahead of him, kind of prepare for his job. Our output is measured by the group, and it is up to the group to help each other out. Maybe the other groups also have a Joe to contend with.

BENTON: In other words, you would be in favor of giving it a try to see what happens.

HANK: Why couldn't we do this? Most of these instruments are clustered, which means a rather hard job to get into. It seems to me Joe's trouble is that he is getting old and not too handy with his fingers. Now the ignition dial is off to one side all by itself, put Joe on there. He might be able to handle that. There are only two bolts he has to handle. It's out in the open and clear. Maybe we could do something like that.

BENTON: We wouldn't be sure just which position, but we would be able to find out if we made any changes around here whether there were any differences like that.

> Hank still resists and again refers to Joe's deficiencies. Benton accepts Hank's suggestion of putting Joe in an easy position and treats it as a further development of the plan of changing positions. Note that Hank accepts the plan when he feels he has participated.

HANK: That's right. We'll go along on that.

BILL: But that doesn't take care of the monotony problem. We get sort of tired doing the same thing every day.

BENTON: I think Hank's idea was if we kept a lookout while we were shifting around, that Joe might find some of these positions that he likes better. Is that the idea, Hank?

> Bill, who seems to have appreciated the rotation plan, wants the plan to incorporate the monotony problem, but Benton defends Hank's idea and doesn't push for more. This gives Bill a chance to support the rotation plan and make it his own. Benton is now emphasizing the acceptance phase of the conference and is pacing the development of ideas in accordance with the degree of acceptance.

HANK: Yes, I think so. We could still go along with the changing and just skip those slow positions each time. That would still give the rest of us a variety of work.

> Notice that Hank, who has held out for keeping production up and believes that rotation will make Joe even more of a bottleneck, now is ready to accept rotation for those who will profit from it.

JOE: Why don't you pick out all the easy jobs on these panels, the easiest places to work on and let me do those parts? These young fellows can do the difficult jobs.

HANK: Oh, they are all easy.

BENTON: That kind of a solution would involve a study of the various positions first, wouldn't it? It's a matter of trying out these changes, and after we've tried them for a while we could find out just how difficult it is to change. We could also find out whether there are some jobs that are harder or easier or if some of them suited our nature better than others. We would then have learned some more things about this assembly job. That would mean that we would have to try these different positions out first because if we talk about it, we might not agree.

> Benton is here accurately summarizing the ideas agreed upon, and he is not pushing for the rotation solution or attempting to add additional features.

> *In summarizing the development of the group's thinking Benton is clarifying the points of agreement and at the same time leaving*

room for further progress. In doing this he is causing the participants to consider similar problems at the same time, thus keeping the thinking from spreading in various directions. This is characteristic of a developmental discussion and is effective when opposition has been removed. Previously Benton moved too fast, and as a consequence various kinds of oppositions distracted forward progress.

HARRY: Why don't we try it that way? Each one shift one step? Say next Monday I'd take Bill's job, and we'd all shift down one and try it for a week.

SAM: A week at a time in each job?

HARRY: Yes.

BENTON: What about you, George?

GEORGE: Oh, I'd go along with the trial.

HANK: It would be O.K. with me if they do it for a week at a time. A day at a time is too short a time, it seems to me.

BENTON: It was Bill's suggestion of every hour.

Benton makes one more try to see if the true rotation plan, which spreads the work and reduces boredom, might be acceptable. In stating that hourly rotation was Bill's plan he is indicating that he is not trying to impose ideas on the group and is reminding them of ideas previously suggested.

ALL: Too much changing. No.

The group's response is clear. Obviously the group is not ready for such a plan at this time. Let's observe what happens when Benton tries to improve the plan the group has agreed upon.

HANK: I think we ought to give it a trial for a week in each position so a man can get the idea, can get the feel of the job. It's no use trying to do it for an hour and then jumping to the next position.

BENTON: What about every two days?

HANK: When we get this thing settled I think we could probably cut the time down—maybe every day make a change.

BENTON: That doesn't take care of Harry's monotony. Could we do it by shifting every hour or every two hours?

Benton raises the monotony problem and supports the hourly rotation idea, but gets nowhere.

JIM: Every half day is better. If you shift every hour there will be jobs that will be partly done. Then you will have to start in and finish them.

BENTON: Every two hours?

He tries a compromise with no better results.

JIM: Every half day maybe.

JOE: I go along with that half-day stuff.

HANK: Let's decide that after we learn all the jobs.

HARRY: Every hour brings too much confusion into it.

BENTON: We do agree this far, I believe, that we would change from time to time and try that out, is that right?

> Benton tests for agreement and finds the group together. Apparently he alone is not satisfied.

ALL: Yes.

BENTON: The question now is, how often should we make those changes?

> *He tries to make the frequency of rotation the new issue, but it is obviously not a difficult problem for the men, since they experience no disagreement. Thus we find Benton attempting to manipulate the group, and this does not work. The job of the discussion leader is to facilitate group thinking, not to control it.*

HARRY: Isn't that something we could find out later—how often we should change?

HANK: The problem right now is the bottleneck that is slowing us up, and it seems to me that we've got to agree that we're going to leave Joe in one spot, and when we find that spot for him, he stays there.

BENTON: Now we've got the suggestions of once every hour, we have every half day, and every day. That would take us seven days before we got all the way around.

> Benton summarizes but inaccurately reflects the group viewpoint. He also points out that daily rotation will require seven days to test the positions. Note that the group does not find this a difficulty.

JOE: I think we should change every Wednesday.

BENTON: Every week?

JOE: Wednesday—not Monday—in the middle of the week.

BENTON: How many like this changing every hour the best?

ALL: No.

BENTON: Every half day?

ALL: No.

BENTON: What about every day?

HANK: That's O.K.

GEORGE: That's for me.

BENTON: Now we have the idea of changing positions in order to find out what jobs are easier. We also had originally suggested making changes in order to take some of the boredom out of the work, and also making the changes so that we could help each other out. Now if we changed every day or every week, how could we do that?

> Benton has tested for agreement on the frequency of rotation and finds the group in agreement, but not with him. He suggests some disadvantages that infrequent rotation might have.

> *Again Benton is attempting to channel group thinking in a direction they are resisting. When resistance to a plan is present, the*

leader should deal with resistance rather than attempt to improve the quality of thinking.

HANK: I don't think we've got to help each other out. What we are trying to do, it seems to me, is find a place for Joe where he can keep up with the rest of us.

BENTON: Suppose we can't. In other words, the time-and-motion men said the jobs are all the same. They have tried them out. Now they may be wrong.

JOE: Aren't there some pieces on this panel that are easier to put on than others? The average of all the pieces that go on the panel gives you the time that it takes to finish the panel. Maybe at the end of a week's time we could reshuffle the things that the boys put on these panels.

BENTON: That was worked out.

JOE: One job would be a little easier than another one.

BENTON: That was worked out by the time-and-motion engineers, and they said they were the same. Now they may be wrong.

> Benton has tried to supply facts, but notice that the group is not with him. The group is set to reject any of his contributions.

JIM: They may not be easier for a given man.

BENTON: Supposing that the problem was one of differences in position. Now how many think that the bottleneck is due to a difficult position? (*Three members raise their hands.*) The rest of you don't feel that way.

> Benton tests the group to see if the group will reject the notion that the positions are unequal and finds limited support. Note that in putting the question to the group he has not stated the issue as the group sees it, but instead is making the group's position appear unsound.

BILL: I don't think one position is any more difficult than another.

HANK: I want to modify that statement—the positions are probably the same for the average person. You put a person in there that hasn't the ability to handle small things, then different positions wouldn't be the same for him.

BENTON: Of course all of these things on the instrument panel are pretty simple, Hank.

> Benton is arguing. The group has put him on the defensive.

HANK: That's right.

SAM: We have two problems.

BENTON: That's right. Broken down into two problems, we want to find out whether the positions are equal, and we want to change to redistribute the work. The changing would redistribute the work, trying it out for a day or a week at a time would give us a way of finding out what the difficult positions are. Now something in between, you see, changing frequently would redistribute the load and give us a chance for variation. Changing occasionally would only give us an idea of trying out the various jobs. Now if we changed somewhere in between, we might accomplish both things at the same time, is that right?

> Benton should have explored Sam's two problems, but instead he supplies what he regards as the two problems before the group. He states the two problems well and suggests a compromise between two plans. Note that he is doing a selling job, not a conference-leader job. Time has run out, and he is under pressure.

JOE: Could be. Think you ought to bring in the music, too.

> Joe distracts him by changing the subject.

BENTON: I'll tell you, I'll do all I can to hurry the music, although I don't have too much to say around here. I'm pretty much confined to this subassembly unit. It's just a matter of time, however. What we are disagreeing on primarily is how often the changes should be made. Now that's one of those things that we can work out by trying.

> Benton is acceptant and turns back to the problem. He is now ready to experiment to find the proper time to change.

JOE: I don't think we should change every hour. I don't think we should change every half a day, either, because I feel good in the morning, but after I've had my lunch, why, I don't feel so good. I'd rather just stay right there and finish that day because I've gotten used to what I'm doing.

> Notice that Joe knows that Benton wants frequent changes and takes a position against them.

BILL: That sounds pretty good to me. I mean, you got to look at this thing from Joe's standpoint, too, if we are going to benefit at all.

JOE: That's enough for a starter.

BENTON: That would always keep that pressure on you, Joe, that you talked about—of having these parts piled up.

> Benton points out that the plan does not favor Joe, but notice that Joe is not impressed with Benton's point.

JOE: These lads are going to take care of that. That's their trouble. They are all trying to fix me up. I'll go along with that and see what we can get out of it.

HARRY: I think it would be interesting to see, as these changes are made, whether the bottleneck is always at Joe's position or whether you'll get to some point where they will more or less even out and Joe will find his spot.

BILL: That's what I have been advocating right along.

HANK: Change every day until we find that out.

BENTON: In other words, you just want to solve one problem.

> Benton finds the group agreeing and tries once more to get the group to think about the total picture.

SAM: I think by trying to solve one problem first, it might eliminate the bottleneck.

BENTON: And let the monotony go?

> Benton tests the group's willingness to drop the monotony problem and finds that it has been shelved.

SAM: For the present.

BENTON: Do you like that better?

HANK: Oh, I don't think we ought to drop that one by any means, but I think if we find a spot for Joe where he can work, keep up with us, why, let him stay there.

BILL: Maybe Joe likes all the spots.

HANK: He doesn't like the spot he's in now.

BENTON: The idea is to try each position for one day, and then we will take up the next problem in our next meeting. That would be in a week, wouldn't it?

> Benton summarizes and plans for the next. Note that the point of agreement is exactly what it was before Benton tried to impose his solution on the group.

HANK: That's right.

BENTON: And then in the next step, of course depending upon what we've found—

HARRY: Might change everybody but Joe, is that it?

BENTON: It's possible, or Joe might want to change, too, so the next thing would be to try changing—or making plans to redistribute the work if this is necessary. The next week gives us an opportunity to work in different positions and at different paces—right? So we try this plan for a week and then we will talk some more about this. How does that sound?

> Benton accepts the group's solution and checks for agreement, leaving the door open for any changes or improvements.

ALL: O.K. All right.

BENTON: Now in the meantime, fellows, if there are any other things you notice about it, why, bring them up next week when we talk about the jobs again. O.K.?

> Here Benton is alerting the group to problems so that they can again raise questions without feeling that they have had a change of heart. Thus the same problems may be again discussed in the light of the week's experience.

ALL: O.K.

GEORGE: Don't forget the Muzak.

BENTON: No, I won't forget that.

12

The Supervisor's Dealings
with Individuals

Introduction

Up to this point we have considered the supervisor as a group leader. Although this may be one of his more important functions in building group morale, it does not constitute the whole of a supervisor's human relations functions. As the supervisor he is in a position to make certain changes in the work situation, and he also must have face-to-face dealings with employees as individuals.

In describing the subject matter of a human relations training program in Chapter 2, the topics of causation, individual differences in ability, motivation, and fatigue were included. A knowledge of these subjects (35) helps the supervisor to analyze situations and to create conditions that are conducive to better and more pleasant work. Although discussions with the group might lead to improvements in the work situation, it is also possible that a supervisor skilled in this area might be more effective if he could function as a source of information and thereby serve as a "resource" person. Thus a democratic supervisor can become more effective if his training includes subject matter, in addition to his duties as a discussion leader. It is also possible for the supervisor to be an autocratic leader and still make changes in the situation which promote good employee relations. This merely means that some aspects of human relations are not strictly related to the form of leadership, even though one type of leadership may make more effective use of the material than the others.

The supervisor has face-to-face dealings with individuals when he makes work assignments; gives help and training on the job; inducts and trains new employees; inspects a man's work; discusses an employee's progress with him; interviews employees for any one of several reasons; and discusses an employee's personal problems with him.

In order to aid the supervisor in performing these activities, the subjects of individual differences, attitudes, frustration, interviewing, and nondirective counseling have been incorporated in the program. Again it can be said that an autocratic as well as a democratic supervisor can perform most of these duties by having the essential skills and knowledge in these areas.

Perhaps the greatest disadvantage to the autocratic supervisor in performing the functions listed above would be his difficulty in carrying out nondirective counseling, and it is perhaps for this reason that it is generally believed that employee counseling must be performed by persons not in positions of authority.

Since this book is primarily concerned with democratic leadership, it should show how this form of leadership fits in with some of the other supervisory duties. In other words, how will the training in democratic supervision transfer to the supervisor's other activities, those having to do with making changes or improving the situation and those having to do with relationships with individuals? If training in supervising a work situation, in developing good interpersonal relationships, and in democratic leadership is of three different types, then the supervisor has three distinct roles to play, and this might be confusing to employees as well as to supervisors. However, if the three kinds of training are variations of each other and supplement each other, then democratic leadership and democratic supervision become overlapping functions and supplement each other.

The remainder of the chapter will attempt to show how training in democratic leadership relates to various duties the supervisor performs. Although these duties may be classified as those influencing situations and those having to do with persons, the latter duties will be further broken down into a variety of more specific functions.

It should not be supposed, however, that supplementary training in these functions is not needed. The purpose of this chapter is to show how training in democratic leadership is consistent with and aids these other functions.

The Supervisor as a Manipulator of the Work Situation

The supervisor may be in a position to determine an office or work layout, the lighting, location of phones, job methods, job schedules, flow of materials, crowding at elevators, location of time clocks, location of his desk, housekeeping, location of tables or benches for eating, his own tours of inspection, safety precautions, etc. He may make changes in some of these which theoretically would improve efficiency or safety, and in this sense he may be compared to a time-study man, a safety engineer, or a lighting expert. As a matter of fact, various technical experts now commonly used to promote efficiency and safety may be considered as supplementing the supervisor as controllers of the work situation. They have been added because the job of creating effective work situations has become too complex for the supervisor to handle alone.

Whichever way improvements in the situation are made, the problem of change is involved. Whether or not change is an improvement, it tends to be resisted because insecurity and suspicion are aroused. Failure to accept change may often counteract the benefits that the change should produce, and some of these undesirable consequences may persist for years. Thus changes in the situation always involve the problem of acceptance, and hence involve people as well as situations.

In order to facilitate improvements, suspicion and insecurity must be removed. If these are unfounded the method of participation is highly effective, and it is at this point that democratic leadership is involved.

To be consistent with training in democratic leadership the supervisor, in so far as he can manipulate or change the situation, can function as an expert. As an expert he supplies information, not decisions. He can ask questions that will cause the group to consider aspects he, as an expert, finds important. An important function of an expert is to discover problems and locate difficulties. These functions are entirely consistent with democratic leadership, since skill in leadership will aid him in putting problems in such a way that progress is made.

It seems, therefore, that the supervisor, as an expert, can make improvements in the situation if he introduces them as problems to the group. He or other experts can supply essential information and thus advance the knowledge of the group. The only thing he sacrifices is the decision-making function, but this is offset by the gain in acceptance and any information the group may supply from its knowledge of the situation.

An important consideration in introducing improvements in a work situation is to locate a mutual interest. If a company wishes to increase productivity by introducing new equipment and reducing the number of employees, it is difficult to find a mutual interest, and, consequently, cooperation will be at a minimum. However, if the new equipment will cause some jobs to be upgraded, if no employees will be dropped in the process, and if the company's increased efficiency will put it in a better competitive situation, all stand to gain.

Finding mutual interests is not difficult in problems having to do with safety, reducing waste, better housekeeping, increasing quality, reducing boredom or fatigue, handling emergencies, and improving service, since employees as well as management stand to gain when safety, smooth-running operation, and good relations are at stake. But when changes occur that can be seen as threats or when changes are made arbitrarily, management's motives are questioned and mutual interest is lacking.

The Hawthorne investigations (51) clearly revealed that employees are willing to try out many changes, even those affecting productivity, when they are allowed to participate. Similarly, the study of Coch and French (12), discussed in Chapter 1, demonstrated how changes were favorably accepted by employees when a participation method was used and that, without participation, the changes introduced undesirable results in the form of longer training and lower productivity.

In one office the problem of using a new type of business machine was introduced to employees by asking them whether they would test the machine and evaluate its effectiveness. This stimulated interest and resulted in a favorable acceptance of the machine. In another office the same machine was introduced arbitrarily, and employee resistance continued for months.

Employees likewise will experiment with various ways of doing a job, providing their help is requested. The supervisor may introduce methods he wishes to have tested, and invariably employees evaluate them in terms of efficiency. Frequently employees suggest improvements, so that cooperative problem solving replaces defensive and critical reactions. It is only when changes are arbitrarily imposed that suspicion is aroused, and this is quite natural when we realize that arbitrary methods are always used when one wishes to satisfy himself and is not concerned with the other person involved.

It appears that the supervisor's control over the situation is enhanced if he functions primarily as an expert and permits the group to participate in the decision. This conclusion seems justified because more changes can be made and accepted by this method and because the changes that are made not only reflect the knowledge of experts but also recognize the experience of the operators. If efficiency experts, as well as supervisors, made changes with proper consideration of the human element there would be less evidence to support the belief that employees oppose efficiency and progress.

Employee Contacts

Introduction. The supervisor has many dealings with individuals in running the day-to-day job, and at first it may appear that these are entirely unrelated to his leadership function. However, many activities in this area involve values having to do with favoritism, pettiness, regimentation, fair interpretation of rules, and persecution. These reactions are not dependent merely upon the relationship between the supervisor and a given employee; the employee reacts not only to his own treatment, but also to the way he feels the supervisor treats others. Any question of fairness thus involves an individual's judgment of the way he sees the supervisor's treatment of him in comparison to others.

Although certain individuals tend to be hypersensitive and see themselves as persecuted, the group aspect of the problem remains. As in group discussion, when it is necessary to protect the minority individual, so in personal dealings it may be necessary to be especially considerate of hypersensitive persons.

The group influence is also apparent when individual dealings with people involve prestige. Prestige is an individual feeling, but it derives its importance from the way an individual perceives his status in the group. If other persons feel an individual is shirking, doing too much, playing up to the supervisor, working only when the supervisor is looking, getting others in wrong with the supervisor, or taking too much time off for sickness, the individual in question is reacting not only to the supervisor's conduct but also to the group's conduct. Thus a man's behavior (insubordination, stubbornness, reluctance, etc.) may seem unreasonable in the light of the supervisor's conduct, but it would make sense if the total situation were known.

It seems that, whenever there is reason to believe that an employee's personal relations with the supervisors are unnatural, difficult, or strained, it would be worthwhile to examine the situation to see if a group aspect to the problem may be present. A group meeting to discuss questions such as fair distribution of work, preferred jobs, more reasonable rules, etc., might bring some of the problems to the surface.

However, after being made aware of these considerations, the supervisor can still profit from his knowledge of democratic leadership. In dealing with individuals he loses the interaction of a group of individuals, but he can retain his sensitivity, his willingness to explore with questions, his use of participation in solving problems, and his appreciation of the value of obtaining expression of feelings (permissiveness). In addition he can profit from his knowledge of motivation and attitudes in order to create job interest and better understanding. The use of these skills can be made more apparent if we examine the more specific situations in which an individual and a supervisor make contacts.

Free Contacts. Many contacts that a supervisor makes with individual employees are not an essential part of the job routine. For example, when employees report for work they are or can be seen by the supervisor. Similarly, the supervisor meets employees in the corridor, the elevator, and during lunch periods. On all of these occasions interpersonal relations occur and impressions are made. The nature of these impressions influences the type of cooperation obtained on the job as well as the over-all attitude of the employee. To disregard these contacts is to overlook an important opportunity for improving employee-management relations.

The Hawthorne Study (51) clearly demonstrated that a work situation is a social situation, regardless of whether management wishes it to be so or not. The same study showed that a free situation was more conducive to good relations and productive effort than a regimented one. Democratic supervision also depends upon having employees feel free to express themselves. It follows, therefore, that anything that can be done to reduce unnecessary restraints and to promote a happy atmosphere will favor the purposes of a democratic work group.

Since all employees report for work, the supervisor has a daily opportunity to contact each employee in his group. The time required to have a few words of greeting with each will be repaid many times. Supervisors who make a big issue of a few minutes lost in getting started are more concerned with obedience to rules than to productivity. A supervisor who is glad to see employees and who permits employees to express greetings with one another can cause an office force to start off work in a happy frame of mind. When one discovers that an employee may brood for a day wondering if something is wrong because the supervisor did not speak to her or notice her in the restaurant, one realizes how important such small details can become. Such a report was taken to a supervisor, and he was amazed that he could be so badly misunderstood. Since he had only a friendly feeling toward the girl, he might wonder about the girl's sanity; yet such things happen too often to be dismissed as peculiarities.

Naturally the supervisor should feel friendly toward employees when he sees and greets them because, if he is concerned with the time lost or regards greetings as foolish drivel, he cannot speak sincerely. A supervisor with a critical attitude will be in constant conflict with democratic supervision.

In addition to friendly greetings when employees report for work, there are other important functions that can be performed in these occasional few minutes that supervisors are thrown with employees. Small talk frequently reveals worries and troubles about which a supervisor should know if he is to make proper assignments and pass unbiased judgments of work performance. Often a contact of this type reveals the need of an interview or of counseling. One supervisor complained because a woman's work showed a decline, and he was on the verge of letting her know that her work was unsatisfactory. He felt that she had lost her job interest since becoming married. In an office of 30 men and women he alone was unaware of the fact that the woman was pregnant and was having a period of morning distress. A little time spent on non-job matters might easily have prevented this erroneous judgment.

Employees often feel that they are not treated as human beings, and, although most companies emphasize the importance of individual treatment, they do not teach supervisors how or when to do this. Contacts not essential to the job routines offer the best opportunities to build up this phase of human relations. In group discussions common problems and the importance of reaching agreements in the group are emphasized, so that the pronoun "we" is highlighted. There also is a place for the "I."

Each employee is unique with respect to his private life. A supervisor can know that one of them has a son in college, that another won the bowling contest, and that still another has a sick child. One office girl can be "high" because she got her engagement ring, another is worried over a broken romance, and a third has to hurry home because she must shop for groceries before dinner. Occasional little visits create opportunities for learning these things if the supervisor is interested and understanding in his attitude, and, when he knows these things, he perceives reasons for behavior changes and need not invent unrealistic motives. Frequently he can make adjustments and relieve insecurities. He should not feel obligated to give advice and counsel; he will be more helpful if he merely listens and understands.

Employees who are given time for little considerations of this sort will feel free to go to the supervisor with problems and questions.

Whether or not a supervisor's door is "open" does not depend upon whether he announces his availability but upon the kind of experiences employees have when they talk to him. With good relations established during free contacts, the problem of contacts in other areas and for other purposes is greatly simplified.

As in any kind of society, differences in position or rank represent barriers that interfere with understanding and free expression. These barriers create a social distance, and the greater the social distance, the more difficult and the more restrained the social relations. Since a given supervisor occupies a higher position in the company hierarchy than do those who report to him, it is difficult for his employees to feel close to him. Although a given supervisor may feel quite unaware of his superior position, it is likely to be felt by those who report to him. They see him not only as a specific personality but as an individual with power. This power factor is constant, so that all supervisors incur some of the same reaction. Thus, a supervisor is judged not only by what he does but by who he is.

Further, the more steps in the organizational chart that one person is removed from another, the greater this power factor becomes. This means that a department head's behavior will have quite different meanings to employees and intermediate management personnel. When differences in level become great, it takes a striking personality to offset the dominating influence that the position has on people's perception. This leads employees to react to top management almost wholly as powers, rather than as human beings, and they tend to regard them as more nearly alike than they do other human beings. Thus the term "brass" becomes one that includes them all, and employees react to them with similar emotions.

Social distance thus represents a barrier to good communication, and since those who have prestige frequently are less aware of it than those who react to it, persons in prestige positions tend not to allow sufficiently for this factor in their dealings with subordinates. It is in informal contacts that much can be done to remove this obstacle to communication and to reduce this social distance. During such contacts a man's position in the organization is incidental to the discussion, and as a consequence the relationship can approach that of a visit between two human beings. In this manner employees can learn to perceive their superiors as specific persons, and this learning can carry over to other relationships. Thus, although social distance is an unavoidable barrier, good unofficial contacts can serve to lower the wall between superiors and employees.

Merely having visits from a member of management two steps removed from the immediate supervisor created a new feeling of "belonging" in a group of switchboard operators in a large company. Previously they felt isolated and quite unrelated to the direct functions of the company. A few pleasant visits of a company official to their office, at intervals of a week or more, immediately became the subject of conversation of both the girls and the supervisor in charge.

In another company low morale was found in a group of employees who worked some distance from the main office. Analysis of the causes revealed that a major factor was lack of personal contact between top management and this group. Other groups located closer to the main office were less critical of top management, it seemed, because circumstances permitted contacts with them. Thus telephone contacts may keep higher management informed of the operations, but they do not permit higher management to give the employees that personal touch which is so essential to good understanding.

Job Assignments. Some work is so routine that a job assignment is not made by the supervisor but is apparent from the job situation. In such cases this duty may not be a problem for the supervisor. In other situations the job assignments are largely a routine matter but nevertheless each assignment is an act, and the way the assignment is made influences the acceptance of the task. In such instances the supervisor may, from time to time, inquire how the man feels about the job, whether he thinks his load is about right, whether he has ideas about the job he would like to discuss sometime, what aspects of the job he likes best and least, etc.

When jobs are less routine and require planning and instruction, the opportunities for participation are greater. Instead of the foreman's presenting all the details (some of which the man may already know, but the extent of whose knowledge is not known to the foreman), he may ask the man to contribute what he knows and then supply additional knowledge. Whenever a person with superior knowledge tells another what the other already knows, he is talking down to the individual. Under such conditions attention is poor, even if a certain amount of irritation is not present. When, however, a person builds upon what another already knows, he not only permits the other person to gain some recognition but also creates a situation in which further knowledge is welcomed.

If the situation permits some planning the supervisor can state the problem and ask the man how he thinks it can best be done. By the good use of questions he can stimulate consideration for details that are overlooked. As in group discussion, he can upgrade the thinking by asking questions or having the man explore other possibilities so that a choice can be made. Presenting alternate solutions for the employee's suggestions discourages thinking and does not create high motivation.

Job Inspection. Most jobs require a foreman to pass judgment on the quality of a man's workmanship or on the amount of work he does. Unpleasant aspects of this duty are the resentment of the employees and an apparent unwillingness on their part to want to do the "right" thing. Men frequently regard inspection as a form of spying or a desire on the part of the foreman to find fault. Since the foreman's attention is usually attracted to work that is unsatisfactory, the men feel that they receive criticism much oftener than they receive praise. As we found in group decision, a common reaction to fault finding is defensiveness or hostility. Since men frequently fail to admit mistakes or deny a charge, the foreman is motivated to catch the men "red-handed." This behavior then becomes analogous to spying, so that a bad situation becomes aggravated.

The assumption that all men cannot perform equally on a job is an essential prerequisite to successful job inspection. When a foreman is critical of behavior that an individual is unable to control, he creates a frustrating experience in the individual and motivates others in the group to come to the man's rescue by slowing down or supporting him in other ways. The correction of conditions that arise because a man is *unable* to perform his job satisfactorily requires an interview in which the foreman and the man together work out the problem of finding a job with duties that are suited to the man's ability.

If we now exclude conditions in which deficiencies point to inadequate ability, then the conditions remaining involve problems of motivation, attitudes, and learning. The problem of correction implies that these conditions can be made more favorable.

If a man wants to do a good job he has a receptive attitude and is motivated to learn or improve. However, if the foreman wants a good job he, instead of the man, has the motivation; and if he criticizes the work he tends to create a defensive attitude in the worker.

Piece rates, promotions, and competition may be used to create motivation, but these are incentives superimposed on the job. Can good human relations introduce motivation into the activity itself and develop a favorable attitude?

In the first place, the foreman's evaluation should include recognition of aspects of the job that are well done. Regardless of the nature of a man's performance, some phase of it is relatively good. When the foreman recognizes a man's best points, the defensive attitude gradually disappears. If a man makes excuses he is defending himself. Excuses should be accepted. To question excuses causes them to become the subject of conversation, and this leads to more insecurity and excuse making. In accepting excuses the foreman reduces insecurity and encourages the man to talk freely and to face the real problem. Thus the discussion can be turned into one of solving problems rather than one of haggling over details.

Participation also has a place in such contacts. Questions such as the following should stimulate discussion.

1. "Are there any difficulties on this job that I can help you work out?"

2. "What part of the job do you like best?"

3. "What part of the job do you find easiest?"

4. "What part do you have most difficulty with?"

5. "Is there any phase of the job that we can help you with?"

6. "Do you think you have disadvantages in comparison with others?"

In getting the man to talk about his problems the permissive foreman causes critical attitudes to be expressed, and these will be followed by a problem-solving attitude which leads to constructive suggestions. Often a man will ask for assistance or training, and when he does so he feels that the foreman is helping him rather than criticizing him. When fear is not present people want to improve. Improvement on the job is an objective that the foreman and the workman share. It is this common interest that develops into a constructive discussion, and this common interest must be located before the two can work together for a common objective. When a man points out his own weaknesses he is ready to correct them, but when a foreman points them out the workman feels required to defend himself. Thus the key to correction is to make a person feel free to analyze himself without fearing that he will lose something if he admits he is lacking.

Generally speaking, a man is able to make accurate judgments of his abilities in comparison with others. It is only when emotional adjustment is poor that people overestimate or underrate their abilities. Since a great many poor adjustments hinge on insecurity or a feeling of rejection of one form or another, any permissive or understanding treatment tends to increase the accuracies of self-judgments.

Thus we find that training in democratic leadership is related to effective skills in carrying out the task of job inspection in that the supervisor:

1. Uses statements of problems rather than criticisms to determine the content of discussion.
2. Listens much more than he talks and thereby attempts to discover the existing attitudes.
3. Shows a permissive attitude by trying to understand the employee's side of the picture.
4. Uses questions to cause the whole issue to be explored.
5. Obtains participation in solving problems raised.
6. Presents information and facts without passing judgments.

It will be noted that these same skills are used in nondirective interviewing and counseling, which merely means that leadership skills and certain interviewing and counseling skills overlap. The similarity between discussion leadership and face-to-face dealings with individuals was pointed out in Chapter 1 and might be reviewed at this point.

One important factor present in group procedures which is not available in individual contacts is the use that is made of the group. Thus social pressure or the expression of opinion of other members of a group is not available to the foreman in individual contacts. This perhaps represents a true loss, but the effectiveness of the remaining techniques is not hampered by this omission.

On the other hand, the individual treatment allows for a more personalized handling in that specific needs and interests can sometimes be satisfied, and the goals that are set by a man may conform to his individual ability. Thus improvement in one phase of the work or another may become an individual goal and take on more reality because it is a personal one. Also, more attention can be given for clearing up misunderstandings, specific attitudes, and personal threats or fears. In many instances the gains made by the personalized treatment more than offset those which ordinarily materialize when group discussion is used.

It is frequently argued that a supervisor cannot use these procedures in upgrading a man's work because the union demands that faults be clearly expressed and made known to the man. This requirement grows out of the ruling that a man must be sufficiently warned before he can be discharged. Regardless of how one feels about the effectiveness of using threats to obtain compliance, such agreement with the union make warnings (verbal or written) an essential prerequisite to discharge. Thus it follows that if discharge is the foreman's anticipated objective then he must conform to the union agreement. In furnishing these warnings, however, there is no need to include blame. As a matter of fact, the foreman can sincerely express regret that the warning has become necessary and hope that improvement will make discharge unnecessary.

The situations in which the type of contact described above can be used, therefore, are confined to those in which improvement rather than discharge is the foreman's objective. Since studies of motivation reveal that constructive methods are more effective than threats, the constructive approach should be used whenever possible. Although threats sometimes seem to be effective, one often overlooks the undesirable behaviors that frequently accompany their use. Thus if one threatens to discharge a man for his low production the man might respond with higher production (if he is able), but he may become less cooperative, take less care of his equipment, increase his waste, or show more absenteeism. Only when punishment is experienced as justified can one expect it to have a true corrective effect.

In training supervisors to use the constructive approach to job inspection, role playing as discussed in Chapter 4 is perhaps the most effective. A knowledge of principles does not readily lead to action, and principles serve their purpose best if used as a basis for analyzing role-playing cases attempted in training sessions. In such cases the reactions to destructive criticism, to threats, and to degrading remarks are readily illustrated. In contrast, the use of friendly approaches by the supervisor soon leads to an objective evaluation of work performance. The following excerpt from a case illustrates how a man will analyze his own performance rather than defend himself if permissively approached.

The workman in question was on a soldering job and, although he worked fast enough, his work was messy. One day, in walking through the shop, the supervisor had the following contact.

SUPERVISOR: How are things going, Walt?
WALT: O.K. I'm keeping up with the job and am ahead of the bogey.
s: Do you feel we are rushing you?
w: Sometimes.
s: What do you have the most difficulty with?
w: Oh, I guess some of the stuff is a bit dirty—the solder doesn't stick.

s: I see—what happens then?
w: Sometimes you have to do it over—slop a lot of solder on it.
s: Yeah. That isn't so good.
w: No. It doesn't look good—takes a lot of solder too.
s: Do you have any ideas on how to correct that?
w: Yes. One way is to have the stuff cleaner. Another is to use a stronger flux.
s: Have you talked it over with the other fellows?
w: No—I had no reason to. Isn't everything O.K. on your end?
s: I was just wondering if there might not be a way of helping things out in case you had any special problems.
w: I don't have any special problems outside of being rushed once in a while.
s: Your main problem is to get the solder to stick.
w: Yeah.
s: You mentioned cleaner material and a different flux. Do you have any other suggestions?
w: (*Pause*) I seem to have more trouble than some of the others with this solder.
s: Would you like to go over and watch some of the other fellows and see how they make out?
w: Yeah—I don't have time ordinarily to do that.

At this point the supervisor and Walt observed the work of a couple of other men, and Walt discovered a little trick that the others used which he thought worked very well. He decided to try it and thanked the supervisor for his help. The quality of his work improved almost immediately.

On-the-Job Training. Many foremen have the responsibility of training or supplementing the training of new employees. Since new employees are insecure and want to be accepted they are motivated to cover up deficiencies and to be very cautious in their behavior and speech. The supervisor is likely to mistake this retiring behavior as one of cooperation and may oversell the job and the duties. Since the learner is likely to be quiet, the supervisor is in a situation in which he feels called upon to do a lot of talking.

When one has much to learn, the description of the job objectives may seem extremely high and may create discouragement and experiences of failure (Maier [35], Chapter 12). Objectives or goals must be comparable to one's ability if they are to serve as effective incentives. A study by Coch and French (12) showed that employees who were just below standard in their production were more likely to quit than those doing above or well below standard. Those who were well below standard, it seems, were not discouraged because they did not expect to reach the standard and were willing to settle for less. Of course those who performed above standard experienced success and job satisfaction. When supervisors talked about goals closer to the level of ability of the individual performers, the problem of labor turnover for this middle group was largely solved.

Inexperienced employees can be most effectively motivated if the objectives of improvement are kept within reach of the individual's development. Thus if the supervisor permits his expectations of an employee's work to develop with the employee's progress he can keep motivation high and prevent discouragement. A little reflection on one's own experience in learning a skill will give one an idea of how discouraging a highly skilled person's performance can be to a beginner. The supervisor can prevent discouragement in new employees if he introduces new aspects of the job in progressive steps.

It should also be emphasized that one learns more by doing than by watching demonstrations. Praising correct approaches and suggesting substitute ways for incorrect operations is the constructive way to help. Labeling something as wrong not only discourages, but it does not tell what should be done. Brief periods of observation and the allotting of time to practice between contacts with the supervisor exert less strain on the person than does close supervision.

Human relations are important throughout the learning process. Bavelas (see Maier [35], p. 225 ff.) found that teaching trainers some of the leadership methods in human relations greatly accelerated the learning process in a sewing operation. There are many opportunities for (a) permitting participation, (b) listening to the learners' difficulties, and (c) encouraging the expression of attitudes. Objectives also can be arrived at through discussion, so that the goals set for the individual conform to the learner's motivations and feelings. The use of general questions to explore the employee's sources of discouragements, his difficulties, and his feelings of inadequacy is highly desirable. If the trainer is permissive these attitudes are expressed, whereas if the trainer appears critical these feelings are hidden and develop into unfavorable attitudes.

It will be noted that many of the points discussed above are similar to those encountered in job inspection. This merely means that the effective human relations procedures apply to both training and inspection, and hence the suggestions mentioned in the previous section need not be repeated here. An important difference is that in job training the employee is less defensive than in job inspection. This makes job training the easier duty, but the use of good human relations procedures still remains important because it is at this time that first impressions are being established.

Training in groups is easier than training individually because no one person feels he is under critical scrutiny. Thus a person might be hesitant to raise questions by himself, but does so in a group. As a matter of fact, only one person need speak up in a group to have all benefit by the question. Training in groups also allows for group discussion and even group decisions. Under these conditions the supervisor is more likely to be in a constructive frame of mind, and the group gains from the advantages associated with the group-decision approach. It is in training problems that the distinction between the supervisor as an expert and as a leader must most clearly be made. While training, he is most often in the role of an expert, and he must function as a source of information without imposing his will on the learners.

Induction of New Employees. Since a work group actually constitutes a small society, a new employee finds himself in a situation similar to that of the person who moves into a new community. Others are looking him over to see what kind of person he is and evaluating his every move to determine whether or not he is acceptable. When there are status factors or cliques in the group the situation is further complicated. The newcomer must not attach himself to any one group too early because his future position may depend upon how he receives overtures from one group or another. If he seems too friendly to members of one group he may be rejected by the opposed group, and if he is not friendly enough to certain persons he may be regarded as "high hat." How can he conduct himself properly when others know the group structure and he does not? How can a person know that in a particular group college men are put to a certain test, that men transferred from the West Coast are "orange juicers," that men who wear bow ties are "aping the boss," or that good family connections make you a "stooge"?

In work groups the social situation often is complicated further. If the new employee is replacing a person it makes a difference whether the previous person was advanced or discharged, whether he was popular or unpopular, or whether he belonged to one group or another. If the new worker represents an addition to the group it makes a difference whether his presence affects the security of some of the group members, whether his assignments and duties were wanted by others, whether his work helps others by reducing their load of work, or whether he assumes duties taken away from others.

Because of complicating factors such as those mentioned above, it is quite natural for a group to neglect a new employee or place him in situations where he will be looked over carefully. Either of these behaviors will make the new employee feel strange and insecure.

It is a common experience to find employees quitting shortly after they are hired. In other words, the labor turnover for new employees is highest at the outset. In one study Scott and Clothier (55) showed the turnover to be 1026 per cent for employees of less than one month of service, but for employees with one to three months of service the turnover dropped to 226 per cent. Although many factors influence the rate of labor turnover, it is apparent that one of the factors, at least, is the problem of finding a place in a work group. In the author's interviewing of employees who had recently been promoted to new jobs in new work locations, the employees mentioned (a) being lonely, (b) finding the new associates different or aloof, (c) being unsuccessful in finding friends, and (d) being made to feel inferior. Some talked of quitting, and some were trying to find ways to get back on their old jobs (at reduced pay) without causing their former associates to think that they had failed.

It seems that the situation faced by new employees is not one that the supervisor can entirely remedy by himself. To what extent can he use group meetings to help create a favorable reception? To what extent can employees participate in the selection of new personnel, the planning of their duties, and the clarification of the need for them? The addition of a new person to a work group represents a change that involves everyone, and it is for the acceptance of change that group discussions and decisions are so effective. Thus the methods of democratic leadership can be directly applied to the induction problem, which on the surface seems to be entirely a management problem.

A realization of the problems faced by new employees also suggests other approaches. In the first place, it is clear that introducing a new employee to the members of the group is not enough. Even the attentions and formalities associated with familiarizing new employees with company policies, benefits, activities, promotions, etc., which frequently are given during the first week, often are not sufficient. Attaining group membership may require several weeks or more, and during this time the supervisor must be sensitive to the new employee's feelings. By having visits with the new employee, spaced over the period of adjustment, and by making these visits primarily a matter of letting the employee talk about things that concern him, the supervisor can discover the kind of progress the new member is making. Thus the listening type of interview becomes a tool that a supervisor might use.

The supervisor is also in a position to manipulate factors in the situation. The way he groups his workers or teams, the way he arranges relief periods, and where he seats new employees are examples of the supervisor's influence on the situation. Furthermore, he can give certain employees the responsibility of seeing that the new employee gets acquainted with persons of similar tastes and age, and he can give this responsibility to group members who are generally accepted. He can even go so far as to use the induction of new employees to remedy factionalism in the group.

In one office there was a split between the old and the young women employees. The clear-cut division was sharpened by the fact that for a period of 5 years few employees were hired, but thereafter there was rapid expansion and a great deal of hiring. This pattern of hiring created a situation in which there were 87 women with more than 10 years of service, 11 women with 5 to 10 years of service, and 432 girls with less than 5 years of service. This distribution of age groups readily aided the classification of the women into "old" and "young" girls, with only 11 women falling on the border line. The older girls felt there was discrimination in favor of young girls. The young girls were promoted more rapidly than they had been, and they reached ceiling wage rates more quickly because of the change in the union contract. But perhaps most important of all was the fact that the number of old girls was growing relatively smaller while the number of young girls was increasing; the new employees seemed to be "taking over" and so constituted a threat. The fact of the matter was that the "old girls" were hostile toward the younger generation and openly expressed this attitude. The younger girls countered and referred to the old girls as "old biddies," "sour pusses," "cranks," etc. There was practically no contact between them at company social functions, and cooperation on the job was poor.

An induction procedure was introduced which gave the old girls the responsibility of showing new employees around, taking them to lunch, training them on office routines, etc. This responsibility served, on each induction occasion, to give some particular older employee (depending on the specific work group) prestige and the feeling of recognition she so sorely needed. As a result she was on her good behavior when she contacted the younger girls with her protégée. The younger girls found that the older women were quite nice and reciprocated with pleasant manners. In a short time this procedure brought a decline in the tension and better cooperation, and new employees reported favorably on the induction procedure.

It seems then that the induction process can be facilitated by the use of group methods and individual contacts and by making changes in the situation. The important thing in making these adjustments is to have a good understanding of the situation in a given work group and then approach the condition as a problem to be solved.

Concluding Remarks. Generally speaking, employee contacts have certain common objectives. These include (*a*) making the employee feel secure in his relationship with individuals with whom he has contacts; (*b*) developing job interests; (*c*) increasing motivation for constructive behavior; (*d*) motivating the individual to seek a level of accomplishment geared to his ability; (*e*) discovering and preventing misunderstandings arising from differences in attitude; and (*f*) becoming aware of personal off-the-job problems. We have pointed out how skills in democratic leadership aid the supervisor in accomplishing these objectives. A knowledge of the subject of motivation, perhaps, would supply the most information for improving working conditions and understanding the needs of people. The subject of motivation would also supply the essential background for appreciating the value of constructive ways of motivating as against the use of fear or punishment. The latter methods are used to train people in *what not to do* and should be substituted, whenever possible, by training in *what to do* or in *what is wanted.* The positive method requires more thought and planning, but it avoids frustrating people and the development of unfavorable attitudes in them. Instead, it draws attention to goals and suggests the procedure of substituting good methods for undesirable methods. Negative approaches attempt to remove undesirable behaviors, but it is easier to substitute a different behavior for one that is not wanted. Thus if a person is told, "Try doing it this way," he feels better about giving up his old behavior than if told, "Don't do it that way."

The subject matter of attitudes also has value in improving employee contacts, but it becomes even more important in improving interviewing skills. The important thing in preventing misunderstandings is to discover the other person's point of view and make this the starting point for reaching an understanding. As long as one attempts to sell one's own point of view, one motivates the other person to protect and defend his. Consideration on the part of the supervisor for the attitude of the employee causes the employee to give consideration to the supervisor's problem. This is contrary to one's natural inclination because one's own point of view is clear and dear to him and so is given all the attention in a discussion.

Interviews

Introduction. An interview may be considered an off-the-job contact between the supervisor and an employee in the sense that the employee leaves his work to discuss something with the supervisor. A time and place is arranged, and as a consequence the interview becomes somewhat more formal than a job contact. To reduce the formality and strain, consideration should be given to permitting the employee to participate in setting a time that meets his convenience and holding the interview in a place that does not put the supervisor at an advantage.

Since a person is much more at ease in a familiar place than in a strange place, interviews progress better if strangeness of surroundings can be reduced. If the offices have been previously visited by employees and if the furnishings are not too elegant to create reserve, this problem is partly solved. Furthermore, if the supervisor has used his office for group discussions of job matters, the problem of putting the employee at ease has been largely solved. The author frequently uses a desk placed in corridors or in a corner of the work space for interviewing employees about their problems. In the Hawthorne plant the coffee shop was used. An executive once asked why his talks with his department heads were so much better when he visited them than when he asked them to come to his office. One answer to this is the familiarity of the location of the interview.

Frequent interviews for various purposes also accomplish this end and tend to remove the possible unpleasant anticipations that may accompany an interview. On many occasions a forthcoming interview produces anxiety in the employee because the event is associated with something being wrong.

Most of the skills associated with democratic leadership can be used in an interview. Each interview can raise a problem in which the employee can participate. Although one lacks the interchange of experience which is available in a group discussion, some of this can be made up by the supervisor in the somewhat greater use of questions to explore the territory.

The importance of finding a mutual interest, so desirable in group discussions, also applies to the interview (7, 21). However, the mutual interest is now one between the company (or supervisor) and a particular employee rather than between the company (or supervisor) and a group of employees. This difference allows for more specific interests, but it also requires a greater knowledge of the individual's needs and how they differ from those of other persons. Since the individual knows his needs perhaps better than the supervisor, the supervisor must get the employee to talk and express his needs. It is the creation of a free and easy relationship between the interviewer and the interviewee that is commonly referred to as gaining *rapport*.

The method for exploring a person's interests and needs not only requires understanding listening but is greatly aided by the use of general questions (7, 13). General questions are recommended initial approaches in interviewing and are effective because they allow the employee to talk about those things which are his greatest concern. Specific questions groove the conversation and at the same time may be misconstrued as inquisitiveness.

The subject of attitudes becomes the most important subject matter for making sense out of the interview procedures. The objective of the interview is to discover the employee's attitude or frame of reference and then to work out the problem from this as the starting point. As in group decision, one must assume the existing attitudes and solve the problem so as to integrate or reconcile them. To impose an outside and different frame of reference results in a basic conflict which never is allowed to be resolved.

As in free contacts, motivation concepts should not be overlooked. The supervisor should accept the needs of an individual regardless of whether he himself has similar needs. Many of our needs are acquired, and, like attitudes, they are influenced by the group with which one associates and identifies himself. Thus different age groups, men and women, skilled and unskilled groups, and management and nonmanagement employees may be expected to have different needs and consequently different work and life objectives. Failure to recognize the needs in another person makes us misconstrue his motives and consequently to misunderstand his behavior.

Although certain common objectives and methods characterize the various interviewing situations, each one has its own objective. Thus employment, transfer, promotion, employee evaluation, and exit interviews have specific objectives or purposes of their own. Each of these raises its own specific problems, so that the applications of the same principles may be somewhat different. We will briefly discuss the interviewing problems associated with each type of interview in order to illustrate the use of the principles.

Employment Interview. The employment interview immediately creates the problem of finding a mutual interest. It is the interest of the applicant to obtain the job for which he has applied and that of the interviewer to screen applicants. Under these circumstances the applicant is motivated to hide his weaknesses and to exaggerate his virtues. Furthermore, he does not truly reveal his interests. If asked whether he minds taking his turn working nights he is not likely to give a true answer and then, as so often occurs after he is hired, he is found to be uncooperative in this respect.

Without a mutual interest, responses to questions, even those to which the applicant knows the answer, are not dependable. For this reason it is desirable whenever possible to obtain factual information from other sources and to give various kinds of employment tests. One cannot even depend upon a person's manner and appearance because the applicant is motivated to make the most of these when applying for a job. Some employment agencies even coach applicants on how to make a good impression on the interviewer. All one discovers from such observations is whether a person has learned how to behave and dress, not whether he will behave and dress well on the job.

If a person wishes to discover an applicant's interests and his true attitudes the interview cannot be made a condition of employment. However, if the applicant is hired on the basis of other criteria (including an interview to check such factors as physical appearance, visible physical handicaps, use of English, and manner of speech), he may be interviewed to determine his placement. The applicant and the company have a mutual interest here. The applicant wants a job on which he can use his strongest abilities and on which his weaker abilities will not be a handicap; he wants a job that interests him; and he wants a job that will give him an opportunity to achieve some of the goals he has set for himself. The company too wants to place the applicant so as to accomplish these things, and if the interviewer states these as company objectives the objectives make sense and are believed by the applicant. However, if the expressed interests of the company are such as to indicate a gain for the company only, the person has no reason to cooperate; and if the company expresses an interest merely in helping the applicant, then the applicant is likely to be suspicious and on guard. It is only when both stand to gain and when these mutual gains are apparent that we can hope to obtain cooperation in placing the individual. Usually applicants who are interviewed by the supervisor (rather than the employment department) are concerned with placement rather than with being hired. Since our concern is with aiding the supervisor in his interviews, the problem of finding a mutual interest is not so serious.

Once a mutual interest is established the placement interview is relatively easy. The interviewer may use questions to explore freely, being guided of course by the principle of beginning with general questions and working toward the more specific. Questions are useful to channel the interview, and, since the placement interview has this purpose, the interviewer's questions should be such as to explore the essential territory. Initial questions should be broad enough to permit the applicant to talk rather than to give brief answers. It is in getting the applicant to talk that one learns how he feels and thinks. Thus the question, "How do you feel about night work?" is likely to produce a more detailed response than the question, "Do you mind working nights?"

Listening for feelings and mirroring the feelings expressed gives far more valuable information for gaining an appreciation of the other's viewpoint than listening for factual details. Thus an interviewee may make many factual statements, but the interviewer should mainly listen for indications about how he feels and should respond to such statements by referring to the feeling. The fact that a person feels he got a bad deal on all of his previous jobs is important, but the factual details may be quite misleading. Since attitudes are always loaded with feeling, one understands them best when one understands the feeling content of a remark. Questions and responses made by the supervisor should frequently contain the phase "you feel" or "you think" because they make it easier for the person to talk about them. Because facts are easy for a person to talk about, it is not necessary to supply help in this respect.

One way of testing a good interview is to determine the relative amount that the interviewer and the interviewee talk. The person who talks the most is the one who is really interviewed. If the interviewer talks the most then the interviewee has learned more than the interviewer. In such cases the purpose of the interview has been defeated.

In developing skills in this type of listening and this way of responding, the principles of democratic leadership and nondirective counseling are being directly applied to interviewing. These skills are essential to establishing a permissive relationship. People come closer to each other when the expressed feelings become understood and are accepted.

A unique feature of the employment interview is the aspect of supplying information. The interviewer possesses many facts about the company which are of concern to the applicant. However, instead of supplying these facts in a routine manner, he may permit himself to be questioned. If he asks, "What are some of the things you would like to know about the company?" the applicant is free to obtain information on matters that concern him. Such information is of interest to him so that the interviewer obtains his full attention. In addition the interviewer learns the things that interest applicants in general and the applicant in particular.

Transfer Interviews. Transfers from one job to another involving no change in pay may have a variety of interpretations. The employee in question may see the transfer as the foreman's way of getting rid of him or as the equivalent of a promotion; he may see the transfer as leading to a dead-end job or as opening the way for new opportunities; he may see the new job as a threat to his security or as a way of having attention thrown his way; and he may see the new job as a move to put him on the shelf or as one making a better use of his abilities. Whether the transfer is given an unfavorable or a favorable interpretation by the employee will greatly depend upon his attitude toward the company and his supervisor; upon his emotional and job security; upon his personal needs and ambitions; and upon the way the transfer is presented to him. Since many of these details are unknown to the supervisor it is important that he discover the employee's interpretation as soon as possible so as not to permit anxiety to build up during the interview. This means that the first objective in a transfer interview is to discover how the employee feels about a transfer to such and such a job.

If the employee is told that a job exists in a particular unit and is asked how he feels about filling it he undoubtedly will have questions to ask. The supervisor can then answer them instead of giving this information at the outset and making it appear as a sales talk. In supplying the facts relevant to the employee's interests, the supervisor supplies information that is wanted and in the order that it is wanted. He learns something about the employee's needs, insecurities, and attitudes from the nature of the questions, and he can learn more about them by asking the employee to elaborate on how he feels. In no case should the supervisor refer to expressed fears as unrealistic, but instead he should let the employee discover their unrealistic nature by encouraging him to talk about them. Thus in the first part of the interview the employee will talk about his feelings and the supervisor will supply information as it is requested. The information supplied should not be in the form of what the foreman or the company desires, but should be purely factual.

When the employee understands the nature of the new job and the supervisor understands the employee's point of view, there is a good possibility that a mutual interest can be found. Certainly the finding of a mutual interest would be more difficult before an understanding had been reached.

On one occasion an employee was on the verge of a nervous breakdown because he had been transferred five times within a year. He felt he was being pushed around and not wanted anywhere. The company, however, was grooming him for an important promotion and was moving him around so that he would be acquainted with various types of operations. Because he made a bad impression with the supervisors on his last three jobs, he was not promoted. How much of this bad impression was caused by the man's failure to understand what was behind these changes? Could a mutual interest have been found without promising the man something before the proper official decisions had been made?

It seems that in most instances a general expression of opinion and feeling about the new job and its implications will reveal that, if the company's decision to move a man is sound, it will also appear as an advantage to the man. Unfounded fear or suspicion is perhaps the most difficult barrier, and the free expression of feelings on the employee's part should dispel these.

However, if the discussion does not reveal a common gain, doubts are raised as to the wisdom of the transfer. If these doubts are valid it follows that the decision to transfer a person should not be made until after the interview. If this is made a condition of the transfer the problem of the transfer interview is simplified. The employee can be permitted to participate in the decision as in the group-decision method, and if this is done satisfaction is greatly increased and possible fears are largely eliminated.

In giving an employee a choice of this kind the interviewer must also clarify some other matters. Often choices are given, but the employee does not feel free to make a choice. He wonders whether turning down a transfer will close the door to future changes, will indicate that he is uncooperative, or suggest that he has no ambition. In order to avoid misunderstandings in these areas, the honest exchange of feelings should be made, with the employee having the benefit of the supervisor's feelings, too.

If the foreman has the problem of transferring one person in his group in order to reduce his force and to make up a deficiency of men in another group, employees interviewed should not only be encouraged to state how they feel about the change but should also be asked to suggest alternatives. However, this type of problem could best be handled by the group-decision method, where all would benefit by the exchange of opinions and no one would feel that he had been singled out for special consideration or treatment.

Sometimes it is essential to move a person because he does not fit the job he is on. When problems of this sort arise the interviewed employee should be allowed to participate in analyzing his skills on the present job. (The merit or progress interview will be discussed later in this chapter, with indications of how a person may participate in analyzing his strong and weak points.) If the employee recognizes that he has strong and weak points, the problem of finding a job at the same level, but one which requires a different pattern of abilities, becomes one which allows participation. In such instances it is best if alternatives can be presented.

The method of giving employees a choice is always helpful. Presenting a person with a choice between two possible job changes gives him less feeling of being regimented, and it has the desirable effect of allowing him to participate in a part of the decision. Introducing a choice also makes for a more satisfactory interview because it creates a broader front on which to explore interests, feelings, and attitudes. Thus in discussing the pros and cons of two or three jobs the interviewee must, of necessity, make many comparisons and differentiations and hence reflect a great variety of opinions.

The Promotion Interview. Perhaps the interview with which the supervisor has least trouble is the one in which he interviews a man who is being promoted or who is receiving a wage increase. Nevertheless, this interview should receive some consideration because a successful interview may prevent future problems. Also associated with such interviews is the problem of interviewing persons who may have expected the promotion. Let us first consider interviewing the individual who is receiving the promotion.

Frequently supervisors ask whether announcements of promotions and increases in pay do not furnish good opportunities for telling a man about his weaknesses. Such persons want to know whether the good news should precede or follow the bad. Questions of this sort reveal the fact that it is unpleasant for supervisors to talk to employees about their faults, and so they seek ways of getting this job done under pleasant circumstances. Yet it seems undesirable to spoil an opportunity to praise and give employees a pleasant experience merely to get an unpleasant job done.

Although the announcement of a promotion should ordinarily produce a pleasant experience, it should not be viewed as entirely lacking in conflicting emotions. Anxiety may be present over the new things that must be learned, the self-confidence in the job that must be acquired, the position in the group that must be built up, and the added responsibilities that must be carried. Sorrow at leaving one's associates and the giving up of former duties may also be present. In some instances the unpleasant feelings may exceed the pleasant. These mixed emotions sometimes cause the employee to appear unappreciative and so disappoint the supervisor. It often happens that persons who seem to want a promotion really want attention or recognition. In such cases an opportunity to turn down a promotion would be a more satisfying experience than receiving the promotion. Needless to say the above problems are not associated with announcements of pay increases.

Because mixed emotions are associated with promotions it is important to explore the employee's feelings by asking if he would be interested in an opening that represents a certain advancement. This question stimulates the employee to ask questions which can be handled in the same way as in the transfer interview. In answering questions put to him, the supervisor will undoubtedly have the opportunity to report the duties and responsibilities associated with the new job. He should describe these in terms of extensions of certain duties the employee now performs, the old functions that no longer will be performed, and the functions and duties that will be entirely new. The employee should also be given some idea of the job objectives and the activities that will be most important. Although the supervisor may be confident that the employee can fill the job, he should not let his confidence prevent him from letting the employee express his doubts and fears. Too much reassurance may build false confidence or prevent the employee from talking out his fears. If an employee cannot make up his mind he, of course, should be given time to think it over, but this thinking by himself should not be substituted for time he might use in exploring the problem with the supervisor. The supervisor may well invite the employee to return to him with questions that might occur while thinking things over.

The interview should also make clear that failure to accept the position will not create an unfavorable impression (assuming that this is true). Rather, in case the employee declines the promotion, it is well to inquire into the kinds of positions that would interest him.

If the employee accepts the position he should be given as much aid as possible. His anxieties on the new job may be reduced if he knows beforehand something about the idiosyncrasies of his new boss; the situation into which he will move; the abilities which are especially essential and on which he will be judged; the areas in which he will have to develop the most; the training goals he will have to meet; and the things he will not be expected to know. An invitation to come back for a talk while he is learning the new job will aid him in his adjustment, not only because such a visit would serve as an opportunity to relieve himself of anxieties, but also because it would send him to the new job with a feeling that he had someone's support while bridging the gap between the old and the new relationships.

In interviewing persons who failed to receive the promotion the supervisor should inform them that they had been considered for the job and that the person who was chosen seemed to fit the requirements of the specific opening the best. In no way should the supervisor point out the shortcomings of those who failed to be selected. The purpose of such interviews should be to give recognition to persons who placed second or third, not to criticize them for failing to take first place. Persons who came close to qualifying have reason to feel encouraged because there will be future opportunities and because their work is receiving attention.

The supervisor should make a brief statement to the effect that these persons received consideration and that he (or a committee or his superior) reached a given decision. This should be followed by the supervisor's question on how they feel about the decision. An interest in the employees' feelings about the decision not only indicates concern over their interests but also invites both favorable and unfavorable criticism.

Since the opinion of an employee is requested, it should be accepted without question and the supervisor can honestly say, "I'm glad to know that."

There are times when the supervisor may learn things that may place him on the defensive or cause him to doubt his decision. It is well for him not to protect himself but to concede that he may have overlooked something and therefore be appreciative of the criticism. If he allows himself to be criticized he also makes it possible for the employee to be generous after having gotten his critical comments out of his system. If the supervisor doubts the wisdom of his decision he will have learned something that will aid him in the future. This will be to interview certain employees before he makes his final decision. Under such circumstances he can make his decision with the aid of existing opinions and facts from his group.

Some supervisors have found that posting notification of a job vacancy and its qualifications simplifies the promotion problem. After the job is posted, all employees who are interested may apply and are interviewed. When this is done persons with most seniority, who might logically have to be considered, may fail to apply. These very employees might feel by-passed under other conditions, but now they have no such feeling. It seems that employees with high seniority have face-saving problems because others offer them sympathy whenever seniority is violated. When they do not apply for a position they escape being by-passed and in many instances exert their influence by recommending persons who clearly lack seniority. Where this method is used, supervisors frequently have successfully promoted highly capable persons having the least seniority in the group. Often these are the employees that management would like to select for promotion but fears to promote because of the potential unfavorable reactions. The emphasis on seniority is primarily stimulated by conditions where favoritism and insecurity prevail. When there is an increase in trust in the company and no fear of retaliation, the emphasis on seniority declines. One way of establishing this trust is to extend employee participation to promotion problems.

At the present time the author is testing the group-decision procedure in this area of decision making. Facts about ability and attitudes in the group are both important. Perhaps the best way to combine these is to permit group decisions in making recommendations and to have objective studies of qualifications determine the final choice.

Evaluation Interview. Many companies have periodic interviews with employees (at intervals of six months or more) in order to go over their development. Such interviews are more common for new employees than for older ones, and they are perhaps more common for supervisory personnel than for the nonsupervisory. Although companies that advocate the practice believe it is sound, they often find it difficult to enforce. When supervisors are asked about the practice some insight is obtained into their reluctance to carry it out. If the supervisor gives an honest account of the employee's good and bad points he often finds himself in a position where he has to prove his estimate because the employee resents his criticism. Although surveys show that employees want to know where they stand, supervisors often feel that what employees really want is to be told they are doing a good job, regardless of whether or not their performance warrants it.

In order to circumvent some of the problems various kinds of rating and evaluation systems have been tried out. Plans that use a committee of supervisors to evaluate an employee's merits and demerits avoid the difficulty of putting the supervisor on the spot. In such instances it is made clear to the employee that the evaluation is merely a committee opinion, based upon impressions which may or may not be true. It is then suggested that the purpose of the discussion is to determine what the employee can do to improve the impressions.

Companies using group-evaluation procedures report favorable responses and improvements in employees, and it is likely that these effects are in part due to the following:

1. The supervisor who presents the evaluation is not placed in a position where he has to defend it, since it is not his evaluation.

2. The supervisor does a good job in presenting the evaluation to the employee because he has first discussed the employee in a conference with other supervisors.

3. Petty criticisms are eliminated.

4. The employee is able to start the next year with a clean slate and will be observed by several persons who are looking for improvement and so are sensitized to finding and praising it if and when it occurs.

Although it is desirable to study plans of this sort, the main objective here is to determine what can be accomplished by an evaluation interview, regardless of the specific company procedures that are set up.

The problem of establishing a mutual interest is not difficult in this type of interview. The employee wishes to be a success on the job, and the supervisor ordinarily wishes this, too. The trouble is that misunderstandings arise and set up barriers. On the one hand, the employee's motivation to succeed causes him to cover up his deficiencies and to protect himself against criticism. On the other hand, the supervisor's motivation to get the employee to do a good job sensitizes him to errors and violations of rules, and so he is more inclined to stress these things than he is to observe acceptable behaviors. At times he may become irritated and as a consequence may show frustrated reactions rather than make constructive suggestions. In return for these frustrated reactions the employee becomes uncooperative or hostile, and then things go from bad to worse. Thus two persons, each having motives acceptable to the other, may defeat each other's accomplishments and prevent the reaching of a common objective.

The best method of avoiding such misunderstandings is to make the evaluation interview a problem for discussion in which both participate. However, before doing this the supervisor should determine the employee's feelings and point of view about his job. Questions such as the following help the supervisor accomplish this:

1. How have things been going with you?
2. Are you developing as you would like to?
3. Do you see any ways in which we can be more helpful?

If the employee mentions problems or worries, it is important that he be given time to talk about them, regardless of whether they involve the company or his personal life. The supervisor should neither interrupt nor offer advice if the employee wants to talk. The mere opportunity to talk about the problem is helpful. If discussing these problems prevents a continuation of the interview, another date can be made to fulfill this purpose. It is unlikely that an interview could succeed while the employee is disturbed or worried.

After the supervisor has a feeling for the employee's point of view, the problem of analyzing the employee's job aptitudes can be raised. First, the supervisor should learn the activities or duties in which the employee feels he is most accomplished. After the employee has discussed his virtues he can be asked to consider the activities in which he feels inadequate, or on which he would like help, or in which he feels less accomplished. The objective of the interviewer in such instances is to have the employee evaluate his strong and his less outstanding aptitudes. The expressed purpose of this analysis is to determine whether the company is doing what it can to make the best use of a person's ability.

After this analysis the problem of what the company, the supervisor, and the employee can do to make the relationship more satisfying should be discussed in detail. In most instances the employee will suggest things he can do. When he makes the suggestions himself he is motivated to carry them out, and the danger of developing the feeling that he has been criticized is entirely avoided.

Suppose that this analysis leaves a number of things unsaid. For example, the employee may not have mentioned the fact that his relations with other employees are poor or that his tardiness record is bad. What can be done to draw attention to areas that the employee overlooks or avoids? Control over such matters can be gained by using questions and raising problems.

In this instance the interviewer may raise the problem of the fairness of employee evaluations. He can point out that supervisors gain impressions of employees and judge them regardless of whether or not they are instructed to perform this function. This leads to the problem of determining the behaviors to which supervisors actually pay attention, and a discussion can be held regarding which of these behaviors are given too much or too little weight. The reasons why supervisors react as they do can also be discussed.

Finally, after various injustices have been considered, the problem of how best to help the employee can be discussed. In this stage of the discussion the supervisor becomes a person who can assist the employee in reaching his objectives.

The extent to which an analysis of this kind need be made will, of course, depend upon the degree to which the employee requires improvement. Since the interview is difficult primarily when the employee is deficient, we have described the process with this problem in mind. However, it is likely that a much better understanding of employee attitudes would be gained if a similar process were used with all employees, regardless of their merit.

Supervisors will primarily object to this method of letting employees evaluate themselves, on the ground that people do not know their own deficiencies. However, studies on self-evaluation strikingly indicate that most people are good judges of themselves and have a good idea of how others see them. This being so, it appears that the reason we get a different impression about the accuracy of self-evaluations is that under most circumstances people are motivated to cover up their deficiencies. Thus it follows that, if an evaluation interview is held under permissive conditions and a mutual interest is established, most persons would make an accurate evaluation of themselves.

Persons who are found to either over- or underestimate their abilities and their standing in a group are likely to have adjustment problems. In the light of this trend it is quite unlikely that such individuals would profit from having their own estimates questioned by the supervisor. On the other hand, a few of the permissive-type interviews might lead to some personal insights, and, even though the initial purpose of the interview might not be achieved, some fringe benefits in the form of a better employee-supervisor relationship and better adjustment on the part of the employee might be achieved.

In order to give the reader some feeling about how the type of interview described above might proceed, some excerpts from a case are included.

In this instance George Morgan, an office manager, is interviewing a first-line supervisor, Jim Spence. Jim, 49 years old, is a work-minded individual, and the morale in his group is very poor. Many requests for transfers come from his unit, and employees resist transfers into his unit even when the move represents an increase in pay. A few years ago he was made a supervisor largely on the strength of his thoroughness and sense of responsibility.

M: Well, Jim, it's time for our periodic interview on job progress. How have things been going since our last talk?
s: Oh, about the same I guess.
M: How has your load been?
s: Pretty heavy. Maybe it wouldn't be so bad if I had better people, but I've got the worst bunch I ever had.
M: Are there any things that we can do to help out on that problem?
s: (*Pause*) No, I guess not—I guess it's my problem and I'll have to work my way through it.

Various operations on the job are then discussed.

M: Jim, what phases of your job do you like best?
s: Oh, I think getting things out that have a regular schedule. Just so long as rush jobs don't come up and disrupt the program, everything is fine. I like things that are systematic and can be planned carefully. That's when I'm at my best.
M: Would you say that your conscientiousness and thoroughness in regard to meeting schedules were your strongest points?
s: Yes, I think they are. I consider myself very conscientious, and I don't believe I've ever missed a due date or been late to work. I never go out for coffee like a lot of the others do, either.

A discussion along this line is continued for several minutes.

M: Now, what are some of the phases of your job that you like least—or bother you most?
s: Oh, I don't know. (*Pause*) I think it's the complaining of some of the people—and having to keep them in line. The trouble with people nowadays is that they don't have a sense of responsibility.

A number of illustrations are given, and the supervisor listens with understanding, nodding and accepting the interpretations given without any question.

M: Could we then say that the most unpleasant phases of your job have to do with people and the problems they create?

S: Yes, I guess that is about it. Of course, I don't like the idea of having to train so many people either. The turnover around here is too high, and I seem to get more of it than the others. If it weren't for the heavy turnover I wouldn't have so many around who need such close supervision.

M: You feel then that if something could be done to reduce the turnover your job would be a happier one.

S: Yes, that would help a lot, but what can be done?

M: Can you think of any way in which I can help?

S: Well— Is there any way in which we could screen out people before we hire them? The other supervisors seem to get people who stay longer.

M: Would you like us to send you more people to look over before you make a choice?

S: That might help. (*Pause*) On the other hand, they all seem O.K. at the start, and they all say they intend to stick with the job. They don't keep their promises—so what can one do?

Other explorations are made and the ideas discarded. Morgan tries to be understanding throughout and makes no criticism or suggestions.

M: Well, we have a number of ideas there. Now if any of them look good and you think I can help out, feel free to let me know and we can talk some more about these things.

S: —You know— Well— (*Long pause*) Do you think that maybe I'm too strict? I know other supervisors give their employees more freedom and leeway. Maybe I'm off the beam there. What do you think?

M: Well, I don't know, Jim. As far as the company is concerned there are authorized rest pauses, and we have the company restaurant open for coffee. We like to leave the interpretation of these things up to the supervisors.

S: Yes, and as I think about it, I think that's the way it has to be. (*Pause*) Say, George, suppose I went up for coffee like some of the others do and sometimes stayed 20 minutes or more. What would you say?

M: Do you think it would interfere with the job?

S: Oh, no—I wouldn't spend time away if I were behind. Maybe the relaxation would help me.

M: Well, do you think I'd have a good reason to object then?

S: No, I guess you wouldn't. (*Pause*) You know, I think I've been too much of a fuss-budget.

The rest of the discussion deals with changes Jim was going to make, and in connection with the discussion he brings up some of his off-the-job problems. When he leaves he is in a very good mood.

This interview shows how Jim Spence was caused to mention the very things that his boss wanted to have brought up for discussion.

However, it is unlikely that Jim would have even accepted constructive criticism. Jim had rationalized his difficulties with his group and probably would have talked about the need for discipline and pointed out that this was needed to get the job out. Morgan reported that Jim showed a definite improvement after this interview. The interview was one of Morgan's first attempts with this type of approach.

Where it is felt that the employee is receptive to a critical evaluation or if time does not permit the nondirective type of interview discussed above, a more directive approach may be satisfactory. If this is done the principles of motivation should be applied, in that positive rather than negative approaches should be made. Thus the supervisor, Jim Spence, might be told that he is doing a conscientious job in getting work out and that since he has this phase of his job well under control, he might like to consider broadening his interests. If he shows a constructive interest in the suggestion the complexity of some of the human relations phases of the job might be raised, and it might be pointed out that the company is becoming more and more aware of the importance of developing good employee relations. This approach might lead to a discussion of some of Jim's problems and a statement of willingness on his part to accept help. At this point Morgan can suggest some of the methods that might be tried out, and then give Jim a chance to participate in selecting ideas from those discussed and to try out those ideas that appeal to him. He should be asked to report on the outcome of his trials, and in this way he will receive stimulation and guidance. Since new ideas will replace old ones, the method of substitution will be used in this approach. The substitution method is far more effective than the operative method (training a man to stop doing something that is wrong) both because it is constructive rather than destructive and because it is more likely to be experienced as training than as criticism.

We have described two approaches to the task of attempting to upgrade the work of an individual in an evaluation interview. The first, the nondirective approach, is more time-consuming and has its greatest value when an attitude change is required and when the individual is on the defensive. When an individual is receptive, the problem of attitude conflict is not so great a barrier as when the person is on guard because of insecurity. In such instances the approach may be guided largely by motivation principles. The degree to which the interviewer should apply motivation principles and attitude-change concepts thus depends upon the interviewee's state of mind. This amounts to saying that the skill of an interviewer is dependent, in part, upon his ability to sense the state of mind of another person. A little preliminary talk or a general understanding of the person's background will often supply supplementary information for this diagnosis.

The Exit Interview. Regardless of whether a person is leaving a company for voluntary reasons or is being discharged and regardless of whether a resignation is avoidable or unavoidable, an exit interview should be held because of valuable information it may supply with regard to studies of placement, morale, and supervisory training (35). The stated reasons an employee gives for leaving a company are not necessarily the real causes. A girl might give marriage as her reason for quitting and then immediately work elsewhere after her marriage, and a man may give undesirable hours for quitting and then take a job across the street with the same hours. Frequently an employee does not know his real reason for quitting. All he knows is that he doesn't like his job. One man requested a transfer from a stockroom job because he couldn't stand the paint smell. A month later he turned down the transfer when it was offered on the grounds that it didn't bother him any more. The real reason, however, for the request of the transfer was the foreman's conduct. Training the foreman in human relations caused the smell of paint to cease being a source of irritation and changed the man's views of the job.

The source of mutual interest in an exit interview is that the company wants to improve its human relations, and any ideas that an employee can contribute to making things more pleasant for other employees are of value. To an employee leaving the company this makes sense, and at the same time he himself is interested in offering advice and criticism. Sometimes he is sufficiently hostile toward the company so that the opportunity to find fault will be welcomed, and expressing his views will serve as a form of relief. However, regardless of whether the employee cooperates constructively or destructively, he goes away feeling better toward the company and its management.

The essential requisite in interviewing, after establishing a mutual interest, is to be a good listener and accept all criticism with appreciation. The interviewer's attitude should be that of a reporter who wants to learn how another person feels and not that of a reformer who wants to change someone else's mind. Making notes may actually facilitate matters because it shows a willingness to accept statements, but before this is done the interviewee's permission should be obtained in order to make it clear that statements made will not be held against the person. If the employee wishes a letter of recommendation it should be made clear that the results of the interview cannot hurt him in any way.

Because the permissive type of interview often changes attitudes it is desirable to hold interviews some days before a person quits. When a satisfactory employee states an intention of leaving the company, he should be interviewed at this time. If the employee expresses complaints he might be asked to reconsider and give his permission to be interviewed again. This procedure permits the employee to change his mind without having to save face or be reluctant to change his mind. Instead he can come back for the second interview and announce that he has good news. One supervisor saved several good employees by getting behind the expressed reason for quitting and asking the employee to reconsider. Several girls worked after marriage, although they had given marriage as the reason for quitting. However, it is only after an employee has felt free to examine the total situation that a reconsideration has anything new to add.

The principles to follow in an exit interview are primarily the same as those involved in a complaint, except that the interviewer may have to make it easy for the employee to complain when he is interviewed about leaving the company. Exploratory questions are helpful, and these should lead to considerations of relations with other employees, the way the job fits into the employee's off-the-job interests, and finally the way conditions at home affect the job. Home problems cannot be separated from job problems, since both exist in the same individual.

On one occasion two women employees were discharged within a week because they refused to take their turns in exchanging shifts as they had agreed to do when they were hired. One of the girls was asked to quit because she refused to work nights. She was going to night school and didn't want to interrupt her studies. The other girl was asked to quit because she refused to work days. She and her husband worked nights and shared an apartment with her girl friend and the girl friend's husband. The husband of the other couple worked days, and the wife didn't work. Had the girl changed from night work to day work her husband would have been left alone in the apartment with her girl friend all day long. This she refused to permit.

Only after he had discharged the second girl did the foreman discover that his problem of covering the shifts would have been soluble by making adjustments in his group. It came to his attention because other employees complained about the unfairness of the discharges and brought the details to his attention. Instead of discovering reasons behind the refusals of two girls to change shifts, he had tried to be fair and treat all employees alike by demanding that all take turns on the shifts. The group-decision method or interviewing procedures would have suggested solutions to the problems by methods that employees considered fair.

Training Methods for Contacts and Interviews

A knowledge of the subjects of attitudes, frustration, motivation, and the basic principles that apply to contacts and interviews is not enough for developing skill in these areas. Intelligent supervisors violate practically every principle when given an assignment immediately after this training. The failure to use the principles is not due to lack of comprehension or to lack of acceptance, but rather it stems from the fact that an actual situation may not act as a stimulus to call up this information. When placed in a specific situation the person recalls the things he has learned and done in such situations, and so the result is that he conducts an interview pretty much as he has in the past. Even if he goes into the interview with the intention of applying what he has learned, he succeeds only for a brief period. Once the interview is under way the expected responses may not be forthcoming, and so the plan no longer is in effect. From this point on he forgets his plans and reacts to the events of the interview, paying attention to the responses rather than the principles.

This does not mean that a knowledge of principles has no value. Rather it means that something must be added to the training to permit the principles to become a part of the person. Role playing and subsequent discussion and analysis in terms of principles supply a necessary link between principles and practice. In Chapter 4 the methods of role playing were discussed, and a number of role-playing cases that are suited to training in handling contacts and conducting interviews were included. Other cases from within the company should be included, the selection being made on the basis of problems that are of most concern to the group.

A valuable supplement to training in these areas is the development of skills in nondirective counseling. Although these counseling skills have a value in themselves for dealing with disturbed employees, the same methods apply whenever one is confronted with an attitude problem in employee contacts and in interviews. Furthermore, training in nondirective counseling develops a person's sensitivity for the feelings of others. If one is sensitive to feelings one can recognize the presence of human relations problems and conduct oneself accordingly. Thus, like skill in group discussion, the technique of nondirective counseling transfers valuable skills to other types of face-to-face dealings with people.

13

Nondirective Counseling

Introduction

The purpose of counseling is to aid an emotionally disturbed individual in making a better adjustment to his job and life. Since a well-adjusted employee of a given level of ability is more effective on the job than a disturbed one, it is of interest to management to concern itself to a reasonable degree in furthering emotional adjustment. Industry has recognized the need for furnishing aid in physical health, and it is beginning to become concerned with mental health. How soon psychiatrists will be generally represented in the company medical departments is a matter of speculation, but the interest of supervisors in dealing with problem employees can no longer be doubted. One of the most acceptable subjects in human relations training is frustration and the techniques for dealing with it. When a sample of 120 employees of a large utility were asked whether they would like to have someone in the company that they could go to and talk to about their problems, over 80 per cent indicated that they liked the idea. Another 15 per cent favored the idea if it would not become a kind of spy system.

Since companies have not as yet employed counselors or psychiatrists in any great numbers, it is advisable to consider what the supervisor might do in the direction of dealing with frustrated employees. The author has gradually expanded this aspect in the follow-up of the human relations programs largely because of the demand for more help from all levels of supervision. After some training the supervisors have requested follow-up training to sharpen their own skills instead of feeling that the company should move in the direction of furnishing counseling services.

Because training in counseling develops skills that are useful to a discussion leader and is an aid in dealing with all interpersonal relations on the job, any time spent on the subject would be useful even if it did not develop all the essential counseling skills. However, the prospects that even limited training in counseling will be of some value in performing the counseling function are assured by the fact that training in leading group discussions facilitates training in counseling. Thus the mere fact that counseling skills and leadership skills require similar attitudes and similar methods makes the training in both an efficient procedure.

Before a supervisor is encouraged to serve as a counselor it is important to be satisfied that the procedures taught cannot be misused so as to do more harm than would result from the approach used by an untrained supervisor. Furthermore, the procedure encouraged should show promise of aiding the counseled person in making adjustments to life.

A new approach to counseling, known as *nondirective* or *client-centered* (52, 53), satisfies these qualifications in that it can be highly effective and yet can have no harmful effects if improperly used. This type of counseling is in contrast to directive counseling, in which a diagnosis is made and treatment or advice is given. Thus nondirective counseling does not preclude other types of counseling, and yet it can function effectively for persons who are not sufficiently disturbed to require psychiatric care or for those who are unlikely to receive it. As a matter of fact, the result of nondirective counseling interviews may be that the client discovers his need for help and so is more likely to seek psychiatric aid than if he had not had this experience.

The essential need for a disturbed person is to (1) obtain relief from his frustrated condition, and (2) adjust himself to the problems in his life which are causing his frustration. An additional possibility when a supervisor functions as the counselor is that the supervisor may be able to change the frustrating situation when the source of frustration is on the job (35).

The Objectives of Nondirective Counseling

Obtaining Relief. A person becomes frustrated when he finds himself in a problem situation which he feels compelled to face and at the same time finds himself unable to deal with. Thus the problem as well as the person's view of the problem determines whether a given condition will become frustrating. In a well-adjusted condition a person approaches problems with problem-solving behavior, but when pressures are present and problem solving approaches fail, the problem-solving behavior is replaced by emotions of anger and fear, and then the behavior ceases to be creative and constructive. Instead the person becomes hostile, childish, and stubborn, and as a result he makes conditions worse, particularly when his problem situation involves other people. In order to correct the frustrated condition one must reverse the process through which frustration was experienced and help the individual return from his state of frustration to a problem-solving state of mind. Once he is in a problem-solving state of mind he at least establishes the possibility of solving the problem. Thus the first step in correcting a frustrated condition is to remove at least some of the frustration.

This is best accomplished by getting the frustrated behavior expressed. Ordinarily our early education includes training in the direction of making us hold back our real feeling, since unpleasant feelings are not socially acceptable. This means that the acquired barriers to the free expression of feeling must be lowered if a person is to be helped. A person may have many pockets of unexpressed hostilities, and each of these must be located so that the feelings associated with frustrating experiences can be released. The more distant and deep-seated these experiences are in our experience, the more difficult it is to release them. If our frustrations go back to being rejected by our parents in our childhood the location of these feelings and their release are more difficult tasks than when the frustration occurs in a specific situation, such as having someone cut in ahead of us in traffic when we are late and on our way to the office. Such differences in the difficulty of locating frustrations are matters of degree, and they require different degrees of skill in helping an individual to release feelings.

Once a person has released some of his hostilities he feels better, and he becomes more inclined to see his condition as a problem rather than as something others are doing to him. Expression takes attention away from one's own feelings and makes it possible to consider the situation and other people in a more objective way. Until this state of mind is established the person is unreceptive to constructive suggestions, and any suggestion that he should change is met with resentment. To a frustrated person a suggestion that he should change is regarded as an attack on him, and this merely aggravates the very condition that is to be corrected. Punishment has a similar effect in that it makes the expression of hostile behavior more difficult and also is regarded as an attack on the person who is punished. The result is that punishment increases the frustrated condition rather than corrects it.

In order for a counselor to be an aid to a frustrated person he must create a situation in which the expression of feelings is easy and of such a nature that the person does himself or others no harm. It is the counselor's task to create such a condition or atmosphere, and his skills depend largely upon his ability to create such a condition.

Locating and Solving a Problem. Once frustration is reduced a person is able to get away from his own feelings and look for the source of trouble. When he is no longer busy blaming others for his condition, he can explore his situation for the real difficulty. However, if the source of frustrations goes back a number of years it is not easy to locate the real problem. One man blamed his poor wages and lack of recognition on the job for his frustration. It was only after considerable exploration that he discovered that his wife's homosexual tendencies were at the bottom of his disturbed state of mind. Because of his wife's earlier background he felt inadequate in his marriage, and this attitude of inadequacy was reflected in other areas, so that he had a mental set to see the behaviors of others as forms of discrimination and rejection. Thus his real problem was one he had pushed in the background, and hence he had failed to face it.

Problem solving can be accomplished only if the difficulty or obstacle is located. Such behavior is constructive only when an individual takes the attitude of exploring what he himself can do to overcome the difficulty. As long as he expects conditions to change or believes someone else must change things he is not solving his problem, but is remaining apathetic. Thus the responsibility for solving a problem must be accepted by the individual who has the problem.

If a counselor is to be an aid to a frustrated person he must stimulate the disturbed person to explore his feelings about various people and events so as to locate the problem; he must impose responsibility on him by failing to assume it himself; and he must help him find solutions that are acceptable to the person himself. The most acceptable solutions are the ones a disturbed individual discovers or invents himself, and this means that the counselor should not supply the solutions.

Correcting the Situation. The counselor is not always able to change or correct the frustrating situations in which a disturbed person finds himself, but the possibility should not be overlooked. For example, the counselor's wise handling of the parents may correct a feeling of parental rejection in the frustrated children. Thus if a 5-year-old child begins wetting the bed shortly after the arrival of a new baby the situation may be pointed out to the parents, and they may be receptive to the suggestion of giving the older child more attention and love. If the bed wetting is caused because the parents quarrel, then it becomes apparent that the parents are in need of counseling. Advising them to give more love to the child would have little value. However, if counseling of the parents results in a happier home situation, the difficulty has been corrected for the child.

A job situation offers similar possibilities for correction. If a supervisor discovers that an older woman employee is lonesome and feels rejected, he may correct the situation by more considerate treatment of her and by giving her extra attentions, such as special assignments on the job. Through group discussions he can protect minority individuals who often feel rejected and cause them to be accepted by the group. He can further utilize the group-decision method by using it to locate problems and accepting the group's solutions by putting them into practice. Where high producers are unpopular in the group (as is often the case), he can cease using their superior performance as examples to others and refrain from expecting the others to do as well. One of the important values of giving supervisors training in counseling as compared to training staff personnel in counseling is that supervisors are able to make changes in the work situation when it becomes a source of frustration.

In one work situation inspectors and painters were having constant disputes, and morale was very poor. Since the job was set up on a piece-rate basis, inspectors were asked to have each painter correct the defects on his own parts. This meant that painters were constantly being interrupted, and these interruptions were becoming a source of frustration. After the source of frustration was discovered, the work routine was changed so that an extra painter went along with inspectors and made all corrections. Defects were charged to the various painters, but the interruptions were eliminated. The change in the work pattern solved the problem completely.

If a large number of persons show signs of frustration in a job situation, it is a pretty good sign that there is a source of frustration on the job. Locating and removing the frustration then becomes an effective method for reducing frustration. The use of the group-discussion and group-decision methods frequently aids the supervisor in discovering the presence of frustration on the job and also aids him in finding remedies that are acceptable.

Requisites of Nondirective Counseling

Since nondirective counseling is a safe method to use, an inadequately trained individual will do no harm even if he applies the method only in part. Rather, if a supervisor replaces only some of the poor procedures he previously used he will already be doing some good. Since everyone receives advice and criticism from others, a reduction in these cannot be regarded as harmful. It is when people take the advice of unqualified advisors that harm may be done. Because nondirective counseling is a method for stimulating people to solve their own problems, the worst that can happen is that the method will fail to do any good. It follows then that supervisors with different degrees of skill in nondirective counseling will be able to aid varying numbers of employees. This being so, the degree of skill desired can be left up to supervisors themselves. Since a limited amount of skill has some value, a brief discussion of some of the basic requirements is included. Those who wish more knowledge may pursue the subject further (13, 49, 51, 52, 58).

An Acceptant Attitude. An acceptant attitude means that the nondirective counselor accepts a person's remarks as a true statement of feelings, regardless of what the person says, and he accepts the person as a member of society. Thus he is neither shocked nor bored, critical nor gullible, and he neither agrees nor disagrees with the statement. If the person contradicts himself, changes his views, admits something he has just previously denied, the counselor accepts the statements as they occur. He does not subject the expression of feeling to any logical analysis, since feelings follow a different kind of logic. His objective is to try to understand how the person feels and not to make a diagnosis or offer advice.

Accepting a person as a member of society is very important because emotionally disturbed people are likely to feel ashamed, rejected, or different. If someone can accept them as true members of society they are already helped in part.

In discussing the group-decision process (Chapter 6) it was pointed out that minority individuals should be protected. In doing this the group leader is aiding the individual to be accepted by the group and is also helping the individual to feel wanted and to become a true group member. One of the values of the organization known as Alcoholics Anonymous is that a person joining is both accepted and understood by the group.

Belief in a Person's Ability to Solve His Problem. If a person is to adjust himself to life *he* must make the adjustment, and he is more likely to change his behavior if he himself decides to do something differently than if advised to do it. In order to make the adjustment, however, the disturbed person must first discover his problem and then decide on a solution. To accomplish these things he must assume the responsibility and not lean on others for support. It is only when a counselor has faith in a person's ability to solve a problem that he can effectively avoid offering help or advice. Ordinarily a disturbed person asks for help, and a counselor must have sufficient skill to turn the responsibility back to the client. A person is not truly adjusted to life until he can make his own decisions, and one of the causes of poor adjustment is that of having had parents who did not let their children acquire this responsibility as they matured. The nondirective counselor imposes this responsibility on persons who ask for advice by making remarks such as, "You feel you would like me to tell you what to do," or by stating that it might be a good idea to talk things out and that when this is done certain ideas might develop. Such methods invariably cause the person to go on talking about things. If you have had people ask for advice you may have observed that such persons actually resist suggestions by saying, "I have tried that," or "That wouldn't work."

The aspect of counseling in which responsibility for solving problems is passed on to those who must carry out a plan is also involved in the group-decision approach. The leader presents the group with problems, and the group members are asked to decide on the solution they wish to put into practice, after having given the problem due consideration.

Listening Skills. Relief from a frustrated condition is obtained through the expression of hostile and regressive behaviors and feelings. Ordinarily such behaviors are socially unacceptable, and as a consequence barriers are set up to discourage such expression. Even when such behaviors are expressed, they are likely to be of such nature that they irritate or antagonize others. The result of these unfavorable reactions is to place the frustrated person at a greater disadvantage than he was at the outset. Since persons ordinarily are not aided by others in the expression of frustrated behavior, it is necessary to help them channel their expression in ways that are harmless and acceptable. Play therapy and the listening type of counseling do this. In play therapy a child can break up boxes and hammer rag dolls, thereby expressing destructive behavior without getting into trouble.

When a person listens to another's expression of hostility and shows by his manner that he understands, frustrated tensions are released and no harm is done.

Once hostility is expressed a person can become more calm, and in this state of mind he may discover his real problem and even solve it. However, more frequently additional skills on the part of the counselor are needed to solve frustrations that are deep-seated and extend into the person's past. Nevertheless it can be said that listening alone will reduce the emotional state aroused by a frustrating incident.

Although permitting a frustrated person the opportunity to express feelings by listening to him seems easy to carry out, it is somewhat difficult for most people to learn. This is because in listening one must stop reacting as one usually does in conversation. Instead of soothing or calming down a person, disagreeing, or accusing him of being unreasonable, or taking his side and sympathizing with him, the listener passes no judgment at all but merely understands and encourages the person to talk about his feelings. These permissive behaviors on the part of the counselor tend to cause the frustrated individual to become less cautious in his expressions and hence to stop holding back his true feelings.

Because listening is difficult to learn we have found it advisable to train supervisors also in a further technique of nondirective counseling. This technique may be called the method of *responding to feelings* or the technique of reflecting feelings. Some knowledge of this method supplements listening because it gives the counselor something to do and say.

Reflecting Feelings. The technique of reflecting feelings is similar to that used by a discussion leader when he mirrors the ideas expressed in group discussion. In this capacity the leader makes summary statements and points up the important phases of a discussion. The counselor likewise rephrases what the client expresses but pays particular attention to feelings. Thus feelings of confusion, hostility, and guilt may be restated or rephrased, and in doing this the counselor shows that he understands and accepts the individual. This conduct on the part of the counselor encourages further expression of feelings and leads to the expression of feelings that are difficult to face. A common phrase for the counselor to use is, "You feel that . . ." or "You think that . . ."

For example, an employee talks about an instance when he was by-passed and reports that he was not given opportunities to learn new jobs. He says, "If I'd had some of the opportunities that others have had, I could have made good, too. But everyone around here has it in for me. What chance have I got?"

The supervisor responds by saying, "You feel that you haven't had a fair chance in the past and that supervisors have discriminated against you."

Such a response encourages further expression as follows, "Yes, and I'm just as good as the rest of the fellows. Of course, some of them go out of their way to get on the good side of a boss, but I never could stand people who try to be white-haired boys."

Eventually the employee discovered, during this type of interview, that his attitude may have had a bearing on his advancement, and this discovery led to a change in his attitude and in his subsequent conduct.

The technique of reflecting feelings not only aids a disturbed person by helping him to express his feelings, but it also leads to the realization that the employee himself contributed to the situation. When this occurs he discovers that his problem is to make a different kind of contribution. Once a person discovers that he has contributed to a difficulty he sees the behavior of others in a different light. Instead of blaming them and expecting them to change, he realizes that he can do something about things. Thus after frustration is released and expressed a person can begin facing and solving problems.

The techniques of both reflecting feelings and listening aid the problem-solving aspect of a counseling interview and the phase having to do with releasing feeling through expression. Since the two techniques serve a similar function, developing skill in reflecting feelings can become an aid to skillful listening, particularly since the reflecting approach requires one to listen for the expression of feelings. This listening for feelings, which we might call *selective listening,* requires the counselor to pay strict attention to the remarks expressed, and as a result he becomes less inclined to talk or interrupt. Furthermore, he ceases to be bothered by pauses and soon discovers that pauses are not openings for another to fill in, but often represent hesitations and difficulties that a disturbed person has in expressing his true feeling. In this struggle to find adequate expression the person frequently clarifies his feelings and experiences new insights. The counselor's skill in reflecting may help these insights along, but he should still respect pauses because they also make the other person feel responsible for filling them in.

The Use of Questions. Once the state of frustration has passed and a person is thinking and feeling constructively, a counselor has opportunities to be helpful. He not only can reflect the constructive feelings as they are expressed but may also encourage exploratory thinking without seeming to pry into the other's affairs. Thus he may ask such questions as, "What would you do if that didn't work out?" and "What is likely to happen in case you try acting differently?" He can open up explorations of other possibilities by asking, "Have you tried going over your plan of action in detail?" or "Is there any possibility that someone might object to that?" These questions should contain no attempt to criticize or evaluate but should be given with the idea of exploring things together. Since the counselor does not know the answers he is merely exploring.

Once a person ceases to be on the defensive and is looking for solutions questions become thought provoking, and as long as the questions are of a constructive nature they serve as an aid to problem solving. When a person is truly in a problem-solving state of mind, one may even drop hints and suggest possibilities just so long as one does not try to sell a solution. Such remarks as, "Do you know of anything that pleases him?" "Have you tried any other approaches?" or "Is there any possibility that he might be jealous?" are suggestive and yet permit the other person to find his own solution. As soon as suggestions are interpreted as an attempt to sell a solution there is a tendency for mutual interests to disappear, and confidence in the counselor may be lost. The counselor must never be seen as one who takes sides or as one who becomes critical and impatient.

Although we have indicated the value of carefully supplied suggestions, this is a deviation from the strict use of nondirective counseling. However, the author's researches (38) indicate that receptiveness to suggestions occurs once a state of motivation is well established. Receptiveness in individuals has the same basis as in group discussions. When individual persons or groups are in a problem-solving state of mind they welcome help; it is only when insecurity, suspicion, or active frustration are present that the nondirective approach is so essential.

Role-Playing Cases of Temporary Frustration

Many problems confronting the supervisor are temporary frustrations in the sense that work pressure, a deadline, or an argument often create a condition of frustration. Since the condition does not persist and the problem situation passes, all that needs to be done is to aid the person to obtain relief through free expression of feelings. Experience in handling such cases can perhaps best be obtained in a training program through the use of role playing.

In order to illustrate the type of case that lends itself to training in listening and behaving in a permissive, acceptant manner, one of the role-playing cases developed for this purpose is included.

THE CASE OF THE FRUSTRATED SUPERVISOR

The following case can be used with two persons acting out the roles before a group of observers, or it can be used in a large training group with as many as 75 pairs of persons acting out the parts with each other. (See discussion of multiple role playing on pp. 146–157.)

For groups unfamiliar with role playing it is desirable to involve all persons in the role playing so that no one is placed in an embarrassing situation. In this manner everyone can have a first-hand experience of how difficult it is for a person to remain angry and hostile when he can express himself freely.

The role-playing case involves two persons: Jim Wells, a division supervisor, and Bill Jackson, a first-line supervisor. Bill Jackson is placed in a frustrating situation, and Jim Wells is given leads that incline him to listen and draw Bill out.

If the role playing is to be carried out in a large group the members are first divided into pairs. One member of each pair is given a copy of the role for Jim Wells, and the other member is given a copy of the role for Bill Jackson. The members are asked to study their own roles only and not to exchange papers because they will be asked to act out their parts with each other. When enough time has been given for all persons to become familiar with their roles, it is advisable to have the Bill Jacksons rise. It is then suggested that the cue for beginning is for Bill to seat himself, thus indicating his arrival in Jim's office.

Role for Jim Wells, division supervisor: You are the supervisor of a division employing about 75 men and women and 6 first-line supervisors. You like your job and the supervisors and employees who work for you, and you feel that they cooperate with you in every way.

This morning you noticed that one of your first-line supervisors, Bill Jackson, was rather late in getting to work. Since Bill is very conscientious and was working on a rush job, you wondered what had happened. Bill is thoroughly dependable, and when something delays him he always tries to phone you. For this reason you were somewhat concerned and were about to call his home when one of Bill's men, a young fellow named Joe Blake, came in. Joe is a good-natured kid

just out of high school, but this time he was obviously angry and said
that he was not going to work for Bill another minute and was going
to quit unless you got him another job. Evidently Bill had come in,
started to work, and then lost his temper completely when young Joe
didn't do something quite right.

Although Bill occasionally has his bad moods, it is unlike him to
lose his temper this way. This latest rush job may have put him
under too much pressure, but even so his outburst this morning seems
difficult to explain on any reasonable grounds. You feel, therefore,
that something must be seriously wrong, and if you can get Bill to
talk about whatever it is that is bothering him you may get the situation straightened out. Anyway, you are determined not to get into an
argument with Bill or criticize him in any way. Instead you are going
to try to get him to talk about his troubles, listen to what he has to
say, and indicate that you understand how he feels about things. If
Bill seems more angry than Joe's mistake would reasonably justify
you might suppose that there is something more behind all this, and
Bill would probably feel a lot better if he got it off his chest. If Bill
is thoroughly angry with Joe you may suggest that Joe be fired in
order to demonstrate that you have not taken Joe's side in the matter.

You talked with Joe for several minutes, and, after he had told his
side of the story, he felt better and was ready to go back on the job.
You just phoned Bill and asked him to drop around when he had a
chance. Bill said he'd come right over and is walking toward your
office now.

Role for Bill Jackson, first-line supervisor: You have just come to
work after a series of the most humiliating and irritating experiences
you have ever had. Last night your next-door neighbor, Sam Jones,
had a wild, drunken party at his house that kept you awake most of
the night. Jones is a blustering, disagreeable man who has no consideration whatever for others, so when you called him at about 3:00
A.M. and told him to be less noisy, he was abusive and insulting.
Things quieted down later on, but when you finally got some rest
you overslept.

Since you were in the midst of a rush job at the company, you
skipped breakfast to hurry to work, and, as you were leaving the
house, you noticed that someone had driven a car across one corner
of your lawn and had torn out several feet of your new hedge. You
were certain that Jones or one of the drunks at his party had done it,
so you ran right over to Jones's house, determined to have it out with
him. He not only denied everything but practically threw you out
and threatened to knock your teeth out if you didn't shut up and
behave yourself, and you know that he is big enough to do it.

When you came to work, more than an hour late, your nerves were
so ragged that you were actually shaking. Everything conceivable
had gone wrong, and then the last straw was when you discovered
that Joe Blake, a young high-school recruit, had made a mistake that
delayed you several hours on your rush job, or at least it would have

if you hadn't caught him in time. Naturally, you gave him a good
going-over for his carelessness. Blake said he wouldn't take that kind
of abuse from anyone and walked out on you. You noticed that he
went in to see your supervisor, Jim Wells. Obviously he is in there
accusing you of being rough on him. Well, you don't like that kind
of an attitude in a young squirt, and if he has gone in there squawking
you'll make him wish he'd never been born. You have had all you
can stand, and the big boss had better not get tough with you because
he'll have one hell of a time getting the job done without you. Jim
had that sniveling brat in there and talked to him for quite a while
before he phoned you to come in. Gabbing when there's work to be
done—that's certainly a hell of a way to run things. You are on your
way to Jim's office now and have no intention of wasting time on
words.

Group Analysis. After about 10 minutes practically all persons will
have finished their role playing. A few questions put to the group
can be used to bring out the following results:

1. Practically none of the Bill Jacksons were able to stay angry, and
most of them will indicate that they feel much better.

2. Nearly all the Jim Wellses will have done a pretty good job of
listening.

3. In practically all instances Jim gets Bill to talk about his other
frustrations.

4. In cases in which Jim Wells asked Bill Jackson whether he
thought Joe ought to be discharged, it turns out that Bill responded
by starting to say some nice things about Joe.

5. In almost every instance the persons who had the role of Jim
Wells believe that Bill will go back on the job and straighten things
out with Joe.

6. Most of the persons who played the role of Bill Jackson feel that
they will get things straightened out with Joe, and nearly half of them
indicate that they feel better about their neighbor.

Values Derived. Demonstrations of this type show that listening
and getting another person to talk have an important place on the
job. When one uses the lecture method to discuss the usefulness of
listening, it is common for persons to react by thinking it would look
foolish or by asking what a listener is supposed to do when asked a
question. An experience with role playing shows that the listening
situation isn't so uncomfortable as many imagine, and most persons
do a pretty good job of getting the other fellow to talk if they have the
mental set to do it.

Sometimes persons playing the role of Jim Wells offer advice to Bill Jackson. A little discussion of a few such illustrations soon demonstrates that the advice added nothing, and if the advice was critical of Bill's conduct it turns out that Bill didn't like it.

If one wishes to produce a contrasting experience the situation can be repeated, but with Jim Wells instructed to reprimand Bill. When this is done the interview usually goes from bad to worse, and frequently Bill quits his job in anger.

Role playing with simple cases of frustration such as described above clearly illustrate that, with a minimum of skill, an angry person can be transformed into a rather reasonable individual within a few minutes. However, many true-life cases are not this simple, so that one should not expect magical results on all occasions. Nevertheless, the fact that a few moments of listening can often be effective should not be overlooked.

Recognizing Persons with Background Problems

General Considerations. In contrast to a person who is angry or disturbed by a specific situation, we often find individuals who are confused, unable to make decisions, very sensitive or touchy, withdrawn from others, or uncooperative and belligerent. Such persons react to minor situations in what seem to be unpredictable ways. These persons often are our problem employees, and we can easily separate them from others because they are a constant source of difficulty. Unfortunately such individuals are a source of irritation, and consequently we are inclined to feel hostile rather than helpful toward them.

One can be quite sure that such individuals' problem behavior is not entirely caused by the situation to which they are reacting, but that a given situation merely serves as an incident that releases feelings which have their basic origin somewhere else. Attempts to prevent disturbing incidents may be of some aid, but preventing the expression of problem behavior is not a cure. Frequently these incidents can furnish the opportunity to make contact with the individual and permit an approach to the real problem. Since supervisors often are on hand when some incidents occur, they are frequently in a good position to capitalize on these incidents and use them as opportunities for counseling. A counselor, who is less available, would have to create his own opportunities to stimulate expression of feeling.

It is a safe assumption that the real sources of disturbance of most problem employees are not in the work situation and that the frustrated reactions are responses to incidents rather than to causes. The skilled supervisor may use these outbursts as points of contact and then attempt, by exploratory questions and a permissive attitude, to encourage expression on off-the-job matters and thereby get to the real causes.

However, a good many examples of poor emotional adjustment cannot be recognized so readily as our clear-cut cases of problem employees. These fringe cases may be even more numerous than the clear-cut problem employees. In such instances one may use as a guide the principle that, if an emotional response to a given situation is out of proportion to what the situation warrants, then the person must have had some background experiences which have supplemented the immediate situation. It is desirable to locate these background experiences and to continue exploring for them in a backward direction. The origin of such experiences frequently goes back to early childhood, and these memories must be recalled. Usually a disturbed person is unable to get away from talking about the immediate situation and experiences closely associated with it because someone interferes with his free expression of feeling by disagreeing or asking for proof. The elimination of such interferences often is all that is needed to get a disturbed person to talk about off-the-job problems.

In order to illustrate how background problems may easily be overlooked, let us examine the history of a problem employee and see how his background problems were missed because the supervisors who interviewed him paid too much attention to the things he complained about and not enough attention to the feelings that were hidden behind his matter-of-fact statements. Supervisors often claim that they know all the background of a case, but invariably their listening falls short of the major objectives of counseling.

THE CASE OF THE LINEMAN

A lineman who worked for a utility had been a source of difficulty in the company for nearly 20 years. He always wanted a different job and constantly requested transfers. His record showed that he had been given at least four opportunities to learn higher-level jobs and he had failed to make good each time. Transfers to other areas were ineffective, and all foremen reported the same difficulties with him. At the present time he was receiving wages for a more highly classified job which he had been given an opportunity to learn and on which he had failed. Management had made this concession of paying him wages beyond his job classification because it was felt that a reduction in pay would disturb him. Although this pay difference was not too well received by his associates, who were actually more skilled, the company was determined to do what it could to keep him satisfied.

He now had a new foreman and in an interview told the foreman of the poor treatment the company had given him. As he saw it, he had not received the needed help on jobs, he had not received proper training on jobs he wanted, and he had received no real breaks or considerate treatment from anyone. He now had to have a desk job, he said, because his feet hurt and he could not climb poles.

The foreman sent him to the medical department for examination, and the doctors reported that nothing was wrong with his feet. When the foreman discussed the medical report with him, he became hostile and said that his own doctor did find trouble. However, he refused to give his doctor's name.

The foreman next sought help by taking the problem to his human relations training group. He wanted to know what kind of job would make the lineman happy.

Since the lineman's dissatisfaction with his treatment appeared to be greater than the facts indicated, it seemed reasonable to suppose that there were other factors in the lineman's experience which might bear on the matter. The foreman, therefore, was asked what he knew about the lineman's home life. The foreman had considerable information about this, as did all the men who knew the lineman. The following statements represent what was common knowledge to employees who knew the lineman.

1. When the lineman was a little over 20 years old he married a woman over 40 years of age.

2. He divorced this wife when he was 40, but his wife received the home. His attitude toward her, expressed freely after a few drinks, indicated that she had been the dominant member and he resented the way she ran things.

3. Shortly after divorcing his first wife, he married a 20-year-old girl and had two children from this marriage.

4. After 5 years he was in the process of divorcing his second wife, but because of the housing shortage continued to live at the same address while the divorce was in process.

5. While awaiting his divorce he was "carrying on" with a woman in her thirties, and the affair was regarded as a scandal in the community.

In the light of these facts it is questionable whether sore feet and company experiences were at the bottom of the lineman's problems. It seems likely that his difficulties preceded his first marriage and went back to his childhood. Apparently he needed someone to mother him when he married at the age of 20. Later on he rebelled and went to the opposite extreme in choosing his second mate. At no time did his relations with women seem to solve a problem; rather these behaviors indicated a desire to avoid solving problems.

In order to aid the lineman, the foreman had to induce him to talk about his off-the-job relationships. In all supervisory interviews with the lineman job matters had been the subject of discussion, and disputes over facts and the like prevented the discussion from getting off these subjects.

After the foreman had received some training in nondirective interviewing he again interviewed the lineman. In his first subsequent interview he found that he was able to get the lineman to talk about his off-the-job problem. The lineman felt that a lot of people "had it in for him" and that few people really understood him. The foreman did not follow up the interview, but he found that he was able to get along with the lineman, and the subject of sore feet was never mentioned again.

Case Discussion for Attitude Training

General Considerations. In discussing case material a group is required to think in terms of specific actions rather than general principles. When using case material for counseling training, a group of persons can review the natural responses that might have been made to an employee's remarks, and the proper response may be contrasted with these. By this approach a group of individuals can experience their own natural reactions and detect which of them is appropriate to the nondirective counseling interview.

If we permit a group of supervisors to voice various possible reactions that a typical supervisor might have made to an employee's remarks, they can include their own reaction tendencies without exposing what they would have done. In this manner all group members who participate actively in the discussion are permitted to correct themselves silently, without feeling that they must defend their positions. This approach creates a receptive discussion climate and allows the group to learn substitute reactions without having face-saving problems.

Since listening and reacting to the feelings of others require the withholding of our own feelings, this type of training is more than an intellectual process. Persons must experience some "gut" feelings themselves in order to experience the full importance of listening. By permitting group members to become involved in the details of a case, some of this "gut" feeling is aroused.

In order to create this type of discussion, case material must be available in considerable detail. Specific remarks that an employee makes have to be put to the group so that they can discuss the various supervisory responses that might have been made. These supervisory responses are then analyzed to determine the effects the various responses might have had on the individual.

To clarify the type of discussion process intended, a detailed analysis of a case is included here.

CASE OF MISS EVERETT

Background: Miss Everett is middle-aged and has been employed by the company for over 15 years. She is single, and her progress in the company has been average or somewhat less than average. For some years she has been receiving the maximum wage for her classification. Her rating is that of an average employee. Miss Everett has a comfortable apartment in the city and lives alone. In appearance she is plain looking. Her social behavior is retiring, and she is never seen at company social functions. On the job she associates primarily with the older group of employees, who are in the minority.

The interview described below was conducted by Mr. Jones, who was in charge of an accounting unit. Mr. Sullivan was Miss Everett's immediate supervisor in the section in which she worked, but Mr. Jones was acquainted with all the employees and handled all policy and controversial matters. Both Mr. Sullivan and Mr. Jones considered Miss Everett something of a problem. At the time of the interview Mr. Jones was in a human relations training group, and the assignment for the week was to try the listening approach on the next employee complaint.

One day Miss Everett came to Mr. Jones's office and said she would like to talk with him. Mr. Jones asked her to be seated and made brief notes on a pad held on his knee and out of sight of Miss Everett. After Miss Everett was seated, and without any other approach, she said:

MISS E: (1) "The only pay increases that I have had in 10 years are where the top rate has been raised. Everyone gets those increases. I think I should get an increase once in a while that isn't due to the top being raised."

> *Discussion Question 1:* What do you think an ordinary supervisor would say at this point, and how would Miss Everett have reacted?
> *Probable Reactions to Q1:* "You are getting the top pay for your classification now, and you have been getting that for some time."
> "You are asking for more pay than your classification allows."
> "We can't pay anyone more than the ceiling rate."
> *Summary Comment:* It seems then that critical comments would have caused trouble. Now let's find out what Mr. Jones actually said.

JONES: (1) "I have been thinking a lot about wage matters lately and, although I have some ideas that might be helpful, I would like to hear what ideas you have."

MISS E: (2) After this comment by the supervisor, Miss Everett continued to talk about wages, saying, among other things: "A girl with a good attendance record should be given an increase for that reason alone."

Discussion Question 2: What sort of a reply do you think the average supervisor would make to this remark?

Probable Reactions to Q2: "You are asking for a raise just because you come to work every day."

"Other girls have good attendance records, too."

"Productivity and cooperativeness also have to be considered."

Summary Comment: These are things that other supervisors might say or do, and the effects would have not been too good. Let's see what Jones did.

JONES: (2) Instead of getting himself involved in an argument, he listened attentively, nodding his head understandingly and letting Miss Everett do the talking.

MISS E: (3) The next thing she came up with was: "New girls come into the office and they get increases whether they are any good or not." She talked around this point for several minutes and mentioned names.

Discussion Question 3: How do you think most supervisors would react to remarks like that, and what would have been the result?

Probable Reactions to Q3: "When you were new you got increases, too."

"That isn't true, and you know it isn't true."

"You are making a very unfair accusation."

"With a remark like that you're just asking for trouble."

Summary Comment: Such responses would certainly have led to quite an argument, wouldn't they? Suppose we see what Jones did.

JONES: (3) Rather than saying anything or showing resentment in any way, Jones continued to listen. Occasionally, when the girl finished a remark, he would simply nod his head or say, "I see," to indicate that he was paying attention to what she was saying and that he understood how she felt.

MISS E: (4) It was not long until she came to her next point: "Lots of girls working for the company get more money than I do, and I'm just as good as they are." Here again she went on at some length to illustrate what she meant.

Discussion Question 4: What do you suppose an ordinary supervisor would say in that situation?

Probable Reactions to Q4: "Yes, but your ratings have never been above average."

"Lots of girls who work here get less than you do, too."

"I've already told you that you are getting top pay for your classification."

"What you're saying is that we don't pay on the basis of merit at all."

Summary Comment: Most supervisors might have begun to get angry at this point, and let the girl know it, but that would have prevented the development of further points. Let's examine how Jones handled it.

JONES: (4) Whatever Jones's real feelings might have been, he still continued to listen and encouraged Miss Everett to do the talking.

MISS E: (5) She spent the next several minutes developing the following statement: "There is a lady who works for another company who gets $70 a week, and this company is making lots of money now, and if others can pay those salaries so can this company."

Discussion Question 5: What kind of a reply would you expect a supervisor to make to that idea?

Probable Reactions to Q5: "Well, if that is the case, then why don't you get a job with this other company?"

"Some girls in that company get less than you do, too."

"You are accusing us of being stingy with our pay."

"You forget that we have a pension plan and they don't."

Summary Comment: Such comments might have put her in her place, but they wouldn't have helped her get rid of her feelings. Suppose we find out what Jones had to say, if anything.

JONES: (5) The supervisor showed neither approval nor disapproval but merely listened attentively to what she had to say, making occasional comments, such as, "I see," and "I understand."

MISS E: (6) The supervisor's understanding manner helped her come to her next point. It was something like this: "I have had to fight for every raise I ever got, and that's what I'm doing now."

Discussion Question 6: Let's take a look at some natural reactions to such a remark and see what they would have accomplished.

Probable Reactions to Q6: "You certainly are, sister, and you're not getting very far, either."

"If you used some of that energy on your job you might get somewhere."

"How about trying to be cooperative and see how that works."

Summary Comment: Some supervisors might have become sarcastic at this point and would have made her even more belligerent. Let's see what Jones did.

JONES: (6) Instead of getting into an argument, he let her go on talking, while he sat back and listened.

MISS E: (7) This manner seemed to encourage her to go on, and the next thing she talked about centered around this remark: "You brought a new girl into our unit the other day. If you had given us girls in the unit a raise then we would have worked harder and you wouldn't have needed to hire the new girl."

Discussion Question 7: How might a typical supervisor be inclined to react to such an idea, and what would his comments have aroused?

Probable Reactions to Q7: "Who do you think is running this unit, you or me?"

"You're just sore at the whole world. Why don't you go home and sleep it off?"

"You've got your nerve asking for a raise when you admit you've been loafing."

Summary Comment: Again we see that the usual reactions would have accomplished little. Let's see whether Jones defended what he had done.

JONES: (7) This accusation didn't bring a rise out of Jones at all. He merely listened as he had before, and this led the girl to express her feelings further and get to her next point.

MISS E: (8) "If there's no more money for me here why don't you transfer me? They have lots of good jobs in other departments and they don't work as hard as I do."

Discussion Question 8: What sort of things might this lead a supervisor to say?

Probable Reactions to Q8: "If that's what you want, I'll be only too glad to do it."

"Frankly, I don't think they'd take you."

"A minute ago you admitted you were loafing; now you're saying you work too hard."

"This company doesn't have another job at higher pay that you are capable of doing."

Summary Comment: Most answers to such a criticism would have led to disagreements over facts. Suppose we find out how Jones reacted.

JONES: (8) As before he had no particular remark to make. He apparently felt that things were going quite well because all he did was to listen and there was no point in distracting her.

MISS E: (9) Having gotten this criticism of Jones off her chest she was able to go on and say: "If I were pretty you'd give me an increase."

Discussion Question 9: What do you suppose the average supervisor would say after a remark like that?

Probable Reactions to Q9: "Now you are just being silly and childish."

"How dare you accuse me of playing favorites!"

"You ought to be fired for saying that."

"It isn't my fault if you're not pretty."

Summary Comment: It's becoming pretty obvious that Jones gets farther by not contesting her accusations, but it's not always easy to do.

JONES: (9) Even this remark didn't seem to bother Jones. He continued to listen, indicating by a brief comment that he understood how she felt about things, and let her go on talking. For the next several minutes her comments were something like the following:

MISS E: (10) "You don't want me here. You just want young girls. I'm getting old, so I guess that I should get out."

> Discussion Question 10: What do you think the ordinary supervisor would say in this situation?
> Probable Reactions to Q10: "I never said anything of the kind."
> "Unless you get back on the beam, that might be a good idea."
> "It isn't that you are old; it's just the way you're behaving that gets you into trouble."
> "Now you know it isn't that bad."
> Summary Comment: It seems that neither anger nor sympathy would have helped things.

JONES: (10) This didn't bring about a change in his methods at all. He showed interest in what she had to say but expressed no opinions.

MISS E: (11) After expressing her feelings about not being wanted she began to cry.

> Discussion Question 11: What do you suppose would be the usual reaction of a supervisor in this case?
> Probable Reactions to Q11: Would become embarrassed.
> Try to comfort the girl.
> Might act as if he didn't notice the crying.
> Summary Comment: It seems one would have to say something, but most things would not be appropriate. Let's see how Jones handled this situation.

JONES: (11) He passed the Kleenex and waited while she cried.

MISS E: (12) After composing herself somewhat she said: "No one pays any attention to me any more."

> Discussion Question 12: What do you think would be a supervisor's natural response to such a comment?
> Probable Reactions to Q12: "Do you think it's as bad as that?"
> "Maybe if you were more sociable you'd have some friends."
> "If you kept busy maybe you wouldn't notice such things."
> Summary Comment: It seems it might be quite natural to attempt to console her by disagreeing or to suggest things she ought to do. Let's see how Jones restrained his remarks.

JONES: (12) He nodded his head, and there was a long pause which indicated to him that she was thinking hard.

MISS E: (13) A few moments later she remarked: "All my troubles seem to have started since my father died. Since then things haven't gone good for me." She then told about how she used to go and visit her father weekends and vacations and how glad he was to see her.

> Discussion Question 13: At this point most supervisors would have come to realize that Miss Everett was a lonesome person and would have begun to feel differently about her. Would it have been wise to console her or to offer advice? Would she have talked that way to the typical supervisor?
> Probable Reactions to Q13: "She should not have been advised."
> "Neither consolation nor advice would help."
> "Most supervisors wouldn't have gotten her this far."

Summary Comment: It seems that Miss Everett is beginning to discover her real problem by herself. Note how her hostility has disappeared.

JONES: (13) Mr. Jones interjected such remarks as "I see," and "I certainly can understand that," but offered no advice. His feelings of anger which he previously repressed were all gone now, and he began thinking of little attentions he might show her during the day.

MISS E: (14) Her first constructive statement followed when she said: "If I could find another girl to live with maybe things would be better, but I can't find anyone I like." She continued to discuss this point and talked about how few people she really knew well enough to live with.

Discussion Question 14: Is Miss Everett sufficiently over her frustrated feelings now to be receptive?
Probable Reactions to Q14: "Not quite."
"No, she still says she doesn't like people."
"Why take a chance when things are going so good?"
Summary Comment: Although there has been a distinct change in Miss Everett's attitude, it seems unwise to push a good thing now.

JONES: (14) He felt no need to comment and was afraid that any mention of people he could suggest to her would be unsatisfactory. He therefore let her fill in the pauses.

MISS E: (15) Finally she became more cheerful and smiled when she said: "I won't be working very long anyway. I'm buying a $25 war bond every week, and that has mounted up and with my pension I can get along all right."

Discussion Question 15: Note that she completely contradicts the first point she made in the interview. What could one say to that?
Probable Reactions to Q15: "I thought you needed more money."
"You're tucking away a lot more than I ever could."
"You are contradicting yourself, aren't you?"
Summary Comment: Such comments would obviously cause trouble and would show how completely we misunderstood her changes in feeling.

JONES: (15) It seemed to Jones that she was over her frustration, and so he engaged her in conversation. He asked her what she intended to do when she retired, and the matter of traveling came up. They then spent about half an hour exchanging traveling experiences.

MISS E: (16) Suddenly Miss Everett looked at her watch, expressed surprise, and said: "My! I've taken a lot of your time. Thank you very much for being so kind." She then left, smiling as she went out. (This entire conversation took about two hours.)

Discussion Question 16: Suppose we take a few minutes to analyze what happened in this interview. Notice that at the end of the interview she thanked the supervisor. Why do you suppose she did that? (Discuss to permit group interaction.)

Probable Reactions to Q16: She felt better.

She felt that she had been shown consideration and understanding.

She got a lot of things off her chest.

She saw through her problem and seemed ready to do something about it.

Discussion Question 17: What was the real cause of this girl's troubles? (Discuss and after each suggestion from your group ask what the evidence is.)

Probable Reactions to Q17: She was confused and disturbed.

She felt she was being pushed aside.

She was lonely. (This is the correct response.)

Discussion Question 18: What do you think would have happened had the supervisor replied to this girl with the kinds of comments we felt an average supervisor might have used? (Discuss any different ideas suggested by your group.)

Probable Reactions to Q18: There would have been hard feelings on both sides.

The real problem would not have been recognized.

The interview would have ended in an argument.

Other employees besides the girl might have thought the supervisor was harsh and unfair if she came back to the job in an upset condition.

Summary: It seems that, by listening, the supervisor made it possible for both himself and the girl to gain in several ways during the interview.

Apparently the girl felt better after she had talked out her troubles.

As she talked, the real cause of her problem became clear to both her and the supervisor, and they came to understand each other better.

Follow-Up Interview of Miss Everett: We have seen how listening brought about a change in our own frame of reference concerning Miss Everett. We also noticed that toward the end of the conversation she not only seemed to realize the nature of her real problem but, when she mentioned finding another girl with whom she might live, she seemed to be heading toward a solution. Mr. Jones also felt that her attitude on the job had improved. He made it a point to chat with her when he passed near her desk, and he gave her little "extra jobs" to do for him. She seemed friendly and very cooperative in these contacts.

In view of the marked change that took place in this girl's outlook during the first interview and subsequent improvement on the job, the supervisor felt that it would be a good idea to follow up with a second interview to see how she felt about things. About 5 months after the first interview Mr. Jones asked Miss Everett if she could spare the time to come to his office for a visit. She seemed very anxious to come, and after a few pleasantries Jones proceeded as follows:

JONES: (1) "You and I had a talk some months ago, and I was wondering how things were going with you now."

MISS E: (1) "Much better. Things are so much better. But there is one thing. (*Pause*) I don't know how to say it. (*Pause*) But when Miss Aldrich [the senior clerk] was on vacation they always used to put me in charge, but now another girl does the assigning. All over the company I know they always put the girl who is next in line in charge."

> *Discussion Question 1a:* What kind of behavior do we have here?
> *Probable Reactions to Q1a:* She seems to be happy about some things.
> She is critical about some things.
> She is thinking straight instead of showing frustration.
> She is being polite and reasonable.
> *Discussion Question 1b:* Although Miss Everett still has problems, do you notice any difference in her attitude?
> *Probable Reactions to Q1b:* Her complaint is reasonable.
> There is an answer to her question.
> She isn't blaming anyone but is raising a problem.
> *Discussion Question 1c:* How could one respond to her statement?
> *Probable Reactions to Q1c:* Say nothing.
> Ask her what should be done.
> *Summary Comment:* Whatever we do, it should be in the form of drawing her out. Let's see what Jones actually said.

JONES: (2) "You feel that there has been some change."
MISS E: (2) "Yes. I talked with Mr. Sullivan [the immediate supervisor] about it, and he said that because the senior clerk was only to be away for two weeks he thought it was unnecessary to put anyone in charge. But that hurt me because I had always been in charge before, and I always thought I was next in line."

> *Discussion Question 2:* The response of Jones immediately drew out some further expression of feeling. Now how should he react to these new feelings?
> *Probable Reactions to Q2:* "You feel Sullivan hasn't treated you fairly?"
> "You feel that they are trying to get rid of you?"
> *Summary Comment:* We would have to be careful not to indicate disapproval, accuse her of feelings she hasn't expressed, or get her talking about the facts of the case. Rather the concern should be with her feelings. Here is how Jones reacted to the feelings she expressed.

JONES: (3) "I can see that your feelings have been hurt."
MISS E: (3) "Yes, and no one has ever told me that I wasn't doing a good job."

> *Discussion Question 3:* What would you say about the feelings behind these remarks?
> *Probable Reactions to Q3:* She is receptive and should be given some facts.
> She would be able to see other sides of the question if given a chance.
> She is still bothered about being overlooked.

She can see reasons for some things, but not for others.
She is still causing trouble.
Summary Comment: It seems that listening would be awkward
and that something has to be said to move things on. Might this
be the place for an exploratory question? Jones thought so.

JONES: (4) "Was the work very heavy while Miss Aldrich was away?"
MISS E: (4) "Oh, no, there wasn't much to do. Everything was all
caught up. Of course that other girl sits right near Miss Aldrich's
desk, and maybe Mr. Sullivan didn't think about it because the work
wasn't heavy and he hasn't been on that job very long."

Discussion Question 4a: Apparently Jones's question was a good
one. Suppose Jones had volunteered the explanations offered by
Miss Everett instead of letting her find them? How would that
have worked out?
Probable Reactions to Q4a: She's more likely to accept things
she suggests.
She might have felt criticized and stopped being so helpful.
She would have proved him wrong.
Discussion Question 4b: Now that Miss Everett is open-minded
one can explore the situation with her, but supplying answers
might put her back on the defensive. However, now that she has
supplied some answers to her own question how should that be
handled?
Probable Reactions to Q4b: Assure her that her answer is correct.
Not say anything.
Try to get her to talk about other things.
Summary Comment: It seems that if Jones is trying to understand how she feels he should not show that he favors any interpretation or encourage her to jump to any quick conclusions. It
seems also that the particular subject has been exhausted and that
the discussion should be broadened. Let's see how Jones handled
it.

JONES: (5) "It could have been that way. How are other things
going with you?"
MISS E: (5) "Good. I have such a nice place to live now. There
are twelve girls in the place. I always have to laugh, I never get any
place where there are any men around. But, then, it's nice when
you go to the bathroom and there are no men waiting around. Each
girl has her own room, and we have a nice big parlor where we can
entertain. Most of the girls work at the same company. (*Pause*)
You know, I appreciate your asking me to come in, I really do. My,
I feel so important. I like my work so much, too. On my vacation
I was up to see my sisters. One of them has three boys in the
service. This war certainly makes us think a lot different. I like the
new location of my desk too. (*Pause*) Was that all you wanted?"

Discussion Question 5: The fact that Miss Everett talked so
freely about her own affairs shows how much at ease she felt with
Mr. Jones. But now she puts a direct question to him. Should
he answer it and, if so, why?

Probable Reactions to Q5: Yes, it is not loaded with feeling.
Yes, she has a right to know.
Summary Comment: Since Miss Everett seems now to be over
her former signs of frustration and is in a conversational attitude,
the need for Mr. Jones to explore for hidden feelings on this subject seems not so necessary. Let's see what he actually said.

JONES: (6) "Oh, I wanted to see how things were going with you."
MISS E: (6) "Well, everything is all right, but I think that when
Miss Aldrich is away I should be in charge, but maybe that will be
straightened out next time." At this point she talked about visiting
her sisters who live in a small town and how they thought the city
in which she lived was "wicked." She laughed at some of the small-
town ideas and talked very happily about events. "I spoke to Mr.
Murphy [the department head] the other day about three months'
service I had with the company about a year before I started to work
permanently. He said that he would look it up and let me know, but
I haven't heard from him yet. I thought it would be nice to have that
three months bridged, and then I would have that much more service
when I retire."

Discussion Question 6a: Since Miss Everett again brought up
the problem of being put in charge of things when Miss Aldrich
was away, this must be considered important. How should it be
handled?
Probable Reactions to Q6a: With her changed attitude she could
handle it.
If she isn't put in charge the company ought to have very good
reasons.
Mr. Jones undoubtedly will put her in charge because he now
feels more confident in her ability.
Discussion Question 6b: Miss Everett also raised the problem
of having her service bridged. Is she being reasonable about this?
Probable Reactions to Q6b: Very constructive attitude.
She is making a reasonable request.
She is doing what any sensible person would do.
Discussion Question 6c: What do you think is bothering her
most in her last statement?
Probable Reactions to Q6c: The fact that Mr. Murphy hasn't
given her an answer.
She feels Mr. Murphy has ignored her.
Summary Comment: Although Miss Everett is showing a healthy
attitude, this doesn't mean that she accepts everything as right.
(Since Miss Everett changed the subject, Jones made no comment
about putting her in charge, but the next time Miss Aldrich was
away Mr. Sullivan and Mr. Jones did put her in charge and she did
a good job.) On the question of bridging service Mr. Jones felt
that some facts he knew about were important, and so he offered
the information.

JONES: (7) "Well, Mr. Murphy has been on his vacation. He just
returned, and perhaps he hasn't obtained the answer yet. Would
you like to have me see what I could do?"
MISS E: (7) "Yes, I would." (*She prepares to leave.*)

Discussion Question 7: How do you think Miss Everett will accept the ruling on bridging her service if the answer is "no"?
Probable Reactions to Q7: She will not take it too well.
She is now ready to accept the facts without feeling that the supervisors are against her.
Depends on how she is told.
Summary Comment: There may be differences of opinion about how a person like Miss Everett would take an unfavorable ruling. In this instance bridging service was not allowed because service had to be 6 months or more to permit it to be counted. Miss Everett accepted the ruling, saying, "I am glad to know that. I know some girls had their service bridged, so I wondered about mine."

JONES: (8) "I'm glad that things are going well for you, and come in again sometime." (*Standing at desk*)
MISS E: (8) "My! I feel good, and thank you very much." (*Exit*)

Discussion Question 8: How do you feel about this follow-up interview? Would you say it was a good idea?
Probable Reaction to Q8: Yes.
Discussion Question 9: What did the interview do for the girl?
Probable Reactions to Q9: It made the girl feel more secure.
She received further attention.
The supervisor let her know that she hadn't been overlooked or forgotten.
The girl had an opportunity to bring up several problems and discuss them.
It helped to establish a more friendly relationship than was possible in the first interview.
Discussion Question 10: Why didn't the question of retiring come up?
Probable Reactions to Q10: She probably forgot about it.
She likes her job better.
She is perhaps happier with the job than she would be without it.
Discussion Question 11: In what ways was the interview a help to the supervisor?
Probable Reactions to Q11: He found out how the girl was getting along.
He was able to help the girl solve problems before they frustrated her.
He learned how the girl felt about things.
He was able to see how constructive she could be.
Discussion Question 12: What was there about the way the supervisor handled this interview that made it worthwhile?
Probable Reactions to Q12: He was friendly and acceptant.
He showed a sincere interest in the girl's problems.
He did a good job of listening and reacting to her feelings.
He responded to her remarks with statements that helped her talk.
Instead of giving advice, he let the girl work out her own solutions.
He asked good exploratory questions.

He supplied information when it was a source of help, but not when it could be construed as criticism.

Summary: Apparently the follow-up interview helped both persons involved by providing a means for solving minor problems before they became frustrating, and at the same time it furnished a basis for the employee and the supervisor to understand each other better. If this is true, then perhaps friendly interviews of this sort afford one way to prevent frustration as well as to furnish a remedy.

Practice in Reflecting Feelings

General Considerations. Once a group has an appreciation for the value of encouraging the expression of feelings, certain skills and confidence must be developed. This means practice. Role playing permits opportunity to practice elementary skills, but in order to refine these skills further one needs standards for comparison.

Training material, in the form of stenographic transcriptions of phonographically recorded cases in counseling, is needed for this next step. Fortunately, such material is available. Snyder's *Casebook of Non-directive Counseling* (58) supplies a number of complete cases, with descriptive comments on what is happening. Such case material has been found very effective for training in the skill of reflecting feelings. Since the mere reading of case material is a passive process and requires little attention and thought, something must be added to the case material to make its study an active process. One method is to have a discussion after each response made by a client. The purpose of the discussion is: (1) to analyze the feelings expressed; (2) to permit trainees to try their hand at reflecting the feeling; and (3) to compare the actual response of the counselor with those suggested by the trainees. After the counselor's reflective response is read, the next reaction of the client is read, and this reaction of the client is again analyzed as above.

This approach not only stimulates a high degree of attention but also permits trainees to experience progress in their skills. Even in the study of a single case one finds a high degree of improvement between the beginning and the end. The method also allows the trainer to point up certain problems that arise in connection with the process of reflecting feelings. Some of these problems are as follows:

1. How to get a reluctant person to talk.
2. How to differentiate between expressed feelings and the true unexpressed feelings.

3. How to avoid sympathizing and criticizing when one is reflecting feelings.

4. How to evaluate the importance of various feelings expressed.

5. What to do when two different feeling areas are expressed.

6. How to observe changes in feelings and how to help the expression move to deeper feelings.

7. How to distinguish between constructive and nonconstructive statements and to observe how the former occur after periods of hostility.

8. How to discover the stage at which constructive feelings can safely be reflected without leaving important hostile feelings unexpressed.

9. How to leave the door open for future contacts.

Problems of this type occur in most cases, and they are much more meaningful if they are raised in connection with real problems and if the trainees are permitted to participate in solving them.

In order to illustrate how case material may be translated into practice in reflecting feelings, a discussion guide which has been found effective is included here. The case used is taken from Snyder (58).[*] It is one of the shorter ones and in this sense is not typical, but it is sufficiently dramatic to show how the technique of reflecting feelings leads to expression. The particular case is also of interest because the client had been given advice and sympathy from various sources, and it becomes clear in the interview how and why these approaches completely failed. Most listeners jump to conclusions and feel they understand a person's situation too soon. As soon as they think they have a correct diagnosis, they tend to abandon the nondirective counseling approach. Case material usually demonstrates that the first several hunches on diagnosis are completely wrong. When enough has been expressed to reveal the true problem, it is usually found that the client also has made the discovery.

CASE OF MARJORY WINKLER AS USED FOR PRACTICE IN REFLECTING FEELINGS

Introduction (Read by Discussion Leader): When frustrations are close to the surface, so that they can be expressed easily, listening is usually sufficient to furnish relief to the individual. However, when

---

[*] Acknowledgment is here made to W. U. Snyder and the Houghton Mifflin Company for permission to reproduce the lines spoken by the counselor and the client from the Case of Marjory Winkler.

frustrations are deep-seated or go back to an individual's early life, listening may not be sufficient to bring about the expression of the real frustration. When we deal with such cases, we use the method of listening, but along with it we use the additional skill of *reflecting feelings*.

In order to get the feeling of what is meant by *reflecting feelings* and how it is done, let's analyze an actual case, that of Marjory Winkler. Although this is a true case, the name of the person has been changed. For this demonstration, we will need the help of one of you to play the part of the counselor and one of you to act as Marjory Winkler. (It is desirable that the two role players have a rehearsal.)

After each remark that Marjory, the client, makes we will pause for discussion in order to see how we would have reflected feelings had we been the counselor. Now here is some background material on the case as quoted from Snyder.

Miss Marjory Winkler was referred to the counselor by a physician, who reported the following symptoms; loss of weight, nervousness, crying spells, and fainting attacks. The physician stated that there were no apparent physical causes for the symptoms.

The client, an eighteen-year-old girl, had undergone plastic surgery, and it had changed her appearance completely. She was now a very attractive girl. The physician had insisted that she accept the counseling before he would continue with any further treatment of her physical condition.

(At this point the counselor should be seated and the participants alerted to begin.)

I. COUNSELLOR: (*Stands up as Miss Winkler enters.*)
    MISS W.: "Well, here I am. This is all perfectly silly, but the doctor *insisted* that I come in and see you. I promised the doctor that I would come for *one* hour and here I am."

> *Discussion Question 1a:* What are the feeling words here?
> (Discuss.)
>   *Probable Reactions:*
>   *Good Reactions*
>   She doesn't *need* counseling.
>   The doctor *insisted*.
>   She *promised* to come.
>   *Poor Reactions*
>   Hostile toward counseling. (This feeling may be there, but it is an interpretation and not what she actually has said.)
>   Here I am. (This is a fact, but it expresses little or no feeling.)

Hostile toward doctor. (She has not said this, so that if
it is true it is not an expressed feeling.)
Discussion Question 1b: What would you say in order to reflect
those feelings? (After two or three suggestions from the group,
continue with comment to group below.)
Comment to Group: Now let's find out how the counselor reflected them in his response. (Ask counselor to read his part in II.)

II. COUNSELOR: "You're here because of the doctor's insistence and
not because you feel any need for it."
MISS W: "Yes, that's it exactly. The doctor says there isn't anything wrong with me physically—that all my symptoms are because
I am emotionally disturbed about things. Well, that's a lie. I'm
not emotionally disturbed about anything."

Discussion Q2a: What are the feelings she is expressing?
(Discuss.)
Probable Reactions:
Good Reactions
Doctor says I'm emotionally disturbed.
That's a lie.
I'm not emotionally disturbed.
Poor Reactions
Angry with doctor. (This is an interpretation, but she
has not expressed this.)
Nothing wrong physically. (Not loaded with feeling.)
Discussion Q2b: If you were the counselor what would you say
to reflect those feelings? (Discuss a few suggestions and proceed.)
Comment to Group: Let's see what the counselor said. (Ask
counselor to read his part in III.)

III. COUNSELOR: "You feel that the doctor is wrong when he says
that you are emotionally upset to the extent that . . ."
MISS W: "I have nothing to worry about. I have all the money I
want. I live at the sorority house and have lots of friends. I'm getting
good grades. What could be bothering me?"

Discussion Q3a: What are the words that show feeling here?
(Discuss.)
Probable Reactions:
Good Reactions
Nothing to worry about.
What could be bothering me?
Poor Reactions
I have all the money I want.
Lots of friends.
I live at the sorority house.
(These points are not the main feeling but are justifica-
tions.)
Discussion Q3b: How would you reflect those feelings? (Dis-
cuss as indicated above.)
Comment to Group: Now suppose we find out how the counselor
picked up these feelings and what happened when they were
reflected back to the girl.

IV. COUNSELOR: "You feel that you have lots of advantages and there is apparently nothing that could be bothering you."

MISS W: "Yes, I think that sums it up." (*Begins to cry.*) "This is one of the things he said indicated that I was upset about something."

> *Discussion Q4a:* What feelings are there in this? (Discuss.)
> *Probable Reactions:*
>   *Good Reactions*
>   Crying.
>   Doctor says I am *upset.*
>   *Poor Reactions*
>   That sums it up.   (Little or no feeling.)
>   This is an indication.   (Absence of feeling.)
> *Discussion Q4b:* What would you say in order to reflect these feelings? (Discuss, then ask group to write down their ideas.)
> *Comment to Group:* Let's find out what the counselor said next.

V. COUNSELOR: "The doctor felt that the tears were caused by some emotional disturbance."

MISS W: "For no reason at all I cry. I just feel like crying and never stop crying. I don't know why."

> *Discussion Q5a:* What is the feeling here? (Discuss.)
> *Probable Reactions:*
>   *Good Reactions*
>   For *no reason at all* I cry.
>   *Feel* like crying.
>   *Never stop* crying.
>   I *don't know* why.
>   *Poor Reaction*
>   She is broken-hearted about something. (This is jumping
>   to conclusions.)
> *Discussion Q5b:* How would you reflect her feelings? (Have group members write out reactions and discuss differences.)
> *Comment to Group:* Let's find out what the counselor said.

VI. COUNSELOR: "You don't know why you get those feelings that you never can stop crying."

MISS W: "Oh, *I* know why."

> *Discussion Q6a:* What feeling do you get out of this? (Discuss.)
> *Probable Reactions:*
>   *Good Reaction*
>   Does know why she cries.
>   *Poor Reactions*
>   Disagreement with counselor. (Is not the point.)
>   She contradicts herself. (True, but this should not be
>   pointed out to her.)
> *Discussion Q6b:* What would you say to the girl if you were the counselor?
> *Comment to Group:* The counselor reflected the feeling in this way.

VII. COUNSELOR: "You think you know why you do it."

MISS W: "I had an operation. It's just a very natural nervous reaction."

Discussion Q7a: What feeling is she expressing in these remarks?
(Discuss.)
Probable Reactions:
Good Reactions
It's a *natural reaction* to operation.
Only what one would expect.
It's obvious.
Poor Reactions
I had an operation.   (This is a fact, not a feeling.)
She feels run-down.   (She does not say this.)
Too much pain and discomfort.   (No evidence of this.)
Discussion Q7b: How would each of you reflect this?
Comment to Group: Let's see how the counselor put it.

VIII. COUNSELOR: "You think it's the natural aftermath of your operation."

MISS W: "It was my face. I was terribly ugly as a child. My nose and chin." (*Bitter and sarcastic tone of voice*) "One day this summer Mother said to me, 'I've made arrangements for you to go to New York and have some plastic surgery. You will stay at the New Yorker and should be able to come home by August.' That's all. Not asking *me* how *I* felt. Not giving a damn. And I had to go. It was such a shock and when it was all over and I looked in the mirror, there was another person. I even had my hair done over—a rinse. The ugly duckling was gone." (*Extreme bitterness*) "Pretty swell job, don't you think?"

Discussion Q8a: How could we summarize the main feelings she expressed here?   (Discuss.)
Probable Reactions:
Good Reactions
Dislike of mother's orders.
Mother was inconsiderate.
Disappointment over results of operation.
Feeling like another person.
Poor Reactions
She didn't want to go.   (Perhaps, but she hasn't said this.)
She hates her mother.   (She may, but she has not said so.)
It isn't her appearance that she is bitter about; it's something else.   (May be true, but not expressed yet.)
She can't get used to her new looks.   (She hasn't said so.)
Discussion Q8b: There seem to be many different feeling areas here. Notice that they seem to center around hostility toward her mother and inability to accept the change in her appearance. Which one of these feeling areas should be reflected? Would each of you write out how you would reflect it?
Discussion Q8c: How many of you reflected the feeling toward the mother? How many reflected the feeling about the change in appearance? (Discuss reasons.)
Comment to Group: Both feeling areas are important, as we shall see later. Usually, when a question like this arises, the counselor reflects the last one expressed, so as to help continuity of expression. Other important feeling areas will come to expression later. Let's see what the counselor did.

IX. COUNSELOR: "A swell job, but you're not very happy about it."

MISS W: (*Low voice*) "How would you feel? I look entirely different. No one recognizes me." (*Voice rises.*) "I feel like a cheat and a crook. I'm a masquerader. I'm not *me*. I'm artificial. And I *had* to come back *here*. And no one knew me. Not the sorority girls, or the professors. And when they found out what had happened—I told them right away—(*voice drops*) they said, 'How wonderful! Why, you're beautiful. You're lucky you could afford it!' And I thanked them and pretended that I was tickled, but deep down inside of me my very soul cried out, 'Fraud! Fraud! Fraud!'" (*Crying*)

> *Discussion Q9a:* What are the feelings she is expressing now? (Discuss.)
> *Probable Reactions:*
> *Good Reactions*
> She feels like a cheap imitation of her real self.
> She feels like a fake.
> *Poor Reactions*
> She feels misunderstood by her friends. (She does not say this.)
> She feels like a stranger among her own friends. (Real feeling is that of a counterfeit or fake.)
> The operation was too much for her nerves. (She has now gone beyond that in expressing feeling.)
> *Discussion Q9b:* How do you think the counselor reflected these feelings? (Ask members to write their opinions on a slip of paper.)
> *Comment to Group:* Let's find out how the counselor reflected these feelings, so as to see how well we have done.

X. COUNSELOR: "Even though the girls you knew admired the change in your appearance, you couldn't feel that it was fair. You felt like a fraud."

MISS W: "I cried myself to sleep many a night. Then one of my profs talked to me and he said, among other things, that a person who lost an eye wore a glass eye, and a person who lost an arm or a leg wore an artificial limb, and it was considered a godsend. 'You're no more of a fraud than they are,' he said. 'No more of a fraud than all the girls who wear rouge and lipstick and who permanent their hair. You had the advantage of correcting a flaw of nature. There isn't any reason for you to feel as you do about it.' And so—(*begins to cry again*) and so, I got over it."

> *Discussion Q10a:* How would you describe what the professor was doing here? (Discuss.)
> *Probable Reactions:* He was giving her advice.
> He was trying to console her.
> He was trying to reason with her when actually she was frustrated.
> He was using logic to try to change her feelings.
> *Summary:* Apparently the professor gave her advice and tried to console her and tell her how she should feel about things. Isn't this just exactly what most people do in a situation like that?

Discussion Q10b: Do you think this approach actually helped her solve the problem? (Probable reaction is "no," "evidently not," etc.)

Discussion Q10c: What are the feelings she is bringing out here?

Probable Reactions:

   Good Reactions

      Unhappy.

      Told she was not a fraud.

      Got over it.

   Poor Reactions

      Any specific points made by professor. (These are not feelings, but are purely logical.)

      Cried herself to sleep. (This is a fact, not feeling.)

      Doesn't really feel better. (She hasn't said this.)

Discussion Q10d: Which of them would you reflect? (Ask group to write out their opinions.)

Comment to Group: The counselor summed up the feeling and reflected it as follows.

XI. COUNSELOR: "After he talked it over with you, you were able to accept it and you got over your feelings."

MISS W: "Yes." (*Long pause*) "Yes." (*Resigned tone of voice*) "It doesn't bother me now. It is an improvement. God knows it is. The doctor thought that that was what was troubling me. I know he did. He said, 'Sometimes when people have radical changes occur in their physical make-up it's difficult to adjust to it.' I know he would bet his year's income that it's because of the plastic surgery that I'm so upset. But he's wrong."

Discussion Q11a: Have any of you noticed who is doing the most talking so far—the counselor or the girl? (Probable reaction is "the girl.")

Discussion Q11b: About what percentage of all the words spoken have been the counselor's? (After two or three guesses from your group point out that so far the percentages are: the counselor 25 per cent, Miss Winkler 75 per cent.)

Comment to Group: Let's go over Miss Winkler's last remark again so that we can analyze it. (Repeat Miss Winkler's speech above.)

Discussion Q11c: What is the feeling in what the girl has been saying here? (Discuss.)

Probable Reactions:

   Good Reactions

      The doctor thinks the surgery is the real reason for her disturbance.

      The doctor is wrong.

   Poor Reactions

      It doesn't bother me now. (She has progressed past this point.)

      She knows what is really the matter. (Perhaps, but she has not said so.)

      Operations often cause trouble. (An argument, not a feeling.)

There is something else that she cannot or will not discuss. (Good point, but she has not said this.)

Discussion Q11d: If you were the counselor how would you reflect these feelings? (Ask your group to write down a reply.)

Comment to Group: Let's see what the counselor said in his next comment, and then see how the girl reacted.

XII. COUNSELOR: "You feel sure that the doctor has your case diagnosed incorrectly."

MISS W: "I know he has." (*Pause of several minutes*) "A person can't spend a lifetime hating someone as badly and completely as I hate my mother and not have it tear their nerves to pieces. As long as I can remember I have *hated* her and wished she would *die*. She was so *dominating*, she killed my father. She drove him to suicide. I—I found him. She killed my sister. She committed suicide, too. Just to get away from *her*. She is like a vampire—sucking the life's blood out of her children. The plastic surgery was incidental. I have been used since I was a child as a convenient housemaid. Mother was starting a business of her own. She was a dynamic *power*. Every energy she had was poured into making a success. And she did. She has a chain of stores now. And all of us remaining children have money in our own names. She wants us to help in the business. One of my sisters is a partner now. Another sister got married, and, when Tom didn't 'fit in,' Mother caused a separation and now Louise is home—brooding but docile. Now she wants me to take over another branch. And won't she be surprised when she discovers that the minute I'm twenty-one out comes my money and away I go, never to return again."

Discussion Q12a: Here we have very strong feelings. What are they? (Discuss.)

Probable Reactions:

Good Reactions

She hates her mother and wishes she would die.

Her mother made life so unbearable for others that her father and sister killed themselves.

Her mother dominated and degraded her.

She doesn't want to see her mother again.

Poor Reactions

She resents her mother's success at the expense of the family. (Feeling is much deeper than this.)

Money and success aren't important as compared to happiness. (She is too frustrated to weigh values; her feelings are complete hate.)

Discussion Q12b: Why do you suppose she didn't pour out these feelings when she mentioned her mother earlier? (Discuss.)

Probable Reactions: It was difficult to talk about, and other feeling areas had to be explored first.

Her frustration was too deep-seated to be brought out right away.

She had to talk about less hateful feelings first.

She was too frustrated at first to show aggression.

She may have been ashamed of these feelings.

Discussion Q12c: How would you reflect these feelings? (Ask the members of your group to write down a reply and compare it with what the counselor will say.)

Comment to Group: Listening and reflecting feelings seem to have brought out something new here. Let's see whether the counselor was shocked at this or whether there was simply a reflection of the girl's feelings.

XIII. COUNSELOR: "Your life has been made most unbearable by your mother's domination, and those feelings are—"

MISS W: "This is the first time in my life that I have ever told anyone that I hated my mother and wished she would *die.* I *should* feel so ashamed of myself. It's a crime, I suppose. But I don't feel ashamed."

Discussion Q13a: What feeling words are there in these remarks? (Discuss.)
Probable Reactions:
   Good Reactions
      She feels ashamed.
      Can't feel ashamed.
   Poor Reactions
      First time she talked this way. (This is factual.)
      Her feelings are justified.
      She thinks she has said more than she should have.
      (This is not expressed.)
Discussion Q13b: How would you reflect if you were the counselor? (Ask group to write what they would say.)
Comment to Group: Let's find out how the counselor sensed the girl's feelings and reflected them.

XIV. COUNSELOR: "You suppose that perhaps you should feel guilty about the feelings you have expressed, but somehow you can't."

MISS W: "I'm probably hard—like she has been toward me."

Discussion Q14a: What is her feeling here? (Discuss.)
Probable Reactions:
   Good Reactions
      She feels she is hard.
      Her mother was hard.
      Her mother made her hard.
   Poor Reactions
      The hatred has had a permanent effect on her. (This may
         be true, but she hasn't said so.)
      To be hard was the only way to get along. (Not expressed.)
      Her mother had it coming. (This, if expressed, would be
         a justification for her feelings.)
Discussion Q14b: What would you say if you were the counselor? (Have group discuss briefly their suggested responses.)
Comment to Group: The counselor's reply was this.

XV. COUNSELOR: "You think you might have acquired some of the hardness your mother extended toward you."

MISS W: "Yes." (*Pause*) (*Then, in a pleasant tone of voice*) "I don't really think it is necessary *now* that I even waste my time wishing she would die. I don't believe that is exactly fair." (*Pause*) "Surely I can stand on my own two feet even though she is alive."

> *Discussion Q15a:* How do these remarks differ from anything she has said so far? (Discuss.)
> *Probable Reactions:* Much of her hatred seems to have disappeared.
> She is showing some consideration as to what is fair.
> She is exploring the possibility of a solution to her problem.
> *Discussion Q15b:* What feelings is she expressing? (Discuss.)
> *Probable Reactions:*
>   *Good Reactions*
>   Feeling less hateful.
>   Continuing to hate is unfair.
>   Her mother has a right to live.
>   Bad feelings are unnecessary.
>   *Poor Reactions*
>   Hating is a waste of time. (This is a reason for not hating, not the main feeling.)
>   I will ignore her from now on. (She has not said this, nor does it correspond with her other feelings.)
> *Discussion Q15c:* If you were the counselor how would you reflect the feelings in these last remarks? (Discuss one or two suggestions briefly.)
> *Discussion Q15d:* Since her remarks show a trend in the direction of facing and solving a problem, should these be encouraged? (Probable reaction is "yes.")
> *Comment to Group:* The counselor sensed the change in feeling and outlook by reflecting her constructive feelings in these remarks.

XVI. COUNSELOR: "You think perhaps the wish that your mother might die is no longer necessary."

MISS W: "I've made up my mind. I know now what I'm going to do. You see, my life has been really intense hell. You can't imagine how I had to live as a child. I was a little kitchen slave. I did all the housework—the cooking and scrubbing and washing. I was ugly and she never got me anything nice to wear. I went to school and I didn't have one friend in school. I buried myself in my books. I crept to school and I crept home and the only words I said were the few I said to the teachers. They pitied me. I know now that they did. I didn't know it then. I felt so miserable and unhappy. I worked so hard. I just *had* to get the best grades in the school—it was the only thing I could do. But I never got any praise for it from my mother. And my father never said anything. My mother was the ruling force in the house. I hated her. She never said a kind word to me. It was always orders. 'Get supper ready early tonight.' 'Do the washing after you get home from school.' 'Scrub down the bathroom. Do you want to live in a hog pen?' And never any recreation. She didn't care how I looked then. My hands—I used to hide

them! They were so rough and ugly and red. Always! And then *
—I was the youngest. The others were helping in the business. And
she didn't care about my face then. Or my clothes. I wore the drab-
best clothes—the castoffs—but it was cheaper that way. She treated
me like a dog—worse than a dog. She would have stopped and
patted a dog once in a while. She was cold. She never showed me a
bit of affection. I didn't her, either. And she and my father would
go for days without speaking. She would snarl at him—call him a
lazy, no-good bum—and say that he couldn't earn a living for his family. He—poor soul *—I used to wish that she would die. I would
stand in the door sometimes when she went out to work, and hope
that she would get killed. Then I would feel terrible and afraid, and
watch and watch for her to come home, and then when she did it was
the same thing all over again. Then one day *—I never went to any
of the school affairs. I didn't have time. Besides, I never wanted to.
At least, I didn't think I wanted to. And, besides, I didn't have any
friends and I was miserable around the school. All I did was to go
to school and come home, and work like a slave and then *—then I
would stay up most of the night studying because I had to get good
grades. It was the only thing I ever had—the best grades, and the
other kids hated me for it because the teachers would point out how
I always had the best grades and the best papers. And then one day
—well, he took all he could, I suppose. I found him. I went down
in the basement to get some potatoes for the supper, and he was
there. And I shall never forget how I felt. I just wished she would
die. I wished she would never get home again. I wished that so
strongly that I got sick. For years I have carried that wish in my
heart. I couldn't get rid of it. It came between me and everything."
(*Pause*) "No, don't say anything yet. It has been with me so long.
For years. But you see—it's just occurred to me, really right now,
that I'm big enough to live and let live. I was really putting off facing a decision by hoping that something would happen to her. But
it's up to me. I really pity her. She must be in hell herself. She
hasn't any friends. No one wants to be a friend of a person like her.
She is lonely and despised."

> *Discussion Q16a:* What is the nature of her feelings here?
> (Discuss.)
> *Probable Reactions:*
> *Good Reactions*
>> Still hostile, but she is describing more how she used to
>> feel, not so much how she feels now.
>> She had been an object of degradation by her mother. Her
>> mother was a hated tyrant.
>> Finding her father dead was the most horrible experience
>> of all.
>> Now there is room in the world for both her and her
>> mother.

* Speech block caused by inability to discuss father's suicide.

Her mother is paying part of the price of her tyranny.
Her mother is to be pitied, not hated.

Poor Reactions

The girl has found a solution. (Not yet expressed; there
are loss of hatred and possible alternatives to hatred.)
She has largely forgiven her mother. (Not mentioned, nor
is it the issue.)

Discussion Q16b: Notice that, almost until the end, the girl has
started to say something several times and then changed the subject. What was she about to say? (Correct reaction is: "Finding her father in the cellar.") If group does not notice this go
over the speech again. Also count the number of times she has
started to mention her father and then held back. These points
in her speech are indicated by asterisks.

Discussion Q16c: Why do you think she has backed away from
talking about this when it is so important? (Discuss.)

Probable Reactions: It was too horrible to talk about right away.
She couldn't bring herself to go through with it until the end.
She has tried to put it out of her mind.

Discussion Q16d: In what ways is the girl helped by being able
to make this speech?

Probable Reactions: She is able to express her feelings about her
father's death.
She has relieved herself of more of the old, pent-up hatred
against her mother.
She finally faces feelings she has tried to avoid.
Her feelings change from hatred to pity.

Discussion Q16e: How would you explain the change in behavior?

Probable Reactions: She has expressed her hatred.
She is no longer frustrated because all her pent-up feelings have
been expressed.
Listening gives her a chance to talk out her feelings.
Listening and reflecting feelings has brought out the whole
trouble by getting to the real cause of frustration.

Comment to Group: Now let's find out what the counselor said.

XVII. COUNSELOR: "You feel that your mother is really an object of
pity—that she's probably unhappy, and miserable, and lonely."

MISS W: "Yes. But she's able to live her life, and *I* still live mine
and avoid her as much as possible. Perhaps some day we can even
become reconciled to one another on a fifty-fifty basis."

Discussion Q17a: What kind of behavior is the girl showing
now? (Discuss.)

Probable Reactions: She is still somewhat hostile toward her
mother, but she sees solutions to her problem.
She even discusses the possibility of getting along with her
mother.
This is problem-solving rather than frustrated behavior.

Discussion Q17b: What do you think would be a good way to
reflect the girl's new feelings? (Discuss one or two suggestions
briefly.)

Comment to Group: Let's see what the counselor said and see
to what extent he reflects her constructive feelings.

XVIII. COUNSELOR: "You hope that someday you may be able to get along in a—"

MISS W: "Yes. So you see I really didn't need to come here. I know the doctor had good intentions. He meant all right. But, well, I'm not—" (*Notices the time.*) "Have I been here an hour?"

> *Discussion Q18:* What is your impression of her statement that she didn't need to come? (Discuss.)
> *Probable Reactions:* She found the answers to her problem by herself.
> The counselor did such an effective job that the girl wasn't even aware of the counselor's contribution.
> The solution was completely her own.
> She wasn't yet aware of the change in herself.
> She knew she was helped but didn't want to admit it.
> *Comment to Group:* Failure to recognize and appreciate the counselor's contribution is not typical. Most persons feel they have been helped and say so.

NOTE: The following dialogue should be read without interruption for questions.

XIX. COUNSELOR: "The time seemed to pass quickly."

MISS W: "Well!" (*Stands up.*) "I'll not be back. Thanks so much for your time."

COUNSELOR: "You don't feel that it will be necessary to make any other appointment."

MISS W: "No. Well, good-bye."

COUNSELOR: "Good-bye."

At this point Miss Winkler left, but a few minutes later she returned.

MISS W: Would you mind giving me your telephone number in case something *should* come up, and I should want to see you again?

COUNSELOR: All right. (*He gives the information.*)

MISS W: Thank you. Good-bye. (*She leaves.*)

> *Discussion Q19a:* How many of you think that the girl's behavior will actually improve after this one interview? (Count hands and indicate proportions.) (Discuss reasons for any differences of opinion that may arise.)
> *Discussion Q19b:* Do you think that the girl and her mother will be able to get along with each other after this, or is there too much bitterness between them? (Discuss as your group wishes.)

Summary of Follow-Up Information: The counselor did not see the girl again. However, two items of follow-up information were subsequently given to the counselor. They were as follows:

Three months after this contact Marjory eloped with a young man whom she had known since entering the college. The physician reported that she seemed quite happy in her marriage.

A report two years later added the information that Marjory's mother had suffered a stroke which had left her a helpless invalid.

When Marjory learned of her mother's illness, she went home and volunteered to care for her mother. In a very short time Marjory and her husband had met this situation in an interesting manner. The husband had taken over the business for his mother-in-law, and Marjory was assuming the responsibility for her mother's care and also for the home. Voluntary reports from several sources indicated that things were moving along smoothly, that everyone seemed to be making the best of the situation, and that Marjory seemed to be disclosing an understanding, kindly, and friendly attitude toward her mother. How much, if any, of this was due to the counseling is purely a matter of speculation. The follow-up report is included as an interesting bit of information.

Concluding Remarks

The training suggestions given in the foregoing pages are by no means intended to produce polished counselors in a group of supervisors. However, with some skill in democratic leadership and a good understanding and appreciation of the subjects of attitudes and frustration, a considerable degree of skill will be achieved by many supervisors. Furthermore, supervisors are found to be very anxious to obtain training in this area, and many are willing to devote more time and study to the subject than are included in a training program. They see many ways in which the skills described can be used, and many report highly successful results in their first attempts.

For follow-up training it is not necessary to introduce new training methods. The same method, with practice on new cases, seems entirely adequate.

To stimulate motivation the follow-up training should include reports of experience with the method. When supervisors discover what they themselves can accomplish, much of the fear associated with new procedures disappears.

Professional counselors may be concerned with the use of methods when practiced without complete competence. The same concern may be directed at the use of democratic skills unless perfection is approached. However, it must be remembered that both counseling and leadership are already practiced by supervisors. Anything that is done in the direction of improving existing practices is all to the good. Once it is discovered that the skills employed by professional individuals are useful there will be much more acceptance of professionally trained personnel in industry, and these individuals can then serve to handle the more difficult problems and at the same time become an aid to refining the supervisors' skills.

It has already been pointed out that the practice of good human relations is not a specific skill, but rather is an integration of a number of skills and attitudes. In refining any one skill all others are improved, since the essential skills are related and interdependent. Counseling skills are an aid to democratic leadership and to all types of face-to-face contacts. At the same time they give the individual who uses them a much greater appreciation and understanding of the other person and his problems.

BIBLIOGRAPHY

1. Allport, G. W. Catharsis and the reduction of prejudice. *J. soc. Issues*, 1945, **1**, 3–10.
2. Axline, V. M. *Play therapy*. Houghton Mifflin Co., Boston, 1947, 379 pp.
3. Barron, Margaret E. Role practice in interview training. *Sociatry*, 1947, **1**, 198–208.
4. Bavelas, A. Morale and the training of leaders. Chapter 8 in *Civilian morale* (ed. by G. Watson), Reynal and Hitchcock, New York, 1942.
5. Bavelas, A. An analysis of a work situation preliminary to leadership training. *J. educ. Soc.*, 1944, **17**, 426–430.
6. Bavelas, A. Role-playing and management training. *Sociatry*, 1947, **1**, 183–191.
7. Bingham, M. V., and Moore, B. V. *How to interview*. Harper & Bros., New York, 1941, 263 pp.
8. Bradford, L. P. Supervisory training as a diagnostic instrument. *Person. Admin.*, 1945, **8**, 3–7.
9. Bradford, L. P., and Lippitt, R. Building a democratic work group. *Personnel*, 1945, **22**, 142–152.
10. Bradford, L. P., and Lippitt, R. Role-playing in supervisory training. *Personnel*, 1946, **22**, 358–369.
11. Canter, R. R. A human relations training program. *J. appl. Psychol.*, 1951, **35**, 38–45.
12. Coch, L., and French, J. R. P. Overcoming resistance to change. *Human Rel.*, 1948, **1**, 512–532.
13. Erickson, C. E. *The counseling interview*. Prentice-Hall, Inc., New York, 1950, 174 pp.
14. French, J. R. P., Jr. Retraining an autocratic leader. *J. abn. and soc. Psychol.*, 1944, **39**, 224–237.
15. French, J. R. P., Jr. Role-playing as a method of training foremen. Pp. 99–116 in *Human factors in management* by S. D. Hoslett, Harper & Bros., New York, 1946.
16. Haas, R. B. Action counseling and process analysis. *Psychodrama Mono.*, 1948, **25**, 32.
17. Hamilton, J. L. The psychodrama and its implications in speech adjustment. *Quart. J. of Speech*, 1943, **29**, 61–67.
18. Haiman, F. S. *Group leadership and democratic action*. Houghton Mifflin Co., Boston, 1951, 309 pp.
19. Hariton, T. Conditions influencing the effects of training foremen in human relations principles. Doctorate dissertation, University of Michigan, 1951.
20. Hendry, C. E., Lippitt, R., and Zander, A. Reality practice as educational method. *Psychodrama Mono.*, 1947, **9**, 32.
21. Kinsey, A. C., Pomeroy, W. B., and Martin, C. E. *Sexual behavior in the human male*. W. B. Saunders Co., Philadelphia, 1948, 804 pp.

22. Lewin, K. The dynamics of group action. *Educ. Leadership*, 1944, **1**, 195–200.

23. Lewin, K. Group decision and social change. Pp. 330–344 in *Readings in social psychology* (ed. by T. M. Newcomb and E. L. Hartley), Henry Holt & Co., New York, 1947.

24. Lewin, K. *Resolving social conflicts.* Harper & Bros., New York, 1948, 230 pp.

25. Lewin, K., Lippitt, R., and White, R. K. Patterns of aggressive behavior in experimentally created social climates. *J. soc. Psychol.*, 1939, **10**, 271–299.

26. Lippitt, R. An experimental study of the effect of democratic and authoritarian group atmospheres. *Univ. Iowa Stud. Child Welf.*, 1940, **16**, 43–195.

27. Lippitt, Rosemary. The psychodrama in leadership training. *Sociometry*, 1943, **6**, 286–292.

28. Lippitt, Rosemary. Psychodrama in the home. *Psychodrama Mono.*, 1947, **22**, 22.

29. Lippitt, R. *Training in community relations.* Harper & Bros., New York, 1949, 286 pp.

30. Lippitt, R., Bradford, L. P., and Benne, K. D. Sociodramatic clarification of leader and group roles, etc. *Sociatry*, 1947, **1**, 82–91.

31. Maier, N. R. F. Reasoning in humans. I. On direction. *J. comp. Psychol.*, 1930, **10**, 115–143.

32. Maier, N. R. F. Reasoning in humans. II. The solution of a problem and its appearance in consciousness. *J. comp. Psychol.*, 1931, **12**, 181–194.

33. Maier, N. R. F. Reasoning in humans. III. The mechanisms of equivalent stimuli and of reasoning. *J. exp. Psychol.*, 1945, **35**, 349–360.

34. Maier, N. R. F. An aspect of human reasoning. *Brit. J. Psychol.*, 1933, **24**, 144–155.

35. Maier, N. R. F. *Psychology in industry.* Houghton Mifflin Co., Boston, 1946, 463 pp.

36. Maier, N. R. F. A human relations program for supervision. *Indust. and Labor Rel. Rev.*, 1948, **1**, 443–464.

37. Maier, N. R. F. Improving supervision through training. Pp. 27–42 in *Psychology of labor-management relations* (ed. by Arthur Kornhauser), Indust. Relations Research Assn., Champaign, Ill., 1949.

38. Maier, N. R. F. *Frustration: The study of behavior without a goal.* McGraw-Hill Book Co., Inc., New York, 1949, 265 pp.

39. Maier, N. R. F. The quality of group decisions as influenced by the discussion leader. *Human Rel.*, 1950, **3**, 155–174.

40. Maier, N. R. F., and Reninger, H. W. *A psychological approach to literary criticism.* D. Appleton and Co., New York, 1933, 154 pp.

41. Maier, N. R. F., and Solem, A. R. Audience role-playing: A new method in human relations training. *Human Rel.*, 1951, **4**, 279–294.

42. Maier, N. R. F., and Zerfoss, L. F. MRP: A technique for training large groups of supervisors, etc. *Human Rel.*, 1952, **5**, no. 2.

43. Meyer, H. H. A study of certain factors related to quality of work-group leadership. Doctorate dissertation, Univ. of Michigan, 1949.

44. Moreno, J. L. Inter-personal therapy and the psychopathology of inter-personal relationships. *Sociometry*, 1937, **1**, 9–76.

45. Moreno, J. L. *Psychodrama.* Vol. I. Beacon House, New York, 1946, 429 pp.

46. Newcomb, T. M. *Personality and social change.* Dryden Press, New York, 1943, 225 pp.
47. Phillips, J. Donald. Report on discussion 66. *Adult Educ. Jour.,* 1948, **7,** 181–182.
48. Pigors, P. J. W., McKenney, L. C., and Armstrong, T. O. *Social problems in labor relations.* McGraw-Hill Book Co., Inc., 1939, 325 pp.
49. Porter, E. H. *An introduction to therapeutic counseling.* Houghton Mifflin Co., 1950, 223 pp.
50. Preston, M. G., and Heintz, R. K. Effects of participatory vs. supervisory leadership on group judgment. *J. abn. and soc. Psychol.,* 1949, **44,** 345–355.
51. Roethlisberger, F. J., and Dickson, W. J. *Management and the worker.* Harvard Univ. Press, Cambridge, Mass., 1939, 615 pp.
52. Rogers, C. R. *Counseling and psychotherapy.* Houghton Mifflin Co., Boston, 1942, 450 pp.
53. Rogers, C. R. *Client-centered therapy.* Houghton Mifflin Co., Boston, 1951, 560 pp.
54. Salter, A. *Conditioned reflex therapy.* Creative Age Press, New York, 1949, 359 pp.
55. Scott, W. D., and Clothier, R. C. *Personnel management.* A. W. Shaw Co., New York, 1923, 643 pp.
56. Shaw, Marjorie E. A comparison of individuals and small groups in the rational solution of complex problems. *Amer. J. Psychol.,* 1932, **44,** 491–504.
57. Shoobs, N. E. Psychodrama in the schools. *Sociometry,* 1944, **7,** 152–168.
58. Snyder, W. U. *Casebook of non-directive counseling.* Houghton Mifflin Co., Boston, 1947, 339 pp.
59. Watson, G. B. Do groups think more efficiently than individuals? *J. abn. and soc. Psychol.,* 1928, **23,** 328–336.
60. Zander, A., and Lippitt, R. Reality-practice as educational method. *Sociometry,* 1944, **7,** 129–151.